COLLEGIATE REVERSE DICTIONARY

Compiled by Gregory S. Donges, B.A., M.Litt., Ph.D.

ISBN 978-1514325902

Introduction

Use of this book should be self-explanatory. It is assumed that anyone with at least a high school education will know the words in the main headings (i.e., the words on the left margin in the text), and using those words, will be able to look up sought-for descriptive words.

The following are not included: 1) archaic and obsolete words and definitions; 2) words listed in conventional dictionaries as "Chiefly British"; 3) fancy, "three-dollar" words when simpler and more commonly-used words suffice; 4) slang terms.

"A group of" before the name of an animal should be read and written as the word given in boldface type, followed by the type of animal, e.g., "A group of bears – **sloth**" should be read and written as *a sloth of bears*.

Plural and adjective forms are given where that form may not follow common rules. The type of verb (transitive or intransitive) is included where this may not be clear from the definition.

The notation "sing./pl." after a noun means that the singular and plural forms are the same.

All nouns that describe a specialized area of study and end in –ics, such as politics and ekistics, are to be used with a singular verb, except as noted. In the Biology section, the heading Biology is bolded in order to draw attention to the fact that it has several subheadings. This system is also used in the Government, Plant and Poetry sections.

Divination is used in several places herein and means the supposed act or art of prediction or the revelation of occult knowledge.

And finally, one definition that didn't seem to fit in anywhere else:

The study of three-dimensional properties of objects or matter usually observed two-dimensionally - **stereology**

Abbreviations

adj. – adjective
Anat. – anatomy
Archit. – architecture
Biol. – biology
Bot. – botany
Chem. - chemistry
e.g. – for example
esp. – especially
f. – feminine or female
m. – masculine
misc. – miscellaneous
n. – noun
Pathol. – pathology
Physiol. – physiology
pl. – plural
pret. – preterite (tense)
q.v. – which see
sing. – singular
usu. – usually
v.i. – intransitive verb
v.t. – transitive verb
Zool. - zoology

A

Abdomen:
>   Surgical incision into the abdominal wall – **laparotomy**

Absent without permission, esp. from school, duty or work – **truant,** n. **truancy** or **truantry**

Academic world, the – **academia**

Accepting willingly – **acceptant**

Account:
>   An examination of accounts or records (to check their accuracy); to examine accounts and records for this purpose –
>   **audit** (v.t./v.i.), n. **auditor**

Accuse:
>   To accuse in return – **recriminate** (v.t.), n. **recrimination**
>   A retort accusing an accuser of a similar offense or similar behavior – **tu quoque**

Acid:
>   Tending to form an acid or containing an excess of acid-forming substance – **acidic**
>   Of, relating to or producing acetic acid or vinegar – **acetous**
>   Capable of being made into an acid – **acidifiable**
>   To make or become slightly acid – **acidulate** (v.t./v.i.)
>   To remove the acid from or reduce the acid content of – **deacidify** (v.t.)
>   Containing excessive acidity – **hyperacid,** n. **hyperacidity**
>   Acidity that is below normal – **hypoacidity**
>   Without normal acidity – **anacid**
>   Neutralizing acid; a substance that neutralizes acidity – **antacid**
>   An abnormal increase in the acidity of the body's fluids – **acidosis**
>   The state, quality or degree of being acid – **acidity**
>   To make or become acidic – **acidify** (v.t./v.i.), n. **acidifier**
>   Not readily decolorized by acid – **acid-fast**
>   Growing well in an acid medium – **acidophilic**
>   Having both acid and alkaline (q.v.) properties – **amphoteric**

Acrobat (see also Rope):
>   An acrobat who performs on a tightrope, trapeze, etc. – **aerialist**

Across:
>   Situated or lying across – **crosswise; transverse**
>   Something that is situated across or lies across – **transverse**

Action:
>   Something that incites or rouses to action – **incentive; stimulant; stimulus**
>   To provoke to action – **goad; incite** (both v.t.)
>   Quick, lively action – **alacrity**
>   To make inactive – **benumb** (v.t.)
>   Loss or impairment of the ability to decide or act independently – **aboulia; abulia**
>   The action of two or more substances, organs or organisms to achieve an effect of which each is individually incapable
>   – **synergism; synergy**; adj. **synergetic** or **synergic**

In action; causing action or change; in a state of action – **active**

To act subtly or with restraint – **underplay** (v.i.)

Excessively or abnormally active – **hyperactive**, n. **hyperactivity**

Serving to lower the rate of vital activities; an agent that does this – **depressant**

Mental or physical inactivity – **lethargy**; **sluggishness**; **torpor**

    Spiritual torpor – **acedia**

A period of inactivity; something that produces a cessation of activity - **quietus**

Add:

    To add on or attach, as a smaller thing or area to a larger – **annex** (v.t.)

    To add as a supplement – **append**; **attach**; **subjoin** (all v.t.)

Adjustment, accurate mechanical – **tram**

Adultery:

    A man whose wife has committed – **cuckold**

    Of or involving adultery; born of adultery - **adulterine**

Advancement:

    One who opposes intellectual advancement and political reform – **obscurant**

Afternoon:

    Of, relating to or occurring in the afternoon – **postmeridian**

Age:

    Under legal age; someone who is under legal age – **minor**

    The state of being under legal age – **minority**

    The period during which one is legally underage – **minority**; **nonage**

    A person who has reached full legal age – **major**

    The state of having reached full legal age; legal age status - **majority**

    Beyond the proper or required age – **overage**

    Of the same age or antiquity – **coeval**, n. **coevality**

    Relating to, characteristic of or proceeding from old age – **senile**

    One who is 40 years old, or in his forties; of, being or characteristic of a person in his forties – **quadragenarian**

    One who is 50 years old, or in his forties; of, being or characteristic of a person in his fifties – **quinquagenarian**

    One who is 60 years old, or in his forties; of, being or characteristic of a person in his sixties – **sexagenarian**;

        sexagenary

    One who is 70 years old, or in his forties; of, being or characteristic of a person in his seventies – **septuagenarian**

    One who is 80 years old, or in his forties; of, being or characteristic of a person in his eighties – **octogenarian**

    One who is 90 years old, or in his forties; of, being or characteristic of a person in his nineties – **nonagenarian**

    One who is 100 years old or older; of, being or characteristic of a person 100 years of age or older – **centenarian**

Aging:

    The study of the physiology and pathology of old age – **geriatrics**; **gerontology**

Agreement:

    Sharing the same opinions or views; being in complete agreement; based on or marked by complete agreement –

        unanimous, n. **unanimity**

Agriculture (see also Farm/Farmer):

    The study or science of agriculture – **geoponics**; adj. **geoponic**

Of or relating to agriculture and rural affairs – **georgic**; **georgical**; **rustic**

The growing of a cultivated crop and a sod-forming crop in alternating strips following the contour of the land, in order to minimize erosion – **strip-cropping**

To prepare and improve (land) for raising crops – **cultivate**; **till** (both v.t.)

To tend or grow (a plant or crop) – **cultivate** (v.t.), n. **cultivation**

Green crops for feeding confined animals - **soilage**

An agriculturally or horticulturally derived plant - **cultivar**

That can be cultivated - **cultivable**

An organism, esp. a cultivated plant such as maize, of a kind not known to have a wild or uncultivated counterpart – **cultigen**

A second crop, as of hay, in a season – **rowen**

To grow a second crop between the rows of another; to plant a crop between the rows of (another crop) – **intercrop** (v.i./v.t.)

Suitable for plowing - **arable**

Plowed but left unseeded during a growing season; the act of plowing land and leaving thus inactive; the state or period of being thus inactive; to make (land) thus inactive by plowing; to plow and till (land), esp. to get rid of weeds – **fallow** (adj./n./v.t.)

To exhaust the fertility of (land) by overcultivation – **overcrop** (v.t.)

Suitable for cultivation (as land) – **arable**

The application of soil and plant sciences to soil management and crop production – **agronomy**, n. **agronomist**

The science of soils in relation to crops – **agrology**

Air:

Of or relating to air – **pneumatic**

The study of the mechanical properties of air and other gases – **pneumatics**

The study of the forces exerted by air or other gases in motion – **aerodynamics**

The study of the air or atmosphere – **aerography**

The study of the equilibrium of air or other gases, and of the equilibrium of solid bodies, such as aerostats, floating in air or other gases – **aerostatics**

The science of measuring air – **aerometry**

Not penetrable to air; to make impenetrable to air – **airproof** (v.t.)

Carrying air – **aeriferous**, n. **aerofication**

Having the form of air – **aeriform**

An upward current of air – **updraft**

A rising body of warm air – **thermal**

A backward flow of air - **backwash**

To blow, displace or scatter with gusts of air – **whiffle** (v.t.)

A rapidly spiraling column of air – **tornado**; **tourbillion**; **tourbillon**; **vortex** (pl. **vortexes** or **vortices**); **whirlwind**

To force air upward from the earth's surface, as when a cold front overtakes and under-cuts a warm front – **occlude** (v.t.)

Extreme or irrational fear of air, drafts, or airborne matter - **aerophobia**

Aircraft:

Of or relating to aircraft or aeronautics; designed for aerial use – **aero**

The design and construction of aircraft – **aeronautics**

Alcohol:

Of or relating to alcoholic drink; inclined or addicted to drinking – **bibulous**, n. **bibulosity**

An insatiable craving for alcohol – **dipsomania**, n. **dipsomaniac**

Total abstinence from alcoholic beverages – **nephalism**; **teetotalism**

One who abstains from such beverages - **nephalist**; **teetotaler**; **teetotalist**; **teetotaller**

To saturate, mix or treat with alcohol – **alcoholize** (v.t.)

Algae (sing. alga):
    Like algae – **algoid**
    The study of algae – **algology**
    A growth of algae at or near the surface of a body of water – **water bloom**

Alien, the legal status of an – **alienage**

Alive:
    To remain alive or in existence – **survive** (v.i.) (q.v.)

Alkaline:
    The quality or state of being alkaline – **alkalinity**
    To make or become alkaline – **alkalify**; **alkalize** (both v.t./v.i.)
    Attracted to or growing best in alkaline soils – **basophile**; **basophilous**
    Increased alkalinity of the body fluids – **alkalosis**
    The process of becoming alkaline – **alkalescence**; **alkalescency**, adj. **alkalescent**
    A substance that neutralizes or counteracts alkalinity – **antalkali**

Allergy:
    Inducing allergy; of or acting as an allergy-inducing substance – **allergenic**
    A doctor who specializes in treating allergies – **allergist**

Alloys (mixtures of metals):
    An alloy of copper and zinc – **brass** (q.v.)
    An alloy of copper and zinc used in making cheap jewelry – **tambac**; **tambak**; **tombac**; **tomback**
    An alloy of copper and tin – **bronze**
    An alloy of copper with 10% tin – **gunmetal**
    An alloy of copper and tin to produce imitation gold – **ormula**
    An alloy of silver and gold – **electrum**
    An alloy of sulfur with silver, lead or copper having a deep black color – **niello**, pl. **nielli** or **niellos**
    An alloy, mainly of copper, tin and zinc, resembling gold – **oroide**
    An alloy of mercury with one or more other metals – **amalgam**
    To separate the metals in an alloy by melting some constituents while leaving others solid – **liquate** (v.t.)
    Consisting of an alloy of three elements – **ternary**

Almond:
    Of or like almonds – **amygdalate**; **amygdalic**; **amygdaline**
    Shaped like an almond – **amygdaloid**
    Made or garnished with almonds - **amandine**

Alone:
    Occurring, carried out or made alone; existing, living or acting without others; standing alone – **solitary**
    Withdrawn from society – **recluse**; **solitary**
    One who lives alone – **recluse**; **solitary**; **solitudinarian**
    The quality or state of being alone – **isolation**; **solitude**
    Extreme or irrational fear of being alone – **autophobia**
    The state of being in solitary confinement – **reclusion**
    A person who has retired to a solitary place for a life of religious seclusion – **anchorite**; **anchoret**; **hermit**, n.
        anchoritism; **hermitry**; **hermitship**, adj. **anchoritic**

A woman who is an anchorite – **anchoress**

Alphabet:
A teacher or learner of an alphabet; having reference to the alphabet – **abecedarian**; **abecedary**
The application in the evolution of an alphabet of a pictorial symbol or hieroglyph for the name of an object to the initial sound alone of that name; the naming of a letter by a word whose initial sound is the same as that which the letter represents – **acrology**; **acrophony**

Alps (see also Mountain):
Of or relating to the alps or any mountainous region – **alpestrine**

Alteration (change):
Causing alteration; something that causes alteration – **alterant**; adj. **alterative**

Altitude:
At the highest altitude – **culminant**

Aluminum:
Of or containing aluminum, alum or alumina - **aluminous**

Ambiguity:
Ambiguity resulting from uncertain grammatical construction – **amphiboly**; **amphibology**, adj. **amphibolous**
To use ambiguities or evasions – **tergiversate** (v.i.)

Among other persons – **inter alios**

Among other things – **inter alia**

Amount:
A tiny amount – **scintilla**; **trace**

Ancestor:
The earliest ancestor or forefather – **primogenitor**
A direct ancestor – **progenitor**
Direct descent from an ancestor – **ancestry**; **lineage**
Belonging to or being in the direct line of descent from an ancestor – **lineal**
Relating to or characterized by development from more than one ancestral type – **polyphyletic**
Of or relating to an excessive veneration of ancestors or tradition – **filiopietistic**

Anger:
Easily angered; marked by or resulting from anger – **irascible**
A long, angry speech, usually of censure or denunciation – **diatribe**; **harangue**; **obloquy**; **tirade**
To become angry or inflamed – **rankle** (v.i.)

Angle:
Having equal angles; a line having equal angles – **isogonal**; **isogonic**
Of, relating to or composed of right angles – **orthogonal**
Having no angle – **agonic**
Angled or swept backward – **backswept**
To make angular; to become angular – **angulate** (v.t./v.i.)
An angle less than 90° – **acute angle**

An angle greater than 90° - **obtuse angle**

Any angle other than a right angle – **oblique angle**

The theory or science of measuring angles – **goniometry**

Animal (misc. terms):

Of, relating to or resembling an animal – **bestial**

    To make bestial – **bestialize**

To make (a person) resemble a beast; to change into animal matter – **animalize** (v.t.)

Having an animal form – **theriomorphic**; **theriomorphous**

The biological study of the distribution of animals – **zoogeography**

The biological description of animals – **zoography**

The study of animals; the animal life of a particular area; the characteristics of an animal group or category – **zoology**

An instinctive inclination or propensity in animals to perform certain actions – **appetence** (pl. **appetences**);

    appetency, pl. **appetencies**

The study of animal behavior in relation to habitat – **ethology**

The worship of animals – **theriolatry**; **zoolatry**

Belief in animal gods – **zoolatry**; **zootheism**

The attribution of animal characteristics or qualities to a god; the use of animal forms in symbolism, literature or graphic representation - **zoomorphism**

Of or like a wild animal – **feral**; **ferine**

Affecting wild animals – **sylvatic**

The breeding of special stocks and races – **stirpiculture**

An official record of the pedigree of purebred animals, as horses and dogs; a book in which such records are published – **studbook**

A plane dividing a bilaterally symmetrical animal into right and left halves – **median plane**

    Of, relating to or lying in the median plane – **median**

The animal lore of a race or people; the systematic study of such lore – **ethnozoology**

Of or relating to the geographic distribution of animals (fauna) – **faunistic**

Feeding on animal matter – **zoophagous**

Any animal having somewhat the appearance and character of a plant – **zoophyte**, adj. **zoophytic, zoophytical**

An animal that lives in the dwelling place or burrow of another kind of animal; being or living as such – **inquiline**

Aquatic animals living on the surface of a body of water – **infauna**

An animal that lives underground – **subterrestrial**; **troglodyte**

A hornless animal, as a cow or sheep - **pollard**

An abandoned young animal – **stray**; **waif**

To lodge and feed (an animal) in a stall for the purpose of fattening – **stall-feed** (v.t.)

A team of animals used to pull or draw a load – **draft**

    A pair of draft animals – **span**

    Two or more draft animals used to pull a vehicle or piece of farm machinery; a vehicle together with the animal or animals harnessed to it; a group of animals exhibited or performing together; to harness or join (animals, e.g.) together thus; to haul or transport with such a group of animals; to drive such a group of animals – **team** (n./v.t./v.i.)

    One who drives a team - **teamster**

A file of animals chained together in transit - **coffle**

A wild or vicious animal – **outlaw**

Serving as a warning of danger – **sematic** (used of conspicuous colors of a poisonous or noxious animal)

To drive from a lair or den; to loose from a kennel – **unkennel** (v.t.)

A pound for animals – **penfold**; **pinfold**

An animal castrated after sexual maturity – **stag**

    A castrated animal, esp. a horse – **gelding**

A hybrid between a stallion and an ass that differs from a mule in having a bushier tail and a body disproportionately large in comparison to the legs - **hinny**

The care and breeding of domestic animals, as cattle, sheep, horses, etc. – **animal husbandry**

    The technology of animal husbandry – **zootechny**; **zootechnics** (sing./pl.)

    Of or relating to herdsmen, shepherds and others involved in animal husbandry – **pastoral**

Measurement and comparison of the sizes of animals or animal parts, esp. the measurement of bulk – **zoometry**

To cut into or dissect the body of a living animal, esp. for research purposes – **vivisect** (v.t.), n. **vivisection**

An attraction to, preference for or erotic fixation on animals – **zoophilia**, adj. **zoophilic**

A lover of animals, esp. one opposed to vivisection – **zoophile**

An extreme or irrational fear of animals or animal spirits – **zoophobia**

An extreme or irrational fear of contact with animal fur or skin – **doraphobia**

Dissection of animals – **zootomy**

Imitative of animal behavior – **zoomimic**

A person trained and authorized to treat animals medicinally – **veterinarian**; **veterinary surgeon**

The medical science of the diagnosis and treatment of animal diseases and injuries – **veterinary medicine**

A very small animal, esp. one that cannot be seen without a microscope – **animalcule**; **animalculum**

An animal that is one year old or has not completed its second year – **yearling**

A young fur-bearing animal – **kit**

Abandoned by its mother and reared by hand – **cade**

An animal, as a lamb or calf, fattened for slaughter – **fatling**

An animal's viscera or inner organs – **entrails**; **purtenance**

The art or process of preparing, stuffing and mounting the skins of dead animals for exhibition in a lifelike state – **taxidermy**

A set of three animals, as hounds – **leash**

A pack animal, such as a horse or mule – **beast of burden**; **sumpter**

A male animal with one or two undescended testicles – **ridgeling**; **ridgling**

Having variegated markings, esp. black and white spots; an animal having such markings – **piebald**

Animals, mythical:

    A figure having, typically, the body of a lion and the head of a man, hawk or ram; a winged monster with a lion's body and the head and breasts of a woman – **sphinx**

        A sphinx having the head of a ram – **criosphinx**

        A sphinx having the head of a man and the body of a lion – **androsphinx**

    A creature with a man's head, trunk and arms, and a horse's body and legs – **centaur**

    A legendary sea creature with the head and trunk of a beautiful woman and the tail of a fish – **mermaid**

    A creature similar to a mermaid but with the head and trunk of a man – **merman**

    A horselike creature having a single horn growing from the center of its forehead – **unicorn**

    A serpent with a head at each end of its body – **amphisbaena**

    A serpent hatched from a cock's egg and having the power to kill by a look – **basilisk**; **cockatrice**

    A fire-breathing monster represented as having a lion's head, a goat's body and a ser-pent's tail - **chimera**

    An animal with the body and hind legs of a lion, and the head and wings of an eagle – **griffin**; **griffon**; **gryphon**

    A monster with the body and hindquarters of a horse and the head and wings of a griffin – **hippogriff**; **hippogryph**

Anniversary (see also Year):

    A third anniversary – **triennial**

    A fifth anniversary – **quinquennial**

    A tenth anniversary or its celebration – **decennial**

    A fifteenth anniversary or its celebration – **quindecennial**

    A fiftieth anniversary or its celebration – **semicentennial**

    A special anniversary, esp. a fiftieth – **jubilee**

A 100th anniversary or its celebration; of or relating to such an anniversary or celebration – **centennial**

A 150th anniversary or its celebration - **sesquicentennial**

A 200th anniversary or its celebration – **bicentenary**; **bicentennial**

A 300th anniversary or its celebration; of or relating to such an anniversary or celebration – **tercentenary**; **tercentennial**; **tricentennial**

A 400th anniversary or its celebration; of or relating to such an anniversary or celebration – **quadricentennial**

Answer:
Yielding a precise answer, as a computational system guaranteeing accurate solution – **algoristic**

Ant:
Of or relating to ants – **formic**; **formican**; **formicine**
Resembling an ant – **formicine**
A group of ants – **colony**
The study of ants - **myrmecology**
The dwelling of a colony of ants – **formicary**
Inhabiting a single nest – **monodomous** (used of ant colonies)
Inhabiting several nests – **polydomous** (used of ant colonies)
An artificial ant nest – **formicarium**
An insect of a foreign species that lives more or less permanently in an ant colony – **myrmecophile**, adj. **myrmecophilous**
A substance used for killing ants – **formicide**
Dependence upon or attraction to ants – **myrmecophilism**; **myrmecophily**
Feeding on ants – **formicivorous**; **myrmecophagous**; **myrmotherine**
Having wingless males – **ergatandrous** (used of ants)
Extreme or irrational fear of ants – **myrmecophobia**

Antelope:
A group of antelope – **herd**
A male antelope – **buck**
A female antelope – **doe**
A young antelope – **kid**

Antenna (pl. antennae):
A small antenna – **antennule**
Having long antennae – **longicorn**
Having branched antennae – **ramicorn**

Antidote, acting as an – **alexipharmic**

Antiques:
Of antiques – **antiquarian**
The study or love of antiques – **antiquarianism**

Antiquities:
One who collects or studies antiquities – **antiquary**, adj. **antiquarian**
The study or knowledge of antiquities, esp. prehistoric ones – **paleology**, n. **paleologist**

Antler:
Having antlers – **antlered**
A set of antlers – **rack**

Anus:
  Of or relating to the anus – **anal**
  Near the anus – **adanal**

Apartment:
  An apartment in which the rooms are connected in a line, with windows at the front and rear – **railroad flat**

Ape:
  A group of apes – **shrewdness**; **troop**
  Relating to, characteristic of or resembling an ape – **simian**

Apex:
  Located below or near an apex – **subapical**
  Opposite to or directed away from the apex – **abapical**

Aphids, of or relating to – **aphidian**

Apology:
  A formal and satisfactory apology to an offended person – **amende honorable**

Appeal:
  To appeal to earnestly – **adjure**; **entreat** (both v.t.)

Appendage:
  A slender, flexible appendage, as a tentacle – **cirrus**, pl. **cirri** (Zool.)
  Of, relating to or being an appendage - **appendicular**

Appendix (body part):
  Of or relating to the appendix – **appendical**; **appendiceal**; **appendicial**
  A small appendix – **appendicle**
  Surgical removal of the appendix – **appendectomy**
  Inflammation of the appendix – **appendicitis**

Appetite – see Eating

Applause:
  A group of persons hired to applaud at a performance – **claque**
  An act of applauding; a round of applause - **plaudit**
  An enthusiastic outburst of applause – **ovation**

Apple:
  Of, relating to or characteristic of an apple – **pomaceous**
  Of the apple family of plants and trees – **malaceous**

Approach:
  To approach and speak to first – **accost** (v.t.)

Arbor:
  To interlace or plait (twigs or branches, e.g.), esp. in making an arbor – **pleach** (v.t.)

Arc, shaped like an – **arciform**

Arch:
  The inner curve of an arch – **intrados**
  The outside curved surface of an arch – **extrados**
  A row of arches – **arcuation**
  An acutely pointed arch – **lancet arch**
  Relating to an arch with a rise less than half its span – **surbased**

Archeology:
  An archeological site regarded as definitively characteristic of a particular culture – **type-site**
  A nonprofessional archeologist – **pothunter**

Archery:
  One fond of or expert at archery – **toxophilite**
  Of or relating to archery – **sagittary**; **toxophilite**
  Of or relating to archers – **toxophilite**
  The love of archery – **toxophily**
  Archery equipment collectively – **tackle**
  The distance an arrow can be shot – **bowshot**
  The ability of the bow to propel arrows – **cast**
  The distance the bowstring is pulled back – **draw**
  The pattern of the arrows on the target – **group**
  The notch in the end of an arrow which is placed on the bowstring and holds the arrow on the string; to place the arrow on the string – **nock** (n./v.t.)

Arctic:
  Of or resembling regions just south of the Arctic Circle (the parallel of latitude 66°33' north) – **subarctic**
  Of or designating the zoogeographic region that includes the northern areas of the earth – **Holarctic** (divided into the Nearctic and Palearctic regions)

Area:
  Over a wide area; scattered over a wide area - **broadcast**

Argument (see also Reason/Reasoning):
  Of or relating to argument or controversy; given to argument – **eristic**; **eristical**
  One devoted to logical argument - **controversialist**; **eristic**
  The art or practice of argument or controversy – **polemics**
  The art or practice of argument, esp. based on specious grounds – **eristic**
  To overwhelm by argument – **confute** (v.t.)
  An advance in argument from antecedent to consequent - **consecution**
  An argument in which one of the propositions is understood but not stated – **enthymeme**
  A plausible but fallacious argument; deceptive or fallacious argumentation – **sophism**, **sophistry**
  The art or practice of arriving at the truth by disclosing the contradictions in an opponent's argument and overcoming them – **dialectic**
  An argument or debate marked by the reckless or incorrect use of words – **logomachy**
  Disproof of a proposition by demonstrating the absurdity of its inevitable conclusion – **reductio ad absurdum**
    Argument by the reductio ad absurdum - **apagoge**
  Dislike, distrust or hatred of argument – **misology**, n. **misologist**

Arm (body part):
  Congenital absence of arms – **abrachia**

Arms (military; see also Nuclear):
  A storehouse for arms – **armory**; **arsenal**

Armpit or analogous part – **axilla**, adj. **axillar**; **axillary**

Arrange:
  To arrange or draw up, as troops in battle order; an orderly arrangement, esp. of troops – **array** (v.t./n.)
    The act or process of arraying; something arrayed – **arrayal**
    A one-dimensional array – **vector**
  Abnormal arrangement, as of organs or parts of the body or of geological strata – **heterotaxis** (pl. **heterotaxes**);
    heterotaxia, pl. **heterotaxias**

Arrow (see also Archery):
  To feather (an arrow) – **fletch**; **wing** (both v.t.)
  Of or like an arrow – **sagittary**
  Shaped like an arrow – **beloid**
  Shaped like an arrowhead – **sagittate**; **sagittiform**
  The bending and springback capability of an arrow – **spine**
  The portion of an arrow that touches the bow when in position for shooting – **breast**
  A blunt or unbarbed arrow – **butt shaft**
  A maker of arrows – **fletcher**
  The wooden shaft of an arrow – **stele**, pl. **steles**
  A portable case for arrows; the arrows held in such a case – **quiver**
  Divination by drawing arrows at random from a container – **belomancy**

Art/Artist:
  A knowledge of, love for, or taste for fine objects of art – **virtu**
  The description, history or analysis of symbolic art or artistic symbolism – **iconology**;
    iconography
  A recurrent thematic element used in an artistic work – **motif**
  To draw or paint upon a canvas or other flat surface – **limn** (v.t.)
  The thick application of pigment to a canvas or panel in painting; the body of pigment so applied - **impasto**
  An artistic work that broadly mimics an artist's characteristic style and holds it up to ridicule – **parody**
  A work of art applied directly to a wall or ceiling – **mural**
  The art, style or process of making one pictorial composition by closely arranging or superimposing many pictures or
    designs – **montage**
  An artistic composition of materials and objects pasted over a surface – **collage**
  A method of making a design by placing a piece of paper on top of an object and then rubbing over it, as with a pencil
    or charcoal – **frottage**
  The art of painting on fresh, moist plaster with earth colors dissolved in water; a painting executed in this fashion –
    fresco
  The art of painting on stone – **lithochromy**
  A painter of landscapes – **landscapist**; **paysagist**
  Decoration produced on pottery or ceramic by scratching through a surface of plaster or glazing to reveal a different
    color beneath – **sgraffito**
  To soften the lines or colors of (a drawing) by rubbing lightly – **scumble** (v.t.)
  The art or process of producing designs or pictures by burning or scorching with hot instruments – **pyrography**
  Print-making through the silk-screen process – **serigraphy**, n. **serigrapher**
    An original print produced by serigraphy - **serigraph**
  A work of art composed of three hinged or folding panels – **triptych**
  To draw, engrave or paint in dots or short strokes – **stipple** (v.t.)

The practice or technique of applying dots or tiny strokes of color elements to a surface so that when seen from the distance the dots or strokes blend luminously together – **pointillism**; **pointillisme**, n. **pointillist** or **pointilliste**

Excessively ornate or intricate – **rococo**

A style of painting that creates an illusion of photographic reality; such a painting or effect – **trompe l'oeil**

A painting medium in which pigment is mixed with water-soluble glutinous materials, such as size or egg yolk; painting done in this way – **tempera**; **tempora**

The sum of an artist's lifework – **oeuvre**

Artistic ability, quality or workmanship – **artistry**

Traditionalism or conventionalism in art, literature, music, etc. – **academicism**

Representation in the same artwork of two or more events that occurred at different times – **synchronism**

The style of an earlier period in painting or other arts – **archaicism**; **archaism**

A style in art characterized by haziness and lack of definition – **obscurantism**, n. **obscurantist**

A vertical Japanese scroll painting – **kakemono**

Artery:
Inflammation of an artery – **arteritis**
Within an artery – **intraarterial**
Of, relating to or connecting boty arteries and veins – **arteriovenous**
Surgical removal of the inner lining of an artery – **endarterectomy**
Inflammation of the inner lining of an artery – **endarteritis**

Ashes:
Like, consisting of, or of the color of ashes - **cinereous**

Ass:
Of or like an ass – **asinine**
A group of asses – **drove**; **herd**; **pace**
A male ass – **jack**
A female ass – **jenny**
A young ass – **colt**; **foal**

Assembly, an unlawful or questionable – **conventicle**

Assume:
The act of assuming; something taken to be true without proof or demonstration – **assumption**
Of or marked by assumption – **assumptive**

Astronomy (cranology; see also Planet, Space, Stars, Sun, and Universe):
The dynamics of celestial bodies – **astrodynamics**
Description or mapping of the heavens – **astrography**
The geological study of celestial bodies - **astrogeology**
The position of a celestial body when it is on the opposite side of the sun from Earth – **superior conjunction**
A configuration in which the Earth lies on a straight line between the sun and a planet – **opposition**
The point farthest from the Earth in the orbit of the moon or a man-made satellite – **apogee**
The point in orbit of greatest or least distance of a celestial body from a center of attraction – **apsis**, pl. **apsides**
The point in the orbit of a revolving body nearest the center of gravity about which the body moves - **pericenter**
Of or caused by both the sun and the moon – **lunisolar**
The dividing line between the bright and shaded regions of the disk of the moon or an inner planet – **terminator**
The bright band or region around a celestial body – **aureole**
A small celestial body with an intense gravitational field that is believed to be a collapsed star – **black hole**

Rapid variation in the light of a celestial body caused by turbulence in the Earth's atmosphere – **scintillation**; **twinkling**

To reach the highest point above an observer's horizon – **culminate** (v.i.) (used of stars and other celestial bodies)

A faintly colored luminous ring around a celestial body visible through a haze or thin cloud – **corona**

A faint, glowing spot in the sky, exactly opposite the position of the sun – **gegenschein**

The worship of heavenly bodies – **astrolatry**

Any of numerous orbiting celestial bodies with typical diameters between one and several hundred miles – **asteroid**; **planetoid**

Atlantic:

On this (the speaker's) side of the Atlantic – **cisatlantic**

Atmosphere:

The study of the air or atmosphere – **aerography**

Of or designating the Earth's atmosphere and the space beyond – **aerospace**

The outermost portion of the Earth's atmosphere – **geocorona**

The science dealing with atmospheric phenomena – **meteorology**

Meteorologic conditions in a small region – **micrometeorology**

The branch of meteorology dealing with the observation of the atmosphere by means of balloons, airplanes, etc. - **aerology**

The study of the Earth's upper atmosphere – **aeronomy**

The study of atmospherics, esp. using electronic detectors – **sferics**; **spherics**

Atom:

Within an atom – **intra-atomic**

An electrically charged atom or group of atoms – **ion**

To convert partially or completely into ions – **ionize** (v.i./v.t.)

A negative ion – **anion**

A group of two or more atoms that acts as a single atom and goes through a reaction unchanged, or is replaced by a single atom – **radical**

The movement of one or more atoms from one position in a molecule to another – **migration**

Occurring as single atoms – **monatomic**

Having two atoms per molecule - **diatomic**

Having three atoms per molecule – **triatomic**

Of or relating to atomic nuclei; using or derived from the energy of atomic nuclei – **nuclear** (q.v.)

The study of the forces, reactions and internal structures of atomic nuclei – **nuclear physics**

The physics of atomic, molecular, nuclear and subnuclear systems – **microphysics**

The technology of nuclear energy – **nucleonics**

Of or relating to the spatial arrangement of atoms in a molecule – **steric**

Attachment:

An organ or structure of attachment – **holdfast** (Biol.)

Permanently attached or fixed – **sedentary**; **sessile** (both Zool.)

Stalkless and attached directly at the base – **sessile** (Bot.)

Situated nearest the point of attachment – **proximal**

Attached to something on one side only – **semidetached**

Attack:

Susceptible to attack – **vulnerable**

To lie in wait for and attack from ambush – **waylay** (v.t.)

Attention:
A focal point of attention and admiration – **cynosure**
To withdraw (oneself) entirely from attention – **efface** (v.t.)

Attraction:
Mutual attraction, esp. between a man and a woman – **affinity**

Auction:
Someone who bids at an auction to raise prices for the owner – **by-bidder**

Authenticity:
Of doubtful authenticity – **apocryphal**

Author:
Of or relating to an author – **auctorial**
Of doubtful authorship – **apocryphal**

Authority:
Authority or power to act for another; a document giving such authorization - **proxy**
Refusing to submit to authority – **recusant**

Average:
Numerical average – **mean**
    Arithmetic mean of the squares of a set of numbers – **mean square**
The difference, esp. the absolute difference, between one set of numbers and their mean - **deviation**

Avoidance:
Causing avoidance of an unpleasant or painful stimulus – **aversive**

Awl, shaped like an – **subulate** (Biol.)

Ax (or axe):
An ice ax used in mountain climbing – **piolet**
Shaped like the head of an ax – **dolabriform**

Axis (pl. axes):
Relating to or forming an axis; located on, around or in the direction of an axis – **axial**
Tending to grow or form along a vertical axis – **orthotropic**
Away from the axis – **abaxial**
Having only one axis; of or along a single axis – **uniaxial**
Having or mounted on a common axis – **coaxial**
Involving or having three axes - **triaxial**
Of, relating to or being on the side toward the stem or axis – **adaxial**
Arranged on or turned to one side of an axis – **secund**

B

Back:
  In the direction of the back – **dorsad** (Anat.)
  Of, toward, on, in or near the back – **dorsal**
  The part of an organ or appendage analogous to the back – **dorsum**
  At, close to or toward the back – **posterior**; **retral**

Bacteria:
  Resembling bacteria in appearance or action – **bacteroid**
  Having bacteria as a cause – **bacteriogenic**
  To cause a change in by means of bacteria – **bacterize** (v.t.)
  A bacterially produced anti-bacterial agent – **bacteriocin**
  The dissolution of bacteria; chemical decomposition caused by bacteria – **bacteriolysis**
  Inhibiting or arresting bacterial growth without killing the bacteria – **bacteriostasis**
      An agent that produces bacteriostasis – **bacteriostat**
  A substance that destroys bacteria – **bactericide**
  Destroying or inhibiting the growth of bacteria; any of certain chemical substances that have the capacity to destroy or
      inhibit the growth of bacteria – **antibiotic** (adj./n.)
  The seat of bacterial growth in a living organism – **nidus**
  The study of bacteria – **bacteriology**, n. **bacteriologist**
  The microscopic study of bacteria – **bacterioscopy**
  The ability of bacteria to be genetically transformable – **competence**
  A rod-shaped bacterium – **bacillus**, pl. **bacilli**
      Of, relating to or caused by bacilli – **bacillary**
      A bacillus that is short and oval in shape – **coccobacillus**
      Extreme or irrational fear of bacilli – **bacillophobia**
  A bacterium with a spherical or oval shape – **coccus**, p. **cocci**

Badgers, a group of – **cete**

Bagpipe:
  To play on the bagpipes; to produce a shrill, piercing tone (on the bagpipe); the shrill sound made by a bagpipe – **skirl**
      (v.t./v.i./n.)

Bail (Law):
  A person to whom property is bailed – **bailee**
  A person who bails property to another – **bailer**; **bailor**
  The process of providing bail for an accused person – **bailment**

Bakery specializing in French pastry – **patisserie**

Balance:
  Equally balanced – **equiponderant**; **equiponderate**

Baldness – see Hair

Ball or globe, to form into a – **conglobate**; **conglobe**

Ballet:
  A man who trains a ballet company – **ballet master**; **maître de ballet**

A woman who trains a ballet company – **ballet mistress**

A female ballet dancer – **ballerina**; **danseuse**

A male ballet dancer – **danseur**

The leading male dancer in a ballet company – **premier danseur**

The leading female dancer in a ballet company – **prima ballerina**

The director of a ballet – **régisseur**

A member of a ballet company who dances usually as part of a small group and who ranks below the soloists –
    coryphée

A ballet enthusiast – **balletomane**

A full turn of the body on the tip of the tow or on the ball of the foot; to perform such a turn – **pirouette** (n./v.i.)

A ballet step or series of such steps – **pas**, pl. **pas**

A ballet figure or dance for two persons – **pas de deux**

A male dancer who is the partner of a ballerina, as in a pas de deux – **danseur noble**

A leap with one leg extending forward and the other backward – **jeté**

A leap straight upward in which the dancer crosses his legs or strikes his heels together while coming down –
    entrechat

A series of short turns performed in a straight line across the stage - **chaîné**

A position in which one leg is extended straight backward and the arms are extended, one forward and one backward
    – **arabesque**

A gliding step to the side – **glissade**

A movement in which the legs are bent while the back is held straight - **plié**

A movement in which the dancer lifts one leg to the front, side or back, and returns it to the supporting leg – **battement**

A broad leap with a battement to the front, side or back – **ballonné**

A position on the extreme tips of the toes – **pointe**

An extravaganza ballet that features a dancing clown and other figures of fantasy - **harlequinade**

An obsession with ballet - **balletomania**

Bandage:

    A bandage applied in overlapping opposite spirals to immobilize a digit or limb – **spica**

Barb:

    A small barb or pointed projection – **barbule**

Barbarism:

    Of, relating to or characteristic of barbarians - **barbaric**

    To make or become barbarous, crude or savage – **barbarize** (v.t./v.i.)

Barber:

    Of or relating to a barber or barbering – **tonsorial**

Barge:

    A heavy barge used for freight – **hoy**

Bark (tree part):

    Covered with, containing or resembling tree bark – **barky**

    Growing or living on tree bark – **corticolous**

    A person or machine that takes bark off a tree or prepares bark – **barker**

Baron:

    Of, relating to, suited to or befitting a baron – **baronial**

    The domain of a baron – **barony**

Barrier/Barricade:

A protective barrier - **redoubt**

A barrier consisting of trees and shrubs that reduces erosion and protects against the effects of wind storms – **shelterbelt**

A ditch or moat serving as a barrier against an enemy, e.g., around a castle – **foss**; **fosse**, pl. **fosses**

A line of fortifications enclosing a castle or town; the area or town thus enclosed - **enceinte**

A barricade or bank (as of earth or sandbags) built up to provide shelter against shrapnel, strafing or overrun of landing space – **revêtement**; **revetment**

A fence of pales (stakes) forming a defensive barrier or fortification; one of the pales of such a fence – **palisade**

To surround with or as if with a rampart or other defensive barrier – **circumvallate** (v.t.)

A defensive barrier across a rampart or trench, as a bank of earth thrown up for protection from enfilade fire – **traverse** (see also Firearms)

Base:

Of, relating to, located at or forming a base – **basal**

A square block serving as a base; the squared base of something – **plinth**

To make basic – **basify** (v.t.)

Basket:

A basket of flowers or fruit – **corbeil**; **corbeille**

Bass (fish), a group of – **shoal**

Bath:

Of a bath or bathing – **balneal**

The act or action of bathing – **balneation**

The science of the therapeutic use of baths, esp. with mineral waters – **balneology**

The treatment of disease by the use of baths – **balneotherapy**; **balneotherapeutics**

Bay:

To put, shelter or detain in or enclose by a bay – **embay** (v.t.)

A wide bay formed by a bend or curve in a shoreline – **bight**

Beach - see Shore and Tide

Beads:

A string of beads that a person fingers to keep the hands occupied – **worry beads**

Resembling a string of beads – **moniliform**

Beak:

Either part of a bird's beak – **mandible**, adj. **mandibular**

Having a beak in which the tips of the mandibles cross – **metagnathous**

A small beaklike part – **rostellum**, adj. **rostellate**; **rostrum**, adj. **rostrate**

Bear:

A group of bears – **sloth**

A male bear – **boar**

A female bear – **sow**

A young bear – **cub**

Of or characteristic of a bear – **ursine**; **arctoid**

Having the form or appearance of a bear – **ursiform**

Beard (see also Hair):
  Beard growing – **pogonotrophy**
  The study of or a treatise on beards – **pogonology**
  Having a beard or tufted hairs resembling a beard – **barbate** (Bot.)

Beat:
  To beat more quickly than normal – **palpitate** (v.i.) (said of the heart)
  To beat with a stick – **cudgel**; **drub**; **fustigate** (all v.t.)
  A beating with a stick or cudgel, esp. on the soles of the feet; to inflict such a beating on – **bastinado**
  To beat severely – **flog**; **welt** (both v.t.)
  The unlawful beating of another person – **battery**
  To beat or pound together, as in a mortar – **contuse** (v.t.)

Beauty:
  One who cultivates superior or excessive appreciation of the beautiful – **aesthete**; **esthete**
  A critic concerned with the theory of beauty and the fine arts – **aesthetician**; **esthetician**
  The pursuit of the beautiful; the cult of beauty and good taste – **aestheticism**; **estheticism**
  Eternally beautiful – **amaranthine**
  Marked by stately or voluptuous beauty - **junoesque**
  A preparation designed to beautify the body by direct application; serving to beautify the body – **cosmetic**
    One whose occupation is manufacturing, selling or applying cosmetics – **cosmetician**
    The study of cosmetics or the skill of applying them - **cosmetology**

Beaver:
  A group of beavers – **colony**
  A young beaver – **kit**; **kitten**; **pup**

Bed:
  Out of bed - **astir**
  A straw bed or mattress – **pallet**
  A low bed on casters – **truckle bed**; **trundle bed**
  A bed that folds or swings into a closet for concealment – **Murphy bed**
  A canopy over a bed – **tester**

Beer:
  Smelling of, tasting of, affected by or produced by beer - **beery**
  An establishment where malt liquors (beer, e.g.) are made – **brewery**, **brewhouse**
  Something prepared by the process of brewing; the process of brewing – **brewage**
  The chemistry that deals with fermentation processes in brewing – **zymurgy**
  A science that deals with fermentation - **zymology**

Bees:
  Of or relating to bees – **apian**, **apiarian**
  A group of bees – **colony**; **swarm**
  Having to do with the care of bees – **apiarian**
  A person who keeps or tends bees – **apiarist**
  A place where bees are kept for their honey – **apiary**
  The raising and care of bees; beekeeping – **apiculture**
  The scientific study of honeybees – **apiology**
  Feeding on bees – **apivorous**
  A shelter for a colony of domestic bees – **hive**

A beehive made of straw - **skep**
Replacement of a queen bee by a superior or younger one – **supersedure**

Beetle:
A long-horned beetle – **longicorn**
Of or relating to blister beetles – **meloid**

Begging:
Depending on begging for a living; someone who depends on begging for a living - **mendicant**
To beg humbly or earnestly, as by praying – **supplicate** (v.i.), n. **supplication**
One who supplicates – **petitioner**; **supplicant**

Beginner – see Novice

Beginning:
Relating to a beginning - **inceptive**
Beginning to exist or appear – **incipient**, n. **incipience** or **incipiency**

Behavior:
Immoral behavior – **obliquity**
Irrational behavior – **irrationalism**
The study of relationships between mental processes and behavior – **psychology**
To explain (behavior) psychologically – **psychologize** (v.t.)
The study of behavior and its interpretation in terms of simple and complex reflexes – **reflexology**, n. **reflexologist**, adj. **reflexological**
The study of psychological reactions – **reactology**, n. **reactologist**, adj. **reactological**
An emotional shock that creates substantial and lasting damage to the psychological development of the individual – **trauma**, pl. **traumas** or **traumata**
The psychological study of the relationships between physical stimuli and sensory response – **psychophysics**
The diagnosis of psychic disorders – **psychognosis**
The measurement of psychological variables such as intelligence, aptitude, etc. – **psychometrics**
The study of correlations between behavior and physiology – **psychophysiology**
The study of phenomena, such as telepathy, clairvoyance and psychokinesis, that are not explainable by known natural laws – **parapsychology**
Of or relating to phenomena that are both physiological and psychological – **psychosomatic**
The study of man as a psychosomatic unity – **organismic psychology**
The practice and technological use of psychology – **psychotechnics**
The generation and development of psychological processes, personality or behavior - **psychogenesis**
Behavioral analysis in terms of motives or drives; interaction of various mental or emotional processes – **psychodynamics**
The application of the findings and methods of experimental, clinical and social psychology to industrial problems – **industrial psychology**
The application of psychological methods and results to the solution of practical problems, esp. in industry – **psychotechnology**
The analysis and classification of mental data – **analytic psychology**
The branch of psychology that deals with pleasant and unpleasant states of consciousness and their relation to organic life - **hedonics**
The aspect of mental or behavioral processes directed toward action or change and including impulse, desire, volition and striving – **conation**
The doctrine that observed behavior provides the only valid data of psychology – **behaviorism**, n. **behaviorist**, adj. **behavioristic**

A doctrine that psychology must be based essentially on data derived from introspection – **introspectionism**

One whose behavior and attitudes differ from the norm or from accepted moral and social standards – **deviant**; **deviate**; **deviator**, n. **deviance**; **deviancy**

The modification of behavioral traits through psychological means, as reinforcement and aversion therapy – **behavior modification**

Continued or repetitive activity or actions, e.g., the uncontrollable repetition of a gesture, word, phrase, etc. – **perseveration**

A person having a personality disorder, esp. one marked by aggressively antisocial behavior – **psychopath,** adj. **psychopathic,** n. **psychopathy**

An emotion, feeling or mood as a factor in behavior – **affect**

An irresistible impulse to act irrationally – **compulsion**

Belching:

An act or instance of belching – **eructation**

To bring up (gas) from the stomach by belching – **eruct** (v.t./v.i.)

Belief:

A false belief – **delusion**

The practice of expressing beliefs, feelings, etc., that one does not hold or possess; an act or instance of this – **hypocrisy**

One given to hypocrisy – **hypocrite**, adj. **hypocritical**

One who holds no particular belief, creed or dogma – **anythingarian; nothingarian**;

A belief or conception derived from sense perception and therefore regarded as not necessarily true - **prolepsis**

The attempt or tendency to combine or reconcile differing beliefs, as in philosophy or religion – **syncretism**

To reconcile or attempt to reconcile (differing beliefs, e.g.); to combine differing beliefs – **syncretize** (v.t./v.i.)

Bell:

Of or relating to bells or the ringing of bells – **tintinnabular; tintinnabulary; tintinnabulous**

The ringing or sounding of bells – **tintinnabulation**

A small tinkling bell – **tintinnabulum**

One who tolls a bell; a bell for tolling – **toller**

Shaped like a bell – **campaniform; campanular; campanulate; campanulated**

A bell tower, esp. a freestanding one – **campanile**

A stationary set of chromatically tuned bells in a tower; a composition arranged or written for such a set of bells; to play such a composition or set of bells – **carillon** (n./v.i.)

The study of bell casting and ringing - **campanology**

A pattern or order in which bells are rung (in music) - **change**

An alarm bell or the ringing of a bell for the purpose of alarm – **tocsin**

Belt:

A broad belt worn over one shoulder and across the chest, with pockets for carrying ammunition, etc. **– bandoleer; bandolier**

A belt worn across the chest to support a sword or bugle – **baldric**

A beltlike structure, band or marking – **cingulum**, adj. **cingulate** or **cingulated** (Biol.)

Bending/Bent:

A bending; a bent part or bend – **flection; flexion**

Bent downward – **inflexed** (Bot.)

Bent downward toward the base – **reclinate** (Bot.)

Bent downward at a sharp angle – **deflexed** (Bot.)

Bending or twisting around; to bend or twist around – **circumflex**

To bend or curve in and out – **sinuate** (v.i.), adj. **sinuous**
Bent in an outward curve – **bandy**
Bent or curved backward – **reflex**; **anaclastic**; **recurvate**; **recurved**; **retroflex**; **retroflexed**; **retrorse**
A backward bending or curving – **anaclasis**; **retroflexion**
Bent at an abrupt angle; jointed so as to be capable of bending thus – **geniculate**; **geniculated**
Not bending – **rigid**, n. **rigidity**

Berry:
Resembling a berry in texture – **baccate**
Having the form of a berry – **baccate**; **bacciform**
Feeding or living on berries – **baccivorous**
Bearing berries – **baccate**; **bacciferous**

Bet:
To win two bets from (a person) at one time – **whipsaw** (v.t.)

Better (see also Improvement):
To make or become better – **improve**; **ameliorate**; **meliorate** (all v.t./v.i.)
Something that ameliorates – **ameliorant**

Bid:
Able to be bid – **biddable**

Bile (liquid secreted by the liver):
Of, relating to or containing bile – **biliary**; **bilious**
Suppression of biliary flow – **cholestasis**
A decrease or absence of bile secretion in the small intestine – **acholia**

Binding, morally or legally – **obligatory**

Biography:
A biography of a person written by himself – **autobiography**, adj. **autobiographic**, **autobiographical**, n. **autobiographer**
A worshipful or idealized biography – **hagiography**, adj. **hagiographic**, **hagiographical**, n. **hagiographer**

Biology – Associations:
An association between two organisms – **mutualism**
The relationship of two or more different organisms in a close association that may be but is not necessarily of benefit to each – **symbiosis**, adj. **symbiotic** or **symbiotical**
One of the organisms in a symbiotic relationship – **symbiont**; **symbiote**
A symbiotic relationship in which one organism dominates and uses another to its own advantage – **helotism**
An association between two organisms that is harmful to one of them - **antibiosis**
An organism that grows, feeds, and is sheltered on or in a different organism while contributing nothing to the survival of its host – **parasite** (q.v.), adj. **parasitic**, n. **parasitism**

Biology – Classification:
The theory, principles and process of classification – **taxonomy**
Standard categories of biological classification – **kingdom**, **phylum**, **class**, **order**, **family**, **genus** and **species**
A member of the same genus as another plant or animal - **congener**
A group of organisms sharing common characteristics in varying degrees of distinction that constitute one of the categories in taxonomic classification, such as phylum, class, order, etc. – **taxon**

A taxonomic group of organisms classified together on the basis of homologous features traced to a common ancestor - **clade**

The classification of organisms in an ordered system designed to indicate natural relationships – **systematics**

A subdivision of a taxonomic species, usually based on geographic distribution – **subspecies** (sing./pl.)

The sole member of its group, such as a species that also constitutes a genus - **monotype**

A taxonomic category forming a subdivision of a species and consisting of naturally occurring or selectively bred individuals having varying characteristics; an organism belonging to such a category – **holotype**

A specimen of an organism taken from the area typical for that species – **topotype**

A taxonomic category forming a subdivision of a species and consisting of naturally occurring or selectively bred individuals having varying characteristics; an organism belonging to such a category - **variety**

A group of organisms of the same species, having distinctive characteristics but not usually considered a separate breed or variety – **strain**

Intermediate in characteristics between two related or similar taxonomic groups – **osculant**

To have or share osculant characteristics – **osculate** (v.i.)

Biology – Fields of study (see also Animals and Plants):
The biological study of:
The geographic distribution of plants and animals – **biogeography**

Essential and typical life processes, functions and activities – **physiology**

The form and structure of organisms and their elements – **anatomy**

The anatomy of specific physiological areas – **topology**

Period phenomena such as flowering, breeding and migration, esp. as related to climate - **phenology**

The cultivation of fruits, vegetables, flowers and plants – **horticulture**

The formation, early growth and development of living organisms – **embryology**

The factors producing degeneration in offspring – **cacogenics**; **dysgenics**

Malformations, monstrosities, or serious deviations from the normal type – **teratology**

Biological rhythms – **chronobiology**

The organs of animals and plants – **organology**

The change in proportion of various parts of an organism as a consequence of growth - **allometry**

Microorganisms and their effects on other forms of life – **microbiology**

The structure and development of biological systems, in terms of the physics and chemistry of their molecular constituents – **molecular biology**

Protozoans – **protozoology**

The form and structure of living organisms – **morphology**

The physics of biological processes – **biophysics**

Life beyond the earth's atmosphere, as on other planets – **exobiology**

See also under specific subject.

Biology – Growing/Living Conditions (see also Growth):
The environment in which an organism or biological population usually lives or grows - **habitat**

A region or area where a particular kind of organism lives and thrives – **metropolis**

Living or moving independently – **free-living**

The course of development of an individual organism – **ontogeny**

Late in developing – **serotinal**; **serotinous**

An animal or plant that lives on, in or with another, sharing its food, but is neither parasitic on it nor is injured by it – **commensal**, n. **commensalism**

A commensal organism living on the outer body surface of another organism – **ectocommensal**

An organism that lives on dead or decaying organic matter – **saprophyte**, adj. **sapro-phytic**

An organism that can withstand a hot, dry environment – **xerophil**; **xerophile**

Flourishing in such an environment – **xerophilous**, n. **xerophily**

Having little capacity to resist drought - **xerophobous**

Living in water during an early stage of development and on land during the adult stage - **amphibiotic**

Living under a stone – **lapidicolous** (used esp. of an insect)

Growing on the exterior of a living animal – **epizoic**

Living within the tissues of a host – **endobiotic**

Living on several hosts – **plurivorous**

Having all stages of a life cycle occur on the same host – **antoecious**

Inhabiting a cavity of an animal's body – **coelozoic**

Growing or living in moist places – **hygrophilous**

Living or able to live both on land and in water – **amphibious**, n. **amphibian**

All the tiny organisms swimming in large numbers on or near the surface of the sea - **nekton**

The organisms living on sea or lake bottoms – **benthos**

Spread out flat without definite form – **diffuse**; **effuse** (Bot.)

Extremely profuse in growth – **rampant**; **rank**

Abnormally grown together – **fasciate**; **fasciated** (both Bot.)

Growing in rubbish, poor land or waste; a plant that grows thus - **ruderal**

Grown in the absence of sunlight – **etiolate**; **etiolated**

Growing or living at high altitudes – **alpestrine** (Bot.)

Growing in or inhabiting mountain areas - **montane**

Growing or living in mountainous regions just below the timberline - **subalpine**
  Preferring or thriving in a subalpine environment – **orophilous**, n. **orophyte**

Growing at the tip – **acrogenous** (Bot.)

Growing upward in a spiral that turns from right to left – **sinistrorse** (Bot.)

Growing upward in a spiral that turns from left to right – **dextrorse** (Bot.)

Growing in groups that are close together but not densely clustered or matted – **gregarious** (Bot.)

Growing outward – **enate**

Growing or developing from the top toward the base – **basipetal** (Bot.)

Growing upward from the apex to the base – **acropetal** (Bot.)

Growing or developing on an upper surface – **epigenous** (Bot.)

Growing or developing on a lower surface – **hypogenous** (Bot.)

Growing or lying or along the ground but erect at or near the apex, as some stems – **decumbent** (Bot.)

Movement or growth of an organism in response to heat – **thermotaxis**; **thermotropism**, adj. **thermotactic**

Responsive movement of an organism toward or away from an external stimulus – **taxis**; **tropism**

Growth or movement of an organism toward or away from the sun - **heliotropism**

The tendency of the longer axes of roots or branches to grow at an oblique or horizontal angle – **plagiotropism**

Of, relating to or marked by a tendency in plants to grow or change in response to internal cell pressures as
  distinguished from environmental influences - **nastic**

Movement of an organism in response to the flow of a current – **rheotaxis**

Lasting past maturity without falling off - **persistent**

To replace (a lost or damaged organ or part) by formation of new tissue – **regenerate** (v.t.)

Regeneration of an organ or part characterized by proliferation of new tissue – **epimorphosis**

The regeneration of a part or the transformation of one part into another by means of structural reorganization with
  only limited production of new cells - **morphallaxis**

Biology – Orientation/Position:

Position, esp. normal position – **situs**

Of or on the lower or inner surface of an organ; relating to the lower surface of the body of an animal – **ventral**

Of or on the underside of a surface – **dorsal**

Resting against another part – **accumbent** (Bot.)

Extending downward from the base along a stem, as some leaves – **decurrent**

Modification of the orientation of an organ (as a plant root) as a result of wounding – **traumatotropism**

Rising above the surface of a fluid, as certain aquatic plants – **emersed**

Directed toward a central organ or section – **afferent**
Spreading or branching widely from a point or axis – **divaricate**
Pressed close to or flat against a surface – **appressed**
Converging and touching – **connivent**
Inverted or seemingly turned upside-down – **resupinate** (Bot.)
Thrust outward – **exsert**
Upward or forward – **antrorse**
Facing outward; turned away from the axis of growth – **extrorse**
Facing inward or toward the center – **introrse** (Bot.)
Slanting or curving upward – **assurgent** (Bot.)
Near the central part of the body or a point of attachment or origin – **proximal**
Farthest from the center or the point of attachment – **distal**
Creeping along the ground; crawling – **repent**

Biology – Physical Characteristics (see also Form; see also Plant Parts; see also under specific name or type of part):
Having many divisions, clefts or lobes – **multifid**
Heart-shaped – **cordate**
Having an equal number of parts, organs, markings, etc. - **isomerous**
Lack of structural, organizational or developmental correspondence between bodily parts, arising from differences in origin - **heterology**
Having differing or unequal parts within the same structure or similar structures – **heteromerous**
A slender, tubular or bristlelike process – **style** (see also Point)
A band or bandlike structure that holds an organ or part in place - **retinaculum**
With edges cut deeply into narrow, fringelike segments or lobes – **laciniate** (used esp. of leaves and petals)
A small, rounded prominence or process - **tubercle**
 Resembling a tubercle - **tuberculoid**
A sac-shaped, bottle-shaped or pitcher-shaped organ or part – **ascidium** (Bot.)
A thin, pliable layer of tissue covering surfaces or separating or connecting regions, structures or organs – **membrane**, adj. **membranal** or **membranous**
A fold, crease or wrinkle – **ruga**, pl. **rugae**
 Having many wrinkles or creases (rugae) – **rugose**
 A fleshy, naked outgrowth, such as a fowl's wattles – **caruncle**
A group of organisms having identical genetic but varying physical characteristics – **biotype**
The retention of juvenile characteristics in the adult – **paedomorphism**
Abnormal structural arrangement – **heterotaxia**; **heterotaxis**; **heterotaxy**
An individual with male and female characteristics – **gynandromorphy**
The typical form of an organism as it occurs in nature, as distinguished from mutant specimens that may result from selective breeding – **wild type**
Thin, membranous and dry – **scarious** (Bot.)
Covered with mealy dust or powder – **farinose**
Spiny or prickly – **acanthaceous** (Bot.)
Enlarged or globular at an end – **capitate**
Having a blunt point – **hebetate** (Bot.)
Egg-shaped, with the narrow end attached to the stem – **obovoid** (Bot.)
Marked with many shallow depressions, grooves or pits – **scrobiculate**
Deeply pitted – **alveolate**
The pattern of spots and markings on an animal or plant – **maculation**
Marked by broad bands of color - **fasciate**; **fasciated** (both Zool.)
Darkened or tinged with brown, as a part of an insect's wing – **infuscate**; **infuscated** (both Zool.)
Enclosed or covered with a hardened secretion – **obtect**; **obtected**
Having markings suggesting spectacles – **spectacled**

Resembling surroundings in color or form – **apatetic**

Abruptly truncated, as though bitten or broken off – **premorse**

Forming a single axis at each branching, as some flower clusters – uniparous (Bot.)

Having the stem or support attached to the lower surface instead of at the base or margin – **peltate**

Helpless and dependent when born or hatched – **altricial**

Active and able to move freely from birth or hatching – **precocial**

Erect and almost parallel, as certain branches – **fastigiate**; **fastigiated** (Bot.)

Having a white, powdery covering or bloom – **pruinose** (Bot.)

Having, formed of or divided into small cavities or cells – **locular**

Having a single compartment or chamber – **unilocular**

Divided into or containing two chambers or cavities – **bilocular**; **biloculate**

Divided into or containing three chambers or cavities – **trilocular**

A single turn of a spiral shell – **volution**; **whorl** (both Zool.)

A circular arrangement around a point on an axis (Bot.) – **whorl**; **verticil**

    Arranged in or forming a whorl or whorls – **verticillate**; **verticillated**, n. **verticillation**

An organism with a stony structure - **lithophyte**

Biology – Processes:

The complex of physical and chemical processes involved in the maintenance of life – **metabolism**

The rate at which energy is used by an organism at complete rest – **basal metabolic rate**

The process by which living tissue is changed into waste products of a simpler chemical composition – **catabolism**

The natural or artificial fusion of two organisms - **parabiosis**

A substance that initiates or modifies the rate of a biological process – **biocatalyst**

Capable of being decomposed by natural biological processes – **biodegradable**

An intrinsically patterned cyclical biological process or function – **biorhythm**

The environmentally determined development of characteristics or structures in an organism – **cenogenesis**;
    coenogenesis

The production of complex substances from simple ones by or with living organisms – **biosynthesis**

A state of physiological equilibrium produced by a balance of functions and chemical composition within an organism –
    homeostasis

To shed an outer covering, such as feathers, skin, etc. – **exuviate**; **molt** (v.i./v.t.)

    The material shed in this manner – **exuvation**; **exuvia**; **molt**

The spontaneous casting off of a body part for self-protection – **autotomy**, v.i./v.t **autotomize**

Falling off or shed at a specific season or state of growth – **deciduous** (Bot.)

Withering but not falling off – **marcescent** (Bot.)

Withering or dropping off early – **fugacious** (Bot.)

Dropping off or shedding at an early stage of development – **caduceus**

To burst or split open along a line or slit – **dehisce** (v.i.), adj. **dehiscent** (Bot.)

Breaking away from a natural dividing line – **septifragal** (Bot.)

Not splitting open at maturity – **indehiscent** (Bot.)

Bursting apart, as do some ripe seed parts – **dissilient** (Bot.)

Bursting through or as if through a surface or covering - **erumpet**

Producing salts of lime, as in the formation of eggshells of birds and reptiles – **calcific**

Biology – Reproduction (see also Offpring and Plant Reproduction and Breeding):

The capacity to perform both the male and female sexual functions - **bipotentiality**

Having both male and female organs in the same individual – **androgynous** (n. **androgyne**); **bisexual**;
    hermaphroditic, n. **hermaphrodite**, n. **hermaphrodism** or **hermaphroditism**

Of only one sex; having only one type of sexual organ – **unisexual**

Incapable of sexual reproduction – **infertile**; **sterile**

    A sterilizing agent – **sterilant**

Having no sex organs – **asexual**; **neuter**

Sexually undeveloped – **neuter** (Zool.)

Marked by the alternation of sexual and asexual generations – **heterogonous**, n. **heterogony**

The occurrence of alternating sexual and asexual reproductive cycles – **metagenesis**

True sexual reproduction, with fusion of sperm and egg nuclei – **amphimixis**

Requiring fertilization in reproduction – **gamic**

Occurring or reproducing without the union of male and female cells – **agamic**; **agamous**

Having two types of females, one able to reproduce sexually, the other infertile, as in ants – **heterogynous**

Reproduction during the larval or preadult stage – **paedogenesis**

Reproduction by budding - **blastogenesis**

Asexual reproduction in which a one-celled organism splits into two or more independently maturing daughter cells –
fission

    Reproduction by fission - **schizogenesis**

    Reproducing by fission – **fissiparous**

    Reproduction by multiple asexual fission – **schizogony**

The regularly recurrent period of ovulation and sexual excitement in nonhuman female animals – **estrus**, adj. **estrous**

    Having one estrus cycle per year – **monestrous**

    The period of sexual inactivity that follows estrus – **metestrus**

The regularly recurrent condition of sexual excitement and reproductive activity in nonhuman female animals - **rut**

The branch of veterinary medicine dealing with all aspects of reproduction – **theriogenology**

Biology – misc. terms:

Descriptive botany - **phytography**

A living organism – **biont**

A short-lived organism – **ephemeron**

The macroscopic plant and animal life of a particular region – **macrobiota**

The application of biological principles to the study and design of engineering systems – **bionics**

Occupying the same or overlapping geographical areas without interbreeding – **sympatric** (used of populations of closely related species)

Having unequal responses to external stimuli – **anisotropic** (Bot.)

A small, degenerate or rudimentary organ or part existing in an organism as a usu. nonfunctional remnant of an organ or part that was developed and functional in an earlier developmental stage – **vestige**, adj. **vestigial**

Early development of a vestigial organ followed by regression – **aphanisia**

Poorly or imperfectly developed – **depauperate**

The capacity or tendency of an organism to become widely dispersed – **vagility**

In an artificial environment outside the living organism – **in vitro**

Within a living organism – **in vivo**

An organism in a dormant or resting state – **spore**

All the living organisms in a specific area at a given time – **standing crop**

The racial history of a specified kind of organism or genetically related group of organisms – **phylogeny**

The single specimen used as the first published description of a taxonomic species and later designated as the type specimen – **holotype**

The effect of a given agent, such as a vaccine, upon a living organism – **bioactivity**

To dissect in order to examine the structure – **anatomize** (v.t.)

An indigenous plant or animal – **autochthon**, adj. **autochthonous**

Capable of moving freely in all directions, as the antenna of an insect – **versatile**

Derived or developed from external causes; growing or developing from or on the outside – **exogenous**

The naturalization of a plant or animal in a new habitat or range typically involving successful growth, survival and reproduction – **ecesis**; **establishment**

An instinctually motivated biological striving – **conation**

Of or relating to an environment that is deficient in moisture that is available for the support of plant life – **xeric**; **xerophytic**

Low or deficient in available moisture for the support of plant life – **xeric**

Originating from a source outside the body, esp. from a different species – **heterogenous**

Failure of an organism, organ or part to develop - **agenesis**

Bird (see also Eagle, Falconry, and Nest):

Of, relating to or characteristic of birds – **avian**; **ornithic**; **ornithoid**

A large enclosure for confining birds – **aviary**

The raising or keeping of birds – **aviculture**

The killing of birds – **avicide**

Bird watching – **ornithoscopy**, n. **ornithoscopist**

The anatomy or dissection of birds – **ornithotomy**

Having a fondness for birds – **ornithophilous**

To catch roosting birds at night by blinding them with a light – **batfowl** (v.i.)

A bird too young to leave its nest – **nestling**

A young bird that has recently acquired its flight feathers – **fledgling**; **fledgeling**

Not yet having feathers – **callow**; **unfledged**

A bird kept in a cage as a pet – **cageling**

A bird of prey – **accipiter** (adj. **accipitral** or **accipitrine**); **raptor**, adj. **raptorial**

Of, resembling or typical of birds such as crows or ravens – **corvine**

The back and folded wings of a bird – **mantle**

To cut, remove or bind the wing feathers of (a bird) to prevent flight; to restrain (a bird) from flight – **pinion** (v.t.)

The outer rear edge of a bird's wing; a bird's primary feather - **pinion**

The gape of the mouth of a bird – **rictus**, pl. **rictus** or **rictuses**

All the birds of a specific region or time division – **avifauna**

Divination by observing the flight of birds – **ornithomancy**; **ornithoscopy**

The study of:

Birds – **ornithology**

Young birds – **neossology**

Birds' eggs – **oology**

Birds' nests - **nidology**

Birth (see also Childbirth and Offspring):

Birth, esp. the place, conditions or circumstances of being born – **nativity**

To give birth to – **bear**; **yean** (v.t.)

To give birth to young - **yean** (used of sheep and goats) (v.i.)

To give birth to (young) prematurely – **slink** (used esp. of cows); **slip** (used of animals) (both v.t.)

Of, relating to or accompanying birth; of or relating to the time or place of one's birth - **natal**

The action or process of giving birth to offspring - **parturition**

Of or relating to giving birth; being in labor; about to bring forth young – **parturient**

Existing or taking place prior to birth – **antenatal**; **prenatal**

Occurring near the time of birth – **perinatal**

Of or occurring during the period immediately after birth – **postnatal**

Of or occurring in the period shortly after birth – **postpartum**

Congenital positional abnormality of an organ or part – **ectopia**

The birth of a dead fetus; a viable fetus that is born dead – **stillbirth**

Dead at birth – **stillborn**

Belonging to a place by birth – **native-born**

The state of being the firstborn of the children of the same parents – **primogeniture**

Biting, given to – **mordacious**; **mordant**

Bitumen:
    To treat with bitumen – **bituminize** (v.t.)
    Like or containing bitumen – **bituminous**

Black:
    To make black – **blacken** (v.t.), n. **blackener**
    The process of becoming black or dark; blackness or darkness, as of complexion – **nigrescence**
    Pigmented black or dark – **melanian**; **melanoid**
    Having black or dark skin or hair – **melanous**
    Black as pitch – **piceous** (Zool.)

Bladder (ampulla):
    Of or relating to a bladder – **vesical**
    Not enclosed in a bladder – **acystic**
    Relating to the urinary bladder – **cystic**
    Inflammation of the urinary bladder - **cystitis**
    Surgical removal of part of the urinary bladder – **cystectomy**
    A hernia of the urinary bladder – **cystocele**
    A surgical incision into the urinary bladder – **cystostomy**; **vesicotomy**
    Shaped like a bladder – **ampullaceous**

Blame:
    Deserving of blame – **blamable**; **blameable**; **blameful**; **blameworthy**; **culpable**; **reprehensible**
    To clear of blame – **absolve**; **acquit**; **exculpate** (adj. **exculpatory**); **exonerate**; **vindicate** (all v.t.)
    The act of blaming oneself – **self-recrimination**; **self-reproach**

Blindness (see also Eyes and Vision):
    The study of blindness – **typhlology**
    Snow blindness – **chionablepsia**
    Partial blindness – **meropia**
    Night blindness – **nyctalopia**
    Of or relating to tangible points or dots used for representing words for reading by the blind – **punctiform**

Blister:
    To blister or become blistered – **vesicate** (v.t./v.i.)
    A blistering agent, esp. an agent used in chemical warfare; causing blisters – **epispastic**; **vesicant**; **vesicatory**
    A large blister – **bulla**
    Having a blistered or puckered appearance - **bullate**

Block:
    Resembling a block – **blockish**; **blocky**
    To block (a wheel, e.g.) with a prop to prevent rolling or slipping; a block or wedge so used – **scotch** (v.t./n.)

Blood:
    Of or relating to blood – **hemal**; **hematal**; **hematic**; **hemic**
    Like blood – **hematoid**; **hemoid**
    Consisting of blood – **sanguinary**
    Of the color of blood – **hematic**; **sanguine**
    Relating to or involving blood or bloodshed – **sanguineous**

Mixed or tinged with blood – **sanguinolent**

Filled or covered with blood – **hematose**

Producing blood; originating in or involving the blood - **hematogenous**

Coagulated blood from a wound – **gore**

To drain of blood – **exsanguinate** (v.t.)

To stain or cover with blood – **ensanguine** (v.t.)

Extreme or irrational fear of blood – **hemophobia**

The formation of blood in the body – **hematogenesis**; **hematopoiesis**; **hemopoiesis**

Oxygenation of venous blood in the lungs – **hematosis**

To convert (venous blood) into arterial blood by absorption of oxygen in the lungs – **arterialize** (v.t.)

Causing or promoting the clotting of blood – **thromboplastic**

A blood clot obstructing a vessel or formed in a heart cavity – **thrombus**

Formation, development or presence of a thrombus - **thrombosis**

To inject whole blood or plasma into the bloodstream – **transfuse** (v.t.), n. **transfusion**

Dialysis of the blood – **hemodialysis**

Expectoration of blood from the lungs or bronchial tubes – **hemoptysis**

Bleeding, esp. abnormally great discharge of blood from the blood vessels – **hemorrhage**

A tendency to uncontrollable bleeding – **hemophilia**, n. **hemophiliac**

An agent that stops bleeding – **hemostat**; **hemostatic**; **styptic**

    The action or application of a styptic - **stypsis**

Acting to stop the flow of blood – **hemostatic**; **styptic**; **styptical**

Stoppage of a flow or circulation of blood – **hemostasia**; **hemostasis**

Passage of blood from ruptured blood vessels into subcutaneous tissue, marked by a purple discoloration of the skin - **ecchymosis**

The settling of blood in the dependent parts of an organ or body – **hypostasis**, pl. **hypostases**

Stimulating red blood cell or hemoglobin production – **hematinic**

The number of red and white blood cells in a specific volume of blood – **blood count**

Any of the white or colorless nucleated cells in the blood – **leucocyte**; **leukocyte**

    The formation and growth of leukocytes – **leucopoiesis**; **leukopoiesis**

    A marked increase in the number of leukocytes in the blood – **leucocytosis**; **leukocytosis**

    An abnormally low number of leukocytes in the blood – **leucopenia**; **leukopenia**

The study of blood and its diseases – **hematology**

An abnormally large blood supply – **hyperemia**; **hyperaemia**, adj. **hyperemic**

A measure of the blood's oxygen-carrying capacity – **hematocrit**

A reduction in the normal amount of oxygen in the blood – **anoxemia**

An abnormally high level of glucose (blood sugar) in the blood – **hyperglycemia**, adj. **hyperglycemic**

An abnormally low level of low level of glucose in the blood – **hypoglycemia**, adj. **hypoglycemic**

The presence of abnormally high levels of insulin in the blood – **hyperinsulinism**

An imbalance of the constituents of the blood – **dyscrasia**

A red blood cell (erythrocyte) that has lost its hemoglobin – **ghost**

An abnormally large red blood cell – **macrocyte**

An abnormally small red blood cell – **microcyte**

The protein-containing portion of the blood – **blood plasma**

The presence of sickle cells in the blood – **sicklemia**

Cancer of the blood – **leukemia**

Blood pressure:

    The measurement of blood pressure – **hemadynamometry**

    Causing a rise in blood pressure; an agent that causes a rise in blood pressure – **vasopressor**

    Abnormally high blood pressure – **hypertension**, adj. **hypertensive**

    Abnormally low blood pressure – **hypotension**

Blood relationship - **consanguinity**

Blood vessels:
    Of or relating to blood vessels – **hemal**
    The entry of foreign material into a blood vessel – **intravasation**
    Within the blood vessels – **intravascular**
    The process of new blood vessel formation – **vascularization**
    The arrangement of blood vessels in the body or in an organ or part of the body – **vasculature**
    Affecting blood vessels – **vasoactive**, n. **vasoactivity**
    Constriction of a blood vessel – **vasoconstriction**
        An agent that causes vasoconstriction – **vasoconstrictor**
    Dilatation of a blood vessel – **vasodilatation**; **vasodilation**
        An agent that causes vasodilatation - **vasodilator**
    Causing or regulating vasoconstriction or vasodilatation – **vasomotor**
    An air bubble, detached clot, mass of bacteria or other foreign body obstructing a blood vessel – **embolus**, adj.
        embolic
    Obstruction of a blood vessel by an embolus – **embolism**
    Obstruction of a blood vessel by a thrombus dislodged from a vein – **thromboembolism**
    Of or relating to the blood vessels supplying the brain – **cerebrovascular**
    An alternative passage created surgically between two blood vessels, esp. to avoid an obstruction – **by-pass**; **bypass**

Blossom:
    To blossom out – **effloresce** (v.i.)
    A state or time of blossoming – **efflorescence** (adj. **efflorescent**); **florescence**, adj. **florescent**

Blow:
    To blow or breathe into or on; to treat medically by blowing a powder, gas or vapor into a bodily cavity – **insufflate**
        (v.t.), n. **insufflation**

Blushing, extreme or irrational fear of – **erythrophobia**

Boar:
    A group of boars – **singular**; **sounder**
    A young boar – **calf**; **squeaker**

Boat - see Ships, Boats and Nautical Terms

Body:
    Of, relating to or affecting the entire body – **systemic**
    Of or relating to the body – **corporeal**; **somatic**
    Anatomy of the human body – **anthropotomy**
    Without material body – **incorporeal**
    Having a bodily nature or form – **incarnate**, n. **incarnation**
    Having two distinct bodies – **bicorporeal**
    A dead body – **body**; **cadaver**; **corpse**
    Of or relating to the lap or bosom – **gremial**
    Affecting or located on the same side of the body – **ipsilateral**
    The sensation of bodily position, presence or movement resulting primarily from stimulation of sensory nerve endings
        in muscles, tendons and joints – **kinesthesia**, adj. **kinesthetic**
    Normal functional readiness in bodily tissues – **tonicity**; **tonus**
    Having a short, stocky and powerful physique; someone with such a physique – **pycnic**; **pyknic**

A human body characterized by powerful musculature and a mainly bony framework – **mesomorph**, adj. **mesomorphic**; **somatic**

Lean and slightly muscular – **ectomorphic**, n. **ectomorph** (used chiefly of the human body)

Marked by prominence of the abdomen and other soft body parts – **endomorphic**, n. **endomorph**

Involuntary trembling of the body – **tremor**

Arising within the body in response to environment - **somatogenetic**; **somatogenic**

The physiological and anatomical study of the body – **somatology**

Bone:

Of or relating to bone or the skeleton – **osteal**

A small bone or bonelike structure – **ossicle**

Having a coarse, netlike or spongy structure – **cancellous** (used of bone)

Decay of a bone or tooth – **caries**, adj. **carious**

Composed of, containing or resembling bone – **osseous**; **osteoid**

To change into bone; to become bony – **ossify** (v.t./v.i.)

The formation of bone – **ostosis**

A thin plate of bone – **squama**

A natural outgrowth or process of a bone – **apophysis**

A small, abnormal bony outgrowth – **osteophyte**

A dead bone fragment separated from healthy bone – **sequesterum**, pl. **sequestera**

The surgical repair or alteration of bone; bone grafting – **osteoplasty**

The surgical operation of dividing a bone or cutting out a piece of bone – **osteotomy**, n. **osteotomist**

Surgical fracture of a bone, performed to correct a deformity – **osteoclasis**

A fracture in which broken bone lacerates soft tissue – **compound fracture**

The hard bony tissue surrounding the ends of a fractured bone – **callosity**; **callus**

   Having calluses - **callous**

   The state of being calloused – **callosity**

The anatomical study of bones; the bone structure or system of an animal – **osteology**

The articulation of bone by ligaments – **syndesmosis**

The fusion of two skeletal bones – **syntosis**

The connection of bones by means of attached muscles – **syssarcosis**, pl. **syssarcoses**

The transmission of sound by bone, esp. to the inner ear by the bones of the skull – **bone conduction**

The consolidation of bones or their parts forming a single unit – **anchylosis**; **ankylosis**

   To join or stiffen by ankylosis; to undergo ankylosis – **anchylose**; **ankylose** (both v.t./v.i.)

Inflammation of bone or body tissue – **osteitis**

A malignant bone tumor – **osteosarcoma**

Pathological enlargement of the bones of hands, feet and face, resulting from chronic overactivity of the pituitary gland – **acromegaly**

Softening of the bones – **osteomalacia**

Excessive or abnormal thickening or growth of bone tissue – **hyperostosis**

Of, relating to or derived from bone marrow – **myeloid**

Inflammation of the bone marrow – **myelitis**; **osteomyelitis**

An incomplete dislocation of a bone in a joint – **subluxation**

A malignant tumor of the bone marrow - **myeloma**

Containing bones, as a geological deposit – **ossiferous**

Book (see also Literature and Text):

A small reference book, esp. one providing instructions - **manual**

A book published for distribution to the general public through booksellers – **trade book**

A book published under the real name of the author – **autonym**

A miniature book, esp. of elegant design or format - **bibelot**

An edition of the works of an author, with notes by scholars or editors; an edition con-taining various versions of a text
   – **variorum**

One of the books in a work of several volumes; a large or scholarly book – **tome**

A book or other publication containing a variety of literary works – **miscellanies** (sing./pl.); **miscellany**, pl.
   miscellanies

A book printed prior to 1501 – **cradle book**; **fifteener**; **incunable**; **incunabulum**

Books strange or unusual in subject or treatment – **curiosa**

A place where books are bound – **bindery**

Material that follows the main body of a book – **back matter**

A label usually pasted on the inside cover of a book that bears the owner's name or other identification – **bookplate**

A measurement of books by the number of lines they contain; division of the text into lines, esp. those fitted to the
   sense - **stichometry**

A list of errors in a book with their corrections – **corrigenda**

A type-setting error – **corrigendum**, pl. **corrigenda**

The right-hand page of a book – **recto**

The left-hand page of a book – **verso**

A passion for collecting books - **bibliomania**

A book lover or collector – **bibliophile**; **bookman**

Excessive devotion to or concern with books - **bibliolatry**

A book worshiper – **bibliolater**; **bibliolatrist**

A strong dislike of books – **bibliophobia**

   One who has a strong dislike of books – **bibliophobe**

Love for or the collecting of books – **bibliophilism**; **bibliophily**

Relating to bookbinding (bibliopegy) - **bibliopegic**; **bibliopegistic**; **bibliopegistical**

A bookseller, esp. one dealing in rare or secondhand works – **bibliopole**, adj. **bibliopolic**

A copy of a book – **exemplar**

A copy or copies of a book still held by a publisher when the sale has fallen off – **remainder**

One who steals books – **biblioklept**

One who hides away or hoards books – **bibliotaph**; **bibliotaphe**

A destroyer or mutilator of books – **biblioclast**

One who has a comprehensive knowledge of books and bibliography – **bibliognost**

Production of books – **bibliogony**

The study of the editions, dates, authorship, etc., of books; a book containing such information - **bibliography**

To illustrate (a book) with pictures taken from other books – **grangerize** (v.t.)

A part of a book used as a substitute for an original part of the book – **cancel**

A section of a book or set of books being published in installments – **fascicle**

A publisher's emblem or trademark; an inscription typically placed at the end of a book giving facts relating to its
   publication - **colophon**

Border:
   An ornamental border of two or more bands interlaced in such a way as to repeat a rounded design – **guilloche**
   A border distinguished by color or structure – **limbus** (Biol.)

Born:
   Born out of wedlock – **illegitimate**
   One born out of wedlock – **bastard**; **love child**
   Born after the death of the father – **posthumous**

Boundary:
   The external boundary of something; the sphere or scope of something – **ambit**
   Contained in the same boundaries – **conterminous**; **coterminous**

Having bounds – **finite**
  Beyond the finite – **transfinite**
Unbounded in one direction or dimension – **semi-infinite**
Transcending national boundaries – **transnational**

Bow (as in archery):
  One who makes bows – **bowyer**
  Shaped like a bow – **arcuate**; **arcuated**; **embowed**
  Bowed in an outward curve – **bandy**

Bowels (see also Intestine):
  To cause evacuation of (the bowels); to induce evacuation of the bowels in (a patient) – **purge** (v.t.)
  Something that tends to cause evacuation of the bowels, esp. a medicinal compound – **cathartic**; **purgative**; **purge**

Box:
  A box used to hold paper and other writing materials – **papeterie**
  A small box used to protect a seal tied to a document - **skippet**

Boxing:
  Of or relating to boxing or fighting with the fists – **fistic**; **pugilant**; **pugilistic**

Bragging:
  Bragging or blustering talk or behavior – **fanfaronade**
  Pretentious bragging – **bluster**; **rhodomontade**; **rodomontade**

Brain:
  Of or relating to the brain – **cerebral**; **cerebric**; **encephalic**
  Inflammation of the brain – **encephalitis**
  A brain tumor – **encephaloma**
  Congenital absence of part or all of the brain – **anencephaly**, adj. **anencephalic**
  A disease of the brain – **encephalopathy**
  A bundle of brain nerve fibers – **lemniscus**
  Of or relating to the cerebral cortex - **pallial**
  Of or relating to the brain and spinal cord – **cerebrospinal**
  Of or relating to the brain and the cranium - **craniocerebral**

Bran, relating to or like – **furfuraceous**

Branch:
  Branchlike – **ramiform**; **ramous**
  Branched; branching – **ramate**; **ramose**; **ramous**
  To divide or separate into branches – **fork**, **furcate** (both v.i.)
  To divide or separate into two branches – **bifurcate** (v.t./v.i.)
  Having two branches – **bifurcate**; **biramous** (Biol.)
  Having three branches – **trifurcate**; **trifurcated**
  Having many branches – **ramose**
  Having many small branches – **ramulose**
  Branching in which successive forking into two approximately equal divisions occurs – **dichotomy** (Bot.)
  Having dichotomous branches or axes – **biparous** (Bot.)
  Branching or spreading widely from a point of axis – **divaricate** (Biol.)
  To branch out into numerous subdivisions that lack a main axis – **deliquesce** (v.i.) (Biol.)

To have or form branches – **arborize** (v.i.)

To split up into branches; to send forth branches or outgrowths, shoots or extensions resembling branches – **ramify** (v.i.)

Brass:

Having the color and luster of brass – **aeneous**; **aeneus**

Made of or resembling brass – **brazen**

One who works in brass – **brasier**; **brazier**

The art of engraving on brass – **chalcography**, adj. **chalcographic**

A brass used to imitate gold used for decorative purposes – **mosaic gold**; **ormolu**

Breadth, in the direction of the – **breadthwise**

Breast (mamma):

Of or relating to a breast or breasts - **mammary**

Having breasts (mammae) – **mammiferous**

The surgical removal of a breast - **mastectomy**

A breast lift – **mastoplexy**

Inflammation of a breast or mammary gland – **mastitis**

A condition marked by fat pads in male breasts – **gynecomastia**

Shaped like a breast – **mastoid**

Breathing (respiration; see also Inhale):

Of or relating to breathing – **aspiratory**; **inspiratory**

Suited or fit for breathing – **aspiratory**; **respirable**

Not fit for breathing - **irrespirable**

The study of the respiratory organs – **pneumology**

Used for the drawing in of air – **inspiratory**

Normal breathing – **eupnea**; **eupnoea**

The amount of air that can be forcibly expelled from the lungs following a full inspi-ration – **vital capacity**

Capable of or functioning in exhalation (breathing out) – **exhalant**; **exhalent**

To breathe or blow upon or into – **insufflate** (v.t.), n. **insufflation**

A device for insufflating – **infufflator**

Inability to breathe except in an upright position – **orthopnea**; **orthopnoea**

Abnormally deep or rapid breathing – **hyperpnea**; **polypnea**; **polypnoea**; **tachypnea**

Abnormally rapid or deep breathing in which excessive quantities of air are inhaled - **hyperventilation**

Abnormally slow and shallow breathing – **hypopnea**

To breathe with difficulty, producing a hoarse, whistling sound – **wheeze** (v.i.)

Difficulty in breathing – **dyspnea**; **dyspnoea**, adj. **dyspneic**

Temporary stoppage of breathing – **apnea**; **apnoea**

Constriction of the bronchial tubes – **bronchoconstriction**

A harsh, high-pitched sound in inhalation or exhalation – **stridor**

A heavy snoring sound in breathing – **stertor**

A deep or noisy sigh – **sough**

A condition marked by stale or bad-smelling breath - **halitosis**

A respiratory structure – **spiracle** (Zool.)

Breeding:

The scientific breeding of domestic plants and animals – **thremmatology**

Selective breeding to perpetuate certain qualities or characteristics in a strain of live-stock – **line breeding**

Having only one purebred parent – **half-blooded**; **half-bred**

To produce by the continued breeding of closely related individuals – **inbreed** (v.t.)
The breeding of distantly related or unrelated stocks of animals – **outbreeding**
To breed animals that belong to different strains of the same breed – **outcross** (v.t.)
A group of species capable of interbreeding – **cenospecies**
To breed (plants or animals) selectively to produce new or desired colors – **colorbreed** (v.t.)
Hybrid offspring of parents differing in a single characteristic or genetic factor – **monohybrid**
To breed (a first-generation hybrid) with a parent or member of the parental stock – **backcross** (v.t.)
Increased vigor or capacity for growth arising from the crossbreeding of genetically different plants or animals –
    heterosis; **hybrid vigor**
The supposed influence of one sire on offspring sired by subsequent males on the same female – **telegony**

Brevity:
    Brevity or concise expression – **brachylogy**; **laconicism**; **laconism**
    A condensed expression – **brachylogy**

Bribery:
    Open or susceptible to bribery- **purchasable**; **venal** (n. **venality**); **vendable**; **vendible**

Brick:
    A sun-dried brick of clay and straw; a structure made of such bricks - **adobe**

Bridge:
    Of or relating to bridges - **pontine**
    Located across or beyond a bridge – **transpontine**
    A steel bridge designed to be shipped in parts and assembled quickly – **Bailey bridge**
    A framework composed of vertical, slanted supports and horizontal cross pieces holding up a bridge – **trestle**
        A system of trestles – **trestlework**
    Extreme or irrational fear of crossing a bridge – **gephyrophobia**

Brilliance:
    Great brilliance, as of performance or achievement - **éclat**

Bristle (seta):
    Having bristles – **acicular**; **chaetophorous**; **setaceous**; **setiferous**; **setigerous**; **setose**
    Bristlelike – **setaceous**; **setose**
    Shaped like a bristle – **setiform**
    A bristlelike part – **aciculum**; **arista**
    Densely covered with stiff bristles – **echinate**
    See also Spine.

Broadcast (see also Television):
    To broadcast by television – **telecast** (v.t.)
    To broadcast simultaneously (by FM and AM radio, or by radio and television) – **simulcast** (v.t.)
    To broadcast (a television program) in color – **colorcast** (v.t.)

Broom:
    A bundle of twigs attached to a handle and used as a broom – **besom**

Brother:
    Of or relating to brothers – **fraternal**
    The murder of one's brother; one who has murdered his or her brother – **fratricide**

One of two or persons having one or both parents in common – **sibling**
A younger brother – **cadet**

Brutal:
To make or become brutal – **brutalize**; **imbrute** (both v.t./v.i.)
To treat brutally – **brutalize** (v.t.)

Buffalo:
A group of buffalo – **herd**
A male buffalo – **bull**
A female buffalo – **cow**

Building:
A circular building or hall, esp. one with a dome - **rotunda**

Bulb (plant part):
Of, relating to or characteristic of a bulb – **bulbar**
Shaped like a bulb – **bulbous**
A small section of a separable bulb – **clove**

Bull – see Cattle

Burglary, of or relating to – **burglarious**

Burn:
Of, relating to or resulting in a burn – **pyric**
Capable of igniting and burning – **combustible**; **flammable**; **ignitable**; **inflammable**
Igniting spontaneously when mixed together – **hypergolic**
To burn or sear with a caustic agent or a very hot or very cold instrument (cautery) in order to destroy aberrant tissue –
    cauterize (v.t.)
A mild burn that produces redness of the skin – **first degree burn**
A burn that blisters the skin – **second degree burn**
A severe burn that destroys epidermis and exposes sensitive nerve endings – **third degree burn**

Bury – see Death/Treatment of the Dead and Their Remains

Business:
Privately owned business activities not under state ownership or control; a privately owned business enterprise –
    private enterprise
The privilege of maintaining a subsidiary business within certain premises; the space allotted for such a business –
    concession
The operator or holder of a concession – **concessionaire**; **concessioner**

Butter:
Of, relating to, containing or derived from butter – **butyric**
Resembling butter in appearance, consistency or chemical properties - **butyraceous**

Butterflies – see Moths and Butterflies

Buttocks (nates):
 Having beautifully proportioned buttocks – **callipygian**; **callipygous**
 Excessive accumulation of fat in the buttocks – **steatopygia**; **steatopygy**, adj. **steatopygic** or **steatopygous**

Buying (see also Bribery):
 An obsession for buying things – **oniomania**
 Able to be bought – **purchasable**

C

Cable, operated by a – **funicular**

Café, a small – **estaminet**

Calcium:
  Composed of, containing or characteristic of calcium or lime – **calcareous**; **calcic**
  Derived from calcium or lime – **calcic**
  Composed of, containing or characteristic of calcium carbonate or limestone – **calcareous**
  Of, forming or containing calcium or calcium carbonate – **calciferous**; **calcific**
  Impregnation with calcium or calcium salts – **calcification**
  To make or become stony or chalky by deposition of calcium salts or lime – **calcify** (v.t./v.i.)
  To remove calcium or calcareous matter from (bones, e.g.) – **decalcify** (v.t.)
  An abnormal condition in which calcium salts are deposited in a body tissue – **calcinosis**

Calendar:
  Of, relating to or used in a calendar – **calendrical**
  The insertion of one or more days at regular intervals in a calendar in order to bring it into accord with the solar year; a
    period so inserted – **embolism**; **intercalation**; v.t. **intercalate**; adj. **intercalary**

Calf (body part):
  Of or relating to the calf of the leg - **sural**

Calling:
  Of, relating to, characteristic of or used in calling – **vocative**

Camel:
  A male camel – **bull**
  A female camel – **cow**
  A young camel – **calf**; **colt**; **foal**
  A group of camels – **flock**; **herd**
  A person who drives or rides a camel – **cameleer**
  A two-humped camel – **Bactrian camel**
  A one-humped camel - **dromedary**

Camp:
  A temporary encampment, esp. an open-air one - **bivouac**

Canal:
  A canal deep enough to serve ships – **ship canal**; **shipway**
  A body canal or passage – **meatus**
  An enlargement in a body canal or duct - **ampulla**

Cancel:
  To cancel or nullify by withdrawing, recalling or reversing – **revoke** (v.t.), n. **revocation**, adj. **revocable** or **revocatory**

Cancer:
  Resembling a cancer - **cancroid**
  Of, like or having cancer – **cancerous**; **carcinomatous**
  A cancer-causing substance – **carcinogen**, adj. **carcinogenic**

Exhibiting a likelihood of becoming cancerous – **precancerous**; **premalignant**
The production of cancer – **carcinogenesis**
Destructive of cancer cells – **cancerolytic**; **carcinolytic**
To become cancerous; to develop into a cancer – **cancerate** (v.i.)
Transformation into cancer or a cancerous state – **cancerization**
A condition in which cancers are spread extensively throughout the body – **carcinomatosis**
The study of cancer – **cancerology**
Extreme or irrational fear of cancer - **cancerophobia**

Candle:
A maker or seller of candles – **chandler**
A female chandler – **chandleress**
The business of a chandler – **chandlering**; **chandlery**; **chandling**
A place where candles are stored; commodities sold by a chandler – **chandlery**
A branched candleholder – **candelabra**; **candelabrum**; **girandole**
An ornamental candlestick – **flambeau**, pl. **flambeaus** or **flambeaux**
A bracket attached to a wall for holding a candle or candles – **sconce**
A small spike on which to stick a candle; a candlestick having such a spike – **pricket**
A small or very slender candle – **taper**
A wax candle – **bougie**

Cane plants, a dense growth of – **canebrake**

Canoe:
A canoe made by hollowing out a tree trunk – **dugout**; **piragua**; **pirogue**
A watertight canoe that is fully covered except for an opening in the center – **kayak**

Canopy:
A canopy over a bed – **tester**
A cloth canopy fixed or carried over an important person or sacred object – **baldachin**

Capsule:
Of, relating to or resembling a capsule – **capsular**
In or formed into a capsule - **capsulate**

Captive, one who takes or keeps a person or thing as a – **captor**

Capture, vulnerable to (as a fort) – **expungable**; **pregnable**

Carbon:
Containing or yielding carbon – **carbonaceous**; **carboniferous**
Consisting of or relating to carbon – **carbonaceous**
To reduce or convert to carbon, or to coat or combine with carbon – **carbonize** (v.t.)
To treat with carbon or hydrocarbons – **carburize** (v.t.)
Of or relating to carbon compounds – **organic**
The chemistry of carbon compounds – **organic chemistry**

Carbon dioxide:
The absence of carbon dioxide in the blood or tissues – **acapnia**

Cards:
  The part of a deck (of playing cards) in certain card games left on the table after the deal – **talon**
  An additional hand of cards dealt to the table – **widow**
  A card for fortune-telling or prediction – **tarot**
  A figure or spot on a playing card – **pip**
  Divination by means of playing cards – **cartomancy**

Carp:
  Of or relating to carp or related fish – **cyprinoid**

Cartilage:
  Of or relating to cartilage – **cartilaginous**; **chondral**; **chondric**
  Within cartilage – **intracartilaginous**
  Located beneath a cartilage; partly cartilaginous – **subcartilaginous**
  The development of cartilage – **chondrogenesis**; **chondrogeny**; **chondrosis**
  A cartilage disk that acts as a cushion between the ends of bones that meet in a joint – **meniscus**
  To change into cartilage – **chondrify** (v.i./v.t.)
  Inflammation of cartilage – **chondritis**
  An outgrowth or spur of cartilage – **chondrophyte**
  Improper development of cartilage at the ends of the long bones, resulting in congenital dwarfism – **achondroplasia**
  A cartilaginous skeleton – **chondroskeleton**
    Of or relating to a cartilaginous skeleton – **chondrostean**
  A cartilaginous growth – **chondroma**
  The abnormal softening or cartilage – **chondromalacia**
    The study of cartilages - **chondrology**

Carving:
  Of or relating to carving, esp. on precious stones – **glyptics**; **glyptography**
  The art of carving or incising designs on whalebone or whale ivory – **scrimshaw**
  A design or figure incised beneath the surface of metal or stone; the process of carving a design in this manner –
    intaglio
  An ornament carved in low relief – **anaglyph**

Castle (see also Barrier):
  Belonging to or suggestive of a castle – **castellar**
  To build like a castle; to take the form of a castle – **castellate** (v.t./v.i.), n. **castellation**
  Having a castle; built or formed like a castle; lodged in a castle – **castellated**
  The governor or keeper of a castle – **castellan**; **chatelain**
  The mistress of a castle – **chatelaine**
  The lands appertaining to a castle – **castellany**; **chatellany**
  The outer wall of a castle; the space enclosed by such a wall – **bailey**
  A massive chief tower in ancient castles – **donjon**

Cat:
  Of or relating to a cat or cats – **feline**
  Resembling a cat – **feliform**; **feline**
  A feline characteristic – **felinity**
  A male cat – **tom**
  A female cat – **queen**; **she-cat**
  A group of cats – **clouder**
  A young cat – **kit**; **kitten**

A group of kittens – **kindle**; **litter**
One who loves cats – **aelurophile**; **ailurophile**
Abnormal dislike or fear of cats – **aelurophobia**; **ailurophobia**, n. **ailurophobe** or **aelurophobe**

Catalyst –see Chemistry

Caterpillar:
A group of caterpillars – **army**
Shaped like a caterpillar - **eruciform**

Cattle:
Of, relating to or resembling an ox, cow or similar animal – **bovine** (adj./n.)
A female bovine – **cow**
A young bovine – **bullock** (m.); **heifer** (f.)
A male bovine – **bull**
Of or relating to a bull – **tauric**; **taurine**
An adult castrated bull of the genus *Bos*, used as a draft animal – **ox**, pl. **oxen**
A young ox castrated before sexual maturity and raised for beef - **steer**
Of or relating to the common ox as distinguished from the zebu – **taurine**
A group of cattle or oxen – **drove**; **herd**
A yearling bullock or heifer – **stirk**
A wild range steer or cow that has evaded many roundups – **mossback**; **mossy back**
A driver of cattle – **drover**
One who grazes cattle – **grazier**
An animal, esp. a calf, born prematurely – **slink**
Not pregnant – **farrow** (used of a cow)
A sterile or otherwise sexually deficient female calf born as the twin of a bull calf – **freemartin**

Cause:
Written or said to promote a cause – **tendencious**; **tendentious**
The study of causes or origins – **etiology**

Caustic:
A caustic or corrosive agent – **escharotic**

Cave:
The study of the physical, geologic and biological aspects of caves; the exploration of caves - **speleology**
A person who explores and studies caves – **speleologist**; **spelunker**
A cave deposit or formation – **speleothem**
A cave-dweller – **troglodyte**
An animal restricted to or living in caves – **troglobiont**
Inhabiting caves – **cavernicolous**

Cavern:
Inhabiting caverns – **cavernicolous**
Filled with caverns; like a cavern – **cavernous**

Cavity:
A cavity, hollow or depression, as in a bone – **fossa**; **lacuna**; **locule**; **loculus**
A small fossa – **fossette**
Shaped like a fossa – **fossate**

Filled with cavities – **cavernous**
The formation of cavities in tissue or an organ – **cavitation**

Ceiling:
A decorative ceiling – **plafond** (Archit.)

Celebrity:
To treat (a person) as a celebrity – **lionize** (v.t.)

Cell:
Relating to or resembling a cell – **cellular**
Between or among cells – **intercellular**
Within a cell or cells – **intracellular**
Occurring or found outside a cell – **extracellular**
Having no cells – **acellular**
Consisting of one cell – **one-celled; unicellular**
Having two cells – **bicellular**
Having two distinct cellular layers – **diploblastic**
Consisting of many cells – **multicellular**
A small cell – **cellule**
A cell that has no nucleus – **akaryocyte**
A cell that gives rise to other cells – **mother cell**
A specialized part of a cell that resembles and functions as an organ - **organelle**
Inert material in the protoplasm of a cell – **metaplasm**
Formation and development of cells – **cytogenesis**; **cytogeny**
Killing or tending to kill individual cells – **cytocidal**
Dissolution of a cell – **cytolysis**
Relating to or marked by greatly enlarged cells – **cytomegalic**
Of or relating to pathological changes in cells – **cytopathic**
The change of cells from a normal to an abnormal state – **metaplasia**
A nontumorous increase in the number of cells in an organ or tissue, with consequent enlargement of the affected part
    – **hyperplasia**, adj. **hyperplastic**
The ability of a cell, as an egg, to generate unlike cells and thus to form a new individual part – **totipotence**;
    totipotency
The study of the formation, structure, pathology and function of cells – **cytology**
The chemistry of cells – **cytochemistry**
Classification of organisms based on cellular structure – **cytotaxonomy**

Cellar:
A cellar or cellars collectively; a fee charged for storage in a cellar - **cellarage**

Cement:
Of, relating to, or having the characteristics of cement - **cementitious**

Censorship:
Overzealous censorship of literature, art and the theater because of alleged immorality – **Comstockery**
To censor (a book, e.g.) prudishly – **bowdlerize** (v.t.)

Censure:
Tending to or expressing censure - **censorious**
Deserving of or liable to censure – **censurable**

Center:
   Of, at, or having a center – **centric**
   Moving or directed away from a center – **centrifugal**
   Developing outward from a center – **centrifugal** (Bot.)
   Developing toward the center or axis (Bot.); directed or moving toward a center - **centripetal**
   Having two centers – **bicentric**
   Having the same center – **homocentric**; **concentric**
   Having no center; off center – **acentric**
   To direct toward or come together at a common center – **concenter** (v.t./v.i.)
   Radiating from or converging to a common center - **radial**
   Center of gravity – see Gravity

Ceramics – see Pottery/Ceramics

Ceremony:
   To purify by ceremony – **lustrate** (v.t.), adj. **lustrative**
   Of, relating to or used in a purification rite – **lustral**
   To begin or inaugurate with a ceremony designed to bring good luck – **auspicate**

Certify by signature or oath to be correct, true or genuine – **attest**

Cervix, inflammation of the – **cervicitis**

Chain:
   Of or relating to a chain – **catenarian**
   To form into a chain or linked series – **catenate** (v.t.)
   Consisting or formed of chainlike links – **catenulate**
   To fetter or confine with or as if with chains – **enchain** (v.t.)
   A file of animals, prisoners or slaves chained together in transit; to transport (animals, prisoners, etc.) in this way –
      coffle (n./v.t.)

Chance (see also Luck):
   Of or depending on chance or luck – **aleatory**

Change (see also Mutation and New):
   Radical transformation of figure or appearance – **metamorphosis**, pl. **metamorphoses**; **transfiguration**, v.t.
      transfigure
   Metabolic change of complex molecules into simple ones – **catabolism**
   A period of life when physiological changes take place in the body – **climacteric**
   The process by which simple substances are synthesized into the complex materials of living tissue – **anabolism**
   To change (something) from one nature, form, substance or state into another – **transform**; **transmute**;
      transubstantiate (all v.t.)
      To undergo such a change – **transform** (v.i.)
   The physical transformation undergone by various animals during development after the embryonic stage -
      metamorphosis, pl. **metamorphoses**
      Complete metamorphosis of a developing insect – **holometabolism**
   An act, process or instance of changing from one state, form, activity or place to another – **transition**
   To change into a different, esp. fantastic or bizarre, shape or form – **transmogrify** (v.t.)
   An abrupt or unexpected change in a situation or course of events, esp. in a literary work – **peripeteia**; **peripety**
   Hatred of change or innovation – **misoneism**
   Not subject or susceptible to change – **immutable**

Experienced or expert in predicting shifts, as in the weather or public opinion – **weather-wise**

The failure of a property that has been altered by an external agent to return to its original value when the cause of the alteration is removed – **hysteresis**, adj. **hysteretic**

Change of life:
Female – **climacteric** (adj. **climacterical**); **menopause**, adj. **menopausal**
Male - **climacteric**

Character:
The art of judging human character from facial features – **physiognomy**
The study of character, esp. its development and its variations among individuals – **characterology**, n. **characterologist**
Of mixed character – **mongrel**
　To make mongrel – **mongrelize** (v.t.)

Cheek:
Of or relating to the cheek or cheeks – **buccal**; **malar**
Of or relating to the cheekbone – **malar**
Restoration of a cheek by plastic surgery – **meloplasty**

Cheese:
Resembling cheese – **caseous**

Chemistry:
The simplest structural unit that displays the characteristic physical and chemical properties of a compound – **molecule**
A chemical formula that shows the number of atoms of each element in a molecule of a compound – **molecular formula**
Consisting of or containing only molecules that have two kinds of atoms – **binary**
Formation of a compound from its constituents – **synthesis**
The synthesis of organic substances such as food nutrients, using the energy of chemical reactions – **chemosynthesis**
The property that certain chemicals have of existing in two or more different forms – **allotropism**; **allotropy**
A substance that modifies and esp. increases the rate of a chemical reaction without being consumed in the process – **catalyst**
　The action of a catalyst – **catalysis**
Resitant to chemical change – **stabile**
Attraction of a chemical compound to specific bodily tissues or organs – **organotropism**; **organotropy**
A substance that slows down a chemical reaction - **anticatalyst**
A chemical reaction between an acid and a base – **neutralization**
Forming one color when treated with an acid and another when treated with a base – **amphichroic**
Designating or pertaining to chemical activity at high temperatures – **pyrochemical**
Chemical change caused by heat – **pyrolysis**
A chemical derived from wood – **silvichemical**
A film or stratum of a compound one molecule thick – **mononuclear layer**; **monolayer**
To cause (a solution) to be more highly saturated than is normally possible under given conditions of temperature and pressure – **supersaturate** (v.t.)
To cause (a solid or a gas) to change state without becoming a liquid – **sublimate** (v.t.)
Pertaining to properties that are both physical and chemical – **physicochemical**
The chemical analysis of quantities weighing one milligram or less – **microanalysis**
Chemistry that deals with quantities weighing one milligram or less – **microchemistry**

The chemistry of biological substances and processes – **biochemistry**
The chemistry of the composition and alterations of the earth's crust – **geochemistry**
The chemistry of stars and interstellar space – **astrochemistry**
The chemistry of the interaction of radiant energy and chemical systems – **photochemistry**

Chest (body part):
Surgical incision of the chest wall – **thoracotomy**
Of or relating to the chest – **pectoral**; **thoracic**
Situated or occurring in or on, or worn on the chest - **pectoral**

Chicken:
A group of chickens – **brood**; **flock**
A male chicken – **cock**; **rooster**
A young male chicken – **cockerel**
A castrated male chicken – **capon**
A female chicken – **hen**
A group of hens – **brood**
A young female chicken – **pullet**
A pullet that has been spayed for fattening – **poulard**; **poularde**
A rooster trained for cockfighting – **gamecock**
A person who keeps or trains gamecocks – **cocker**
Divination by means of a rooster encircled by grains of corn placed on the letters of the alphabet which are then put together in the order in which the grains were eaten – **alectoromancy**; **alectryomancy**

Chickweed, of or like – **alsinaceous**

Chiggers, infestation with – **trombiculiasis**; **trombiculosis**

Child/Children (see also Infant):
Of, relating to or befitting a son or daughter – **filial**
A newborn child – **neonate**
A foster child – **fosterling**
An abandoned child whose parents are unknown – **foundling**
A child secretly exchanged for another – **changeling**
A homeless or neglected child roaming the streets – **street Arab**
An orphaned or forsaken child - **waif**
The number of children borne by one woman – **parity**
A woman who has borne only one child – **primipara**
A woman who is bearing her second child or has borne two or more children – **multipara**, adj. **multiparous**
The branch of medicine dealing with the development and care of infants and children, and with the treatment of their diseases – **pediatrics**
A specialist in pediatrics – **pediatrician**; **pediatrist**
The study of the behavior and development of children – **pedology**
The study of the first 60 days of an child's life – **neonatology**
Relating to the correction or treatment of mental and emotional abnormalities in children – **orthogenic**

Childbirth/Conception (see also Birth):
An attitude or policy that encourages childbirth – **pronatalism**
To conceive when a fetus is already present in the uterus – **superfetate** (v.i.)
To undergo the labor of childbirth – **travail** (v.i.)

The presence of fetuses of different ages resulting from the fertilization and development of two or more ova liberated at different periods of ovulation in the same uterus – **superfetation**

The production of a large number of ova at one time – **superovulation**

Manipulation of a fetus in the uterus to bring it into a favorable position for delivery – **version**

A drug that hastens the process of childbirth – **oxytocic**

Inducing or facilitating labor during childbirth; a drug that does this – **parturifacient**

An agent that causes fetal malformations or monstrosities – **teratogen**, adj. **teratogenic**

Difficult childbirth – **dystocia**

A woman who helps women in childbirth – **midwife**

    The work of a midwife – **midwifery**; **tocology**; **tokology**

The branch of medicine concerned with the care and treatment of women during pregnancy, childbirth and the period immediately following - **obstetrics**

A doctor who specializes in obstetrics – **obstetrician**

Confinement of a woman in childbirth – **lying-in**

Being in labor – **parturient**

A surgical incision through the abdominal wall and uterus, performed to extract a fetus – **Caesarean**; **Caeserian**; **Cesarean**; **Cesarian**; **Caeserean section**; **caesarean section**

Delivery of a fetus with the buttocks or feet appearing first – **breech delivery**

Position of a fetus during labor in which the buttocks or feet appear first – **breech presentation**

Faulty or abnormal position, esp. of the fetus in the uterus – **malposition**

An injury or emotional shock sustained by an infant during birth – **birth trauma**

Relating to, resulting from or following childbirth – **puerperal**

The state of a woman while bearing a child or immediately thereafter – **puerperium**

Normal discharge of blood, tissue and mucus from the vagina after childbirth – **lochia**

Excrement in the fetal intestinal tract that is discharged at birth – **meconium**

A childbirth ritual among primitive people in which the father of a neonate goes through the motions of giving birth - **couvade**

Chin, of or relating to the – **genial**; **mental**

China/Chinese:

    The study of Chinese language, literature or civilization – **Sinology**

    A student of Sinology – **Sinolog**; **Sinologue**

    One favoring the Chinese, their interests, characteristics, etc. – **Sinophile**; **sinophile**; **sinophil**

    A custom or trait peculiar to the Chinese – **Sinicism**

    To change or modify by Chinese influence – **Sinicize** (v.t.)

    Conduct felt to suggest the Chinese - **chinoiserie**

Chivalry – see Knight

Choking, extreme or irrational fear of – **pnigophobia**

Choosing, the power or capability of – **volition**; **will**

Chorus, of or relating to a – **choric**

Church:

    Of, relating to or befitting a church – **churchly**

    To free from church control – **laicize** (v.t.)

    An endowment or estate belonging to a church – **patrimony**

    The buying or selling of a church office - **simony**

A doorkeeper at a church – **ostiary**

Cigar, shaped like a – **prolate**

Circular/Encircling (see also Surfaces, curve):
    Something circular or gracefully rounded – **rondure**
    A semicircular arrangement or structure – **hemicycle**
    Moving in a circular path – **gyral**; **gyratory**
    Encircling a part or opening – **orbicular**

Circumstances, a combination of – **conjuncture**

Citizen:
    Of, relating to or befitting a citizen or citizens – **civil**
    Citizens collectively – **citizenry**
    To endow with the rights of citizenship; esp. the right to vote - **enfranchise** (v.t.)
    Or, relating to or belonging to a citizen or citizenship – **civic**

City:
    Of, relating to, characteristic of or belonging to a city – **civic**; **urban**
    The study of civic affairs - **civics**
    To cause to become urban; to impart the styles and manners of a city – **citify**; **urbanize** (both v.t.)
    A city dweller – **urbanite**
    The culture or way of life of city dwellers; the condition of being or becoming urbanized – **urbanism**
    Relating to or connecting urban areas – **interurban**
    A specialist in urban problems – **urbanologist**
    Having a city or cities – **citied**
    An artistic representation of a city – **cityscape**
    The region, area or community outlying a city – **suburb** (q.v.)
    A region beyond the suburbs of a city, typically inhabited by the well-to-do – **exurb**, adj. **exurban**
        An exurban area – **exurbia**
        A resident of an exurb – **exurbanite**
    Designating a city and its populous suburbs – **greater**; **Greater** (e.g., Greater London)
    A region made up of several large cities and their surrounding areas in sufficiently close proximity to be considered a single urban complex – **megalopolis**
    The practices and problems peculiar to cities or to urban life – **urbiculture**
    A great mass or continuous network of urban communities – **conurbation**
    The inhabitants or citizens of a city – **townspeople**
    Restoration of deteriorated urban property, esp. in working-class neighborhoods by the middle and upper classes – **gentrify**

Claim:
    Someone making a claim – **claimant**
    To claim or seize without right – **arrogate** (v.t.)
    To relinquish a claim to; to surrender by deed – **remise** (v.t.) (Law)

Clan:
    Of, relating to or characteristic of a clan – **clannish**
    A person who belongs to a clan – **clansman**
    A woman who belongs to a clan - **clanswoman**

Class:
   A social class separated from others by hereditary, professional or financial distinctions; a social system based on such distinctions; the social status conferred by such a system – **caste**
   The socially select – **haut monde**; **high society**
   The social class comprising those who are supported by wealthy lovers or protectors – **demimonde**
   Fallen or lowered in class, rank or social position – **déclassé**; **déclassée**

Classics, a student or specialist in the – **classicist**

Classification:
   The science, laws or principles of classification – **taxonomy**
   Classification of organisms by use of biochemical criteria - **chemotaxonomy**

Claw (chela, pl. chelae):
   Of, resembling or having a claw or clawlike structure – **ungual**; **ungular**
   Having claws; having a claw-shaped base (Bot.); a mammal having claws – **unguiculate**
   Having three claws – **tridactyl**; **tridactylous**
   Shaped like a claw – **cheliform**
   Bearing a claw or claws – **cheliferous**
   Without claws on the feet – **adactylous** (used of crustaceans)

Clay:
   Of, containing or resembling clay – **argillaceous**; **argillous**
   Formed or molded of clay – **fictile**
   Producing or abounding in clay – **argilliferous**
   Clay thinned to the consistency of cream – **slip**
   To trim off excess clay at the seams of (partly dried pottery ware) – **fettle** (v.t.)

Clean/Cleanse:
   Cleansing power or quality – **detergency**
   Serving to cleanse; a cleansing agent - **abluent**

Cleft:
   Cleft or cloven, as a hoof – **bisulcate**
   Having many clefts forming lobes – **multifid**

Clients collectively – **clientele**

Cliff (scarp):
   A sloping mass of debris accumulated at the base of a cliff – **talus**
   A line of steep, lofty cliffs, esp. along a river - **palisades**
   A very steep or overhanging mass of rock, as a crag or the face of a cliff – **precipice**

Climate:
   The study of climate – **climatology**
   The climate of a specific place within an area contrasted with the climate of the area as a whole – **microclimate**
   The climate of a large geographical area – **macroclimate**
   The study of the effects of climatic conditions on organic life – **bioclimatology**
   The scientific study of the relationship between climate and periodic biological phenomena; the scientific study of such phenomena; the relationship between climate and periodic biological phenomena - **phenology**

Climax, relating to or constituting a – **climactic**

Climbing:
 To climb by gripping with the arms and legs – **swarm** (v.i./v.t.)
 Climbing – **scandent** (Bot.)
 Adapted to or specialized for climbing – **scansorial**

Clock:
 The science or art of making timepieces – **horology**
 An expert in horology; a maker of clocks or watches – **horologist**
 The relativistic slowing of a clock that moves with respect to a stationary observer – **time dilatation; time dilation**

Cloth/Clothing:
 Of or relating to clothes – **vestiary**
 One who makes, designs or deals in fashionable clothing for women – **modiste**
 A heavy cloth woven with rich, complex designs or scenes – **arras; tapestry**
 Richly decorated clothing – **finery; caparison**
  To clothe richly – **caparison** (v.t.)
 Civilian clothing, esp. when worn by one whose regular garb is a uniform - **mufti**
 A corduroy ridge – **wale**

Clouds:
 The science of clouds – **nephology**
 The scientific observation of clouds – **nephelognosy**
 A dense, white, fluff, flat-based cloud with a multiple rounded top and a well-defined outline – **cumulus**
 Shaped like a cumulus cloud – **cumuliform**
 A very dense, vertically developed cumulus with a rather hazy outline and a glaciated top – **cumulonimbus**
 A high-altitude cloud composed of a series of small, regularly arranged cloudlets in the form of ripples or grains -
  cirrocumulus
 A high-altitude, thin, hazy cloud, usually covering the sky – **cirrostratus**
 A high-altitude cloud composed of narrow bands or patches of thin, generally white, fleecy parts – **cirrus**
 Long, narrow formations of cirrus cloud some like a horse's tail in shape – **mare's tail; mare's-tail**, pl. **mare's tails** or
  mares' tails
 A low-altitude cloud typically resembling a horizontal layer of fog – **stratus**
 A low-altitude cloud occurring in extensive horizontal layers with massive, rounded summits – **stratocumulus**
 A low, gray cloud that precipitates rain, snow or sleet – **nimbostratus**
 A uniformly gray cloud that extends over the sky – **nimbus**
 A formation of gray or bluish sheetlike clouds – **altostratus**
 A high formation of roundish, fleecy, white or gray clouds – **altocumulus**
 Wisps of precipitation trailing from a cloud but evaporating before reaching the earth - **virga**
 Wind-driven clouds – **scud**
  A thin mass of wind-driven clouds - **rack**
 Shaped like a turret or row of turrets – **castellatus** (used of clouds)

Clown:
 A circus clown who appears in white makeup and follows a chiefly slapstick routine – **auguste**

Club:
 Shaped like a club; having one end thickened – **clavate; claviform**

Clump:
  To clump, as microorganisms, blood cells, etc. – **agglutinate** (v.i.), n. **agglutination**

Cluster:
  Clustered; gathered into a mass or ball - **agglomerate**; **agglomerative**; **capitate**; **agminate**
  A jumbled mass or cluster – **agglomerate**
  Compactly clustered – **glomerate**, n. **glomeration**
  Arranged in clusters – **agminate**
  Forming a dense cluster - **capitate**
  A bundlelike cluster, as of flowers or leaves – **fascicle** (Bot.)
    Made up of fascicles – **fascicular**
  Growing in compact clusters or small heaps – **acervate** (Bot.)

Coagulation:
    An agent that causes coagulation – **coagulant**
    A coagulated mass – **coagulum**

Coal:
  Producing, containing or relating to coal – **carboniferous**
  The process by which coal is formed from plant materials – **coalification**
  A coal miner; a ship for carrying coal – **collier**
  A coal mine and its buildings, equipment, etc. – **colliery**
  Coal mining by stripping off soil rather than sinking a shaft – **strip mining**

Coast (shoreline):
  Following, by way of, or along the coast – **coastwise**

Coat:
    The coat of a mammal, as distinct from bare skin – **pelage**

Coating:
  A smooth, thin, shiny coating; a coating applied to ceramics before firing or to food; to apply or form such a coating –
    glaze (n./v.t./v.i.)
  Having a glazed surface - **glacé**
  To become covered with a hard coating – **effloresce** (v.i.), n. **efflorescence**
  Covered with a clammy or sticky coating – **viscid**
  A metal coating bonded onto another metal – **cladding**

Coat of arms – see Heraldry

Cocaine:
  The habitual use of cocaine – **cocainism**
  To anesthetize with cocaine – **cocainize** (v.t.)

Coccyx, of or relating to the – **coccygeal**

Cockfights, a person who promotes or attends - **cocker**

Code:
  To reduce (laws, e.g.) to a code – **codify** (v.t.)
  The art or process of writing in or deciphering secret codes – **cryptography**

The procedures and methods used to translate or intercept codes or ciphers – **cryptanalysis**, v.t. **cryptanalyze**
A message or writing in code or cipher – **cryptogram**; **cryptograph**

Coffin:
A stone coffin – **sarcophagus**, pl. **sarcophagi** or **sarcophaguses**
The raised structure on which a coffin rests during a state funeral - **catafalque**

Coiling:
An act of coiling, turning, or folding about a center, core or axis – **circumvolution**

Coins:
Of or relating to coins or currency – **numismatic**
The study or collection of coins or money – **numismatics**; **numismatology**
The act or process of minting coins; coins manufactured in a mint; the impression stamped on a coin – **mintage**
Formed by stamping or punching in – **incuse** (used mainly of old coins)
A coin with the image of a head on one side – **teston**; **testoon**
Having the appearance of a coin that is not for circulation – **prooflike**
A coin containing a minting error – **fido**
Shaped like a coin (circular and flat) – **nummular**; **orbicular** (Bot.); **orbiculate** (Bot.)
A system of coinage in which a unit of currency consists of a combination of two or more metals in fixed proportion –
symmetalism
An imitation coin – **counter**; **token**

Cold (see also Freezing):
Very cold – **gelid**; **icy**
Extremely cold - **frigid**
Causing coldness – **frigorific**; **frigorifical**
The study of the effects of very low temperatures on living organisms – **cryobiology**
The science of low-temperature phenomena – **cryogenics**; **cryogeny**, adj. **cryogenic**
Thriving at low temperatures – **cryophilic** (n. **cryophilia**); **psychrophilic**
Selective exposure of tissues to extreme cold to bring about cell destruction – **cryosurgery**
Use of low temperatures in medical therapy – **crymotherapy**; **cryotherapy**
To cool below the freezing point without solidification – **supercool** (v.i./v.t.); **undercool** (v.t.)
One who lives in a cool northern climate - **hyperborean**
Extreme or irrational fear of cold temperatures – **psychrophobia**

Collapse, a violent inward – **implosion**

College:
Of, relating to or resembling a college – **collegiate**
Involving or representing two or more colleges – **intercollegiate**

Colon (body part):
Surgical removal of all or part of the colon – **colectomy**
Inflammation of the mucous membrane of the colon – **colitis**
The surgical construction of an artificial excretory opening from the colon – **colostomy**

Collection of various items, parts or ingredients – **miscellany**

Color:
Relating to colors or color – **chromatic**

The scientific study of color – **chromatics**

Producing or imparting color - **colorific**

Having only one color; having or producing light of only one wavelength – **homochromatic**; **monochromatic**; **unicolor**

Having two colors – **bicolor**; **dichromatic**

Having two distinct color phases in the adult – **dichromatic** (Biol.)

Having many colors – **polychromatic**; **polychrome**; **polychromic**; **polychromous**; **variegated**; **versicolor**; **versicolored**

Manifesting changes of color - **polychromatic**; **polychrome**; **polychromic**; **polychromous**

Having a changeable color or luster, esp. marked by an undulating narrow band of white light; a gem with such coloring - **chatoyant**

Having the same color throughout – **isochroous**

Having different parts or sections colored differently – **parti-colored**; **pied**

Without enough color – **achromatous**

Lacking the normal amount of color – **pale**; **pallid**; **paly**; **wan**

The total absence of color – **achromaticity**

Designating color having no hue – **achromatic**

To rid of color or render achromatic – **achromatize** (v.t.)

Having no color; colorless – **achromatous**; **achromic**; **achromous**

To change the appearance of, esp. by marking with different colors – **variegate** (v.t.)

Changing in color – **variegated**; **versicolor**; **versicolored**

Sensitive to all colors – **panchromatic**

Lack of normal coloration in a person, animal or plant – **albinism**; **alphosis**; n. **albino**, adj. **albinic**

Darkness of the skin, hair or eyes resulting from high pigmentation – **melanism**

To cause (a plant) to develop without normal green coloring by preventing exposure to sunlight – **etiolate** (v.t.) (Bot.)

A band or streak of color – **vitta** (Biol.)

A broad and distinct band of color – **fascia** (Zool.)

Marked by broad bands of color - **fasciate**, **fasciated** (both Zool.)

A white or light-colored spot on the face of a horse or other animal – **blaze**

Producing a display of lustrous, rainbowlike colors; colorful in effect or appearance – **iridescent**, n. **iridescence**

    To emit or show an iridescent shimmer of colors – **opalesce** (v.i.), n. **opalescence**

A strongly pigmented or pigment-generating organ or organelle – **chromogen** (Biol.)

A substance used as coloring; a substance that imparts a characteristic color to plant or animal tissue – **pigment**

A small, dark-colored area around a center portion – **areola**; **areole** (both Anat.), pl. **areolae** or **areolas**

A change in color caused by variation of the physical conditions to which a body is subjected, as in heating – **metachromatism**

To remove the color from – **decolorize** (v.t.)

Having a pattern of brightly colored diamond shapes – **harlequin**

Column:

    Having the shape of a column; constructed with or having columns – **columnar**

    The use or arrangement of columns in a building – **columniation**

    Having columns at one or both ends, but not along the sides – **apteral**

    A building having a roof or ceiling supported by rows of columns – **hypostyle**

    A series of columns placed at regular intervals – **colonnade**

    Having a row of columns along the front only – **prostyle**

    Having a set of columns at each end, but none along the sides – **amphiprostyle**

    Having columns at both front and back or on each side – **amphistylar**

    Having a row of columns on all sides; a structure with this columniation - **peripteral**

    A series of columns surrounding a temple or other structure, or enclosing a court – **peristyle**, adj. **peristylar**

    A column or pillar with a capital and a base, set into a wall as an ornamental motif – **pilaster**

Not having columns or pilasters – **astylar**

The bulge in columns to correct the optical illusion of an inward curve created by a straight column - **entasis**

A male figure used as a column – **telamon**, pl. **telamones**

A female figure used as a column – **caryatid**, pl. **caryatids** or **caryatides**

Coma:

Of, relating to or in a coma – **comatose**

A partial or mild comatose state – **semicoma**

Comb:

Comblike – **cockade**; **pectinate**

Having a profile like that of a rooster's comb - **cockade**

A comblike structure – **ctenidium** (Zool.)

Having narrow segments or spines resembling the teeth of a comb – **ctenoid** (Biol.)

Having teeth like a comb – **pectinate**; **pectinated**

Comedy (see also Humor):

A continuous series of jokes or comic stories delivered by a single comedian – **monolog**; **monologue**

Of or relating to comedy – **comedic**; **comic**; **comical**

A plotless comedy – **farce**; **harlequinade**

Committee, a member of a – **committeeman**

Communication:

Without the right or means of communicating with others, as one held in solitary confinement – **incommunicado**

The science and technology of automatic data measurement and transmission, as by wire or radio, from remote sources, such as space vehicles, to a receiving station for recording and analysis - **telemetry**

Communication through means other than the senses – **telepathy**

Electrical transmission of sound between distant stations, esp. by radio or telephone – **telephony**

The use of the fingers and hands to convey ideas - **dactylology**

Compensation:

To make compensation to for damage, loss or injury – **indemnify** (v.t.)

Complain:

A lamenting and denunciatory complaint - **jeremiad**

To complain persistently; a persistent complaint – **kvetch** (v.i./n.)

A government official charged with investigating citizens' complaints against the government – **ombudsman**

Comply:

Inclination to comply willingly with the wishes of others – **complaisance**; **compliance**

Compress:

Able to be compressed – **compressible**

Violent compression – **implosion**

Computer:

The part of a computer that interprets and executes instructions – **central processing unit (CPU)**

An action resulting from a single computer instruction – **operation**

The smallest unit of measurement for computer data - **bit**

A group of eight bits, enough to represent a character; a sequence of adjacent binary digits operated on as a unit by a computer – **byte**

The unit of a computer that preserves data for retrieval - **memory**

A computer memory with no moving parts – **static memory**

Allowing access to stored data without regard to data sequence – **random-access**

A sequence of instructions that causes a departure from the normal sequence of instructions – **branch**

A sequence of instructions that repeats until a terminal condition prevails – **loop**

A sequence of instructions that starts the processing of a program entered by means of an automatic input device – **loading program**

A computer program contained within another program that operates semi-independently of the encasing program – **subprogram**

A program that originates, stores and distributes the programs that make up an operating system – **librarian**

A program that transfers data from off-line memory by means of an input or storage device – **loader**

To set to a starting position or value – **initialize** (v.t.)

One of a set of symbols, as letters or numbers, arranged to express information – **character**

Little dots put together in a grid to make a picture - **bitmap**

Computers that are connected to one another – **network**

A device or software that connects two or more networks - **router**

To send a short message to which another computer automatically responds – **ping** (v.t.)

Operating instructions, carried out by CPUs, for computer operations; manuals for computer operation and maintenance – **software**

Software designed to interfere with a computer's normal functioning - **malware**

E-mail used as a broadcast medium by sending the same message to many people who didn't ask for it – **spam**

Advertising software that automatically plays, displays, or downloads advertising material to a computer – **adware**

Computer software that collects personal information about users without their informed consent - **spyware**

A software program capable of reproducing itself and usually capable of causing great harm to files or other programs on the same computer - **virus**

A program that uses computer networks and security flaws to create copies of itself and spreads from computer to computer - **worm**

A computer that uses the services of another computer or a server - **client**

To move or copy a file from a local computer to a remote network or Internet server – **upload** (v.t.)

To copy a file from a remote computer to one's own computer – **download** (v.t.)

A device that converts data from one form into another, or that enables one's computer to talk on the phone or cable TV – **modem** (short for *mo*dulator/*dem*odulator)

Information that a program uses unless you specify otherwise - **default**

A computer program that lets the user enter numbers or text into a table with rows and columns – **spreadsheet**

A word, phrase or alphanumeric character used to identify an item in an information retrieval system – **descriptor**

A basic unit of storage in a computer memory that can hold one unit of information, as a character or word – **cell**

A single file containing a group of files that have been compressed for efficient storage - **archive**

A file that contains information other than text – **binary file**

A magnetic tape or disk containing the original data for a programming system – **grandfather file**; **grandfather tape**

Of or relating to computer input or output data that have not been edited before display – **unformatted**

To scramble (access codes) to prevent illicit entry into a system – **encrypt** (v.t.)

A way of coding the information in a file or e-mail so that it cannot be read by a third party as it travels over a network - **encryption**

A flow chart symbol indicating continuation of a broken line or flow – **inconnector**

The actual time in which a physical process under computer study or control occurs; the time required for a computer to solve a problem – **real time**

The time required for a device to begin physical output of a desired piece of data once processing is complete – **latency**

An arrangement of computer memory elements in one or several planes - **array**

A region on a punch card or magnetic tape in which nondigital information is recorded – **zone**

A procedure in which a table of values stored in a computer is searched for a specified value – **look-up**

Under the control of a central computer, as in a manufacturing process – **on-line**

To interact with a computer on-line – **converse** (v.i.)

A frequent, chronological publication of personal thoughts and web links – **blog** (short for *web log*)

A pre-recorded audio program that can be downloaded for listening on personal com-puters or mobile devices – **podcast**

A high-speed connection to the Internet – **broadband**

The connection of a device to a network via a modem and a public telephone network – **dial-up** (adj./n.)

A system that prevents unauthorized access to or from a private network – **firewall**
(A firewall can be hardware or software, or a combination of both.)

A computer system that provides client stations with access to files as shared resources to a computer network – **server**

The practice of bidding in the last few seconds of an on-line auction in order to avoid being outbid - **sniping**

To control (an industrial process, e.g.) automatically by computer; to become thus controlled – **cybernate** (v.t./v.i.)

A person who has some vital bodily processes controlled by cybernetically-operated devices – **cyborg**

Art obtained by programming a computer to create a design or picture – **computer graphics** (used with sing. or pl. verb)

A very small computer built around a microprocessor – **microcomputer**

A small computer having more memory and higher execution speed than a microcomputer – **minicomputer**

Conceal:
 Tending to conceal or camouflage – **cryptic**; **cryptical**
 Calculated misrepresentation through concealment of the facts; an inference drawn from such a misrepresentation - **subreption**

Conceiving, capable of or relating to – **conceptive**

Concentrate:
 To concentrate by boiling down – **decoct** (v.t.)
 Concentration of emotional energy on an object or idea – **cathexis**, pl. **cathexes**

Concept:
 To form a concept or concepts of; to form concepts – **conceptualize** (v.t./v.i.)

Concern:
 An unselfish concern for the welfare of others – **altruism**, adj. **altruistic**, n. **altruist**

Concerts, to give or perform in – **concertize** (v.i.)

Condensation, a product of – **condensate**

Conduct (see also Etiquette):
 The standard of what is socially acceptable in conduct, speech, etc. – **decorum**; **propriety**
 The study of human conduct – **ethics**; **moral philosophy**; **praxeology**; **praxiology**
 Misconduct, esp. in handling public affairs – **malfeasance**
 Attentive to the finer points of formal conduct and etiquette – **punctilious**
 Unrestrained or lawless in conduct - **dissolute**

Cone:
 Shaped like a cone – **conic**; **conoid**

Shaped like a cone resting on its apex – **turbinal**
A cone with the top sliced off – **frustrum**

Conference – see Meeting

Confined places, extreme or irrational fear of – **claustrophobia**

Conform/Conformity:
One who conforms to the prevailing ways and opinions of one's time or condition for personal advantage – **opportunist; timeserver**
Tending to produce conformity by violent or arbitrary means – **procrustean**

Connections between blood vessels, veins in a leaf, channels of a river, etc. – **anastomosis**
To join by anastomosis; to be connected by anastomosis – **anastomose** (v.t./v.i.)

Conscience, not restrained by – **unconscionable; unscrupulous**

Consciousness:
Above the threshold of consciousness – **supraliminal**
Below the threshold of consciousness – **subliminal**
Consciousness at a rudimentary sensory level – **sentience; sentiency**
The mind being conscious of its consciousness – **apperception**
The suspension of consciousness in order to express subconscious ideas and feelings – **automatism**

Conspiracy, one engaged in a – **conspirator**; adj. **conspiratorial**

Constipation, having or causing – **costive**

Construction:
One who constructs something – **wright**
Of or relating to construction – **geotectonic; tectonic**
The art or science of construction, esp. of large buildings – **tectonics**
An angular military construction - **redan**

Contests:
One who participates in contests simply to win prizes – **pothunter**

Continent:
Between or among continents – **intercontinental**
Spanning or crossing a continent – **transcontinental**
An attitude or policy of favoritism or partiality to a continent - **continentalism**

Contraction:
Capable of contracting or causing contraction – **contractile**
Alternately contracting and expanding – **pulsating; systaltic**
Contracting the tissues or blood vessels – **astringent; styptic; styptical**
A drug or substance having this effect – **styptic; styptical**

Contradiction:
A seemingly contradictory statement that may nonetheless be true – **paradox**
Contradiction in ideas, statements or terms – **antilogy**

An apparent contradiction between valid principles or conclusions that seem equally necessary and reasonable – **antinomy**
A figure of speech in which contradictory ideas or terms are combined – **oxymoron**

Contrary, the quality or state of being – **contrariety**

Control:
An area over which one exercises control - **fiefdom**

Convention, a person who attends a – **conventioneer**

Conversation/Discussion:
A conversation between two individuals – **dialog**; **dialogue**
One who takes part in a conversation or dialogue – **interlocutor**, adj. **interlocutory**, n. **interlocution**
A conversation or scene in which three individuals participate – **trialogue**
To draw out discussions or negotiations so as to gain time – **temporize** (v.i.)
A participant in a discussion - **discussant**
Someone skilled in table talk – **deipnosophist**
A formal conversation – **colloquy**

Convulsion – see Muscle

Cooking:
Of or relating to cooking or a kitchen – **culinary**
The style of cooking; manner of preparing food - **cuisine**
To cook in water just below the boiling point – **coddle** (v.t.)

Copper:
Of, relating to or resembling copper – **cupreous**
Containing copper – **cupreous**; **cupriferous**
The art of engraving on copper - **chalcography**
One who makes articles of copper – **coppersmith**
Copper poisoning – **chalcosis**

Coral, resembling – **coraloid**

Cork:
Of, relating to or resembling cork or cork tissue – **suberose**
To draw the cork from (a bottle, e.g.) – **uncork** (v.t.)

Corporation, a member of a - **corporator**

Corrupt practices, one who defends or engages in - **corruptionist**

Corsets:
A manufacturer, fitter or seller of corsets - **corsetière**

Cortex:
Of, relating to or made up of a cortex – **cortical**
Having a cortex or similar specialized external layer – **corticate**
To remove the cortex from (an organ or structure), esp. in surgery – **decorticate** (v.t.)

Cosmic rays, generated by – **cosmogenic**

Costumes:
    One who designs, makes or supplies costumes – **costumer**; **customier**

Cough drop, a four-sided – **troche**

Council, of or relating to a – **conciliar**

Counted, capable of being – **numerable**

Country:
    To restore or return to the country of birth or citizenship – **repatriate** (v.t.)
        Love of and devotion to one's own country – **patriotism**, n. **patriot**
    Militant devotion to and glorification of one's country – **chauvinism** (n. **chauvinist**); **jingoism**, n. **jingoist**
    Underdeveloped or developing countries – **Third World**; **third world**, n. **Third Worlder**
    Of or relating to the country (as opposed to the city) – **agrestic**; **bucolic**; **pastoral**; **rural**; **rustic**
        To make or become rural – **ruralize** (v.t./v.i.)
        One who lives in a rural area; an advocate of rural life – **ruralist**
        To send or go to the country; to live or stay in the country – **rusticate** (v.t./v.i.)
        The quality or state of being rural; a rural characteristic or trait – **rurality**; **ruralism**; **rusticity**

Courage:
    Courage due to intoxicants or other artificial stimulation – **Dutch courage**; **dutch courage**
    To recover courage or hope – **respire** (v.i.)
    An incitement to courage – **sursum corda**

Court (Archit.):
    An open central court – **atrium**

Court (Law; see also Jury):
    A formal written application requesting a court for a specific judicial action – **petition**
    The judgment of a court of equity, admiralty, probate or divorce – **decree** (q.v.)
    A court ruling – **holding**
    Outside the authority of a court – **extrajudicial**
    Appropriate for or subject to court trial – **justiciable**
    Before a court of law or a judge; not yet decided – **sub judice**
    To fail to appear in court when summoned; to lose (a case) by failing to appear in court – **default** (v.i./v.t.)
    Courts as a whole – **judicature**
    A written order requiring appearance in court to give testimony – **subpoena**; **summons**
    A writ commanding a person to produce in court certain designated documents or other evidence – **subpoena duces**
        tecum, pl. **subpoenas duces tecum**
    A court order forbidding a given course of action – **injunction**
    A writ issued to bring a person before a court or judge in order to release that person from unlawful restraint or
        detention – **habeas corpus**
    One appointed by a court administrator to take into custody the property or funds of others – **receiver**
        The office or functions of a receiver; the state of being held by a receiver - **receivership**
    One guilty of attempting to influence a court illegally – **embracer**

Covering:

    The natural covering of an organ or part – **tunic**

    A covering, as the tough, leathery forewing of certain insects or the inner coat of a seed – **tegmen**; **tegmentum** (both Biol.)

Crab, resembling a – **cancroid**; **carcinomorphic**

Cracks:

    Full of cracks, clefts or crevices - **rimose**

Craftsmanship, of or relating to – **vulcanian**

Cranes, a group of – **herd**

Creosote or cresol, of or relating to – **cresylic**

Crescent:

    Shaped like a crescent – **bicorn**; **lunate**; **lunated**; **lunular**; **semilunar**; **semilunate**

    A crescent-shaped body – **meniscus**

    A small crescent-shaped marking or structure – **lunula**, pl. **lunulae**

    Having crescent-shaped markings – **lunulate**; **lunulated**

Crest, having or forming a – **cristate**; **cristated**

Crime:

    A habitual or confirmed criminal; a fugitive from the law – **outlaw**

    A tendency to return to criminal habits and activities – **recidivism**, adj. **recidivous**, n. **recidivist**, v.i. **recidivate**

    To involve in or charge with a wrongful act, as a crime – **incriminate** (v.t.)

    To treat as a criminal – **criminalize** (v.t.)

    The study of crime, criminals and criminal behavior – **criminology**

    The study of the punishment of crime – **penology**

    Neglect in preventing or reporting a crime – **misprision**

    A member of a criminal organization – **gangster**; **racketeer**

    A woman companion of a gangster – **moll**

    A crime considered more serious than a misdemeanor and punishable by a stronger sentence – **felony**, adj. **felonious**

    One who has perpetrated a felony – **felon**

    Felons as a group – **felonry**

    An offense of lesser gravity than a felony – **misdemeanor**

    An attempt to commit a crime of violence – **attentat** (used esp. of an unsuccessful attempt at a political crime)

    An offense or crime against the ruler or supreme power of a state – **lese majesty**; **lèse majesté**

    One who is guilty of or has been convicted and sentenced for a misdemeanor – **misdemeanant**

Crippled, to cause or become – **becripple** (v.t./v.i.)

Crisis, showing no signs of a – **acritical**

Critical/Criticize:

    To criticize severely – **castigate**; **fustigate** (both v.t.)

    To castigate with harsh or violent language – **objurgate**; **vituperate** (both v.t.)

    One who is overcritical – **hypercritic**, adj. **hypercritical**

Crops – see Agriculture

Cross:
   To put (a person) to death by nailing or binding to a cross – **crucify** (v.t.)
   A person who carries a cross, as in a procession – **crucifer**
   Bearing a cross – **cruciferous**
   Having cross-shaped leaves or petals; crossing or overlapping, as the wings of some insects when at rest – **cruciate**
   Crossed in the form of an X - **decussate**
   Shaped like a cross – **cruciate**; **cruciform**

Crossbow:
   One who employs or bears a crossbow – **arbalest**; **arbalist**; **arbelest**; **crossbowman**
   A crossbow with a steel bow set crosswise in a wooden shaft – **arbalest**; **arbalist**

Crow:
   A group of crows – **murder**
   Of, relating to, typical of or resembling a crow – **corvine**
   Having the form of a crow – **corviform**; **corvine**

Crowds:
   Extreme or irrational fear of crowds – **demophobia**; **ochlophobia**

Crown:
   The act or ceremony of crowning a sovereign or consort – **coronation**
   Shaped like a crown - **coronoid**

Cruelty:
   Delight in cruelty – **sadism**, adj. **sadistic**
   One who delights in cruelty – **sadist**

Crust:
   Of or relating to a crust, esp. that of the earth or the moon – **crustal**
   A loose, scaly crust coating a surface – **scurf**

Crystal:
   Generating or containing crystals – **crystalliferous**
   To assume a crystalline form or structure; to cause to form crystals – **crystalize**; **crystallize** (both v.i./v.t.)
   The science of crystal structure – **crystallography**
   Having properties of a crystal – **crystalloid**
   Having a crystalline structure that is visible only under the microscope – **microcrystalline**
   Having a crystalline structure consisting of crystals too small even to be seen with a microscope – **cryptocrystalline**
   A small needle-shaped crystal – **trichite**, adj. **trichitic**
   Divination by concentrating on a glass or crystal globe with the aim of inducing a physical state in which divination can
      be performed – **crystal gazing**; **crystallomancy**

Cube:
   Shaped like a cube – **cubic**; **cubical**; **cubiform**; **cuboid**

Cucumber, shaped like a – **cucumiform**

Culture, human:

The study of human culture based on archeological, ethnologic, ethnographic, linguistic, social and psychological data and methods of analysis – **cultural anthropology**

The branch of anthropology that describes the varieties of mankind and their geographic distribution – **anthropography**

One who specializes in anthropography – **anthropographer**

The study of cultural heritage and socioeconomic systems in technologically primitive societies – **ethnology**

The ethnology of early man – **paleethnology**; **paleëthnology**

The study of peoples whose cultures are at an early developmental stage – **agriology**

The comparative study of nonliterate cultures – **agriology**, n. **agriologist**

The fusion of diverse cultures or traditions – **hybridism**

To absorb (an immigrant or culturally distinct group) into the prevailing culture; to become absorbed thus – **assimilate** (v.t./v.i.), adj. **assimilative**

A cultural subgroup differentiated by status, ethnic background, residence, religion, or other factors that functionally unify the group and act collectively on each member – **subculture**

Of or relating to two distinct cultures in one nation or geographic region – **bicultural**

Modification of one culture as a result of contact with a different, esp. a more advanced, culture – **acculturation**

To cause to change or to change by the process of acculturation – **acculturate** (v.t./v.i.)

To cause to lose tribal customs by means of acculturation – **detribalize** (v.t.)

Cultural change induced by the introduction of elements of a foreign culture – **transculturation**

The accepted traditional customs and usages of a particular social group – **mores**

The character, disposition, or basic values peculiar to a specific people or culture - **ethos**

The pattern of basic values and attitudes of a people, characteristically transmitted through the arts – **mythos**

A way of thinking or acting adopted by the members of a group as part of their shared culture – **folkway**

An animal, plant or natural object serving as the emblem of a clan or family by virtue of an asserted ancestral relationship – **totem**

A feature of primitive social organization whereby the members of a group identify themselves with totems – **totemism**

Belief in the superiority of one's own ethnic group – **ethnocentrism**

A prohibition excluding something from use, approach, mention, etc., because of its sacred and inviolable nature; a ban or inhibition attached to something by social custom or emotional aversion; an object, act or word protected by such a prohibition – **taboo** (pl. **taboos**); **tabu**, pl. **tabus**

A cultural phenomenon that is transmitted by repetition and replication in a manner analogous to the biological transmission of genes - **meme**

Cup:

A cup-shaped part, structure or indentation – **cupule** (Biol.)

A shallow, cuplike depression or pit – **fovea** (Anat.)

Shaped like a fovea – **foveiform**

A small cup-shaped structure – **calyculus** (Biol.)

Shaped like a cup – **cotyloid**; **cupulate**; **cyathiform**; **scyphiform**

Curare, to poison with – **curarize** (v.t.)

Curtain:

A heavy curtain hung across a doorway – **portière**; **portiere**

A theater curtain – **scrim**

Curve:

The process of curving; the state of being curved – **arcuation**

Curved inward – **incurvate**; **incurved**

To cause to curve inward – **incurvate** (v.t.) (used chiefly as a past participle, e.g., an incurvated column)
Curving inward, as a parrot's beak – **adunc**; **aduncous**
Curved or hooked like a sickle - **falcate**
Having an outward-curving front – **bowfront**
Curving or slanting upward – **assurgent** (Bot.)
Curved downward – **inflexed** (Bot.)
Curved downward at a sharp angle – **deflexed** (Bot.)
Curved downward toward the base – **reclinate** (Bot.)

Cushion, shaped like a – **pulvinate**; **pulvinated**

Cusp:
    Having a cusp – **cuspate**; **cuspidate**; **cuspidated**
    Having two cusps – **bicuspid**; **bicuspidate**
    Having three cusps – **tricuspid**; **tricuspidal**
    An organ or part with three cusps, esp. a tooth - **tricuspid**
    Shaped like a cusp - **cuspate**

Customs officer who boards incoming ships at a harbor – **tidewaiter**

Cut:
    Capable of being cut or split easily – **scissile**
    Capable of being cut smoothly with a knife – **sectile**
    To mark or cut into with a sharp instrument; to engrave into a surface – **incise** (v.t.), n. **incision**
    Having the apex cut off and replace by a plane – **truncated**, v.t. **truncate**

Cycles:
    Consisting or having two cycles – **bicyclic**
    Not cyclic; not in cycles – **acyclic**

Cylinder:
    Of or relating to a cylinder; having the properties of a cylinder – **cylindrical**
    Shaped like a cylinder – **cylindrical**; **cylindroid**
    Cylindrical and smooth-surfaced – **terete** (Bot.)
    Cylindrical and having ridges or swellings- **torose**

Cyst:
    Surgical removal of a cyst – **cystectomy**
    Resembling a cyst – **cystoid**
    To enclose in or become enclosed in a cyst – **encyst** (v.t./v.i.)
    A large or enlarged cyst – **macrocyst**

Czar:
    A czar's eldest son – **czarevitch**
    A czar's daughter; the wife of a czarevitch – **czarevna**
    A czar's wife – **czarina**; **czaritza**

D

Dagger – see Knife

Dairy:
    A man who works in a dairy; a dairy manager or owner – **dairyman**
    A woman who works in a diary – **dairymaid**

Dam:
    A dam placed across a river or canal to raise or divert the water - **weir**

Dampness:
    Dampness, esp. of the air – **humidity**
    To make damp (humid) – **humidify** (v.t.)

Dance/Dancing (see also Ballet):
    Of or relating to dancing – **saltatorial**; **saltatory**; **terpsichorean**
    The art of creating and arranging ballets or dances; the art and technique of dance notation – **choreography**
    The study of dance notation; the recording of dance movement by notation - **choreology**
    A dance for two performers – **pas de deux**
    A whirling dance on the toes – **toedance**
    A dance movement in which a couple or couples swing around the dance floor with hands joined, as in country dancing - **poussette**
    The rhythmic stamping of the heels characteristic of Spanish flamenco dances – **zapateado**
    A sliding or gliding step; to perform such a step – **glissade** (n./v.i.), n. **glissader**
    A woman employed to dance with patrons (of a nightclub, e.g.) for a fee – **taxi dancer**
    A frenzied female dancer – **maenad**; **menad**, adj. **menadic**
    A fancy dance step executed by jumping and striking the legs together - **pigeonwing**
    A jazz dance involving circular group formations with improvised solos and duets – **big apple**; **Big Apple**

Daring, arrogantly or recklessly – **temerarious**

Darkness:
    Able to survive in darkness – **scotobiotic**
    Partial darkness – **semidarkness**
    Overtaken by darkness or night – **benighted**
    Marked by intensity of darkness or gloom – **cimmerian; stygian**

Day:
    By the day; per day – **per diem**
    Exhibiting approximately 24-hour periodicity – **circadian**
    Active or occurring during the daytime, rather than at night; living for one day; opening during daylight hours and closing at night – **diurnal**
    Comprising a sequence of day and night - **noctidiurnal**
    The period between sunrise and noon – **forenoon**
    Of, relating to, occurring or performed during a half-day; occurring or coming approximately once every 12 hours – **semidiurnal**
    The time required for a complete rotation of the earth – **sidereal day**
        A twenty-fourth part of a sidereal day – **sidereal hour**
    Occurring in the course of a single day – **intraday**
    Occurring every fourth day, counting inclusively – **quartan** (used of a fever)

Recurring daily – **quotidian**
Recurring every other day, or, when considered inclusively, every third day – **tertian**
A day on which collectors for a charity solicit contributions, giving each contributor a tag – **tag day**
A hot, sultry day – **dog day**

Dean:
    The office, jurisdiction or authority of a dean; a dean's official residence – **deanery**
    Of or relating to a dean or deanery – **decanal**

Death/Treatment of the dead and their remains (see also Coffin, Funeral, Grave, Killing, and Monument):
    Causing death – **deadly**; **deathly**; **fatal**; **lethal**
      Less than lethal – **sublethal**
    Resembling death – **thanatoid**
    Suggestive of death – **cadaverous**; **deathly**; **Stygian**; **stygian**
    One whose business it is to arrange for the burial or cremation of the dead and to assist at funeral rites – **mortician**; **undertaker**
    A furnace or establishment for the cremation of corpses – **crematorium**; **crematory**
    Ashes remaining after the cremation of a corpse – **cremains**
    A place for keeping the ashes of a cremated body – **cinerarium**, adj. **cinerary**
    An underground chamber or vault, esp. one used as a burial place beneath a church – **crypt**
    An ancient underground burial chamber or series of such rooms – **catacomb**; **hypogaeum**, **hypogeum**, pl. **hypogaea** or **hypogea**
    A place, esp. a funeral home, where corpses are kept prior to burial or cremation – **mortuary**
    A vault with niches for urns containing the ashes of the dead – **columbarium**; **columbary**, pl. **columbaria** or **columbaries**
    A place in which bodies of persons found dead are kept until identified and claimed, or until arrangements for burial have been made – **morgue**
    One who buries (a body) – **inhumer**
    The act or an instance of burying – **inhumation**; **interment**
    Extreme or irrational fear of being buried alive - **taphephobia**
    A rite or ceremony relating to burial – **obsequy** (usu. used in pl. - **obsequies**)
    Urn burial – **hydriotaphia**
    A vault or chamber for burying the dead; a place of burial; a monument commemorating the dead – **tomb**
      To place in a tomb – **entomb**; **inter** (both v.t.)
      To serve as a tomb for – **entomb** (v.t.)
      The tomb of a venerated person - **shrine**
      A large and stately tomb, or a building housing such a tomb or tombs – **mausoleum**
    A place for burying the dead – **cemetery**; **graveyard**
    A burial ground for poor or unknown persons – **potter's field**
    A large and elaborate cemetery belonging to an ancient city – **necropolis**, pl. **necropolises** or **necropoleis**
    A container or receptacle for holding the bones of the dead – **ossuary**
    Occurring or continuing after one's death; born after the death of the father – **posthumous**
    Happening or taking effect after a person's death – **post-obit**
    Approaching the point of death – **moribund**
    At the point of death – **in extremis**
    Made or done just before one's death – **ante-mortem**
    A meditation on death – **thanatopsis**
    The study of death or the dead – **thanatology**
    Not subject to death – **immortal**
      To make immortal – **immortalize** (v.t.)

Death and decay of tissue in a bodily part due to failure of blood supply, injury or disease – **gangrene**, adj. **gangrenous**

To cause to become gangrenous; to become gangrenous – **sphacelate** (v.t./v.i.)

The natural degeneration and death of cells and tissues, as opposed to death from injury or disease and distinguished from death of the entire organism - **necrobiosis**

An obsessive fascination, esp. a sexual one, with death and corpses – **necrophilia**; **necrophily**

One who practices necrophilia – **necrophile**; **necrophilist**

The pathological death of living tissue in a plant or animal – **necrosis**, adj. **necrotic**

The necrotic degeneration of bodily tissue into a cheeselike substance – **caseation**

Muscular stiffening following death – **rigor mortis**

The worship of the dead – **necrolatry**

An announcement of death; a list of persons who have died – **necrology**; **obituary**

A writer of obituaries – **necrologist**

A hymn, composition or service for commemorating the dead - **requiem**

A deceased (dead) person – **decedent** (Law)

Divination by means of communication with and intervention of the dead – **necromancy**

Extreme or irrational fear of death or corpses – **necrophobia**; **thanatophobia**

Debate:

The study or practice of formal debate – **forensics**

The ending of debate in parliamentary procedure – **closure**; **cloture**

Debt:

An unpaid and overdue debt – **arrears**

The state of being in arrears – **arrearage**

An authorization to a debtor permitting temporary suspension of payments - **moratorium**

A certificate or voucher acknowledging a debt – **debenture**

To seize the property of in order to compel payment of debts – **distrain** (v.t.) (Law)

Deceive:

A presentation, as of mingled fact and fancy, designed to deceive - **farrago**

The act or practice of deceiving by the assumption of a false identity – **imposture**

One who has assumed a false identity – **imposter**; **impostor**

To deceive by artful wheedling or tricky dishonesty – **cozen** (v.t.)

Decision:

Loss or impairment of the ability to exercise will power and come to decisions – **abulia**; **aboulia**

The belief in or practice of decision-making in an organized group by a numerical majority of its members – **majoritarianism**

Decompose (putrefy):

Able to be decomposed by natural biological processes – **biodegradable**

Partial decomposition of organic matter by microorganisms; putrefied matter; the state of having been putrefied – **putrefaction**

Of or relating to putrefaction – **putrescent**; **putrid**; **saprogenic**

Subject to putrefaction – **putrescible**

Proceeding from or displaying putrefaction – **putrid**

Double decomposition – **metathesis**, adj. **metathetic** or **metathetical** (Chem.)

Decree:

Having the force of a decree – **decretive**

Of or resulting from a decree – **decretory**

Deer:
  A group of deer – **herd**
  A male deer – **buck**; **hart** (used esp. of a male red deer five years old or older); **stag** (used esp. of a male red deer five years old or older)
  A male red deer in his third year – **spay**; **spayad**; **spayard**
  A two-year-old stag with its first horns – **brocket**
  A female deer – **doe**
  A young deer – **fawn**
  A female red deer – **hind**
  Relating to, resembling or characteristic of a deer – **cervine**
  The flesh of a deer, used for food – **venison**
  The note blown on a hunting horn to announce the killing of a deer – **mort**

Defeat:
  To defeat or best in two ways at once – **whipsaw** (v.t.)

Defense:
  A person who writes or speaks in defense or justification of a doctrine, action, etc. – **apologist**
  Defensible from armed assault – **tenable**

Demand:
  Stubbornly or unreasonably persistent in pressing demands or requests – **importunate**

Demons:
  The study of demons or of beliefs about them; a treatise on demons – **demonology**
  To control or possess by a demon – **demonize** (v.t.)
  A demon alleged to assume a female form in order to have sexual intercourse with men in their sleep – **succubus**
  A male demon – **warlock**

Deny (see also Law):
  To deny to oneself – **abnegate**; **renounce** (both v.t.)

Dependence:
  Psychological dependence on others – **anaclisis**, adj. **anaclitic**

Depths, extreme or irrational fear of – **bathophobia**

Descent (see also Heredity):
  A record or table of familial descent; the study of family histories – **genealogy**
    The art or study of tracing genealogies – **heraldry** (q.v.)
  An originator of a line of descent – **progenitor**
  Having the same mother but different fathers – **uterine** (used of siblings)
  Descended from two ancestral lines or individuals – **diphyletic**
  Of the same lineage or origin, esp. related by blood – **consanguine**; **consanguineous**

Description:
  A description detailing a person's appearance and features, as for police files – **signalment**

Desert:
   The study of desert features and phenomena – **eremology**

Deserve:
   Entirely in accordance with what is deserved or merited - **condign**

Design (see also Graphic Arts):
   The study of equipment design in order to reduce operator fatigue and discomfort – **ergonomics**

Destroy:
   Capable of being destroyed – **destructible**
   Causing or bringing destruction – **destructive**; **ruinous**
   Mutually destructive – **internecine**
   Destruction of property or obstruction of normal operations to defeat or hinder a cause or endeavor – **sabotage**
      One who commits sabotage – **saboteur**

Development – see Biology: Growing/Living Conditions, and Biology: Processes

Devil:
   A little devil – **devilkin**
   The representation of devils or demons, as in art or fiction; actions or behavior of devils; dealings with the devil or devils – **diablerie**
   Worship of or dealings with the devil or demons – **diabolism**; **Satanism**
      One who teaches or practices diabolism – **diabolist**
   Of, relating to or suggestive of Satan or evil – **diabolic**; **diabolical**; **satanic**
      To portray as diabolic – **diabolize** (v.t.)
   The study of the devil or of belief in devils – **diabology**; **diabolology**

Dew:
   Frozen dew forming a white covering on a surface – **hoar**; **hoarfrost**

Diagnosis:
   The art or practice of medical diagnosis – **diagnostics**

Dial:
   The art of using or making dials, esp. sundials – **gnomonics**

Dialogue:
   A writer of dialogue; one who speaks in a dialogue – **dialogist**
   A written dialogue – **colloquy**

Diameter:
   Of, relating to or along a diameter – **diametric**; **diametrical**
   The diameter of the inside of a tube; the bore of a gun or a bullet or shell (of a gun) – **caliber**
   Having equal diameters – **isodiametric**

Diamond:
   Bearing or yielding diamonds – **diamondiferous**
   A small diamond cut from a fragment of a larger stone - **melee**

Diaphragm (body part):
    Of or relating to the diaphragm – **phrenic**
    Inflammation of the diaphragm – **phrenitis**

Diary, one who keeps a – **diarist**

Dice (sing. die):
    The uncertainty of the result in throwing a die – **hazard**
    One of the dots on the face of a die – **pip**
    A throw of dice – **cast**
    The lowest throw at dice – **ambsace**; **amesace**
    To load or manipulate dice fraudulently – **cog** (v.t.)
    One who uses dice in gambling – **dicer**

Dictionary, compilation of a – **lexicography**, n. **lexicographer**

Diet (see also Eating):
    The study of diet and dieting as it relates to health and hygiene – **dietetics**
        One who specializes in dietetics – **dietician**; **dietitian**
    The practice of or belief in eating a diet consisting primarily of vegetables and excluding animal flesh – **vegetarianism**
        One who advocates or practices vegetarianism; subsisting on vegetables, grains, nuts, etc.; composed mainly of vegetables and vegetable products (as a diet) – **vegetarian**
        Vegetarianism in which no animal food or dairy products are consumed, and no products derived from animals are used – **veganism**
        One who practices veganism – **vegan**

Different:
    Consisting of differing elements – **heterologous**
    Composed of unrelated or unlike elements or parts – **heterogeneous**, n. **heterogeneity**
    Lack of structural, organizational or developmental similarity between bodily parts, due to difference in origin – **heterology**

Digestion:
    Of, relating to or assisting in digestion; capable of digesting – **peptic**
    Capable of being digested – **digestible**
    The thick semifluid mass of partly digested food that is passed from the stomach to the duodenum – **chime**
    Good digestion – **eupepsia** (pl. **eupepsias**); **eupepsy**, pl. **eupepsies**
    Beneficial to or stimulating digestion in the stomach – **stomachic**
    Having both digestive and circulatory functions – **gastrovascular**

Digging or burrowing, adapted for use in – **follorial**

Digital:
    To change (data, e.g.) into digital form – **digitize** (v.t.)

Dignity, beneath one's – **infra dig** (adj.)

Dilate, tending to – **dilatant**

Diluting, capable of – **diluent**

Dim, to make – **bedim** (v.t.)

Dimensions:
Of, relating to or having two dimensions – **two-dimensional**
Of, relating to or having three dimensions – **tridimensional**

Direction:
An apparent change in the direction of an object, caused by a change in observational position that provides a new line of sight – **parallax**
In no definite direction – **nowhither**
Having little or no tendency to take a fixed or definite direction or position – **astatic**, n. **astaticism**
Having, operating or moving in only one direction – **unidirectional**
Identical in all directions – **isotropic**
Having properties that vary according to the direction in which they are measured – **anisotropic**
Having different properties in different directions – **aeolotropic**

Disappear:
To disappear gradually – **evanesce** (v.i.), n. **evanescence**, adj. **evanescent**

Discipline:
One who believes in or enforces strict discipline – **disciplinarian**
A very strict (esp. military) disciplinarian - **martinet**
Of, relating to or used for discipline – **disciplinary**; **disciplinarian**
To discipline (one's body and physical appetites) by self-denial and austerity – **mortify** (v.t.)
Lack of discipline or control - **indiscipline**

Discomfort:
A vague feeling of physical discomfort – **malaise**

Discovery:
Something supposed to be a wonderful discovery but turning out to be a hoax or delusion – **mare's-nest**

Discrimination, esp. against women, based on sex – **sexism**

Disease (see also Therapy):
The branch of medicine concerned with the study of the nature of disease and its causes, processes, development and consequences – **pathology**
The scientific study of the diagnosis and treatment of disease through laboratory analysis of clinical specimens – **clinical pathology**
The medical study of the effects of disease on the cellular level – **cytopathology**
The study of diseases of former times as found in fossils and other remains – **paleopathology**
The branch of medicine that classifies diseases – **nosology**
Systemization and description of diseases - **nosography**
The factors that contribute to the occurrence of a disease – **etiology**; **aetiology**
Of, relating to or caused by a disease – **morbid**
Causing disease; generating a sickly state – **morbific**; **morbifical**
The appearance of symptoms of a disease not actually present – **mimesis**
Affecting or peculiar to animals of a particular area or limited district – **enzootic** (used of a disease)
Attacking a large number of animals simultaneously – **epizootic** (used of a disease)
Peculiar to a particular locality – **endemic**
Affecting many individuals throughout an area; widely prevalent - **epidemic**

Epidemic over an especially wide geographic area – **pandemic**

The branch of medicine that deals with epidemics and epidemic diseases – **epidemiology**

A secondary condition in the course of a disease, not necessarily associated with the disease – **epiphenomenon**

Able to be transmitted – **communicable**

Transmission of a disease from an original site to one or more sites elsewhere in the body – **metastasis** (Pathol.)

A disease that can be transmitted from animals to man – **zoonosis**

One recently exposed to a contagious disease – **contact**

To communicate a disease to by transferring its virus or other causative agent into the body; to introduce the virus of a disease into in order to immunize, cure or experiment – **inoculate** (v.t.)

Transmissible by inoculation; susceptible to a disease transmitted by inoculation – **inoculable**

Material used in an inoculation – **inoculant; inoculum**

The prevention of disease; measures necessary to preserve health and prevent the spread of disease – **prophylaxis**, adj./n. **prophylactic**

A crisis in or recurrent intensification of a disease – **paroxysm**

An agent, esp. a microorganism, that causes disease – **pathogen**

An organism that carries pathogens from one host to another - **vector**

The development of a diseased or morbid condition – **pathogenesis; pathogeny**

Wasting accompanying a chronic disease – **tabes**, adj. **tabescent**

Increased severity of a disease after a remission, or recurrence after a brief intermission - **recrudescence**

To reduce the intensity or severity of (a disease) – **mitigate; palliate** (both v.t.), adj./n. **palliative**

Extremely pathogenic – **virulent** (used of a toxin or microorganism)

An infectious or contagious disease – **zymosis**

Producing or breeding infectious diseases; infected with or contaminated by an infectious disease - **pestiferous**

Originating in the body or the cells of the body – **physiogenic; somatogenic**

A bodily tendency or predisposition toward some disease or abnormality – **diathesis**, pl. **diatheses**

Tending to spread, esp. to invade healthy tissue – **invasive**

Of unknown or obscure origin – **cryptogenic; cryptogenous** (used of a disease)

Marked by temporary abatements in severity – **remittent**

A symptom of the onset of a disease – **prodrome**, adj. **prodromal** or **prodromic**

The maximum development of a disease – **fastigium**

Gradual subsiding of the symptoms of a disease - **lysis**

Of or relating to a disease or condition in which characteristic symptoms are manifested - **subclinical**

A general wasting of the body during a chronic disease – **cachexia**, adj. **cachectic**

A disease of unknown origin or cause; a disease for which no etiology is known – **idiopathy**

Medical treatment of disease – **therapeutics**

A physical, biological or human environmental factor occurring in a particular region and favoring the development of a particular disease – **geogen**

A pathological condition resulting from a disease or injury – **sequela**, pl. **sequelae**

The use of chemicals to prevent infectious disease – **chemoprophylaxis**

The treatment of disease with chemicals – **chemotherapy**

Therapy or treatment of disease with remedies that produce effects differing from those of the disease treated - **allopathy**

Treatment of disease by the use of air - **aerotherapeutics**

The treatment of disease using gold compounds - **chrysotherapy**

Extreme or irrational fear of disease - **pathophobia**

Dish:

Shaped like a dish, pan or cup – **patelliform**

Disk, shaped like a – **discoid; discoidal**

Dislocation – see Bone

Dissolve:
Capable of being dissolved – **soluble**; **dissoluble**
To make (substances) soluble in water by the action of a detergent or similar agent – **solubize** (v.t.)
A substance dissolved in another substance – **solute**
To dissolve and become liquid by absorbing moisture from the air – **deliquesce** (v.i.)
To dissolve and assimilate (bone tissue, e.g.) – **resorb** (v.t.)

Dive:
To dive swiftly downward – **sound** (v.i.) (used of a whale or fish)

Divide:
Capable of being divided – **divisible**
To divide or cut into two parts – **bisect** (v.i./v.t.)
Something that bisects, esp. a straight line that bisects an angle – **bisector**
To divide or separate into two parts or branches – **bifurcate** (v.t./v.i.)
To divide or separate into distinct parts – **divaricate** (v.t./v.i.)
To divide by cutting transversely – **transect** (v.t.)
To divide and distribute proportionally or according to a plan – **apportion** (v.t.)

Divorce:
A divorced man – **divorcé**
A divorced woman – **divorcée**
A person charged with having committed adultery with the defendant in a divorce suit – **correspondent**

Doctor (physician):
Induced in a patient by a physician's actions or words – **iatrogenic**
Extreme or irrational fear of going to the doctor – **iatrophobia**

Document:
The exact meaning or actual wording of a document as distinct from its effect – **tenor**
A document written entirely in the handwriting of the individual whose signature it bears – **holograph**
The intentional alteration or destruction of a document – **spoliation**
A written document, such as a vellum or parchment, that has been written upon several times, esp. over remnants of previous writing – **palimpsest**
A clause containing a qualification, condition or restriction in a document - **proviso**
An attested copy of a document – **vidimus**
To make (a document) ready for publication – **edit**; **redact** (both v.t.)
A marginal annotation; an explanatory comment – **scholium**
A list of documents stating how many lines each contains – **stichometry**
An official document from a government granting a privilege, title or dignity - **brevet**
The study of ancient documents and the determination of their age and authenticity - **cliometrics**
The science of deciphering old official documents and of determining their age, authenticity, etc. – **diplomatics**
The study and scholarly interpretation of ancient documents; the documents thus studied - **paleography**

Dog (see also Hounds):
A male dog – **hound**
A female dog – **bitch**
A young dog – **pup**; **puppy**; **whelp**
A group of pups produced at one birth - **litter**

A group of dogs – **kennel**; **pack**

A shelter for a dog; a place where dogs are bred, trained or boarded; to place or keep (a dog, e.g.) in or as if in such a place or shelter – **kennel** (v.t.)

    To loose from a kennel – **unkennel** (v.t.)

  A dog trained to hunt wolves; the offspring of a dog and a wolf – **wolf dog**

A dog trained for coursing (hunting with hounds) – **courser**

The scientific study of the dog – **cynology**

A specialist in the care and training of dogs – **cynologist**

A dog fancier – **cynophilist**

A dog resulting from various interbreedings – **mongrel** (n./adj.)

Doglike behavior - **doggery**

Dome, shaped like a – **domic**; **domical**

Donkey, a female – **jenny**

Dots:

The dot over *i* or *j* - **tittle**

Divination by means of figures derived from even or odd numbers of dots jotted down hastily at random – **geomancy**, n. **geomancer**

Doves, a group of – **dole**; **piteousness**

Down (fine, soft feathers or fibers):

Covered with whitish or grayish down – **canescent**; **hoary**

Covered with fine down – **puberulent**; **puberulous**; **pubescent**

See also Hair.

Drain:

Left within a bodily organ or passage to facilitate drainage – **indwelling**

A place where a drain, sewer or stream discharges – **outfall**

To drain (cider or wine) from the dregs – **rack** (v.t.)

Drama (see also Theater):

Of or relating to drama – **dramatic**; **thespian**

The opening lines esp. of a drama or narrative poem – **protasis**, pl. **protases**

The middle part of a play that develops the main action leading to the catastrophe – **epitasis**

The climax of a play – **catastasis**; **catastrophe**

The group of performers to whom parts are assigned – **cast**

To act (a role) subtly or with restraint – **underplay** (v.t.)

To study or know (a role) so as to be able to replace the regular performer when required; to be engaged in such study; an actor or actress who does this – **understudy** (v.t./v.i./n.)

A minor role in a theatrical production, such as one having no speaking lines; an actor playing such a role – **walk-on**

  An actor employed to play a walk-on, as in a mob scene or spectacle – **supernumerary**

To perform (a role) weakly; to understate (a role) intentionally – **underact** (v.t./v.i.)

Capable of acting many different roles - **protean**

Secondary action or speech taking place while the main action proceeds, esp. on a theater stage – **by-play**

A drama containing elements of both tragedy and comedy – **tragicomedy**

A bragging, swaggering soldier, esp. as a stock character in comedy – **miles gloriosus**

A modern actor or comedian who specializes in comic mimicry or pantomime – **mime**

A short play – **playlet**

A play to be read rather than performed - **closet drama**

A play openly imitating the previous work of another artist – **pastiche**

A play presented by casting shadows of puppets or actors on a screen or wall – **shadow play**; **galanty show**

A dramatic presentation marked by heavy use of suspense, romantic sentiment and a conventionally happy ending; the dramatic genre that encompasses such works – **melodrama**

Melodramatic theatrical performance – **melodramatics**

Modern narrative drama that asks the audience to examine social problems analytically rather than emotionally – **epic drama**; **epic theater**

The dramatic effect attained by leading an audience to understand the incongruity between a situation and the accompanying speeches, while the characters in the play remain unaware of the incongruity – **irony**, adj. **ironic** or **ironical**

Draw:

Drawn back or in, as a cat's claw – **retractile**

Drawn or pulled tight – **taut**

To make or become taut – **tauten** (v.t./v.i.)

Dream:

Of or relating to dreams – **oneiric**

A rapidly changing series of things seen or imagined, as in the figures or events of a dream – **phantasmagoria**; **phantasmagory**

The interpretation of dreams – **oneirocriticism**

An interpreter of dreams – **oneirocritic**

A person or thing that oppresses or burdens like a nightmare – **incubus**, pl. **incubi** or **incubuses**

Divination by dreaming or the interpretation of dreams – **oneiromancy**

Dress (attire):

Dressed too informally – **underdressed**

The act or practice of adopting the dress of the other sex – **eonism**; **transvestism**

One who dresses thus – **transvestite** (adj./n.)

Drift:

To cause to drift gently and smoothly through the air or over water; to convey or send floating through the air or over water – **waft** (v.t.)

The act or state of being wafted – **waftage**

The action of wafting – **wafture**

Drink:

The study or skill of preparing mixed drinks – **mixology**

Fit to drink – **potable**

Drop:

Being in the form of drops; having drops; spotted as if by drops – **guttate**; **guttated**

Drown:

An execution by drowning; a mass drowning - **noyade**

Drug:

The science of drugs, including their composition, uses and effects – **pharmacology**

The branch of pharmacology dealing with the psychological effects of drugs – **psychopharmacology**

The science of preparing and dispensing drugs – **pharmaceutics**

The administering of drugs; treatment by drugs; the art or practice of preparing and dispensing drugs; a place where drugs are prepared, dispensed or sold – **pharmacy**

Kept in stock by pharmacists - **officinal**

The study of drug action on living organisms – **pharmacodynamics**

The study of the absorption, metabolism and action of a drug – **pharmacokinetics**

The branch of pharmacology dealing with crude natural drugs - **pharmacognosy**

The study of hereditary influences to drug response – **pharmacogenetics**

The branch of medicine that studies drugs – **pharmacopedia; pharmacopedics**

Hypersensitivity to a drug – **idiosyncrasy**

Designating a drug available without a prescription – **officinal**

A drug that serves as a remedy for several diseases - **polychrest**

A combined action of drugs that produces a greater effect than the sum of their individual effects – **synergism; synergy**

A substance added to a drug to aid its action – **adjuvant**

A drug or medicine that restores or stimulates; of or relating to a drug that does this - **analeptic**

A drug that dulls the senses, induces sleep and becomes addictive with prolonged use – **narcotic**

　To place under the influence of a narcotic – **narcotize** (v.t.)

　Addiction to narcotics such as opium, heroin or morphine – **narcotism**

Psychotherapy carried out with the aid of sedating or hypnotic drugs – **narcotherapy**

An abnormal desire for drugs – **narcomania**

An addiction to a drug – **toxicomania**

A condition of stupor or unconsciousness induced by narcotics or other chemicals – **narcosis; narcoticism; narcotism**

The paste or plastic combination of drugs from which pills are made – **mass**

Drum:

　Of, relating to or resembling a drum – **tympanic**

　A low continuous beating of a drum that is not as loud as a roll – **ruffle**

　One who plays the kettledrum in a band or orchestra – **timpanist; tympanist**

Dry/Dryness:

　A substance used as a drying agent – **desiccant**

　To dry out thoroughly; to preserve (foods) by removing the moisture; to become dry – **desiccate** (v.t./v.i.)

　To dry up or cause to dry up – **exsiccate** (v.i./v.t.)

　Somewhat dry or arid – **subarid**

　Abnormal dryness, esp. of the skin, conjunctiva or mucous membranes – **xerosis**

　Of, marked by or adapted to an extremely dry habitat – **xeric**

　Something that promotes drying; a substance added (to some paints and medicines) to promote drying; causing to dry; promoting the action of drying– **siccative**

　Extreme or irrational fear of dryness or dry places – **xerophobia**

Duck:

　Resembling a duck - **anatine**

　A male duck – **drake**

　A female duck – **duck**

　A young duck – **duckling**

　A group of ducks:

　　Swimming – **paddling**

　　Collected in the water, e.g., to sleep – **draft**

　　In flight – **team**

Duct:
  A small duct – **ductile**
  Having or secreting through a duct; of or relating to the secretion of a gland having a duct – **exocrine**
  Constriction of a duct or passage – **stenosis**, adj. **stenosed** or **stenotic**

Duel, the art or rules of the – **duello**

Duke or dukedom, of or relating to a – **ducal**

Dull or obtuse, to make – **hebetate** (v.t.)

Dust:
  The study of atmospheric dust and its biological effects – **coniology**; **koniology**
  Covered with mealy dust – **farinose** (Biol.)
  Extreme or irrational fear of dust - **amathophobia**

Duty:
  Careful to perform duties; imbued with or expressing a sense of duty – **duteous**; **dutiful**
  A neglect or wrong performance of official duty - **misprision**
  Extreme or irrational fear of neglect of a duty – **paralipophobia**

Dwarfism – see Cartilage

Dyeing:
  Of or relating to the processes of dyeing or coloring - **tinctorial**

E

Eagle:
    A young eagle – **eaglet**
    A group of eagles – **convocation**
    Of or like an eagle or an eagle's beak – **aquiline**

Ear:
    The branch of medicine that studies the ear and its diseases – **otology**
    The branch of medicine that combines treatment of the ear and throat – **otolaryngology**
    The branch of medicine that combines treatment of the ear, nose and throat – **otorhinolaryngology**
    A pain in the ear – **earache**; **otalgia**, adj. **otalgic**
    Of, relating to or located near the ear – **auricular**; **otic**
    Inflammation of the ear – **otitis**
    Of, relating to or perceived by the ear – **aural**
    Having ears – **eared**
    Having earlike parts or projections – **auriculate**; **auriculated**; **eared**
    The external part of the ear – **pinna**; **auricle**
    Situated around the ear – **periotic**
    Having or related to two ears; hearing with both ears – **binaural**
    Pleasing to the ear – **euphonious**
    Shaped like an ear – **auricular**; **auriform**
    An earlike part, process or appendage – **auricle**
    Having bent or drooping ears – **lop-eared**
    Earwax – **cerumen**

Earth:
    Of or relating to the earth – **earthly**; **tellurian**; **telluric**; **terrene**; **terrestrial**
    To or toward the earth – **earthward**
    Inhabiting or characteristic of the earth – **tellurian**
    An inhabitant of the earth – **earthling**; **tellurian**; **Terran**; **terrestrial**
    The study of the earth and its features, and of the distribution of life on earth, including human life and the effects of human activity – **geography**
    The study of the origin, history and structure of the earth – **geology**
        The geology of ancient times or of a particular former geologic epoch – **paleogeography**
        The physics of geologic phenomena – **geophysics**
    The geologic science of the size and shape of the earth - **geodesy**
    The branch of geology that deals with the materials of the earth and its general constitution – **geognosy**
    A science that deals with the earth – **geoscience**
    A theory or science about the formation of the earth – **geogony**
    Relating to, measured from, or observed from the center of the earth – **geocentric**
    The chronology of the earth's history, as governed by geologic events – **geochronology**
    The study of the earth's magnetic field – **geomagnetism**
    The geologic science of the configuration and evolution of land forms – **geomorphology**
    Of or like the earth, its shape or surface configuration - **geomorphic**
    Of, relating to or occurring on the earth's surface - **surficial**
    To become cut off from contact with the earth's surface, as a cyclone – **occlude** (v.t.)
    The hypothetical surface of the earth that coincides everywhere with mean sea level – **geoid**
    Being under high pressure within the earth – **geopressured**; **geopressurized**
    The process by which the major features of the earth's crust (continents, mountains, etc.) are formed – **diastrophism**
    Of or relating to the force caused by the earth's rotation – **geostrophic**

Of or relating to the earth's internal heat – **geothermal**

Located or occurring on or near the surface of the earth – **subaerial**

Situated or operating beneath the surface of the earth – **subterranean**; **subterrestrial**; **underground**

Occurring or originating on or just below the surface of the earth - **epigene**

Situated or believed to be situated beneath the surface of the earth - **nether**

Of, relating to or located on the opposite side of the earth – **antipodal**

A person who lives on the other side of the earth – **antipodean**

Any two places directly opposite each other on the earth – **antipodes**

Revolving around or surrounding the earth – **circumterrestrial**

Relating to or involving both of the earth's poles – **bipolar**

Extending across or crossing over either of the geographic polar regions – **transpolar**

The study of the earth's topological configuration above sea level, esp. the measurement and mapping of land elevations – **hypsography**

Belonging to a region adjacent to the equatorial area – **subequatorial**

The part of the earth and its atmosphere in which living things exist – **biosphere**

The solid part of the earth; the earth's rocky crust – **lithosphere**

The waters of the earth as distinguished from the lithosphere and the atmosphere – **hydrosphere**

Between the earth and the moon – **cislunar**

Deformation of the earth's crust that forms continents and oceanic basins or parts of these – **epeirogeny**

The soil, sand and other loose material covering the solid bedrock of the earth – **mantle**

A geologic process in which one edge of crustal plate descends below another – **subduction**

A wearing or wasting away, as of glacier or rock – **ablation**

The process by which the major features of the earth's crust, including continents, mountains, ocean beds, folds and faults, are formed – **diastrophism**; **tectonism**

A nearly flat land surface representing an advanced stage of erosion - **peneplain**; **peneplane**

A mountain or rocky mass that has resisted erosion and stands isolated in a plain or peneplain – **monadnock**

The geology of the earth's structural deformation – **tectonics**, adj. **tectonic**

A large upward fold in the earth's crust – **geanticline**

Of or relating to the shape, structure and arrangement of the rock masses forming the earth's crust – **geotectonic**

A depression of the earth's crust between two parallel faults – **graben**

Composed of loosely cemented heterogeneous material – **conglomerate**

Residual deposits of soil, dust and rock particles produced by the action of the wind – **eluvium**

The theory that geologic changes have been caused by catastrophes rather than by gradual and continuing processes – **catastrophism**

The angle of inclination from the vertical of a fault, vein or lode – **hade**

The amount of vertical displacement of a fault – **throw**

The plane along which the break or shear of a fault occurs – **fault plane**

A cliff or escarpment directly resulting from an uplift along one side of a fault - **fault scarp**

Movement toward the center of the earth – **positive geotropism**

Movement away from the center of the earth – **negative geotropism**

The point in the orbit of a satellite of the earth that is nearest to the center of the earth – **perigee**

A tendency to grow or move away from the earth – **apogeotropism**

View of the earth from a high position, as from an aircraft – **airscape**

Headed for the earth – **earthbound**; **earth-bound**

The region of the earth's surface between the tropics of Cancer and Capricorn – **Torrid Zone**; **Tropics**

Of, relating to or located in the Tropics – **equatorial**; **intertropical**; **subsolar**; **tropical**

Of, relating to or being the geographic areas adjacent to the Tropics – **subtorrid**; **subtropical**

Either of two middle latitudes of the earth, lying between 23½° and 66½° north and south – **Temperate Zone**

Of, relating to or occurring within the colder regions of the Temperate Zone – **subtemperate**

Divination using the configurations of earth – **geomancy**, n. **geomancer**

Earthquakes (seisms):
  The study of earthquakes and of the mechanical properties of the earth – **seismology**
  The study of earthquakes – **seismometry**
  The collective phenomena involved in earthquakes – **seismism**
  Of, relating to or exhibiting equal seismic intensities – **isoseismic**; **isoseismal**
  A faint, recurrent tremor of the earth's crust - **microseism**
  Of, subject to or caused by an earthquake or earth vibration – **seismic**
  An earthquake under the sea floor – **seaquake**
  An earthquake occurring at very deep levels in the earth - **bathyseism**
  A minor tremor occurring before an earthquake – **foreshock**
  A minor tremor occurring after an earthquake – **aftershock**
  The point of origin of an earthquake – **focus**
  The point on the earth's surface directly above the origin of an earthquake – **epicenter**
  The intensity, frequency and distribution of earthquakes in a specific area - **seismicity**

Earthworm – see Worm

Eating (see also Food):
  Of or relating to a meal – **prandial**
  Following a meal – **postprandial**; **post-prandial**
  The art of good eating – **gastronomy**
  One who eats heartily and well – **gourmand**; **trencherman**
  Eating and drinking in moderation – **abstemious**
  The art or science of good eating – **epicurism**; **gastronomy**, adj. **gastronomic** or **gastronomical**
      A specialist in gastronomy – **gastronome**; **gastronomist**
  Fit for eating; something fit for eating – **edible**; **esculent**
  Not fit for eating – **inedible**; **uneatable**; **unedible**
  Of or relating to those who customarily eat at the same table; a customary mealtime companion – **commensal**
  The conveyance of food or drink into the mouth - **prehension**
  Lack of appetite – **inappetence**
  Loss of appetite – **anorexia**
  A pathological condition marked by aversion to food and consequent nutritional deficiency – **anorexia nervosa**
  To cause (the body or its flesh) to waste away by excessive fasting – **macerate** (v.t.)
  The eating of earth substances, as clay or sand - **geophagy**
  Abnormally increased desire for food - **hyperphagia**
  Consuming or eager to consume large quantities of food – **ravenous**; **voracious**
  Insatiable appetite – **bulimia**; **polyphagia**; **polyphagy**
  Excessive weight loss combined with distorted body image and the use of forced vomiting to compensate for eating
      binges – **bulimarexia**
  Feeding on or utilizing a wide variety of foods – **polyphagous**, n. **polyphagia**
  An inability to feed - **aphagia**
  Self-devouring - **autophagous**
  The practice of eating in small amounts and only when hungry, and of chewing food thoroughly – **fletcherism**;
      Fletcherism
  One who eats the flesh of other human beings – **cannibal** (n. **cannibalism**); **anthropophagus**, (pl. **anthropophagi**);
      anthropophagite, adj. **anthropophagous** or **anthropophagic**
  The act or practice of eating the flesh of corpses or carrion –**necrophagia**; **necrophagy**, adj. **necrophagous**
  A craving for and eating of unnatural substances that occurs in nutritional deficiency states – **depraved appetite**;
      geophagy; **pica**
  A dining hall in a college or monastery - **refectory**

Ecology (the branch of biology that studies the relationships between organisms and their environments):

The study of the interrelationships between individual organisms or individual kinds of organisms and their environment – **autecology**

The study of the interrelationship of plants and animals in their common environment – **bioecology**

The branch of ecology that deals with the characteristics, relationships and distribution of associated plants - **phytosociology**

The study of the environmental interrelationships among communities of organisms – **synecology**

An ecological community with its physical environment - **ecosystem**

An ecological relationship in which microorganisms are dependent upon one another for nutritional (or trophic) requirements – **syntrophism**

The ecology of cultivated or domestic plants – **agrioecology**

The study of the interaction between ancient organisms and their environments - **paleoecology**

The study of communities and member interactions in nature – **biocenology**

The set of functional relationships of an organism or population to the environment it occupies; the area within a habitat that is occupied by an organism – **niche**

A succession of organisms in a community that constitutes a feeding chain in which food energy is transferred from one organism to another as each consumes a lower member and in turn is preyed upon by a higher member – **food chain**

A complex of interrelated food chains in an ecological community – **food web**

The total mass of living matter within a given volume of environment – **biomass**

An entire community of living organisms in a single major ecological region – **biome**

The animal and plant life of a particular region considered as a total ecological entity – **biota**

A limited ecological region or niche in which the environment is suitable for certain forms of life – **biotope**

A chemical transformation within a living system – **biotransformation**

A series of differing characteristics within members of a species or population, resulting from gradual changes or transitions in the environment – **cline**

An animal or plant species that establishes itself in a previously barren environment – **pioneer**

A stage in ecological development or evolution in which a community of organisms becomes stable and starts to perpetuate itself – **climax**

A normally stable climax community that has been altered by human beings or other influences - **disclimax**

A stage in the ecological succession of a plant or animal community immediately preceding a climax - **subclimax**

An organism or species of an earlier time surviving in an environment that has undergone considerable change – **relict**

The surrounding environment or substance in which a specific organism lives and thrives – **medium**

The likelihood of survival of a specific organism in a specific environment - **biotic potential**

The sum of environmental influences and conditions acting on an organism – **nurture**

Having a narrow range of adaptability to changes or variations in environmental conditions – **stenotopic; stenotropic**

Capable of adaptive response to varying environments – **facultative**

An environmental limit, as of temperature or radiation, beyond which a specified life form cannot survive – **death point**

A local, usually stable population of organisms of the same kind or species – **deme**

Native or limited to a certain region – **endemic**

Successful establishment or an organism in a new environment – **ecesis**

A transitional area between two adjacent ecological communities, as forest and grassland - **ecotone**

Destruction of the natural environment, as by pollutants – **ecocide**

To increase irregularly in number – **irrupt** (v.i.)

The entire sequence of ecological communities successively occupying an area – **sere**

A secondary series of communities that succeeds an interrupted climax community – **subsere**

A sequence of communities beginning in a dry area – **xerosere**

An area marked by distinct physical conditions and populated by communities of certain kinds of organisms – **zone**

The distribution of organisms in biogeographic zones – **zonation**

An ecological region marked by the dominance of certain kinds of animal life – **zoogeographic region**

The smallest unit of a habitat, as a clump of grass or a space between rocks – **microhabitat; microenvironment**
An organism that ingests other organisms or particulate organic matter – **macroconsumer**

Economics (see also Price):
  The exclusive control by one seller or producer of a commodity or service in a particular market – **monopoly**
    Opposed to or regulating business monopolies, cartels, trusts, etc. – **antitrust**
  The market condition that exists when only one buyer seeks the products or services of a number of sellers - **monopsony**
  The market condition that exists when there are only two sellers – **duopoly**
  The market condition that exists when there are only two buyers – **duopsony**
  A market condition in which sellers are so few that the actions of any one of them will affect prices – **oligopoly**
  A market condition in which buyers are so few that the actions of any one of them will affect prices – **oligopsony**
  A national policy of self-sufficiency and nonreliance on imports or economic aid – **autarchy; autarky**
  A dealer or expert in international exchange; a manual listing the exchange values of currencies, weights and measures of many countries – **cambist**
  The branch of economics that studies commercial exchange, esp. its international aspects – **cambism; cambistry**
  Requiring or having a large expenditure of capital (money, equipment, etc.) in comparison to labor – **capital-intensive**
  Requiring or having a large expenditure or labor in comparison to capital – **labor-intensive**
  The study of the overall aspects and workings of a national economy, and the interrelationships among diverse economic sectors – **macroeconomics**
  The study of individual 'decision units' such as the consumer, households and firms, and the way in which their decisions interrelate to determine relative prices of goods, factors of production, etc. – **microeconomics**
  The theory and system of political economy prevailing in Europe after the decline of feudalism based on national policies of accumulating bullion, establishing colonies and a merchant marine, and developing industry to attain a favorable balance of trade – **mercantilism**
  The linkage of economic factors, such as wages, interest or prices, to the cost-of-living index so that they rise and fall within the rate of inflation – **indexation**
  The theory or practice of using only one metal as a standard of money – **monometallism**
  To place (gold) in safekeeping so as not to affect the supply of money or credit – **sterilize** (v.t.)
  Relating to, composed of or controlling all the grades or levels in the manufacture and sale of a product – **vertical**
  Relating to the integration resulting from the merger of firms in the same business – **horizontal**
  Producing a return equal to the sum invested to create or maintain something – **self-liquidating**
  An economic doctrine that opposes government regulation of or interference in commerce beyond the minimum necessary for a free-enterprise system to operate according to its own economic laws – **laisser faire; laissez faire**
  To write off expenditures by prorating over a fixed period – **amortize** (v.t.)

Edge:
  A distinctive edge or border – **limbus** (Biol.)
  Having an edge or margin of a different color – **limbate**
  Meeting at the edges without overlapping – **valvate** (Bot.)
  Folded together with overlapping edges – **obvolute** (Bot.)
  Indented along the edge with small curves – **engrailed**
  Edged with toothlike projections – **dentate**
    Finely dentate – **denticulate; denticulated**

Eel (see also Fish/Fishing):
  A group of eels – **swarm**
  A young eel – **elver**
  Shaped like an eel – **anguilliform**

Effort:
    To do more than is required, ordered or expected – **supererogate** (v.i.)

Egg (ovum, pl. ova; see also Ovary):
    Bearing or producing ova – **oviferous**
    To produce or discharge eggs – **ovulate** (v.i.)
    An immature ovum – **ovule**
    Having the ovule partially inverted or curved – **campylotropous**
    To fertilize (an ovum, e.g.) – **impregate** (v.t.)
    A fertilized ovum – **oosperm**
    Producing many ova at one time – **polytocous**
    Derived from a single fertilized egg – **monozygotic**
    Derived from two separate and separately fertilized eggs – **dizygotic**
    Derived from two eggs (as fraternal twins) – **biovular**
    The development of an egg without fertilization – **parthenogenesis**
    A place where eggs, esp. those of fish or poultry, are hatched – **hatchery**
    To warm eggs, as by bodily heat, so as to bring about embryonic development and the hatching of young – **brood**;
        incubate (both v.t.)
    The number of eggs produced or incubated at one time; a group or nest of eggs – **clutch**
    A group of eggs in a hen's nest – **setting**
    Capable of killing eggs – **ovicidal**, n. **ovicide**
    Producing eggs that hatch outside the body – **oviparous**
    Producing eggs that hatch within the female's body - **ovoviviparous**
    To lay eggs, esp. with an ovipositor – **oviposit** (v.i.)
    Of or relating to the yolk of an egg; having the yellow color of an egg yolk (vitellus) – **vitelline**
    Having the yolk evenly distributed throughout the egg – **isolecithal**
    Having the yolk concentrated at one end of the egg – **telolecithal**
    Having the yolk concentrated in the center of the egg – **centrolecithal**
    The egg case or capsule of certain insects or mollusks – **ootheca**
    Shaped like an egg – **oval**; **ovate**; **oviform**; **ovoid**

Eight:
    An eight-sided figure with eight angles – **octagon**
    Having eight plane surfaces – **octahedral**
    A polyhedron with eight plane surfaces - **octahedron**, pl. **octahedra** or **octahedrons**
    Of or relating to the number 8; consisting of eight members or groups containing eight – **octonary**
    Having eight parts, members or copies; multiplied by eight – **octuple**

Elections - see Political terms

Electricity/Electronics:
    Of, relating to or producing electrical current – **electromotive**
    Having electric potential – **isoelectric**
    The measure of a material's ability to conduct electric charge – **conductance**
    Electric circuits collectively – **circuitry**
    A conducting bar thatcarries heavy currents to supply several electric circuits – **bus**; **bus bar**
    A series of components or networks the output of each of which serves as the input for the next – **cascade**
    An electric circuit consisting of miniaturized components – **microcircuit**
    The branch of electronics that deals with components of miniature size – **microelectronics**
    To vary the frequency, amplitude, phase or other characteristic of (a carrier wave) – **modulate** (v.t.)
    A self-contained assembly of electronic components and circuitry – **module**

Of, relating to or denoting electricity or electric current produced by a chemical action – **galvanic**; **voltaic**

Capable of producing electric current when exposed to radiant energy, esp. light – **photovoltaic**

The science and technology of electronics applied to aeronautics and astronautics – **astrionics**; **avionics**

Electromagnetic radiation produced by natural phenomena such as lightning – **atmospherics**

Consisting of or enhanced by, or as if by, electronic components (as an artificial limb) – **bionic**

Not capable of being electrified by friction - **anelectric**

The flow of electric current without resistance in certain metals and alloys at temperatures near absolute zero – **superconductivity**

An electric current flowing through a superconductor – **supercurrent**

Having the effect of an electric shock; produced as if by an electric shock – **galvanic**

Generating electricity by conversion of the energy of running water – **hydroelectric**

Electricity generated by a heat flow – **thermoelectricity**

Electricity produced by magnets – **magnetoelectricity**

A process in which an industrial facility utilizes its waste energy to produce electricity - **cogeneration**

Interruption of a flow of current – **break**

Of, relating to or having a wide band of electromagnetic frequencies – **broadband**

A faintly visible, relatively slow crackling discharge of electricity without sparking – **brush discharge**

Medical therapy using electric currents – **electrotherapy**

Elephant:

A group of elephants – **herd**

A male elephant – **bull**

A female elephant – **cow**

A young elephant – **calf**

Of or relating to an elephant – **elephantine**

A keeper and driver of an elephant - **mahout**

The periodic state of murderous frenzy of the bull elephant usu. connected with the rutting season – **must**; **musth**

Elevation:

The measurement of elevation relative to sea level – **hypsography**; **hypsometry**

Equality of elevation above sea level – **isometry**

Elf:

Of, relating to or like an elf; made or done by an elf – **elfin**

Of or relating to elves – **elfish**; **elvish**

Elk:

A group of elk – **gang**

A male elk – **bull**

A female elk – **cow**

A young elk – **calf**

Emblem:

Of, relating to or serving as an emblem – **emblematic**; **emblematical**

An emblem or device with a motto – **impresa**

Embryo:

Implantation of an embryo in the lining of a uterus – **nidation**

The growth and development of an embryo – **embryogenesis**

Abnormal development of an embryo – **embryopathy**

The development of more than one embryo from a single egg or ovule – **polyembryony**

Emigrant:
    An emigrant compelled to emigrate for political reasons – **émigré**

Emotion - see Feeling

Empire, of or relating to an – **imperial**

End:
    Of or relating to the ends of the extremities – **acromelic**
    Second from the end – **penultimate**
    Third from the end – **antepenultimate**

Energy:
    The physics of energy and its transformations – **energetics**
    A substance or device that converts input energy of one form into output energy of another – **transducer**
    Needing energy – **endergonic**
    Releasing energy – **exergonic**
    Energy transferred by radiation, esp. by an electromagnetic wave – **radiant energy**
        The rate of flow of radiant energy – **radiant flux**
    Distribution of energy emitted by a radiant source, as by an incandescent body, arranged in order of wavelengths – **spectrum**, adj. **spectral**
    The shattering effect of a sudden release of energy – **brisance**
    Resisting applied energy – **antienergistic**
    Combined or co-operative force or action – **synergy**

England/English:
    In the English manner – **à l'anglaise**
    A person who admires England, its people, customs, etc. – **Anglophil; Anglophile**
    An authority on the English language or English literature – **Anglist; Anglicist**
    A word, idiom or phrase characteristic of or peculiar to British English – **Anglicism; Briticism; Britishism**
    Irrational fear or hatred of England, the English or English ways - **anglophobia**

Engraving:
    To engrave into a surface – **incise** (v.t.), n. **incision**
    The art or process of engraving on copper or steel plate by scraping or burnishing areas to produce effects of light and shadow - **mezzotint**
    The art or process of engraving on gems or the like – **glyptics; glyptography**, adj. **glyptic**
        An engraving of this type – **glyptograph**
    The art or process of engraving on wood or of printing from such engravings – **xylography**
        An engraving or print of this type – **xylograph**
    An engraved or incised symbolic figure – **glyph**

Enter:
    An entering – **ingress; ingression**
    Permission or right to enter - **ingress**
    To cause or allow to enter – **intromit** (v.t.)

Entrails (viscera):
    To remove the entrails – **disembowel; eviscerate** (both v.t.)
    Of or relating to the entrails – **splanchnic; visceral**

Envelope:
   An enveloping wrapper or sheath – **involucrum**

Environment – see Ecology

Enzymes:
   The study of enzymes – **enzymology**
   Participating in enzyme production - **zymoplastic**

Epilepsy:
   Resembling epilepsy or any of its symptoms – **epileptoid**

Equator:
   One who has crossed the equator and been initiated in the traditional ceremony – **shellback**

Erected, capable of being – **erectile** (used esp. of bodily parts and tissues)

Erosion (see also Earth):
   Causing erosion – **erosive**
   Lateral mechanical erosion, as of a valley, by a running stream – **planation**
   Worn away almost to the base, as at the end of an erosion cycle – **senile**
   A closely woven mat of brush and poles used to protect an embankment, dike or dam from erosion – **mattress**
   A sharp ridge with steeply sloping sides, produced by the erosion of the broken edges of highly tilted strata – **hogback**
   To erode or be eroded by abrasion – **corrade** (v.t./v.i.)

Escaping, the art of – **escapology**

Essential (necessary):
   To call for as essential; to advocate earnestly – **desiderate** (v.t.)
   To provide or convey something essential – **purvey** (v.t.)

Ethics (see also Philosophy):
   The study of the ethical and moral questions involved in the application of new biological and medical findings – **bioethics**
   A theory of ethics dealing with or based on the relation of duty to pleasure - **hedonics**

Etiquette:
   Attentive to the finer points of etiquette and formal conduct – **punctilious**
   A fine point of etiquette – **punctilio**
   A violation of etiquette – **faux pas**; **impropriety**; **solecism**

Evaluate:
   To evaluate by a new standard or principle – **transvalue** (v.t.)

Evaporate:
   Evaporating rapidly at normal temperatures and pressures; capable of being readily vaporized – **volatile**
      To make or become volatile – **volatize** (v.t./v.i.)

Evening (see also Night):
   Relating to or occurring in the evening; opening or becoming active in the evening -**vespertine**; **vespertinal**

Event:
  An outline of a hypothesized or projected chain of events – **scenario**
  A significant event in a person's life that indicates a transition from one stage to another, and that may be marked by a ceremony or ritual – **rite of passage**

Everything, fear of – **panophobia**

Everywhere:
  Being or seeming to be everywhere at the same time – **omnipresent; ubiquitous**

Evil:
  One who does evil – **evildoer**; **malefactor**
  The act or practice of doing evil - **evildoing**
  To call down evil upon – **curse; imprecate** (both v.t.), n. **imprecator**, n. **imprecation**
  A delusion of being possessed by an evil spirit – **cacodemonia; demonomania**
  Intended to ward off evil – **apotropaic**
  The use of magic and ritualistic ceremony to ward off evil – **apotropaism**
  The branch of theology that deals with evil – **ponerology**
  Of, relating to or suggestive of evil – **diabolic; diabolical; satanic**
  Invoking evil – **maledictive**

Evolution:
  The evolutionary development of a species of plant or animal – **phylogeny**
  Evolutionary or embryological development of the structure of an organism or part – **morphogenesis**
  A gradual change of form by evolution – **anamorphosis**
  Evolution involving whole species or large groups of organisms – **macroevolution**
  The repetition by a single organism of various stages in the evolution of its species during embryonic development – **palingenesis**
  The gradually increasing concentration of the brain and sensory organs in the head during animal evolution – **cephalization**
  The evolutionary process by which new species are formed – **speciation**

Exaggeration – see Figures of Speech

Examine:
  A person who examines – **examinant**
  Examination of objects with the naked eye - **macrography**

Exchange:
  Capable of being exchanged or substituted – **commutable**

Excrement (see also Filth):
  Of, relating to or consisting of excrement – **stercoraceous; stercorous**
  Extreme or irrational fear of fecal material – **coprophobia**
  Living in excrement – **coprophilous**
  Feeding on excrement – **coprophagous**
  Fossil excrement – **coprolite**
  An abnormal interest in excrement – **coprophilia; mysophilia**
  The study of fecal excrement, including fossil excrement; an obsession with excrement or excretory functions – **coprology; scatology**
  The surgical construction of an artificial excretory opening – **ostomy**

Existence:
  To regard or treat (an abstraction) as if it had material existence – **reify** (v.t.)
  The essential nature or ultimate form of something; what makes something the type of thing that it is – **essence**; **quiddity**
  To ascribe material existence to – **hypostatize** (v.t.)
  A visible trace evidence of something once in existence but existing or appearing no more - **vestige**

Exotic, the quality or condition of being – **exoticism**

Expand:
  Of or relating to expansion – **expansible**
  Capable of being expanded – **expandable**; **expansible**; **expansile**

Experience:
  Relating to or derived from experience – **experiential**
  Felt or undergone as if one were taking part in the experience of another – **vicarious**

Explain:
  Capable of being explained – **explicable**
  To explain away – **gloss**; **gloze** (both v.t., both usu. followed by *over*)
  Critical explanation or interpretation, esp. of a text – **exegesis**, adj. **exegetic** or **exegetical**
    One who is skilled in exegesis – **exegete**; **exegetist**
  An explanation following a word or larger part of a text that limits its application or clarifies its meaning – **epexegesis**, pl. **epexegeses**
  A doctrine that the least possible number of assumptions are to be made in the attempt to explain ascertained facts – **law of parsimony**; **Ockham's razor**
  A deliberately misleading explanation or interpretation – **gloss**
  An explanation accounting for a set of facts that can be tested by further investigation – **hypothesis**; **theory**
    To assert as or from a hypothesis – **hypothesize** (v.t./v.i.)
    Of, relating to or based on a hypothesis – **hypothetical**

Explode:
  To cause to explode; to explode with sudden violence – **fulminate** (v.t./v.i.)
  The setting off of an explosive charge by forcible contact - **percussion**

Extension of a bodily limb beyond its normal limits – **hyperextension**

External (see also Outside):
  Derived from something external – **adscititious**

Extraction, a forcible – **evulsion**

Exude:
  To exude into the surrounding tissues – **extravasate** (v.i.) (Pathol.)

Eye (see also Vision):
  Of or relating to the eye – **ocular**; **ophthalmic**
  Relating to, used by, or involving both eyes at the same time; having two eyes arranged to produce stereoscopic vision – **binocular**
  Of or relating to movements of the eyeball – **oculomotor**
  A rapid intermittent eye movement – **saccade**

The coordinated turning of the eyes inward to focus on a nearby point – **convergence**

The physical and chemical adjustments of the eye, including dilation of the pupil, that make vision possible in relative darkness – **dark adaptation**

A marking that resembles an eye – **ocellus** (Biol.)

The branch of medicine the deals with the eye –**ophthalmology**

    A doctor specializing in ophthalmology – **oculist; ophthalmologist**

A person who makes and sells eyeglasses and lenses – **optician**

The practice or profession of testing eyes for defects in vision, and the prescribing of corrective eyeglasses – **optometry**

A medical examination and analysis of the refractive properties of the eye – **retinoscopy; skiascopy**, n. **retinoscopist**

Of or affecting the pupil of the eye – **pupillary**

Located or occurring between the pupils of the eyes – **interpupillary**

Excessive contraction of the pupil of the eye – **miosis; myosis**

An agent that causes contraction of the pupil; relating to or causing miosis – **miotic**

Prolonged and abnormal dilation of the pupil, as a result of disease or a drug – **mydriasis**

A drug that causes dilation of the pupils – **mydriatic**

Within the eyeball – **intraocular**

Of or resembling the white of the eye – **albugineous**

Located or occurring beneath the orbit (the cavity in the skull that holds the eye) – **infraorbital**

Located above the orbit – **supraorbital**

Located behind the orbit – **postorbital**

The mucous membrane lining the inner surface of the eyelid and the exposed surface of the eyeball – **conjunctiva**

Inflammation of the conjunctiva – **conjunctivitis**

Extreme dryness of the conjunctiva – **xerophthalmia**

Inflammation of the retina – **retinitis**

A movable stalk ending with an eye – **ommatophore** (Zool.)

The transparent anterior portion of the outer fibrous layer of the eye – **cornea**

Surgical removal of all or part of the cornea – **keratectomy**

A cloudy spot on the cornea – **nebula**

A dense, white opacity of the cornea – **leucoma; leukoma; walleye**

    Having leukoma of the cornea – **walleyed**

Inflammation of the cornea – **corneitis; keratitis**

The tough, white, fibrous outer layer of tissue covering all of the eyeball except the cornea – **sclera**, adj. **sclerotic**

    Surgical removal of the sclera – **sclerotomy**

    Inflammation of the sclera – **scleritis**

A medicinal lotion applied to the eye – **collyrium**

The small, optically insensitive area where the optic nerve enters the retina of the eye – **blind spot; optic disk**

The round, pigmented, contractile membrane of the eye, located between the cornea and the lens – **iris**, adj. **iridic**

    Inflammation of the iris – **iritis**

    Surgical removal of part of the iris – **iridectomy**

Inflammation of the eye – **ophthalmia; ophthalmitis**

    Having ophthalmia – **ophthalmic**

Eyestrain, esp. with headache and dimming of vision – **asthenopia**

Opacity of the lens or capsule of the eye – **cataract**

Abnormal smallness of the lens of the eye – **microphakia**

Abnormal protrusion of the eyeball – **exophthalmos; exophthalmus**

A sinking of the eyeball into the orbital cavity – **enophthalmos; enophthalmus**

A watering of the eyes – **epiphora**

A lesion or fissure of the eye or eyelid – **coloboma**

A spasmodic, involuntary motion of the eyeball – **nystagmus**

Eyebrow (supercilium):

 Of or relating to the eyebrow; located over the eyebrow – **superciliary**

Eyelids:

 Of or relating to the eyelids – **palpebral**
 Inflammation of the eyelid - **blepharitis**
 Uncontrollable winking caused by the involuntary contraction of an eyelid muscle – **blepharospasm**
 An inner eyelid in some animals that helps to keep the eye clean – **nictating membrane; nictitating membrane**
 Drooping of the upper eyelid caused by muscle failure – **ptosis**

F

Fables:
A composer of fables – **fabulist**
A medieval collection of allegorical fables about the habits and traits of animals, each fable followed by an interpretation of its moral significance – **bestiary**

Face:
The face, esp. when considered as an indicator of character or mood – **physiognomy**
Having a short or broad face – **brachyfacial**
Having two faces, fronts or facades – **bifacial**
Having or formed by two plane faces – **dihedral**; **two-sided**
Having four faces – **tetrahedral**
A solid having six faces, each a parallelogram - **parallelepiped**

Fact:
By the fact itself – **ipso facto**

Fads:
An inclination for adopting fads – **faddism**, adj. **faddish**
One who has such an inclination – **faddist**
An intense or unreasonable desire or enthusiasm – **craze**; **mania**

Faith (see also Religion):
In good faith – **bona fide**
In bad faith – **mala fide**
Based on or relating to faith or trust – **fiducial**
A reliance, in a search for religious truth, on faith alone – **fideism**, adj. **fideistic**
The branch of theology that deals with faith – **pistology**

Falconry:
A male hawk used in falconry – **tercel**; **tiercel**
A breeder and trainer of falcons; a hunter who uses falcons – **falconer**
The act of rising in flight; the act of swooping down on a hunted bird; to swoop down in attack – **souse** (n./v.i.)
A pair of hawks put in flight together – **cast**
To stitch closed the eyes of (a falcon) – **seel** (v.t.)
To flap the wings wildly in impatience – **bait**; **bate** (used of a falcon) (v.i.)
To spread first one wing, then the other, over the outstretched legs – **mantle** (v.i.) (said of a perched hawk)
A nestling hawk or falcon, esp. one trained for falconry – **eyas**

Family:
Of or relating to the family or household – **domestic**
A family unit making up one household that consists of parents, children and other close relatives – **extended family**
One from whom a family is descended (Law); a branch of a family – **stirps**, pl. **stirpes** (usu. used in the phrase *per stirpes* [by familial stocks; as representatives of the branches of a person's descendants])

Fan (semicircular or wedge-shaped object):
Arranged in folds like those of a fan – **plaited**; **plicate**; **plicated**
Shaped like a fan – **flabellate**; **flabelliform**
A body organ or part that resembles a fan – **flabellum**

Fanatical:
   To make fanatical or act as a fanatic – **fanaticize** (v.t./v.i.)

Fantasy:
   To indulge in fantasies – **fantasize** (v.i./v.t.)
   To make fantastic – **fantasticate** (v.t.)
   A creator of fantasy or fantasia – **fantasist**

Farewell:
   Of, relating to or by way of a farewell or leave-taking – **apopemptic**; **valedictory**
   A farewell address – **valedictory**

Farm/Farmer (see also Agriculture):
   A farm producing vegetables for the market – **truck farm**
   A tenant farmer who gives a share of his crop to the landlord in lieu of rent – **sharecropper**

Fat:
   Of or obtained from fat; fatty – **aliphatic** (said of certain hydrocarbons)
   Resembling fat – **fatty**; **lipoid**; **lipoidal**
   The solid form of fat – **stearin**
   Of, relating to or similar to fat or stearin – **stearic**
   An excessive accumulation of fat in the buttocks – **steatopygia**
   The tendency to become obese – **adiposity**
   The branch of medicine dealing with the treatment of obesity – **bariatrics**
   Excessive discharge of fat in the feces – **steatorrhea**; **steatorrhoea**
   Hydrolysis (decomposition by reaction with water) of fat – **lipolysis**
   Preventing abnormal or excessive accumulation of fat in the liver; having an affinity for lipids – **lipotropic**
      The state or tendency of being lipotropic - **lipotropism**; **lipotropy**
   Of or relating to animal fat; the fat found in adipose tissue – **adipose**
   Adipose tissue whose oxidation is a major source of heat in mammals – **brown fat**
   The solid or semisolid rendered fat of a hog; to make richer with or as if with fat; to insert strips of fat into (meat) before
      cooking – **lard** (n./v.t.)
   The thick layer of fat between the skin and the muscle layers of several marine mammals – **blubber**

Father:
   Of, relating to or characteristic of a father – **fatherly**; **paternal**
   Having no known father – **unfathered**
   An estate inherited from one's father or other ancestor; anything derived from one's father - **patrimony**

Favoritism shown or patronage granted by persons in high office to relatives or close friends – **nepotism**, adj. **nepotistic**
      or **nepotistical**

Fear (dread):
   Causing fear or dread; inspiring awe – **dreadful**
      A place with dreadful associations – **Aceldama**
   Great alarm or dread – **trepidation**
   A nonspecific feeling of fear or uneasiness – **anxiety**
   Fear of everything – **panophobia**
   (See also under type of fear or thing feared)

Feather:
  Having feathers – **feathered**; **pennate**; **pennated**; **pinnate**
  Resembling a feather or plume (large feather or cluster of feathers) – **pinnate**; **pinnated**; **plumate**; **plumose**
  A bunch of feathers or a plume, esp. on a helmet – **panache**
  A tuft of feathers – **tussock**
  A featherlike or plumelike organ or part – **pinnula** (pl. **pinnulae**); **pinnule**, pl. **pinnules**
  One of the parallel filaments projecting from the main shaft of a feather – **barb**
  A bird's primary feather - **pinion**
  A glossy or shining mark on the end of a feather - **spangle**
  A hairlike feather having few or no barbs – **filoplume**
  To pluck the feathers from – **deplume** (v.t.)

Feed (for livestock) – see Livestock

Feeling (see also Sensation):
  Lack of feeling or interest – **apathy**, adj. **apathetic**
  Feeling or exhibiting little emotion – **impassive**; **stolid**
  The ability to feel – **aesthesia**; **esthesia**
  Capable of feeling or suffering - **passible**
  Hardened in feelings, esp. against moral or mollifying influences - **obdurate**
  Feeling as contrasted with sensation, perception or ideation - **sentience**
  Identification with and understanding of another's feelings – **empathy**, adj. **empathetic**
  Sameness of feeling – **sympathy**, adj. **sympathetic**
  A strong feeling of aversion, repugnance or opposition – **antipathy**, adj. **antipathetic**
  Simultaneously conflicting feelings toward a person or thing – **ambivalence**
  An emotional state marked by anxiety, depression and restlessness – **dysphoria**, adj. **dysphoric**

Female:
  Having female form – **gynecomorphous**
  Of or relating to the female sex – **feminine**
  The quality or state of being feminine; a female trait or characteristic – **femineity**; **femininity**

Fence (barrier):
  Jagged glass or a spiked obstacle set in the masonry on the top of a fence or wall to prevent trespassing or escape – **cheval-de-frise**

Fencing (sport):
  One who fences with a foil – **fencer**; **foilsman**
  A sudden movement made in avoiding a thrust – **volt**; **volte**

Fermentation (zymolysis; zymosis):
  The chemistry of fermentation – **zymology**
  Of, relating to or caused by fermentation – **zymotic**
  Capable of causing fermentation – **zymogenic**
  The chemistry of fermentation processes in brewing – **zymurgy**

Fern:
  The study of ferns – **pteridology**
  Shaped like a fern or fern frond – **filiciform**

Ferret:
   A group of ferrets – **business**
   A male ferret – **dog**
   A female ferret – **bitch**

Ferrying:
   The act or business of ferrying; the toll charged for ferrying – **ferriage**

Fertilizer:
   A mixture of decayed organic matter used as fertilizer – **compost**

Festival commemorating the founding of a city, church, etc. – **encaenia**

Fetus:
   Intentional destruction of a human fetus – **feticide**; **foeticide**
   The medical study and treatment of a fetus – **fetology**

Feud:
   A bitter blood feud between two families motivated by the desire for revenge - **vendetta**

Fever (pyrexia):
   Having a fever – **feverish**; **febrific**; **febrile**
   The state of having a fever – **febricity**
   Anything that reduces fever – **antifebrile**; **antipyretic**; **febrifuge**; **refrigerant**
   Inducing fever – **pyretogenic**; **pyretogenous**
   Producing or due to fever - **pyrogenic**
   A fever-producing agent – **febrifacient**; **pyrogen**
   Abnormally high fever – **hyperpyrexia**
   Abnormally high fever, esp. when induced for therapeutic purposes – **hyperthermia**, adj. **hyperthermal**
   Without fever – **afebrile**; **apyretic**
   Chill felt during a fever – **algor**
   The abatement of a fever – **defervescence**
   A fever with periods of chill and sweating – **ague**
   Treatment of disease involving artificially induced fever – **fever therapy**

Fiber:
   To moisten or soak (flax, e.g.) in order to soften and separate fibers by partial rotting – **ret** (v.t.)
   Shaped like a fiber – **fibriform**
   A small, slender fiber – **fibril**
      Having or made up of fibrils – **fibrillose**
      Shaped like a fibril – **fibrilliform**
   A small bundle of nerve or muscle fibers – **fascicle** (Anat.)

Figures of speech (tropes):
   The comparison of two essentially unlike things – **simile**
   The transference of a term from the object it ordinarily designates to an object it may designate only by implicit
      comparison or analogy – **metaphor**
      An exaggerated or elaborate metaphor, the use of such metaphors – **conceit**
      A succession of metaphors that produce an incongruous effect – **mixed metaphor**
   An extravagant or exaggerated statement – **hyperbole**; **hyperbolism**
      To use or express with hyperbole – **hyperbolize** (v.i.)

The use of a more inclusive term for a less inclusive term or vice versa – **synecdoche**

The reversal of the natural or rational order of terms – **hysteron proteron**

An understatement – **meiosis**, adj. **meiotic**

An understatement, esp. one in which an affirmative is expressed by negation of its opposite – **litotes**

The use of an attribute or commonly associated feature or part to designate something; use of the name of one thing for that of something else with which it is associated – **metonymy**, n. **metonym**

A play on words, esp. a pun – **paronomasia**

The attribution of personality to an inanimate object or abstraction – **personification**

The use of a word with the same syntactic relation to two adjacent words, in a literal sense with one and a metaphorical sense with the other – **syllepsis**, adj. **sylleptic**

The combination of incongruous or contradictory terms – **oxymoron**

The conscious repetition of a word or phrase at the beginning of several successive verses, clauses or paragraphs - **anaphora**

The use of a word in a sense opposite to its proper meaning – **antiphrasis**

A sudden breaking off of a thought in midsentence, as if unable or unwilling to continue – **aposiopesis**, pl. **aposiopeses**

The repetition of a word or phrase for emphasis – **palilogy; palillogy**

An apparent concession made to an opponent in an argument that really serves to strengthen one's own argument – **paromologia**

Denial of one's intention to speak of a subject that is at the same time named or insinuated - **apophasis**

Reversal of the expected or 'normal' syntactic relationship between two words – **hypallage**

Reversal of the usual order of the parts of a sentence – **anastrophe**

A digression in which the dead, absent or inanimate are addressed as if present – **apostrophe**

A deliberately paradoxical figure of speech; the use of a forced figure of speech – **catachresis**

A figure of speech in which an absent person is represented as speaking or a dead person as alive and present - **prosopopoeia**

A change from one grammatical construction to another within the same sentence; a sentence in which this occurs – **anacoluthon**, adj. **anacoluthic**

Repetition in the first part of a clause or sentence of a prominent word from the latter part of the preceding clause or sentence – **anadiplosis**

Reversal in the order of words in two otherwise parallel phrases – **chiasmus**

The application of a verb or adjective jointly to two nouns although logically appropriate to only one – **zeugma**

Filament:

Having or utilizing only one filament, such as a thread or wire – **unifilar**

A small, needle-shaped filament – **trichite**, adj. **trichitic**

Fill:

To fill throughout – **impregnate** (v.t.) (adj. **impregnate**); **saturate** (v.t.)

Capable of being impregnated, as an egg – **impregnable**

Film:

A surface film of thickness comparable to that of a single molecule – **molecular film**

Filter:

A filtering substance, as filter paper – **medium**

Filth (see also Excrement):

A devotion to or worship of filth and obscenity – **aischrolatreia**

Covered with filth; abounding in noxious matter – **fecal; feculent**, n. **feculence**

An abnormal attraction to filth – **mysophilia**

An extreme or irrational fear of uncleanliness or contamination – **misophobia**; **mysophobia**

Fins:
   Lacking paired fins – **apterygial**
   Lacking pelvic fins – **apodal**
   Having fins supported by flexible cartilaginous rays – **soft-finned**
   Relating to, designating or marked by a tail fin having two unequal lobes, with the vertebral column extending into the upper lobe – **heterocercal**
   Relating to, designating or marked by a tail fin having two symmetrical lobes extending from the end of the vertebral column - **homocercal**
   Having fins supported by sharp, spiny, inflexible rays – **spiny-finned**
   Having or designating a tail fin in which the vertebral column extends into the tip, with symmetrical upper and lower parts - **diphycercal**

Fine, to punish by imposing a – **amerce** (v.t.), n. **amercement**

Finger:
   Having fingers or fingerlike parts – **digitate**; **digitated**
   Without fingers – **adactylous**
   A fingerlike process or part – **digitations**
   Having abnormally short fingers – **brachydactylic**; **brachydactylous**, n. **brachydactyly**, pl. **brachydactylia** or **brachydactylies** or **brachydactylias**
   Having more than the normal number of fingers – **polydactyl**; **polydactylous**
   Having two or more wholly or partially fused digits; an animal having such fused digits – **syndactyl**; **syndactyle**
   Having five fingers on each hand or foot – **pentadactyl**; **pentadactylate**
   The use of the fingers and hands to convey ideas, as in the manual alphabet used by the deaf – **dactylology**; **sign language**
   To manipulate (a stack of objects) idly between the fingers of one or both hands – **riffle** (v.t.)

Fingernail:
   Resembling a fingernail in shape or texture – **onychoid**
   Fingernail-biting – **onychophagia**; **onychophagy**
   Longitudinal ridging and splitting of the nails of the fingers and toes - **onychorrhexis**

Fingerprint:
   The study of fingerprints as a method of identification – **dactylography**
   The comparison of fingerprints to establish identification – **dactyloscopy**
   A fingerprint that is difficult to see but can be made visible for examination – **latent**

Fire:
   Of, relating to or typical of fire – **igneous**
   On fire – **aflame**; **burning**
   Easily ignited and capable of burning with great rapidity – **flammable**; **inflammable**
   Easily ignited material used as a fire starter – **kindling**
   A piece of wood or rolled paper used to light a fire – **spill**
   The uncontrollable impulse to start fires – **pyromania**, adj. **pyromaniac** or **pyromaniacal**
      One who manifests such an impulse – **pyromaniac**
   Spontaneously igniting in air – **pyrophoric**
   Extreme or irrational fear of fire – **pyrophobia**
   The act or practice of unlawfully setting fire to the property of another or one's own property – **arson**
      One who sets a fire or fires thus – **arsonist**

Of or involving arson; causing or capable of causing fire – **incendiary**

The process of burning designs on material, such as wood or leather, with a heated tool or fine flame – **pyrography**, adj. **pyrographic**, n. **pyrographer**

Divination by means of fire or flames – **pyromancy**

Firearms:

A maker or repairer of firearms – **gunsmith**

The study of the functioning of firearms – **ballistics**

Having a small bore, as a gun – **unrifled**

The range of a gun or projectile – **carry**

The art and science of constructing and operating guns – **gunnery**

A gunshot fired from a concealed place; to shoot at (a person or persons) typically from a concealed and removed vantage point – **snipe** (v.i.), n. **sniper**

The firing of a gun or guns so as to sweep the length of a target; to rake with gunfire lengthwise – **enfilade** (n./v.t.)

Fireworks:

Of, relating to or resembling fireworks – **pyrotechnic**; **pyrotechnical**

The practice of manufacturing or setting off fireworks – **pyrotechnics**

One who manufactures or sets off fireworks – **pyrotechnist**

A firework having a spiral flight – **tourbillion**; **tourbillon**

A rotating and radiating firework – **girandola**; **girandole**

The material in fireworks that produces stars, fiery rain, or other display after explosion - **garniture**

A small firecracker; a broken firecracker the powder in which burns with a fizz – **squib**

First:

In the first place – **imprimis**

First according to historical record or scientific analysis – **aboriginal**

Fish/Fishing (see also Bass, Carp, Mackerel, and Salmon):

Of, relating to or typical of fish – **ichthyic**; **piscatorial**; **piscine**

A group of fish – **run**; **school**; **shoal**

A young fish – **fry** (sing./pl.); **fingerling**; **parr**, pl. **parr** or **parrs**

A young cod or haddock, esp. one split and boned for cooking – **scrod**

A small fish – **fingerling**

Having recently spawned and thus being less desirable as food – **shotten**

The fish of a given region – **ichthyofauna**

Typical of or like a fish; a fish or fishlike vertebrate – **ichthyoid**; **ichthyoidal**

The study of fishes – **ichthyology**

Feeding on fish – **ichthyophagous**; **piscivorous**

The act or practice of feeding on fish – **ichthyophagy**

A person who eats or subsists on fish - **ichthyophagist**

Shaped like a fish – **pisciform**

Having the left side turned uppermost – **sinistral** (used of a flatfish)

Having the right side turned uppermost – **dextral** (used of a flatfish)

Migrating up rivers from the sea to breed in fresh water – **anadromous**

Migrating down river to breed in marine waters – **catadromous**

A fish living at the bottom of the water – **groundling**

Fish sperm, including the seminal fluid – **milt**

A male fish that is ready to breed – **milter**

A fish that produces eggs that hatch within the female's body – **live-bearer**

A fish that carries its eggs and young in its mouth – **mouthbreeder**

A fish cured by being split and air-dried without salt – **stockfish**, pl. **stockfish** or **stockfishes**

A fisherman who uses a hook and line – **angler**

To fish with a rod and a long line that is drawn along through the water – **drabble** (v.i.)

To fish for by running a baited line behind a slowly moving boat; to trail (a baited line) in fishing; to fish by running a baited line behind a moving boat – **troll** (v.t./v.i.)

To draw the hook of a fishing line along the surface of water with a skipping motion; to cause to draw a hook thus – **skitter** (v.i./v.t.)

To fish for eels by thrusting a baited hook or needle into their hiding places; to catch (a salmon, e.g.) by direct snatching with a hook or snare – **sniggle** (v.i./v.t.)

A pen in shallow water, as for confining fish - **crawl**

A fence or wattle (poles intertwined with twigs, reeds, etc.) placed in a stream to catch or retain fish – **weir**

A transverse board in a fishway to check the flow of the current and afford a resting pool for ascending fish - **riffle**

The act of drawing in a fishnet – **draft**

Thin, rounded and smooth-edged – **cycloid** (used of fish scales)

Migration of fish, esp. for spawning; a group or school of fish ascending a river for spawning – **run**

The right to fish in waters owned by another party – **piscary**

Of or relating to fishermen or fishing – **piscatorial**

The breeding, hatching and rearing of fish under controlled conditions – **pisciculture**

Five:

Five times as much; consisting of five parts – **fivefold**; **quintuple**

A set up five persons or things – **pentad**; **quintet**; **quintette**

A group or combination of five things related by common properties or behavior; one of five born at a single birth – **quintuplet**

Multiplied by five; being the fifth of a set of five identical copies; to make five copies of – **quintuplicate** (adj./v.t.)

Having five smaller parts – **pentamerous**

An arrangement of five objects with one at each corner of a square or rectangle and one at the center – **quincunx**

Consisting of five; arranged by fives; of the fifth order or rank – **quinary**; **quinquenary**

Flag:

The study of flags and flag designs – **vexillology**

A person who makes or designs flags – **vexillographer**

Flags collectively – **bunting**

A standard bearer - **vexillary**

A flag with three colors – **tricolor**

A narrow forked flag or streamer – **banderol**; **banderole**

A small flag displayed at the bow of a ship – **jack**

A small distinguishing flag displayed by a yacht – **burgee**

A black flag bearing the white skull and crossbones of a pirate ship – **Jolly Roger**; **jolly roger** (usu. capitalized)

The span of a flag from the staff to the outer edge; the outer edge of a flag – **fly**

A signal with a flag; a flag used for signaling or indicating wind direction – **waft**; **waif**

A flag that hangs from a crosspiece or frame – **gonfalon**

Flap:

A flaplike structure – **lappet**

A flap or lid covering an aperture – **operculum** (Biol.)

Having an operculum – **operculate**; **operculated**

Flashes, to emit in – **fulgurate** (v.i.)

Flask:
Shaped like a flask (having an enlarged base tapering to a narrow neck) – **lageniform** (Biol.)

Flat:
Flattened lengthwise or laterally – **compressed**
Flattened and two-edged – **ancipital** (Bot.)
Abnormally flattened – **fasciate**; **fasciated**

Flattery:
A person who attempts to win favor or advance himself by flattering persons of influence – **sycophant**; **toady**
To obtain through the use of flattery or guile; to use flattery or guile to achieve one's ends – **wheedle** (v.t./v.i.)

Flavor:
Having flavor – **sapid**
Having a strong, esp. agreeable flavor – **sapid**; **savory**

Fleas:
A specialist in fleas – **pulicologist**
An agent that destroys fleas – **pulicide**

Flesh:
Of, relating to, resembling or consisting of flesh – **sarcoid**; **sarcous**
Flesh-colored – **incarnadine**; **incarnate**
Feeding on human flesh – **anthropophagous**
The act or practice of feeding on human flesh – **anthropophagism**; **anthropophagy**

Flight (see also Aircraft):
In fit condition to fly – **airworthy**
The ability to fly; the act of flying – **volitation**
Flying or capable of flying – **volant**; **volatile**; **volitant**
Not yet having the feathers necessary to fly – **unfledged**
Incapable of flying – **flightless**
Aircraft navigation by visual reference to the horizon or to landmarks – **contact flight**; **contact flying**
The part of a missile's flight between burnout and re-entry – **midcourse**

Float/Floating:
Floating on the surface – **supernatant**
To send floating through the air or over water; to float easily and gently – **waft** (v.t./v.i.)
The act or state of being wafted – **waftage**
The action of wafting – **wafture**

Flood:
The state of being flooded – **flowage**
Of or produced by a flood; resembling a flood – **diluvial**
A flash flood – **spate**
Of the time before the flood – **antediluvian**

Flow:
Something that flows in or into, esp. a tributary – **influent**
Flowing out or forth; something that flows out – **effluent**
The action or process of flowing or seeming to flow out - **efflux**

Flow toward a point, as of blood to an organ – **afflux**

A backward flow of water – **backwash**

Intermediate in flow properties between a solid and a liquid; a substance that is intermediate in flow properties between a solid and a liquid - **semifluid**

Flower:

Of, relating to or like a flower or flora – **floral**

Resembling the flower of a rose - **rosaceous**

Without flowers – **ananthous**

Flowers as a whole; the act of flowering or state of being in flower – **flowerage**

To burst forth as if flowering – **effloresce** (v.i.), n. **efflorescence**

The state of full bloom in a flower – **anthesis**

Ornamented with floral designs – **floreated**; **floriated**

The cultivation of flowering plants – **floriculture**

The study of flowers as related to their environment – **anthoecology**

An imaginary flower that never fades or dies – **amaranth**, adj. **amaranthine**

The outer envelope of a flower, composed of petals – **corolla**

Of or resembling a petal – **apetaline**; **petaloid**

Without petals – **apetalous**

Having petals – **petaliferous**; **petalous**

Having two petals – **bipetalous**; **dipetalous**

Having three petals – **tripetalous**

Having distinctly separate petals – **polypetalous**

The protective covering of a flower – **calyx**

One section of a calyx – **sepal**

  Having only one sepal – **monosepalous**

  Having two sepals - **diphyllous**

  Having distinctly separate sepals – **polysepalous**

  Having the sepals united or partially united – **gamosepalous**; **monosepalous**

  Resembling or characteristic of a sepal – **sepaloid**

The central ovule-bearing female organ of a flower – **carpel**

  Consisting of only one carpel – **monocarpellary**

  Having or consisting of many carpels - **polycarpellary**

  Having or composed of united carpels – **syncarpous**

  A group of separate or partially joined carpels – **apocarp**

The pollen-producing organ of a flower – **stamen**

  Having a stamen or stamens - **staminate**

  Having a single stamen; having flowers bearing a single stamen – **monandrous**, n. **monandry**

  Having two stamens – **diandrous**

  Having eight stamens – **octandrious**

  Bearing stamens only – **androgenous**

    An androgenous plant – **androgyne**

  Without stamens – **anandrous**

  A sterile, functionless stamen – **staminode**; **staminodium**

  The transformation of a floral organ into a stamen – **staminody**

  To remove the stamens from (a flower) – **castrate** (v.t.)

Having stamens and pistils that mature at different times - **dichogamous**

Having stamens and pistils in separate flowers; having pistils but not stamens, or stamens but not pistils – **diclinous**

Having no pistils or stamens – **neuter**

Having either stamens or pistils but not both – **unisexual**

The seed-bearing organ of a flower – **pistil**

Having a pistil or pistils; bearing pistils but no stamens – **pistillate**

A plant having stamens and pistils in the same flower – **hermaphrodite**, adj. **hermaphroditic** or **hermaphroditical**

Bearing a single flower – **monanthous**

Bearing flowers – **floriferous**

Bearing many flowers – **multiflorous**

Having flowers of different kinds, esp. both male and female flowers – **heterogamous**

Having flower parts in sets of three – **trimerous**

Having flower parts in sets of four – **tetramerous**

Having flower parts in sets of five – **pentamerous**

Having flower parts in sets of six – **hexamerous**

The state of having perfect flowers of only one type – **homomorphism**, adj. **homomorphous**

Having male and female flowers borne on separate plants – **diecious; dioecious**

Having male, female and bisexual flowers borne on separate plants – **triecious; trioecious**

A compact flower cluster – **glomerule**

A flower cluster that is loosely and irregularly branched – **panicle**

A type of flower cluster in which single flowers grow individually on small stems arranged at intervals along a single larger stem – **raceme**, adj. **racemiform**

An arrangement of flowers in a cluster around the axis of a plant – **anthotaxy**

A typical arrangement of flowers on a stalk or in a cluster – **inflorescence**, adj. **inflorescent**

A dense, headlike cluster of stalkless flowers – **capitulum**

Having an equal number of parts in the floral whorls – **anisomerous**

Composed of or arranged in two distinct floral whorls – **bicyclic**

Bearing flowers directly from the root – **rhizanthous**

The flower head of a composite plant – **anthodium; compound flower**

Unusual regularity in the form of a flower that is normally irregular – **peloria**

Having blossoms that open during the night – **nocturnal**

Having or designating flowers that open and close at specific times – **equinoctial**

Blooming more than once during a season – **remontant**

Blooming in the evening – **vespertinal; vespertine**

Late in blooming – **seritonal; seritonous**

Blossoming before the leaves sprout – **precocious**

A cup-shaped blossom – **chalice**

A fragrant essential oil or perfume obtained from the petals of flowers – **attar**

A small bunch of flowers – **nosegay**

A small bunch of flowers worn by a woman – **corsage**

The Japanese art of flower arrangement with special regard to form, balance and harmony – **ikebana**

Feeding on flowers – **anthophagous; anthophilous**

Fluid:

Of, involving, moved or operated by a pressurized fluid, esp. water – **hydraulic**

The study of the static and dynamic behavior of fluids – **hydraulics**

The dynamics of fluids, esp. incompressible fluids, in motion – **hydrodynamics**, adj. **hydrodynamic** or **hydrodynamical**

The technology of fluids used as nonmoving, nonelectric components of control and sensing systems – **fluidics**

The kinetics of fluids, esp. incompressible fluids, in motion – **hydrokinetics**

Mechanics dealing with the motion and equilibrium states of fluids – **hydromechanics**

The statics of fluids, esp. incompressible fluids – **hydrostatics**

Diffusion of fluid through a semipermeable membrane – **osmosis**, adj. **osmotic**

Osmosis toward the interior of a cell or cavity – **endosmosis**

Normal fullness or tension produced by the fluid content of blood vessels, capillaries or cells - **turgor**

The path of one particle in a flowing fluid – **streamline**

Fluid flow involving rotation about an axis – **vortex** (pl. **vortexes** or **vortices**, adj. **vortical** or **vorticose**); **whirlpool**
Having relatively high resistance to flow – **viscous**
    The condition or property of being viscous – **viscosity**
        Having no viscosity – **inviscid**
Thick and adhesive – **viscid**
Not using fluid – **aneroid**
Inducing absorption of fluids; something that induces the absorption of fluids – **absorbefacient**
Readily taking up fluids or moisture – **bibulous**, n. **bibulosity**
A fluid-containing sac or space in the body of an organism – **cisterna**
Stagnation of a bodily fluid, esp. blood – **stasis**

Fly:
    A group of flies – **business**
    Infestation of human tissue by fly maggots or flies; a disease resulting from such infestation – **myiasis**

Focus – see Eyes, Optics, and Vision

Fog:
    A faint white or yellowish arc-shaped light, similar to a rainbow, often seen opposite the sun in a fog bank – **fogbow**;
        fogdog; **fogeater**; **seadog**
    A bright or clear spot in a fog bank – **fogdog**
    Immobilized by heavy fog; clouded or obscured by fog – **fogbound**

Follow:
    A faithful follower who carries out orders without question – **myrmidon**
    Following successively without interruption – **consecutive**
    Something that follows or comes after – **sequel** (pl. **sequels**); **sequela**, pl. **sequelae**
    An unexpected sequel to a supposedly concluded matter – **afterclap**

Food (see also Eating and Nutrition):
    An article of food – **viand**
    A scrap or leaving of food after a meal is completed – **ort**
    Of or relating to food – **alimentary**
    Fit for human consumption; to provide with food; to lay in food supplies – **victual** (adj./v.t./v.i.)
        A supplier of victuals – **victualer**; **victualler**
    To consume food and incorporate it into the body – **assimilate** (v.t.)
    Incomplete assimilation of food materials – **malassimilation**
    The process by which food is changed into living tissue – **anabolism**
    The exchange of food substances between organisms – **trophallaxis**
    Feeding on minute particles – **microphagous**
    Feeding on organic substances – **heterotrophic**, **holozoic**
    Feeding on plants – **herbivorous**; **phytophagous**
        An animal that feeds on plants – **herbivore**
    Feeding on animal flesh – **carnivorous**
        An organism that feeds on animal flesh - **carnivore**
    Requiring only one kind of food – **monophagous**; **monotrophic**
    Feeding on a limited range of food substances – **oligophagous**
    Feeding on both animal and plant substances – **omnivorous**; **polytrophic**
        An organism that feeds on animal and plant substances – **omnivore**
    Feeding on a variety of foods – **polyphagous**
    Feeding on living prey – **rapacious**

Feeding on dead or decaying matter – **saprophagous**
    An organism that lives on dead or decaying matter – **saprobe**
Feeding on dead or decaying animal matter – **saprozoic**
    An animal that feeds on dead or decaying matter – **scavenger**
The eating of raw food, esp. raw meat – **omophagia**, adj. **omophagous**
    An organism that eats raw food – **omophagist**
The maintenance of bodily nutrition by the metabolism of some bodily tissues, as in dieting – **autophagia; autophagy**
A person whose diet consists chiefly of fruit – **fruitarian**
Characteristically scratching the ground for food – **rasorial**
A taste and relish for good food – **gourmandise**
Excessive intake of food – **overnutrition**
Urgently eager for food – **ravenous**
An appetite for unusual foods – **parorexia**
A craving for unnatural food, such as earth or ashes, occurring esp. in pregnancy or hysteria – **pica**
To pick at one's food – **piddle** (v.i.)
An abnormal craving for food – **sitomania**
An abnormal aversion to food - **sitophobia**
Abstinence from food – **abrosia; fasting**
Young twigs, leaves and tender shoots of plants or shrubs that are fit for animals to eat – **browse**
Dry food, such as hay, used as feed for livestock – **provender**
The cultivation of marine organisms in their natural habitat – **mariculture**
Warmed leftover food – **réchauffé**
To season food heavily – **devil** (v.t.)
A characteristic style or manner of preparing food; food prepared in a particular style or way – **cuisine**

Foot:
    The study and treatment of food ailments – **chiropody; podiatry**
    Of, relating to or occurring on the sole of the foot – **plantar; volar**
    A foot or footlike part – **pes**, pl. **pedes**
    Having feet – **pedate**
    Resembling or functioning as a foot – **pedate**
    Having no feet or footlike appendages – **apodal; apodous; apodus**
    Having two feet – **biped; bipedal**
        An animal with two feet – **biped**
    Having four feet – **quadrupedal; tetrapod**
        An animal with four feet – **quadruped; tetrapod**
    Having six feet – **hexapod**
    Having many feet – **multiped; multipede; polypod**
    Shaped like a foot – **pediform**
    Congenital deformity of the foot, marked by a misshaped appearance often looking like a club; a foot deformed thus –
        clubfoot; talipes
        Afflicted with clubfoot - **taliped**
    Marked by a disk-shaped foot or feet – **discopodous**

Footprint, a fossilized – **ichnite**

Force:
    Incapable of being entered or taken by force – **impregnable**
    To force to act or think in a given way by pressure, threats, etc. – **coerce; compel** (both v.t.)
    Incapable of coercion – **incoercible**
    Lack of vital force as a result of illness – **debility**

Superior or irresistible force – **force majeure**
The ratio of the output force of a machine to the input force – **mechanical advantage**

Forceps, shaped like a – **forcipate**

Forehead:
   Of or relating to the forehead – **frontal**; **metopic**
   The forehead of an animal, esp. when distinctively marked – **frontlet**

Foreigner:
   Extreme or irrational fear of foreigners, strangers or strange things – **xenophobia**, adj. **xenophobic**
      One who has such a fear - **xenophobe**

Forest:
   Of, relating to or characteristic of woods or forest regions; located in or inhabiting a wood or forest; abounding in trees
      – **silvan**; **sylvan**; **sylvatic**
   One who lives in or frequents the woods – **forester**; **silvan**; **sylvan**
   Skill and experience in matters relating to the woods, as hunting, fishing, etc. – **woodcraft**
   Inhabiting forests – **silvicolous**
   The care and cultivation of forest trees – **forestry**; **silviculture**
   To replant (an area) with forest trees – **reforest** (v.t.)
   An open space in a forest – **glade**
   To convert (open land) into forest – **afforest** (v.t.)
   Land covered with forest – **forestland**
      Forestland considered of commercial value – **timberland**

Forgetting (see also Memory):
   The quality or condition of being completely forgotten – **oblivion**
   Something capable of causing oblivion of grief or suffering; something that induces forgetfulness of sorrow – **nepenthe**

Form (see also Biology: Physical Characteristics):
   The study of the form and structure of plants and animals – **morphology**, adj. **morphologic** or **morphological**
   Relating to form – **morphic**; **morphological**
   Primitive in form or structure – **protomorphic**
   Anomaly of form – **monstrosity**; **teratism**; **teratosis**
   Without form – **amorphous**
   Having but one form, as one crystal form – **monomorphic**
   Having the two ends symmetrical in form – **holomorphic**
   Having or occurring in two distinct forms – **biform**; **dimorphic**; **dimorphous**
   Having or occurring in three distinct forms – **trimorphic**
   Having or occurring in a variety or diversity of forms – **diversiform**; **multiform**; **variform**
   Of all forms, varieties or kinds – **omnifarious**
   Readily taking on different forms or shapes – **protean**
   The existence of an organism in two or more distinct forms during its life cycle – **pleomorphy** (adj. **pleomorphic** or
      pleomorphous); **polymorphism**, adj. **heteromorphic**
   Misshapen or abnormally formed – **malformed**
   Having an atypical or irregular form or forms – **heteromorphic**; **heteromorphous**
   An abnormal change of form that gives the appearance of a different botanical species; gradual change of form by
      evolution – **anamorphosis**
   Similarity of form, as in different organisms – **isomorphism**; **isomorphy**, adj. **isomorphic**; **isomorphous**
      An object, organism or group displaying isomorphism – **isomorph**

The occurrence of different forms, stages or color varieties in individual organisms or in organisms of the same species – **polymorphism**, adj. **polymorphic** or **polymorphous**

The manner in which an organism or one of its parts changes form or the manner or order of its development – **morphosis**

Having a basic structure remaining unchanged through a series of developmental changes – **monomorphic**; **monomorphous**

Fort/Fortification:

The act of scaling the walls of a fortification; to climb up and over (a fortified wall) – **escalade** (n./v.t.)

A circular fort of masonry, formerly built on coasts to protect against invaders – **Martello tower**

The art or process of planning or erecting earth fortifications – **vallation**, adj. **vallatory**

The steep outer slope of a fortification – **scarp**

The exterior slope or wall of the ditch in a work of fortification – **counterscarp**

The inner wall of a trench or ditch dug around a fortification; to furnish with such a wall – **escarp** (n./v.t.)

A hastily constructed, temporary fortification that is breast high – **breastwork**

Forty:

A period of forty days – **quarantine**

Fossils:

The study of fossils – **paleontology**

The study of fossil life forms – **paleobiology**

The study of plant fossils and ancient vegetation – **paleobotany**

The study of microscopic fossils – **micropaleontology**

The study of fossilized tracks, trails, burrows, etc. – **ichnology**

The study of fossil excrement – **scatology**

Fossil excrement – **coprolite**

Containing fossils – **fossiliferous**

To convert into or become a fossil – **fossilize** (v.t./v.i.)

Remains of fossil organisms - **reliquiae**

Four:

Having or consisting of four parts or members – **quadripartite**; **quadruple**; **quaternary**; **tetramerous**

Multiplied by four; to multiply by four; to increase fourfold – **quadruple** (adj./v.t./v.i.)

A group or arrangement of four; something composed of four parts – **quaternion**; **tetrad**

Being in fours – **quaternary**

Of or relating to a quarter or quarters; being one of four parts; occurring four times per year – **quarterly**

Divided into four parts – **quadrifid** (Bot.)

Having four angles or sides - **tetragonal**

Fowl:

A pen for domestic fowl – **hennery**

A young fowl, esp. a turkey – **poult**

Fox:

A group of foxes – **earth**; **skulk**; **troop**;

A male fox – **dog**; **vix**

A female fox – **vixen**

A young fox – **cub**

Of, resembling or characteristic of a fox – **vulpine**

The killing of a fox by methods other than by hunting it with hounds; the killer of a fox other than in this way – **vulpecide**

France:
    One who admires France, its people, culture, etc. – **Francophil**; **Francophile**
    A strong favoring of anything French - **Gallomania**
    To make or become like the French – **Gallicize** (v.t./v.i.)
    A French idiom or phrase appearing in another language; a French trait – **Gallicism**
    One who dislikes or fears France, its people, culture, etc. – **Francophobe**, n. **Francophobia**
    French-speaking; a French-speaking person – **Francophone**

Freezing (see also Cold):
    Freezing and storing a corpse to prevent tissue decomposition – **cryonics**
    The study of the freezing points of solutions – **cryoscopy**

Frankincense, producing or bearing – **thuriferous**

Friction:
    The study of the mechanisms of friction, lubrication and wear of interaction surfaces that are in relative motion – **tribology**, n. **tribologist**
    A rubbing away or wearing down by friction – **attrition**
        Worn down by attrition – **attrite**; **attrited**

Friend:
    To act as a friend to – **befriend** (v.t.)
    Having no friends – **unfriend**
    A very close friend or constant companion – **alter ego**

Fringe:
    Fringed – **fimbriate**; **fimbriated**; **laciniate**; **laciniated** (all Biol.)
    A fringelike part or structure – **fimbria** (Biol.)

Frog:
    A group of frogs – **army**
    Of or relating to frogs or toads – **anuran**; **batrachian**
    Extreme or irrational fear of frogs and toads – **batrachophobia**

Frond:
    Having or resembling many fronds – **frondescent**, n. **frondescence**
    Bearing fronds; like a frond - **frondose**

Front, toward the – **anterior**

Fruit:
    Bearing fruit – **fructiferous**; **fructuous**; **fruitful**
    Producing no fruit – **acarpous**
    The cultivation of fruit – **pomiculture**; **pomology**
    The production of fruit – **fructification**
    To bear fruit – **fructify** (v.i.)
    Feeding on fruit – **frugivorous**
    A person whose diet consists chiefly of fruit – **fruitarian**

The time, process or state of bearing fruit – **fruitage**

A grower or seller of fruit – **fruiterer**

Of or obtained from citrus fruits – **citric**

The cultivation of citrus fruits – **citriculture**

A fruitlike structure marked by rows of overlapping scales, such as a pine cone – **strobile**; **strobilus**; adj. **strobilaceous**

An accessory fruit – **pseudocarp**

A plant that flowers and bears fruit only once – **monocarp**

Bearing fruit at the end of the stalk – **acrocarpous**

Any fruit that grows encased in an external covering – **angiocarp**

Any of the small parts (drupelets) composing such fruits as the raspberry; also a grape or any berry – **acinus**, adj. **acinose**; **acinous**

The wall of a ripened fruit – **pericarp**

A fruit whose pericarp is soft and pulpy – **fleshy fruit**

A fleshy fruit having seeds but no stone – **pome**

   Bearing pomes – **pomiferous**

A fruit, esp. a peach, having a stone that does not cling to the pulp – **freestone**

Funeral:

Of, relating to or appropriate for a funeral or burial – **funerary**; **funereal**

One of the persons who carry or attend a coffin at a funeral – **pallbearer**

A funeral rite or ceremony – **obsequy**

A combustible heap (as of wood) for burning a dead body as a funeral rite - **pyre**

A funeral procession - **cortege**; **cortège**

A funeral song or ode – **dirge**; **elegy**; **epicede** (pl. **epicedes**), **epicedium** (pl. **epicedia**); **monody**; **threnody**

Fungus (pl. fungi):

Of, relating to, caused by or characteristic of a fungus – **fungous**

A fungous growth in the body; a disease caused by a fungous growth – **mycosis**

The study of fungi; the fungi native to a region – **mycology**

Capable of inhibiting the growth of fungi without destroying them – **fungistatic**, n. **fungistat**

Resembling a fungus; having a mushroom shape or spongy or fleshy texture – **fungoid**

Infected with or affected by fungus; having a fungous growth – **fungused**

Not supporting fungous growth – **funginert**

Feeding on or in fungi – **fungivorous**; **mycetophagous**

The symbiotic association of the vegetative part of a fungus with the roots of certain plants – **mycorhiza**; **mycorrhiza**

A substance that destroys or inhibits the growth of fungi - **fungicide**

Funnel:

A funnel-shaped bodily passage or part – **infundibulum**

Shaped like a funnel – **infundibuliform**

Fur:

Bearing fur; made, covered or trimmed with fur – **furred**

One whose business is the dressing, selling or repairing of furs – **furrier**

Fur garments and trimmings as a whole; the business of a furrier – **furriery**

Fur used in medieval times to line and trim robes – **vair**

A wavy pattern in fur - **moiré**

Furnace:

One who feeds fuel to and tends a furnace – **stoker**

Futility:

A believer in the futility of human behavior – **futilitarian**

Future:

The study or forecast of potential developments, as in science and technology, using current conditions or trends as a point of departure – **futuristics**; **futurology**

Supposedly direct acquaintance with the future – **prescience**

Pretending to foretell events – **oracular**; **pythonic**

The art or act of foretelling future events by means of signs, omens or alleged supernatural power - **divination**

The art or science of divination; of or relating to the faculty of divination – **mantic**

Divination by the interpretation of omens or portents – **augury**

One alleged to be able to predict the future – **prophet** (q.v.; adj. **prophetic**); **soothsayer**; **vaticinator**; adj. **pythonic**

A sign or omen taken as an indication of the future – **augury**; **portent**

G

Galaxy:
    Occurring or located within the space of a galaxy – **intragalactic**
    Between galaxies – **intergalactic**

Gallbladder:
    Of or relating to the gallbladder – **cystic**
    Surgical removal of the gallbladder – **cholecystectomy**; **cystectomy**
    The presence of gallstones in the gallbladder – **cholelithiasis**

Gambling:
    An attendant at a gaming table who collects and pays bets – **croupier**
    A method of gambling in which one doubles the stakes after each loss - **martingale**

Garden:
    The cultivation of a garden – **horticulture**
    A garden in which vegetables and fruits are grown for household use – **kitchen garden**

Garlic:
    Characteristic of garlic, esp. in odor or taste - **alliaceous**

Garnets, containing - **garnetiferous**

Gas:
    The dynamics of gases – **aerodynamics**
    The branch of dynamics that deals with gaseous fluids - **gasdynamics**
    A mixture of methane and carbon dioxide produced through bacterial action – **biogas**
    Inducing expulsion of gas from the stomach and intestines; something that induces such expulsion – **carminative**
    An apparatus for removing impurities from a gas – **scrubber**
    Being in gaseous form – **gasiform**
    Gas generated in the stomach or intestines – **flatus**
    Gaseous distention of the stomach or intestine – **meteorism**; **tympanites**
    To remove embedded gas from (a solid) by heating – **outgas** (v.t.)

Gears:
    The arrangement of gears in a mechanical device – **wheel·work**

Gel/Gelatin:
    Of, relating to, containing or resembling gelatin – **gelatinous**
    To convert to gelatin or jelly; to coat with gelatin; to become gelatinous – **gelatinize** (v.t./v.i.)
    Formation of a gel – **gelation**
    The separation of a liquid from a gel caused by contraction – **synaerisis**; **syneresis**
    The property exhibited by certain gels of liquefying when stirred or shaken, and returning to the hardened state upon
        standing – **thixotropy**

Gem:
    The study of gems – **gemmology**; **gemology**; n. **gemologist**
    The art of carving or engraving gemstones – **glyptics**; **glyptography**
    Of or relating to carving or engraving on gems - **glyptic**

One who cuts, polishes or engraves gemstones; of or relating to gems or the art of working on them; the art of cutting gems – **lapidary**

A highly polished, convex-cut, unfaceted gem – **cabochon**

A gemstone, as a diamond, cut in a pointed oval shape – **marquise**

Having a changeable luster; a stone or gem with a changeable luster – **chatoyant**

The highest quality or purest luster – **first water** (used of gems)

Genetics:

The functional hereditary unit that occupies a fixed location on a chromosome – **gene**

One of the threadlike bodies in cell nuclei that are composed of genes – **chromosome**

The chromosomal complement of an individual or species – **karyotype**

A chromosome that is not a sex chromosome – **autosome**

Having an excess number of one or more chromosomes – **polysomic**

A structure, function or attribute determined by a gene or group of genes – **character**

The degree or frequency with which a gene manifests its effect – **penetrance**

The control or determination of more than one characteristic or function by a single gene – **pleiotropism**; **pleiotropy**

The genetic constitution of an organism; a group or class of organism having the same genetic constitution – **genotype**

The environmentally and genetically determined observable appearance of an organism – **phenotype**

The degree to which an individual gene can affect the phenotype of an organism – **expressivity**

The condition in which tissues of genetically different types occur in the same organism – **mosaicism**

A gene that determines major qualitative hereditary characteristics – **oligogene**

A hereditary alteration of the genes or chromosomes of an organism - **mutation** (q.v.)

Any of a group of possible mutational forms of a gene – **allele**

A reversal process whereby a gene that has undergone mutation returns to its previous state – **back mutation**

The branch of biology linking the study of genetic inheritance with the study of cell structure – **cytogenetics**

The branch of radiobiology dealing with genetic systems – **radiogenetics**

Derived from the male line – **patriclinous**; **patroclinous**

Derived from the female line – **matriclinous**; **matroclinous**

Being or occurring between generations - **intergenerational**

Geography – see Land, Water, etc.

Geology – see Earth, Mineral, Rock, etc.

Germ (see also Bacteria):

A germ-killing agent – **germicide**; **sterilant**

Free from microorganisms – **sterile**

An agent that kills microbes – **microbicide**

The state of being free of pathogenic organisms – **asepsis**, adj. **aseptic**

An inanimate object or substance that transfers infectious organisms from one individual to another – **fomite**

Able to resist a specific pathogen (bacterium, fungus, etc.) because the proper antibodies or antigens are present – **monovalent**

Extreme or irrational fear of germs – **bacillophobia**; **bacteriophobia**

German/Germany:

An admirer of Germany and German things – **Germanophile**

One who hates or fears Germany and German things – **Germanophobe**

A German practice or idiom; German character or culture – **Teutonism**; **Teutonicism**

To give a German quality to – **Teutonize** (v.t.)

A fear or hatred of Germany, its people, customs, etc. – **Germanophobia**; **Teutophobia**; **Teutonophobia**

Ghost (phantom; eidolon)
   The study of ghosts, phantoms and apparitions – **spectrology**
   The ghost of a dead person – **wraith**
   A supposedly ghostly double of a living person – **doppelganger**

Gift:
   A small gift presented by a store owner to a customer who has made a purchase – **lagniappe**
   A gift or testimonial expressing gratitude, respect or admiration – **tribute**, adj. **tributary**

Gill:
   A gill or similar breathing organ – **branchia**
   Having gills or branchiae – **branchiate**
   Having no gills – **abranchial**; **abranchiate**; **abranchious**

Giraffes, a group of – **herd**

Give up:
   To give up (a claim or right) voluntarily – **waive** (v.t.)
   The intentional relinquishment of a claim or right; the document that evidences such a relinquishment – **waiver**

Glacier:
   The study of the nature, distribution and movement of glaciers and their effects on the earth's topography – **glaciology**; n. **glaciologist**
   A glacier confined by walls of a valley – **alpine glacier**; **mountain glacier**; **valley glacier**
   A glacier perched on the edge of a cliff – **cliff glacier**; **hanging glacier**
   A glacier that terminates in an ocean – **tidal glacier**; **tidewater glacier**
   A glacier on flat land that is not confined to valley walls and spreads out to form a broad apron of ice – **piedmont glacier**
   A glacier that moves in all directions away from its point of origin and completely covers the land except for isolated mountain peaks (nunataks) that project above its surface – **continental glacier**; **ice cap**; **ice sheet**
   Formed or deposited beneath a glacier – **subglacial**
   Located or occurring within a glacier – **englacial**
   Between glacial epochs – **interglacial**
   The face or sheer side of a glacier, resembling a frozen waterfall - **icefall**
   The upper part of a glacier where the snow turns into ice; the field of snow at the head of a glacier; the granular snow typically found in such a field – **névé**
   A deep fissure in a glacier – **chasm**; **crevasse**
   A vertical shaft in a glacier, kept open by falling water and rock debris; a cavity in a glacier – **moulin**
   An accumulation of boulders, stones or other debris carried and deposited in a glacier – **moraine**
   A shallow depression in an undulating glacial moraine - **swale**
   A glacial deposit of gravel or sand containing eroded particles of valuable minerals; a place where such a deposit is washed to remove its mineral content – **placer**
   Rounded by glacial action to a shape resembling a sheep's back – **moutonnée**; **moutonnéed**
   Facing the direction from which a glacier moves – **stoss** (used of a rock or slope in its path)

Gland:
   The study of glands – **adenology**
   Surgical removal of a gland – **adenectomy**
   Glandular; glandlike – **adenoid**; **adenoidal**
   Inflammation of a lymph gland or node – **adenitis**
   The process of internal secretion typical of endocrine glands – **incretion**

Relating to a gland whose secretion is formed by the degeneration of the gland's cells – **holocrine**

Glass:
Of, relating to, resembling or having the nature of glass; obtained or made from glass – **vitreous**, n. **vitreosity** or **vitreousness**
Tending to turn into glass; similar to glass; capable of being turned into glass – **vitrescent**
To change or make into glass or a similar substance, esp. through heat fusion – **vitrify** (v.i./v.t.)
To remove or destroy the glassy quality of – **devitrify** (v.t.)
Glass set or made to be set in frames – **glazing**
To furnish or fit with glass – **glaze** (v.t.)
One who cuts and fits window glass – **glazier**
A glassy or transparent appearance; something translucent or transparent – **hyaline**
Scraps of broken or waste glass gathered for remelting – **cullet**
Extreme or irrational fear of glass – **crystallophobia**; **hyalophobia**

Gliding:
The branch of aviation that deals with gliding – **aerodonetics**
To glide toward the earth with the engine cut off – **volplane** (v.i.)

Globe – see Sphere

Glow:
A reddish-purple glow often seen on mountain tops just before sunrise or after sunset – **alpenglow**
Having a rosy glow - **ablush**

Glue:
Like glue - **glutinous**
To become or cause to become glued or stuck together – **conglutinate** (v.i./v.t.)

Goal:
Directed or tending toward a goal – **telic**
The most remote goal attainable – **ultima Thule**

Goat:
A group of goats – **flock**; **herd**; **tribe**; **trip**
A male goat – **billy**
A female goat – **nanny**; **nanny goat**
A young goat – **kid**; **yeanling**
Of, relating to or suggestive of a goat, esp. in terms of the smell - **hircine**

God:
The study of the question of God and the relation of God to the real world – **theology**
A belief in the existence of a god or gods; a belief in one god as creater and ruler of the universe - **theism**
Belief in the existence of God as the creator of the universe who after setting in motion abandoned it, assumed no control over life or natural phenomena, and gave no supernatural revelation - **deism**
A religious ecstacy in which the devotee believes that he is a god or is inspired - **theomania**
Representation of something or someone in the form of a god; the condition of being formed in the image of God - **theomorphism**
Denial of the existence of God; the quality or state of being godless – **atheism**, n. **atheist**
The doctrine that neither the existence nor the nature of God is known or knowable – **agnosticism**, n. **agnostic**
The worship of a particular god, without denying the existence of others – **henotheism**; **monolatry**

A local deity; a presiding spirit – **numen**, pl. **numina**

Ascription of supreme divine attributes to whichever one of several gods is addressed at the time - **henotheism**

The doctrine of or belief in only one god - **monotheism**

The doctrine of or belief in two gods - **ditheism**

A belief in three gods; a Christian doctrine holding that the Trinity consists of three distinct gods – **tritheism**

A belief in or worship of more than one god or in many gods – **polytheism**

Belief in and worship of all gods – **pantheism**

The identification of a god or gods with matter - **hylotheism**

The belief that God is the focal point of thoughts, feelings, etc. – **theocentrism**; **theocentricism**; **theocentricity**; adj. **theocentric**

A mingling of religious forms and deities - **theocrasy**

The attributing of human characteristics to the gods - **theanthropism**

Both divine and human in nature or quality – **theanthropic**; **theanthropical**

A manifestation or appearance of a god to a person - **theophany**

The attribution of animal form or nature to a deity - **zoomorphism**

Making a god of a person – **apotheosis**; **deification**

The killing of a god; a killer of a god - **deicide**

The origin of the gods; a genealogical account of the origin of the gods - **theogony**

Rule by a god – **thearchy**; **theocracy** (see also Government)

Relating to the gods and spirits of the underworld - **chthonic**

A delusional mental illness in which a person believes he is God or specially chosen by God – **theomania**

Of or worthy of the gods – **ambrosial**; **ambrosian**; **divine**

A battle with or among gods - **theomachy**

The sacramental eating of a god (e.g. in the form of an animal, image or other symbol) as a part of a religious ritual – **theophagy**, adj. **theophagous, theophagic**

Gold:

Of, relating to, derived from or containing gold – **auric**; **aurous**

Bearing gold – **auriferous**

Resembling gold – **gilt**

Gold in powder form – **gold dust**

An artisan who creates objects of gold – **goldsmith**

Adorned with gold – **clinquant**

Made of gold and ivory – **chryselephantine**

The treatment of disease using gold compounds – **chrysotherapy**

To release (gold) from an inactive status and return it to use as a backing for credit and new currency – **desterilize** (v.t.)

Good:

The supreme or highest good – **summum bonum**

Goose:

A group of geese – **flock**; **gaggle** (on water); **skein** (in flight)

A male goose – **gander**

A female goose – **goose**

A young goose – **gosling**

Of or like a goose - **anserine**

Gossip:

A spreader of gossip - **gossipmonger**; **gossiper**

Gossips as a group – **gossipry**

Government by:
 The people, through elected representatives – **democracy**, adj. **democratic**
  To make democratic – **democratize** (v.t.)
 The people directly (not through representatives) - **democracy**; **pure democracy**
 The numeric majority – **arithmocracy**
 Bureaus staffed with nonelective officials – **bureaucracy**, n. **bureaucrat**
  To bring under bureaucratic influence – **bureaucratize** (v.t.)
  A style of language used by bureaucrats, marked by euphemism and jargon - **bureaucratese**
 An elite composed of talented achievers – **meritocracy**
 Scientific technicians - **technocracy**
 The military - **stratocracy**
 A single person having unlimited power – **absolutism**; **autocracy**; **despotism**; **dictatorship**; **monocracy**
  Such a ruler – **autocrat**; **despot**; **dictator**
  One who favors monocracy - **monocrat**
 The best, or the privileged or titled, class of persons – **aristocracy**, n. **aristocrat**
 The worst persons – **kakistocracy**
 Thieves - **kleptocracy**
 Women – **gynarchy**; **gynecocracy**
 Holy men, as priests or saints – **hagiarchy**; **hagiocracy**
 The clergy - **hierocracy**
 A few, esp. a small fraction of persons or families – **oligarchy**
  A member of such a government - **oligarch**
 A monarch (king, emperor, etc.) – **monarchy**
 Two joint rulers – **diarchy**; **dyarchy**
 Three leaders – **triumvirate**; **triarchy**; **troika**
  One such leader - **triumvir**
 Four rulers – **tetrarchy**; **quadrumvirate**
  One such ruler – **tetrarch**; **quadrumvir**
 Five rulers – **pentarchy**
 Seven rulers – **heptarchy**
 The wealthy – **plutocracy**, n. **plutocrat**
 The masses or a mob – **mobocracy**; **ochlocracy**
 Priests or officials claiming divine sanction, where a diety is recognized as the supreme civil ruler – **theocracy**, n. **theocrat**
 A group of elders - **gerontocracy**

Government, systems of:
 A monarchy in which the powers of the ruler are limited to those granted under the constitution and laws of the nation – **constitutional monarchy**
 A system of stringent political and socioeconomic control, intolerance of political opposition, and a strong, highly nationalistic central government – **fascism**, n. **fascist** or **Fascist**; **totalitarianism**, n. **totalitarian**
 A system in which power and administration are concentrated in a central group or institution – **centralism**, n. **centrist**
 A system in which a union of states recognizes the sovereignty of a central authority while retaining certain residual powers; a system in which sovereign power is divided between a central authority and a number of constituent political units - **federalism**, n. **federalist**
 A government in which all individuals have equal power - **isocracy**
 Absolute sovereignty; absolute or autocratic rule - **autarchy**
 A form of government in which love of honor is the dominant motive of the rulers, or in which a certain amount of property is a prerequisite for political office - **timocracy**
 A form of government in which the supreme power rests in the body of citizens entitled to vote and is exercised by representatives they elect directly or indirectly – **republicanism**

A supporter of government by a monarch – **monarchist; royalist**

A state in which the head of government is not a monarch or other hereditary head of state - **republic**

To make republican – **republicanize** (v.t.)

The principle of concentrating major political, economic and related controls in the state at the cost of individual liberty; the support of the sovereignty of the state - **statism**

Government in which power is distributed and limited by a system of laws that must be obeyed by the rulers; advocacy of such a system - **constitutionalism**

The system or principle of ownership and control of the means of production and distribution by the people collectively - **collectivism**

A philosophy, form or system of government dominated by a man or men - **patriarchalism**

A system of government in which trade and professional corporations are the basis of society – **corporate state**

A political philosophy advocating the freedom of the individual, parliamentary systems of government, nonviolent modification of political institutions and governmental guarantees of individual rights and civil liberties – **liberalism**

A theory or system of government in which communities are virtually autonomous and loosely bound in a federation – **communalism**, n. **communalist**

The rule of a family or tribe of men - **patriarchy**

Government – misc. terms:

The art or science of government – **political science; politics** (Note: *politics* is used with a singular verb except when it refers to intrigue or maneuvering within a group [*company politics*], or to one's general position or attitude on political subjects [*His politics are liberal*].).

The doctrine that sovereign power is vested in the people and that those elected to govern, as trustees of such power, must exercise it in conformity with the general will – **popular sovereignty**

The power or right of self-government; a self-governing community or state; the condition of being self-governing - **autonomy**

One who believes in or supports rule by hereditary right – **legitimist**

Supreme power or absolute dominion, esp. over a large area – **empire; imperium**, pl. **imperia** or **imperiums**

A government within a government – **imperium in imperio**

An edict announcing a change in government – **pronunciamento**, pl. **pronunciamentoes** or **pronunciamentos**

The doctrine that all types of government are oppressive and undesirable, and should be abolished; active resistance against the established government – **anarchism**

Absence of any political authority – **anarchy**, adj. **anarchic** or **anarchical**

A leader or advocate of anarchy – **anarch; anarchist**

To convert from private to governmental ownership and control – **nationalize** (v.t.)

To suspend or end a legislative session – **prorogue** (v.i.)

Composed of one legislative chamber – **unicameral**

Composed of two legislative chambers or branches – **bicameral**

A general assembly of all members, esp. of a legislative body – **plenum**

The vested power or right of one branch or department of government, esp. the right of a chief executive, to reject a bill that a legislative body has passed; exercise of this right; the official document communicating the rejection and the reasons for it – **veto** (n./v.t.)

Of, relating to, constituting or in the manner of a legislative or executive body that holds closed meetings – **star-chamber**

Predominance of the military in the administration or policy of a state – **militarism**

The art or practice of conducting international relations, as in negotiating alliances, treaties, etc. – **diplomacy**

One skilled in or working at diplomacy - **diplomat**

A diplomatic official of the highest rank appointed and accredited as representative in residence by one government to another; a diplomatic official heading a nation's permanent mission to an international organization – **ambassador**

A diplomatic agent, as an ambassador, authorized to represent a government - **plenipotentiary**

A person authorized to represent his government in diplomatic dealings with other governments (usu. ranking next below an ambassador) – **minister**

One who holds high office – **Pooh-Bah**

Two people associated in high office or position – **diumvirate**

An officer of the armed forces who is assigned to the official staff of an ambassador, consul general, or minister to a foreign country – **military attaché**

A body of persons appointed by a chief of state or a prime minister to head the executive departments of the government and to act as his official advisers - **cabinet**

Support of or adherence to the principle of rule by a monarch – **monarchism**; **royalism**

The doctrine that the state exists for the individual rather than vice versa – **individualism**

The original covenant by which, according to certain philosophers of modern times, individuals have united and formed the state – **social contract**

A sudden attempt by a group to overthrow a government – **putsch**

A sudden overthrow of a government in deliberate violation of constitutional provisions, esp. by a group of persons who already hold some governmental or military power – **coup**; **coup d'état**

A group of military officers holding state power in a country after a coup d'état – **junta**

Assignment of power and authority to a central leadership – **centralism**

An independent country that is very small in area and population – **microstate**; **ministate**

The policy of state direction and control in economic and social matters – **dirigisme**, adj. **dirigiste** or **dirigistic**

Absolute power, esp. when exercised unjustly or cruelly – **tyranny**, adj. **tyrannic** or **tyrannical** or **tyrannous**, v.i./v.t. **tyrannize**, n. **tyrant**

A subordinate ruler or official; a petty tyrant – **satrap**

The territory or sphere under the rule of a satrap – **satrapy**

Supremacy of authority or rule as exercised by a sovereign or a sovereign state; total independence and self-government; a territory existing as an independent state - **sovereignty**

Of or relating to the affairs of a zone under the joint administration of two powers – **bizonal**

A territory that is considered necessary for the existence or the economic self-sufficiency of a nation - **lebensraum**

A policy of moderation – **moderantism**, n. **moderantist**

A political philosophy of avoiding extremes by taking a midway position – **centrism**

Governor, of or relating to a – **gubernatorial**

Graft/Grafting:

A surgical graft of skin from one part of the body to another or from one individual to another – **skin graft**

Tissue taken from one species and grafted onto another - **heterograft**

Derived from a different species, as a tissue graft – **heterologous**

The surgical grafting of tissue obtained from another person or from a lower animal – **heteroplasty**

Surgical transfer of tissue from a lower animal to man – **zooplasty**

A graft of tissue obtained from a member of the same species as the individual receiving it - **homograft**

Surgical repair or replacement with tissue taken from the same body as that on which the surgery is performed - **autoplasty**

Grain:

Ground grain – **grist**

A storage building for threshed grain – **granary**

To spread (grain) on a frame or floor to germinate, as in malting – **couch** (v.t.)

Resembling or consisting of grain – **frumentaceous**

Grainy in texture; composed or appearing to be composed of grains or granules – **granular**

To form into grains or granules – **granulate** (v.t./v.i.), n. **granulation**

A fee paid for grinding grain at a mill – **multure**

Feeding on grain – **graminivorous**; **granivorous**

Grammar (see also Word):

A specialist in grammar – **grammarian**

Omission of conjunctions from constructions in which they would normally be used – **asyndeton**

The shortening of a word by the omission of a sound, letter or syllable from the middle of a word - **syncope**

A construction in which a form differs in number but agrees in meaning with the word governing it - **synesis**

The way in which words are assembled to form phrases and sentences – **syntax**, adj.
syntactic or **syntactical**

The placing together of phrases, clauses or sentences without coordinating elements such as conjunctions –
parataxis, adj. **paratactic** or **paratactical**

Dependent relation or construction, as of clauses; syntactic subordination – **hypotaxis**

Denoting the first of two third persons referred to in a context – **proximate**

A violation of conventional grammatical construction – **solecism**

Marked by incomplete grammatical construction – **pendant**; **pendent**

Lacking grammatical inflections – **indeclinable**

Grant:

One who makes a grant – **grantor**

One to whom a grant is made – **grantee**

The revoking of a grant – **ademption**

Something, as a land tract, granted esp. by a government to be used for a specific purpose – **concession**

A grant made by a sovereign or legislative body for the support of dependent members of the royal family; to provide
or endow with such a grant – **apanage**; **appanage** (both n./v.t.)

The granting of financial aid; financial aid granted to an individual or organization; a subsidy from a government or
foundation; to provide with such aid or support – **subvention** (n./v.t.)

The return of an estate to the grantor or to his estate after the grant has expired – **reversion**, adj. **reversionary**

One entitled to receive an estate in reversion – **reversioner**

The technique of obtaining grants-in-aid – **grantsmanship**

Granule (small grain or pellet):

To form into granules; to become granular – **granulate** (v.t./v.i.)

The act or process of granulating; the state of being granulated – **granulation**

Covered with granules – **granulose**

Grape:

The cultivation of grapes – **viniculture**; **viticulture**

Ground planted with cultivated grapevines - **vineyard**

The yield of grapes from a particular vineyard or district during one season; the harvesting of a grape crop; of or
relating to such a yield – **vintage**

One who cultivates and prunes grapevines – **vinedresser**; **viticulturist**

Partially fermented grape juice – **must**; **stum**

Shaped like a cluster of grapes – **aciniform**; **botryoid**; **botryoidal**

Graphic Arts:

The study and science of systems of graphic script - **grammatology**

A projection in which the three spatial axes are equally inclined to the drawing surface and equal distances along the
axes are drawn equal – **isometric projection**

A projection in which the projecting lines are perpendicular to the plane of projection – **orthogonal projection**;
orthographic projection

A form of perspective in which parallel lines converge so as to give the illusion of depth and distance – **linear
perspective**

A figure formed by shading in the outline of the shadow cast by an object – **skiagram**

Projection or depiction of shadows; the making of skiagrams – **skiagraphy**

The rendering of an object on a perspective plane – **scenography**

Representation of the forms of solid bodies on a plane surface – **stereography**

Representation of an object at least as large as the object – **macrograph**

A technique of painting or drawing using light and shade to achieve a three-dimensional effect – **chiaroscuro**; **chiarooscuro**

The area between the foreground and the background in a painting, drawing or photograph – **middle distance**

A painting done in different shades of one color; the technique of producing such paintings – **monochrome**, n. **monochromist**

The application of thick layers of pigment to a surface in a painting – **impasto**

A style of painting that creates an illusion of photographic reality – **trompe l'oeil**

Painting on dry plaster – **secco**

The art of painting on fresh, moist plaster with earth colors dissolved in water; a painting executed in this way – **fresco**

Brightly colored and simply designed graphic shapes of billboard proportions – **supergraphics**

A ratio between two portions of a line, or the two dimensions of a plane figure, in which the lesser of the two is to the greater as the greater is to the sum of both, a ratio of approximately .618 to one – **golden mean**; **golden section**

Grasping:

Adapted for grasping, seizing or holding – **prehensile** (Zool.); **prehensive**

Grass:

Of, relating to or characteristic of grasses – **gramineous**

A treatise on grasses – **agrostography**

Feeding on grasses - **graminivorous**

The grass or other vegetation eaten by grazing animals; land covered with grass or other vegetation suitable for grazing animals; the right to graze animals on such land; the business of grazing cattle – **pasturage**

Land suitable for grazing – **pasture land**

A clump of grass – **tuffet**

A second growth of grass appearing on a mown or grazed field – **fog**

Grasshoppers, a group of – **cluster**

Grateful:

The state of being grateful – **gratitude**

An ungrateful person – **ingrate**

Grave (see also Death; Treatment of the Dead and their Remains):

To bury in a grave – **inhume**; **inter** (both v.t.)

To remove from a grave – **disinter**; **exhume** (both v.t.)

A marking stone at the foot of a grave – **footstone**

A marking stone at the head of a grave – **headstone**

A slab of stone laid flat over a grave - **ledger**

One who steals corpses or breaks open a grave to obtain interred valuables – **body snatcher**; **ghoul**; **grave robber**; **resurrectionist**; **resurrection man**

A grave mound – **barrow**; **tumulus**

Gravity:

Movement of an organism in response to gravity – **geolaxis**; **geotropism**

A tendency to grow or move away from the pull of gravity - **apogeotropism**

The tendency of growing parts to become oriented at right angles to the direction of gravitational force – **diageotropism** (Bot.)

The tendency of an organism to be influenced in growth by gravitation so that one side or lateral organ balances another – **geomalism**

Of or relating to the center of gravity – **centrobaric**

Of or relating to a condition of no gravitation – **agravic**

Experiencing little or no gravitational force – **weightless**

Gray:

To make or become gray – **grizzle** (v.t./v.i.)

Grizzled or mottled with gray – **griseous**

Greece/Greek:

One who admires Greece or the Greeks – **philhellene; philhellenist**

A student or admirer of Greek culture – **Hellenist**

Adoption of Greek style, ideas, culture, etc.; the culture of ancient Greece – **Hellenism**

Of or relating to the ancient Greeks or their language – **Hellenic**

To adopt Greek or Hellenistic speech and ways; to make Greek or Hellenistic – **Grecize** (v.t.); **Hellenize** (v.i./v.t.)

A Greek idiom – **Grecism; Hellenism**

The style or spirit of Greek culture; something imitative of Greek style or spirit – **Grecism**

The idea or advocacy of a union of all Greeks in one political body – **Panhellenism**, adj. **Panhellenic**

The collection and compiling of extracts from ancient Greek philosophers to which editorial comments are added – **doxography**

Green:

Becoming green – **virescent**, n. **virescence**

Slightly green – **viridescent**

The abnormal development of a green coloration in plant parts normally not green – **virescence**

Green with vegetation; covered with a green growth – **verdant; virid**

The fresh, vibrant greenness of flourishing vegetation; such vegetation itself – **verdure**

Grinding, capable of – **molar**

Gritty or sandy – **sabulous; sabulose**, n. **sabulosity**

Groin:

Of, relating to or situated in the groin - **inguinal**

Groove:

Having grooves or channels – **canaliculate**

A shallow groove, depression or furrow – **vallecula**

A thin, narrow groove or channel – **stria**, pl. **striae**, adj. **striated**

Marked with fine, close-set grooves or streaks – **strigose**

A narrow, deep groove or furrow - **sulcus**

Having narrow longitudinal indentations – **sulcate** (Biol.)

A decorative motif consisting of a series of long, rounded, parallel grooves; the grooves formed by narrow pleats in a cloth; the act of making grooves – **fluting**

A groove or notch made by a cutting tool; the width of such a groove – **kerf**

Grotesque:

The state of being grotesque; something grotesque – **grotesquerie; grotesquery**

Ground:
    Living on or in the ground – **terrestrial**; **terricolous**
    An organism living on or close to the ground – **groundling**
    Living or occurring on or near the surface of the ground – **epigeal**; **epigean**; **epigeous**
    To chase into an underground hiding place; to hide or burrow in the ground – **earth** (v.t./v.i.)

Group:
    A large group of moving things – **armada**
    A small group of persons who have similar interests and associate frequently – **coterie**

Grouse, a group of – **covey** (family); **pack** (larger groups)

Growth (see also Biology: Growing/Living Conditions):
    Of, relating to or capable of growth – **vegetative**
    Less than normal growth – **hypotrophy**
    Showing fresh growth or vigor – **renascent**
    Growing rapidly – **fungoid**
    To grow or spread abnormally – **vegetate** (v.i.) (Pathol.)
    Continued or continuous growth - **accrescence**
    A nontumorous increase in the size of an organ or part without increase in the number of constituent cells; to grow or cause to grow abnormally large – **hypertrophy** (n./v.i./v.t.), adj. **hypertrophic**
    Growing out or forming an outgrowth, esp. an abnormal, excessive or useless one – **excrescent**, n. **excrescence**, adj. **excrescential**
    To grow with an irregular elliptical or spiral motion – **circumnutate** (v.i.) (Bot.)
    Growth or increase in size by gradual external addition, fusion or inclusion; something added externally to promote such growth or increase; growing together of plant or animal tissues that are normally separate – **accretion**
    Incomplete or arrested development of an organ or part – **hypoplasia**, adj. **hypoplastic**
    Designating a growth or lesion about one-eighth inch in diameter – **miliary**
    A period during which growth or development is suspended – **diapause**

Guard:
    A mounted guard stationed in advance of an outpost – **vedette**; **vidette**
    Being or serving as a guard or protector; one having such power – **tutelary**; **tutelor**

Guilt:
    To extinguish the guilt incurred by – **expiate** (v.t.), n. **expiation**

Gulls, a group of – **colony**

Gums (body part):
    Of or relating to the gums – **gingival**
    Inflammation of the gums – **gingivitis**

Guns – see Firearms

Gypsy (tzigane):
    A male gypsy - **rye**
    Of or relating to gypsies; of the kind or style used or made by gypsies - **tzigane**

H

Half:
  Consisting of only one half of the normal – **dimidiate**

Hair:
  A head of hair - **chevelure**
  Like hair – **trichoid**
  Of or relating to hair - **pilar**
  A hairlike structure – **pilus**
  A hairlike outgrowth - **trichome**
  Covered with hair – **hirsute**; **pilar**
  A heavy growth of hair – **hirsutism**
  Baldness or loss of hair, congenital or acquired – **alopecia**; **atrichia**; **atrichosis**
  Having no hair – **glabrous**; **levigate** (Bot.)
  Covered with dense, soft, silky hair – **velutinous**; **velvety**
  Covered with fine, soft hairs – **downy**; **lanuginose**; **lanuginous**; **pilose**; **puberulent**; **puberulous**; **pubescent**; **sericeous**
  Covered with or made up of thin, soft, entangled hairs – **arachnoid**
  Having wooly hairs – **lanate**; **laniferous**; **ulotrichous**
  Having tufted hairs resembling a beard – **barbate** (Bot.)
  Covered with bristly hairs – **hispid**
  A bristling of body hair, as from fear or cold – **gooseflesh**; **horripilation**
    To produce horripilation – **horripilate** (v.i.)
  Having minute, hooked hairs – **barbellate**
  Having wiry hairs – **ulotrichous**
  A barbed hair on a plant – **glochid**; **glochidium**; adj. **glochidiate**
  A stiff hair or hairlike projection, as a cat's whisker – **seta**, pl. **setae**; **vibrissa**, pl. **vibrissae**
  Having stiff, closely-pressed hairs – **strigose** (Bot.)
  A tuft of hairs – **coma** (Bot.); **tussock**
  Having hairlike tufts – **crinite**
  Having or resembling a tuft of hairs – **comate**; **comose**; **penicillate**
  A dense, brushlike tuft of hairs – **scopula**, pl. **scopulae**, adj. **scopulate**
  A fine, hairlike epidermal growth (Bot.) – **villosity**; **villus**, pl. **villi**
    Having the form or appearance of a villus or villi – **villiform**
  Covered with fine, unmatted hairs – **villose**; **villous** (both Bot.)
  Fine, soft hair, esp. that covering the fetus of certain mammals – **lanugo**
  A microscopic hairlike process extending from a cell surface – **cilium**, pl. **cilia**
    Having cilia - **ciliate**
    Having minute cilia – **ciliolate**
  A condition of ingrowing hairs around an orifice – **trichiasis**
  A lock of hair growing or falling on the forehead – **forelock**
  Having wavy hair – **cymotrichous**
  A roll or knot of hair worn at the back of the head or nape of the neck – **chignon**
  A covering of closely matted woolly hairs – **tomentum**, adj. **tomentose**
  A matted and encrusted state of the hair – **plica**, pl. **plicae**
  Hair that has formed long matted clumps due to lack of washing and combing – **dreadlocks**
  A woman's long hair, esp. when unbound – **tresses**
  To remove hair from – **depilate** (v.t.)
  A cream or liquid used to remove unwanted body hair – **depilatory**
  A person skilled in the use of electrolysis for removing unwanted hair – **electrologist**

A female hairdresser – **coiffeur**
Any disease of the hair – **trichosis**
Chronic inflammation of the hair follicles, esp. of the beard and scalp – **sycosis**
An abnormal desire to pull out one's own hair – **trichotillomania**
The study of hair and its diseases – **trichology**, n. **trichologist**

Hallucination:
A drug inducing hallucination – **hallucinogen**
An abnormal condition or mental state marked by hallucinations - **hallucinosis**
Of or relating to hallucinations – **psychedelic**

Halo – see Light

Hammer:
Capable of being hammered thin – **ductile**
Capable of being hammered or pounded into various shapes without breaking or returning to its original shape – **malleable**
Formed by hammering, stamping or pressing – **incuse** (used of designs of coins and medals)

Hand:
Of, relating to, done by, operated with or used by the hands - **manual**
To make by hand – **handcraft** (v.t.), n. **handcraftman**; **handcraftsman**
Able to use both hands with equal facility; unusually dexterous – **ambidextrous**, n. **ambidexterity**
To control or operate by skilled use of the hands – **handle**; **manipulate** (both v.t.)
Medical therapy that emphasizes manipulative techniques for correcting bodily abnormalities thought to cause disease and inhibit recovery – **osteopathy**
Plastic surgery of the hand – **cheiroplasty**; **chiroplasty**
Having the palm upward – **supine**
To turn and place (the hand and forearm) so that the palm is upward; to assume a position with the palm and forearm upward – **supinate** (v.t./v.i.)
To turn (the inner surface of the hand or forelimb) downward or backward – **pronate** (v.t.)
Using or requiring the use of both hands – **bimanual**
Having hands made calloused or hard by work – **hard-handed**
Of or relating to the palm of the hand – **volar**; **palmar**
Resembling a hand with the fingers extended – **palmate**
A handcuff, fetter or shackle for the hand – **manacle** (n./v.t.)
To feel around with the hands – **grabble** (v.i.); **grope** (v.i./v.t.)
The art or practice of telling one's character, future, etc., by the lines, marks and patterns on the palms of the hands – **cheiromancy**; **chiromancy**; **palmistry**, n. **palmist**
The edge of the palm below the fourth finger (used chiefly by palmists) – **percussion**
Manual dexterity in the execution of tricks - **legerdemain**; **prestidigitation** (n. **prestidigitator**); **sleight of hand**
A hand gesture for conveying a command or message – **sign manual**, pl. **signs manual**

Handicraft, one who is skilled in – **handicraftsman**

Handle:
Having a handle or handlelike part – **ansate**
The handle of a tool – **haft**; **helve**
The handle of a weapon; to fit into or provide with such a handle – **haft** (n.v.t.)

Handwriting – see Writing

Hanging:
Hanging downward; drooping – **cernous** (Bot.)
Hanging down loosely – **pensile**
One employed to execute condemned prisoners by hanging - **hangman**

Happiness:
Producing or tending to produce happiness – **felicific**
A state of freedom from anxiety and emotional disturbance – **ataraxia**, adj. **ataraxic**
The theory or art of happiness – **eudaemonics**; **eudemonics**
A doctrine or system of ethics that evaluates the morality of actions in terms of their ability to produce happiness –
    eudaemonism, eudemonism, n. **eudemonist**
A feeling of elation or well-being – **euphoria**, adj. **euphoric**

Harbor:
One who oversees and enforces the regulations of a harbor – **harbormaster**

Hard:
Very hard; made of an extremely hard substance – **adamantine**
Emotionally hardened; to make or become emotionally hardened – **callous** (adj./v.t./v.i.)
To make hard or callous; to harden – **indurate** (v.t./v.i.)
Firm but easily sliced (as cheese) – **semisoft**
An abnormally hard patch of bodily tissue – **scleroma**
A hardening or thickening of a body part – **sclerosis**, adj. **sclerotic**

Hare:
A male hare – **buck**
A female hare – **doe**
A young hare – **leveret**
A group of hares – **drove**; **trace**
The fur of a hare – **rabbit**
To hunt hares – **rabbit** (v.i.)

Harem:
A female slave or concubine in a harem – **odalisk; odalisque**;

Harmful:
Neither harmful nor helpful – **adiaphorous**

Harvest:
The completion of a harvest; the time of completing a harvest – **harvest home**

Hat:
One whose occupation is the manufacture, selling or repair of hats – **hatter**
Plaited straw, grass or palm leaves for making hats – **sennit**

Hawk:
A male hawk used in falconry – **tercel; tiercel**
A young hawk – **eyas**
Two hawks – **cast** (of hawks)
A group of hawks – **flight**

A cage for hawks, esp. while molting; to put or keep (a hawk) in a cage, esp. when molting; to molt (used of a hawk) – **mew** (n./v.t./v.i.)

Hay (plants that are cut and dried for fodder):
To mow and cure herbage for hay; to make into or feed with hay – **hay** (v.i./v.t.)
One who hays – **haymaker**
An elongated stack or pile of hay, straw or similar material, esp. when covered or thatched for protection from the weather; to heap up (hay, e.g.) thus – **rick** (n./v.t.)
A long row of cut hay or grain left to dry in a field before being bundled – **windrow**

Hazard:
A biological material, esp. if infective in nature, that constitutes a threat to man or his environment – **biohazard**

Head (body part):
Of or relating to the head or skull; located on, in or near the head – **cephalic**
Or or relating to the side of the head – **malar**
Toward the head or anterior section – **cephalad**
Located on or near the front of the head - **procephalic**
The top of the head - **vertex**
Lacking a defined head – **acephalous**
Having two heads – **bicephalous**; **dicephalous**
Abnormal smallness of the head – **microcephaly**, adj. **microcephalic**
A condition in which the head or cranial capacity is abnormally large – **macrocephaly**, adj. **microcephalic**
A congenital abnormality in which the skull assumes a conical shape – **acrocephalia**; **acrocephaly**; **oxycephaly**
An involuntary nodding of the head – **nutation**, adj. **nutational**, v.i. **nutate**
The ratio of the maximum width of the head to its maximum length – **cephalic index**
Having a cephalic index of 75.9 or less – **dolichocephalic** (n. **dolichocephalism** or **dolichocephaly**); **dolichocephalous**; **dolichocranial**; **dolichocranic** (n. **dolichocrany**); **long-headed**; **longheaded**
Having a short, almost round head, the width of which is at least 80 percent as great as the length – **brachycephalic**; **brachycephalous**; n. **brachycephaly**; **brachcephalism**
A head-shaped part – **capitulum** (Anat.)
Forming a headlike mass – **capitate**
The science of measuring the dimensions of the human head – **cephalometry**
The act of shaving the crown of the head; the part of a priest's or monk's head that has been shaven – **tonsure**

Headache:
Severe, recurrent headache marked by sharp pain – **migraine**
A severe headache similar to migraine that can occur several times daily for a period of weeks - **cluster headache**
Pain in one side of the head – **hemicrania**
Pain affecting both sides of the head - **amphicrania**

Heal:
Having healing powers – **therapeutic**
Healing readily – **euplastic**
Used in the healing or treating of wounds; a remedy used in healing or treating wounds – **vulnerary**

Health (see also Disease):
Of or relating to health – **sanitary**
Free from elements that endanger health – **hygienic**; **sanitary**
To make sanitary – **sanitize** (v.t.)
The science of health and the prevention of disease – **hygiene**; **hygienics**; adj. **hygienic**

The pulse rate, temperature and respiratory rate of an individual – **vital signs**

The science that deals with developing human well-being and efficient functioning through the improvement of environmental conditions - **euthenics**

Gradually restoring to health; something that gradually restores health – **alterative**

The condition of being overly concerned with one's health – **valetudinarianism**

A condition of prolonged ill health – **invalidism**

Hearing:

Capable of being heard – **audible**

Of or relating to hearing – **auditory**

Of or relating to the sense or organs of hearing; perceived by or spoken into the ear - **auricular**

Capable of learning chiefly from auditory stimuli – **audile**

The science of hearing defects and their treatment – **audiology**

The sense or power of hearing – **audition**

Impaired hearing due to old age – **presbyacusia**; **presbycusis**

A sound in the ears, as buzzing, ringing or whistling – **tinnitus**

Testing of hearing ability by frequencies and various volume levels - **audiometry**

Heart (see also Pulse):

Of, relating to or near the heart – **cardiac**; **coronary**

The study of the diseases and functioning of the heart – **cardiology**

Of or relating to the lungs and the heart – **cardiopulmonary**

Of or relating to the heart and the blood vessels - **cardiovascular**

Inflammation of the heart – **carditis**

Inflammation of the heart muscle (myocardium) - **myocarditis**

Originating in the heart; caused by a disorder of the heart – **cardiogenic**

Relating to or located on or in the side of the body containing the heart – **hemal**

Within a heart chamber – **intracardiac**

Returning to the heart through the great veins – **venose**; **venous**

Enlargement of the heart – **cardiomegaly**; **megalocardia**

Having a tonic effect on the heart; a substance having such an effect – **cardiotonic**

A pain in the heart region – **cardiodynia**

The recording of electric potentials associated with the electric currents traversing the heart – **cardiography**; **electrocardiography**

Any disease or disorder of the heart - **cardiopathy**

Any disease of the heart muscle, leading to decreased function – **cardiomyopathy**

The restoration of proper heart rhythm by electrical shock – **cardioversion**

To beat more quickly than normal – **palpitate** (v.i.)

Excessively rapid heartbeat – **tachycardia**

A premature beat of one of the chambers of the heart – **extrasystole**

Any irregularity in the force or rhythm of the heartbeat – **arrhythmia**

Heart-shaped – **cordiform**

Having a heart-shaped outline – **cordate**

Heart-shaped, with the tapering end at the point of attachment – **obcordate** (Bot.)

Heat:

The unit of heat equal to the amount of heat needed to raise the temperature of one kilogram of water by one degree Centigrade at one atmospheric pressure - **calorie**

Of, relating to or generating calories – **calorific**

The measurement of the amount of heat evolved or absorbed in a chemical reaction, change of state, or formation of a solution – **calorimetry**

Of or relating to heat – **calorific**; **thermal**

Generating heat – **calorific**; **pyrogenic**; **pyrogenous**; **thermal**

Caused by heat – **pyrogenic**; **pyrogenous**; **thermal**

Utilizing heat; designed to retain body heat – **thermal**

Resistant to heat – **refractory**

Releasing heat – **exothermal**; **exothermic**

Growing warmer – **incalescent**

Moderately warm – **tepid**, n. **tepidity**

    To make or become tepid – **tepefy** (v.t./v.i.)

Intense heat – **fervor**

Extremely hot – **fervid**

The state of being white hot – **candescence**; **incandescence**

The chemistry of heat and heat-associated chemical phenomena – **thermochemistry**

Of or relating to microorganisms that can survive high temperatures – **thermoduric**

The physics of the interrelationships between heat and other energy forms – **thermodynamics**

Subject to destruction, decomposition or great change by moderate heating – **thermolabile**

Loss of heat from the body; decomposition of compounds by heat - **thermolysis**

An engine operated by heat – **thermomotor**

Requiring high temperatures for normal development – **thermophilic** (Biol.)

Permanently hardening or solidifying on being heated – **thermosetting**

To heat (a substance) to a high temperature but below its melting or fusing point, causing loss of moisture, reduction or oxidation – **calcine** (v.t.)

Unaffected by high temperatures – **thermostable**

Therapy by heat – **thermotherapy**

Therapy involving the production of heat in the body by electric currents - **diathermy**

The use of heat produced by high-frequency currents to bring about the localized destruction of bodily tissue – **thermocoagulation**

To heat and then cool slowly to prevent brittleness – **anneal** (v.t.)

The quantity of heat required to raise the temperature of one pound of water by one degree Fahrenheit – **British Thermal Unit (BTU)**

Marked by or causing the absorption of heat – **endothermic**

The quality of being impervious to heat waves – **adiathermancy**

Heat transfer by horizontal currents of air – **advection**

Heat transfer by fluid motion between regions of unequal density – **convection**

A sensory receptor that detects heat – **caloreceptor**

The production of heat, esp. in an animal body by physiological processes – **thermogenesis**, adj. **thermogenic** or **thermogenous**

Hebrew (see also Judaism):

    A scholar who studies Hebrew – **Hebraist**

    A custom or manner typical of the Hebrews; a linguistic feature typical of Hebrew occurring esp. in another language; the character, culture or spirit of the Hebrew people – **Hebraism**

    The Hebrew language as used in the learned writings of rabbis – **Rabbinic Hebrew**

    Of, relating to or typical of Hebrews or their language or culture – **Hebraic**; **Hebraical**

Height:

    The science of measuring altitudes, as by altimeters – **altimetry**

    Extreme or irrational fear of being at great heights – **acrophobia**

    Extreme or irrational fear of being near an object of great height, such as a skyscraper or mountain – **batophobia**

Heir – see Inherit

Hell:
> Of or relating to hell or a lower world of the dead – **infernal**
> A place or condition suggestive of hell – **inferno**

Helmet:
> A helmet-shaped part – **casque**; **galea**
> Having a galea – **galeate**; **galeated**
> Shaped like a helmet – **galeate**; **galeated**; **galeiform**

Hemp:
> Of, relating to or like hemp – **hempen**

Heraldry:
> A person entitled to heraldic arms – **armiger**
> Of or relating to heraldry or heraldic arms; a treatise or book on heraldry – **armorial**
> A figure or device on a coat of arms – **bearing**; **charge**; **heraldic achievement**
> A simple or common charge, as the bend and cross – **ordinary**
> To paint or depict (a coat of arms) with accurate heraldic detail – **blazon** (v.t.)
> The art of accurately describing or representing armorial bearings – **blazonry**
> A shield or shield-shaped emblem bearing a coat of arms – **escutcheon**, adj. **escutcheoned**
> Any of the four sections of an escutcheon – **quarter**
> The inner border of an escutcheon – **orle**
> A wide vertical band in the center of an escutcheon - **pale**
> A boss or knob at the center of an escutcheon – **umbo**
> A figure borne above the escutcheon – **crest**
> Any of the colors, metals or furs used for the fields, charges, etc., of an escutcheon - **tincture**
> A wreath of twisted silks of two alternating tinctures depicted supporting a crest or coronet - **torse**
> A border around a heraldic shield - **bordure**
> Indented at the edge with small concave curves, as on a heraldic bordure or ordinary – **engrailed**
> A self-created coat of arms – **arms of assumption**
> The base on which the shield and accessories stand – **compartment**
> A stylized representation of a four-petaled flower or a four-lobed leaf - **quatrefoil**
> Located on the wearer's right and the observer's left – **dexter**
> Located on the wearer's left and the observer's right – **sinister**
> Symbols showing a family's status (cadency) – **marks of cadency**
> The heraldic color red – **gules** (sing./pl.)
> Sitting – **sejant**
> A heraldic representation of fur – **vair**
> Having a pattern ornamented with small figures, e.g., stars or flowers – **semé**
> A panel bearing the coat of arms of a deceased person – **hatchment**
> Animals depicted on coats of arms:
>> Rearing on the left hind leg with the forelegs elevated, the right above the left – **rampant**
>> With the face turned backward – **regardant**; **reguardant**
>> Facing and walking toward the viewer's right with the further forepaw raised – **passant**
>> Shown in full face, turned toward the viewer – **gardant**; **guardant**
>> Lying down with the head raised – **couchant**
>> With the tips of the head or limbs cut off – **couped**
>> Without feet, used as a crest or bearing – **martlet** (used of a bird)
>> With only the wings extended, as in flying – **volant**
>> A bearing resembling a giraffe but represented with long curved horns – **camelopard**
>> A two-legged dragon having wings and a barbed and knotted tail – **wivern**; **wyvern**

A creature with the head, wings and legs of a rooster and the tail of a serpent - **cockatrice**

Herb:
Relating to or typical of an herb as distinguished from a woody plant – **herbaceous**
A book about herbs and plants, esp. those useful to humans – **herbal**
One who grows, collects, or specializes in the use of herbs, esp. medicinal herbs – **herbalist**

Heredity:
The biology of heredity, esp. the mechanisms of hereditary transmission and variation of characteristics – **genetics** (q.v.)
The study of heredity by cytological and genetic methods – **cytogenetics**
One who advocates the theory that heredity rather than environment determines personality – **hereditist**
The study of hereditary improvement by genetic control – **eugenics**
Causing or relating to the deterioration of hereditary qualities – **dysgenic**

Heresy:
Of or relating to heresy or heretics – **heretical**
A treatise on heresy – **heresiography**
An active opponent of heresy and heretics – **heresimach**
A writer against heresies – **heresiologist**
An originator or chief advocate of a heresy; a leader of a group of heretics – **heresiarch**
To pronounce or denounce as heretical; to denounce as a heretic – **hereticate** (v.t.), n. **hereticator**

Hermit (see also Alone):
The habitation of a hermit; the condition or way of life of a hermit – **hermitage**

Herons, a group of – **siege**

Herrings, a group of – **army**; **glean**; **shoal**

Hide (of an animal):
The tanned or dressed hide of an animal; an article or part consisting of such – **leather** (q.v.)
The untanned hide of a small or young animal; a set or bundle of such hides – **kip**
A hide with the hair and fur still attached; a stripped animal skin ready for tanning – **pelt**
    Undressed pelts – **peltry**
Having unusually dry, stiff skin or hide that adheres closely to the underlying flesh – **hidebound**
The rough hide of a shark or ray – **shagreen**

Highway:
The dividing area between opposing lanes of traffic – **median strip**

Hill:
A hillside shelter - **abri**
Having many small hills or mounds – **tumulose**; **tumulous**

Hip (body part):
A pain or disease of the hip – **coxalgia**
Inflammation of the hip joint – **coxitis**

History:
> The study or knowledge of history - **historiology**
> The writing of history; the principles or methodology of historical study – **historiography**
> The history of mankind in the period before written historical records – **prehistory**
> The study of a culture just prior to its earliest recorded history – **protohistory**
> An expert in the history, literature, etc., of the Middle Ages; a connoisseur of medieval culture – **medievalist**

Hogs, a group of – **drift**

Hold:
> To hold oneself back – **forbear**; **refrain** (both v.i.)
>> To refrain from something voluntarily – **abstain** (v.i.), n. **abstention**
> The fact or condition of holding something, as real estate or an office; the terms under which something is held; the period of holding something – **tenure**
>> Having academic tenure – **tenured**

Hole:
> To pierce or stamp with rows of holes, to allow an easy separation – **perforate** (v.t.)
> Having a hole or series of holes – **perforate**; **perforated**; **pervious**; **pierced**
> Pierced with small holes like a sieve – **cribriform**
> Lacking perforations; having no hole or opening – **imperforate**; **unperforated**
> A hole in a cask, keg or barrel through which liquid is poured in or drained out – **bunghole**

Holiday, of or relating to a – **ferial**

Home/House/Dwelling:
> The construction of a house or its framework by a group of neighbors – **house-raising**
> One who lives in and cares for a house while the occupant is away – **house sitter**, v.i. **housesit**
> Confined to the house – **housebound**
> A dwelling with its outbuildings and adjoining lands – **messuage** (Law)
> A temporary or secondary dwelling – **pied-à-terre**, pl. **pieds-à-terre**
> An overcrowded dwelling place – **warren**
> The act of unlawfully breaking into the home of another – **housebreaking**

Homosexuality – see Sexuality, human

Honey:
> Forming or bearing honey – **melliferous**
> Flowing with honey or sweetness – **mellifluent**; **mellifluous**
> Having, full of, or sweetened with honey – **honeyed**; **honied**

Honor:
> One who receives an honor – **honoree**
> Conferring or showing honor – **honorific**

Hood:
> Shaped like a hood or cowl – **cowled**; **cucullate**; **cucullated**

Hoof (unguis):
> Having hoofs – **ungulate**
> Of, resembling or having a hoof – **ungual**

A divided or cleft hoof – **cloven hoof**

Hook, a part or process shaped like a – **uncus**, adj. **uncal**

Horn:
    Hornlike – **ceratoid**
    Having two horns or horn-shaped parts – **bicorn**
    Having horns that are shed annually, as certain deer – **caducicorn**
    Made of horn or a hornlike substance; of a texture resembling a horn – **corneous**
    Having horns or hornlike projections – **corniculate**; **cornute**; **cornuted**
    A protuberance of bone similar to a horn – **cornu**
    Shaped like a horn - **cornute**; **cornuted**
    A goat's horn overflowing with fruit, flowers and corn, signifying prosperity – **cornucopia**; **horn of plenty**
    Hornless – **muley** (used of cattle); **polled**
    An animal that no longer has its horns – **pollard**
    The blare of a horn – **tantivy**

Horse:
    A group of horses – **herd**; **stable**
    A herd of horses from which ranch hands select their mounts - **remuda**
    An uncastrated adult male horse – **stallion**; **studhorse**; **stud horse**
    A female horse – **mare**
        A mare kept for breeding – **broodmare**
        A group of mares – **stud**
    A young horse – **colt**; **foal**
        A group of colts – **rag**
    The hybrid offspring of a male horse and a female ass – **hinny**
    Equipment, as saddles and harnesses, for horses – **saddlery**; **tack**
    One who makes, repairs or sells equipment for horses – **saddler**
    One who shoes horses – **farrier**
    One who makes bits, spurs and metal mountings for bridles and saddles – **lorimer**; **loriner**
    The practice of eating horseflesh – **hippophagy**, n. **hippophagist**
    Lameness accompanied by spasmodic movements in the hind legs of a horse – **stringhalt**
    A gait between a walk and a run in speed, in which diagonal pairs of legs move forward together – **trot**
    A gait slower than a gallop but faster than a trot – **canter**
    A natural three-beat gait, faster than a canter but slower than a run – **gallop**
        At full gallop; full gallop – **tantivy**, pl. **tantivies** (adv./n.)
    A gait faster than a gallop – **run**
    A rapid gait in which each foot strikes the ground separately – **single-foot**
    Trained in all gaits or paces – **thoroughpaced**
    Trained in the walk, trot and canter – **three-gaited**
    A horse of pure breeding stock; bred of pure stock – **thoroughbred**
    A book registering the pedigrees of thoroughbred horses – **studbook**
    Having a pale coat with reddish-brown flecks – **flea-bitten**
    A horse with a golden or tan coat and a white or cream-colored mane and tail – **palomino**
    A horse having reddish hair mixed with white – **strawberry roan**
    A horse with irregular markings or spots – **paint**; **pinto**
    A horse bred or schooled for riding – **saddle horse**
    A horse given to swallowing quantities of air – **windsucker**
    A horse capable of good speed; a fast trotter or pacer – **spanker**
    A lover of horses – **hippophile**

The study of horses – **hippology**

The art and practice of riding a horse - **equitation**

The art, techniques or practice of expert horsemanship – **haute école**

Of or relating to horsemanship or horseback riding – **equestrian**

A horse or a figure like a horse behind which a hunter stalks game – **stalking-horse**

A woman skilled at horsemanship – **horsewoman**

One who takes charge of horses, as at an inn – **hostler**

A horse race with only one horse entered, won by the mere formality of walking the length of the track – **walkover**

The weight carried by a horse in a handicap race – **impost**

A racehorse that runs well on a wet or muddy track – **mudder**

The racehorses running in a group behind those that set the pace – **ruck**

To disable (a racehorse), esp. by drugging – **nobble** (v.t.)

Guidance of a horse through a series of complex maneuvers by slight movements of the hands, legs and weight – **dressage**

A half-turn to the right or left executed by a mounted horse; to ride a horse executing such a turn or turns – **caracole** (n./v.i.)

A dressage movement in which a horse trots in place with high action of the legs – **piaffer**
　To perform the piaffer – **piaffe** (v.i.)

A vertical leap with a backward kick of the hind legs at the height of the leap - **capriole**

A low leap (of a horse) in which all four feet leave the ground – **gambado**

The renting out of horses and carriages – **livery**

Hotel:

A manager or owner of a hotel or inn – **hotelier**

Hounds:

A group of hounds – **pack**

To hunt or track prey by means of the sense of smell – **scent** (v.i.) (used of hounds)

Hour:

Of an hour or hours – **horay**

Housewife (see also Wife):

The domestic function or duties of a housewife – **housewifery**

Of, relating to or suited to a housewife – **housewifely**

Howl:

To howl, wail or lament loudly – **ululate** (v.i.)

Human (see also Body):

Concern for human welfare – **humanitarianism**

Human beings as a group – **humanity**; **humankind**

Resembling a human being in appearance – **anthropoid**; **humanoid**

Of or relating to all of humanity – **panhuman**

Changing into human form – **anthropomorphosis**

The attributing of human shape to gods, animals, objects, etc. – **anthropomorphism**, v.t. **anthropomorphize**, adj. **anthropomorphic** or **anthropomorphous**

The attributing of human emotions or characteristics to something that is not human – **anthropomorphism** (v.t. **anthropomorphize**, adj. **anthropomorphic** or **anthropomorphous**); **anthropopathism**; **anthropopathy**; **pathetic fallacy**

The study of extinct manlike creatures more primitive than *Homo sapiens* – **paleoanthropology**, adj. **paleoanthropic**

Of or relating to members of the extant species of *Homo sapiens* as compared with other, now extinct species of Homo – **neanthropic**

Having human shape and appearance – **anthropomorphic**; **anthropomorphous**

To pass beyond (a human limit) – **transcend** (v.t.)

Hatred of humanity – **misanthropy**, adj. **misanthropic**

One who hates or distrusts humanity – **misanthrope**; **misanthropist**

The scientific study of the origins and the physical, social and cultural development of humans – **anthropology** (see also Culture, human)

Knowledge of the nature of man – **anthroposophy**

The study of the origin of humans – **anthropogenesis**; **anthropogeny**, adj. **anthropogenic**

Regarding the human being as the central fact orfinal aim of the universe; interpreting reality solely in terms of human values and experience – **anthropocentric**, n. **anthropocentrism**; **anthropism**

An incarnation or embodiment in human form – **avatar**

The worship of a human being as a god – **anthropolatry**

A doctrine or attitude that emphasizes the values, capacities and achievements of human beings – **humanism**

Hummingbirds, a group of – **charm**

Humor:

One who has a good sense of humor; a writer or performer who specializes in humor – **humorist**

A person who makes coarse jokes – **buffoon**

The practices of a buffoon – **buffoonery**

Witty or humorous writings or sayings; short, humorous tales – **facetiae**

Given to jokes and jesting; abounding in jokes; having the character of or containing a joke; sportively humorous – **jocose**; **jocular**; n. **jocosity**

Relating to or indulging in coarse, licentious humor – **ribald**

Ribald language or joking – **ribaldry**

Coarse humor with a satirical or serious purpose; cynical humor - **pantagruelism**

Hump, having a – **gibbous**

Hundred:

A hundred times as much – **centuple**; **hundredfold**

Relating to or divided into hundredths – **centesimal**

Hunting:

A man who hunts – **hunter**; **huntsman**

A woman who hunts – **hunter**; **huntress**

One who hunts game for food, ignoring the rules of the sport – **pothunter**

Of or relating to hunting – **cynegetic**

To unleash or free (a dog or hawk) to pursue game – **slip** (v.t.)

A big-game hunting guide – **shikari**

The hunting of game by stalking or ambushing – **still hunt**

Relating to or used in hunting; given to hunting for sport or livelihood – **venatic**; **venatical**

Animals that are hunted – **venery**

Husband:

The state or practice of having more than one husband at a time – **polyandry**, **polygamy**; adj. **polyandric**; **polyandrous**

Relating to the home territory of the husband's family or tribe – **patrilocal**

The state or practice of having one husband at a time – **monandry** (adj. **monandrous**); **monogamy**, adj. **monogamous**

Protected by a husband – **covert** (Law)

A husband who manages the household while his wife earns most or all of the family income – **househusband**

Hydrogen:

Of, having or relating to hydrogen – **hydric**

To combine with or subject to the action of hydrogen – **hydrogenate** (v.t.)

To remove hydrogen from – **dehydrogenate**; **dehydrogenize** (both v.t.)

Hyena:

Of or relating to a hyena – **hyaenic**; **hyenic**

Resembling a hyena – **hyaenic**; **hyenic**; **hyeniform**; **hyenoid**

Hymn – see Song

Hyphen:

To connect or divide (word elements or syllables) with a hyphen – **hyphenate** (v.t.)

Hypnosis:

Of or like hypnosis – **hypnoid**; **hypnoidal**

Therapy based on or using hypnosis – **hypnotherapy**

To put in a state of hypnosis – **hypnotize** (v.t.), n. **hypnotism**

Psychoanalytic treatment involving the use of hypnosis – **hypnoanalysis**

The process of inducing or entering a hypnotic state – **hypnogenesis**

Hysteria:

One suffering from hysteria – **hysteric**

Causing hysteria – **hysterogenic**

Resembling hysteria – **hysteroid**

I

Ice:

A sheet of ice - **glare**

Covered over or locked in by ice – **icebound**

An avalanche of ice – **icefall**

A large, level expanse of floating ice – **ice field**

A yellowish glare in the sky above an ice field – **iceblink**

A ridge or hill of ice in an ice field – **hammock**; **hummock**, adj. **hummocky**

A flat expanse of floating ice, smaller than an ice field – **floe**; **ice floe**

A belt or ledge of ice that forms along shorelines in polar regions – **ice foot**

A mass of floating ice broken away from a glacier – **iceberg** (q.v.)

The thawing of ice on the surface of a body of water – **ice-out**

A floating mass of compacted ice fragments – **ice pack**

A thin, glassy ice coating – **glaze**

The temperature at which pure water and ice are in equilibrium in a mixture at one atmosphere of pressure – **ice point**

Floating ice driven together into a single mass – **pack ice**

The breakup of ice in a river – **debacle**

The fusion of two blocks of ice by pressure – **regelation**

A large mass of ice broken off the main body of a glacier (q.v.) and remaining behind in a crevasse after glacial movement or melting – **sérac**

An extension of glacial ice into coastal waters that is in contact with the bottom near the shore but not toward the outer edge of the shelf – **shelf ice**

Iceberg:

To break up and lose a portion of itself – **calve** (v.i.) (used of an iceberg or glacier)

A small iceberg – **growler**

Idea:

An idea demonstrably true or assumed to be so – **theorem**

Total lack of ideas – **vacuity**

Pathological obsession with one idea – **monomania**, n. **monomaniac**, adj. **monomaniacal**

A body of ideas reflecting the social needs and aspirations of an individual or group – **ideology**, n. **ideologist** or **ideologue**

A fear or distrust of ideas or reason - **ideophobia**

Ideal:

An ideal place, state or situation – **Utopia**

The most remote ideal attainable – **Ultima Thule**

An ideal serving as a pattern – **archetype**; **exemplar**

An ideal figure – **eidolon**

Identity:

With one's identity disguised or hidden – **incognito**, f. **incognita**

Identifying marks or signs – **indicia**

One who assumes the identity of another – **imposter**; **impostor**

The act or conduct of an impostor - **imposture**

Idol:

The worship of idols – **idolatry**

One who worships idols – **idolater**

Of, relating to, given to or constituting the worship of idols – **idolatric**; **idolatrical**; **idolatrous**
To worship as an idol – **idolatrize**; **idolize** (both v.t.)

Ill will, persistent and intense – **malignity**

Image/Icon:
   Of, relating to or like an icon – **iconic**
   An image regarded as an object of worship – **idol** (q.v.)
   The practice of destroying images, esp. religious images – **iconoclasm**, n. **iconoclast**, adj. **iconoclastic**
   The worship of sacred images or icons – **iconolatry**
   One who worships images or icons - **iconolater**
   The study of images or icons – **iconology**
   An image of an ideal – **eidolon**
   Opposition to the use of images or idols; the worship of objects symbolic of but not depicting a deity – **aniconism**
   An image cause by reflection - **reflex**
   Of, relating to or marked by extremely detailed and vivid recall of visual images – **eidetic**
   A distorted image that looks normal when viewed with a special device – **anamorphosis**
   An arrangement of images reduced in size, as on microfilm – **microform**

Imitation (mimicry):
   Of or relating to imitation – **imitative**; **mimetic**
   An imitator, esp. a second-rate follower of an artist or philosopher – **epigone**
   A grotesque imitation with intent to ridicule; a grotesque, debased, highly inferior imitation - **travesty**
   To ridicule by imitation – **mime** (v.t.)
   To strive to equal or excel, esp. by imitating – **emulate** (v.t.), adj. **emulous**

Immune/Immunity:
   To render immune – **immunize** (v.t.)
   The chemistry of immunologic phenomena – **immunochemistry**
   The medical study of immunity – **immunology**
   The study of the interrelation between immunity to disease and genetic make-up – **immunogenetics**
   Causing immunity – **immunogenic**
   Tending to suppress a natural immune response of an organism to an antigen – **immunosuppressive**
   Treatment of disease by immunosuppressive techniques – **immunotherapy**
   A long-lasting immunity to a disease due to antibody production – **active immunity**
   Immunity acquired by an individual after the transfer of antibodies through injection or by natural means (as by placental transfer to a fetus) – **passive immunity**

Impede:
   Objects, as baggage or provisions, that impede or encumber – **impedimenta**

Important (significant):
   Of supreme importance – **critical**; **crucial**
   Having little or no importance – **cosmetic**; **superficial**
   Not important – **insignificant**; **trivial**; **unimportant**
   Unimportant or superfluous matters – **minutiae** (sing. **minutia**); **trifles**; **trivia**
      To make trivial – **trivialize** (v.t.), n. **triviality**
      With attention to minutiae – **minutely**

Improvement/Melioration:
   To make or become better – **ameliorate**; **improve**; **meliorate** (all v.t./v.i.)

Something that ameliorates – **ameliorant**
The belief that society tends toward improvement and that human effort can further its improvement – **meliorism**
The study of hereditary improvement by genetic control – **eugenics**
An advocate of or specialist in eugenics – **eugenicist**; **eugenist**
The study of the improvement of human functioning and well-being by improvement of environment – **euthenics**

Improvise:
One who improvises – **improvisator**; **improviser**

Inability:
A statement indicating inability to do a particular thing – **non possumus**

Income:
One who owns rentes (government securities yielding income); one who receives a fixed income; one who lives on income from investments – **rentier**

India:
Of or relating to India, its people or their culture – **Indic**

Individuality:
To give individuality to – **individualize**; **individuate** (both v.t.), n. **individuation**

Infant (see also Child/Children):
The state or period of being an infant - **infancy**
Of or relating to infants or infancy – **infantile**

Infection:
The process of infection – **zymosis**
The development of an infection from the time of its entry into or initiation within an organism up to the time of the first appearance of signs or symptoms – **incubation**
Preventing or inhibiting infection; something that prevents or inhibits infection – **antiseptic**
Infection caused by germs or viruses persisting on or in the body - **autoinfection**
A secondary infection caused by a disease already present in the body – **autoinoculation**
Inhibiting of infection by the body – **phylaxis**

Infinite:
An infinite quantity, number or extent – **infinitude**

Information:
The scientific study of the gathering, manipulation, classification, storage and retrieval of recorded knowledge – **informatics**; **information science**
Deliberately incorrect and misleading information leaked esp. by an intelligence agency – **disinformation**

Inhale (see also Breathing):
Used for inhaling; something that is inhaled – **inhalant**
Capable of being inhaled - **respirable**

Inherit:
Capable of being inherited – **hereditary**; **heritable**
One who inherits or is entitled to inherit the estate of another; one who succeeds or is in line to succeed to a hereditary rank, title or office - **heir**

The condition of being an heir – **heirship**

An heir whose right to inheritance can be defeated by the birth of a closer relative – **heir presumptive**, pl. **heirs presumptive** (Law)

A woman who is an inheritor – **heiress**; **heritress**

The right of the eldest child, esp. the eldest son, to inherit the entire estate of one or both of his parents – **primogeniture**

An inheritance from a father or other ancestor – **patrimony**

Limitation of the inheritance of an estate to a particular person or persons – **tail**

Inheritance, through blending, of characteristics intermediate between those of parents widely divergent in those characteristics – **blending inheritance** (Biol.)

Injection:

An injection of fluid into an artery in order to reach tissues – **perfusion**

Injury:

Injury of a soft structure, esp. of the brain, resulting from a violent blow – **concussion**

To injure without breaking the skin – **contuse** (v.t.), n. **contusion**

Following or resulting from an injury – **posttraumatic**

Extreme or irrational fear of injury – **traumatophobia**

Insane – see Mental Illness

Inscriptions, the study of - **epigraphy**

Insect:

A group of insects – **swarm**

The scientific study of insects – **entomology**

A place where living insects are kept or bred – **insectary**

An insect-killing agent – **insecticide**

An organism feeding on insects – **insectivore**

Feeding on insects – **entomophagous**; **insectivorous**

An insect between molts, as during metamorphosis – **instar**

Pollinated by insects – **entomophilous**

Complete metamorphosis of a developing insect – **holometabolism**

An insect in its sexually mature adult stage after metamorphosis – **imago**, adj. **imaginal**

The insect life of a region or habitat – **entomofauna**

Insert:

To insert something foreign into – **interlard** (v.t.)

To insert between printed lines – **interline** (v.t.)

Inserted between the lines of a text – **interlinear**

Inspect (see also Examine):

To make a preliminary inspection of; to make a reconnaissance – **reconnoiter** (v.t./v.i.)

Institution:

Of, relating to or typical of an institution - **institutional**

To commit to an institution; to make into, treat as, or give the character of an institution to – **institutionalize** (v.t.)

Use of institutions for those incapable of self-care – **institutionalism**, n. **institutionalist**

Instruction – see Teaching

Instrument – see Measure

Intellect:
Of, relating to, originating in or apprehended by the intellect – **noetic**
The exercising of the intellect – **intellection**; **intellectualism**
The use of electronic devices to extend human intellect – **intellectronics**
The intellectual elite of a society – **intelligentsia**
A devotion to intellectual activities; an excessive emphasis on intellectual matters – **intellectualism**
A condition characterized by a lack of development of intellectual capacity – **amentia**

International:
The quality or state of being international in principles, character, concern or attitude – **internationalism**, n. **internationalist**
To make international; to place under international control – **internationalize** (v.t.)

Interpretation:
The science and methodology of interpretation – **hermeneutics**
To give a false interpretation to – **gloss** (v.t.)

Intestine:
Of or within the intestine – **enteric**
Intestinal inflammation – **enteritis**
Capable of causing intestinal disease – **enteropathogenic**
Reduced motility of the intestines with retention of feces – **stasis**
Creation of an opening into the intestine through the abdominal wall – **enterostomy**
Surgical incision into the intestine – **enterotomy**

Introduction:
The lines introducing a discourse or play; an introductory act or event – **prolog**; **prologue**
An introductory statement or essay explaining the scope, intention or background of a book – **foreward**; **preface**
The introductory part of a speech – **preface**
An introductory fact or occurrence – **preamble**; **preliminary**
The introduction to a formal document that explains its purpose – **preamble**
Introductory observations; a formal essay or critical discussion that introduces and interprets an extended work – **prolegomenon**, pl. **prolegomena**
A scholarly introduction to a branch of study or research – **isagoge**, adj. **isogogic** or **isogogical**
Introductory to an art or science – **propaedeutic**
An introductory comment before a speech; a preliminary discourse to a longer piece of writing – **proem**

Invitation:
Constituting or having an invitation – **invitatory**

Iodine/Iodide:
To treat or combine with iodine or an iodide – **iodate**; **iodize** (both v.t.)

Irish:
An Irish custom or idiom – **Irishism**
To make Irish in character – **Hibernicize** (v.t.)
An idiom or characteristic peculiar to Irish English or to the Irish – **Hibernianism**; **Hibernicism**
Of, relating to or characteristic of Ireland or its inhabitants; a native of Ireland – **Hibernian**
The English language as spoke in Ireland – **Anglo-Irish**; **Hiberno-English**

Iron:
  Tasting like iron – **chalybeate**
  Of or similar to iron – **ferruginous**
  Containing or yielding iron – **ferriferous**; **ferruginous**
  A worker in iron – **blacksmith**; **ironsmith**
  Products made of iron – **ironware**
  A mass of wrought iron ready for further working – **bloom**

Irritation:
  Involving irritation – **irritative**
  Easily irritated or annoyed – **irritable**
    The quality or state of being irritable – **irritability**
      Abnormal irritability and sensibility to stimulation in any part of the body – **erethism**
  Relieving or lessening irritation – **abirritant**

Islam:
  To convert (someone) to Islam – **Islamize** (v.t.)
  The religious faith, tenets or cause of Islam – **Islamism**
  A follower of Islam – **Moslem**; **Muslim**; **Mussulman**, pl. **Mussulmans** or **Mussulmen**
  A Moslem who knows the Koran by heart – **hafiz**, pl. **hafis** or **hafiz**
  A pilgrimage to Mecca made during Ramadan – **hadj**; **haj**; **hajj**
  One who has made a pilgrimage to Mecca during Ramadan – **hadji**; **haji**; **hajji**
  To slaughter (an animal) for food according to Moslem law – **halal** (v.t.)
  The body of Islamic custom and practice based on Mohammed's words and deeds – **sunna**; **sunnah**
  Title for a Moslem religious teacher or leader – **mulla**; **mullah**
  A Moslem leader who assumes a messianic role – **Mahdi**; **mahdi** (usu. capitalized)
    Belief in or devotion to a Mahdi – **Mahdism**; **mahdism** (usu. capitalized)
      An adherent of Mahdism - **Mahdist**; **mahdist** (usu. capitalized)
  The Moslem summons to prayer, called by the muezzin from a minaret of a mosque - **azan**
  A Moslem holy war against infidels - **jihad**
  A professional jurist who interprets Moslem religious law - **mufti**

Island:
  Of, relating to or being an island – **insular**
  A large group of islands – **archipelago**
  An inhabitant of an island – **islander**

Israeli, a native-born – **sabra**

Italian:
  Italian in character – **Italianate**
  To give an Italian aspect to – **Italianize** (v.t.)
  An Italian custom, trait or expression – **Italianism**; **Italicism**

Italic:
  To print in italic type – **italicize** (v.t.)

Itching:
  Causing itching; a substance that causes itching – **urticant**
  Marked by the presence of itching wheals – **urticate**

Ivy, overgrown or covered with – **ivied**

J

Jail:
   To put (someone) in jail – **incarcerate** (v.t.)

Japanese immigrants to North America:
   First generation – **Issei**, pl. **Issei** or **Isseis**
   Second generation (born in N. America of Japanese immigrant parents) – **Nisei**, pl. **Nisei** or **Niseis**
   Third generation (a N. America-born grandchild of Japanese immigrants to N. America) – **sansei**, pl. **sansei** or **sanseis**

Jaundice (icterus):
   Relating to or having jaundice; used for treating jaundice; a remedy for jaundice – **icteric**
   Causing jaundice – **icterogenic**

Jaw:
   Of or relating to the jaw – **gnathal**; **gnathic**
   The lower jaw – **mandible**, adj. **mandibular**
   Of or relating to the lower jaw – **submandibular**; **submaxillary**
   Having a mandible or mandibles – **mandibulate** (said of insects)
   The pair of bones forming the upper jaw – **maxillae**
   A jaw or jawbone – **maxillary**
   Relating to the two halves of the upper jaw (maxilla) – **bimaxillary**
   Relating to the part of the jaws containing the sockets of the teeth – **alveolar**
   The width of the space between the open jaws or mandibles of a vertebrate – **gape**
   A jaw or jawlike appendage – **gnathite**
   Having jaws that project forward to a considerable degree – **prognathic**; **prognathous**
   Having receding jaws – **opisthognathous**
   Having the lower jaw aligned with the upper so that it does not protrude or recede – **orthognathous**

Jays, a group of - **band**

Jellyfish, shaped like a – **medusoid**

Jewelry:
   A collection of jewelry or trinkets – **bijouterie**
   A piece of jewelry inserted into a perforation in the lip – **labret**

Joint/Joining:
   The actor process of joining – **junction**
   Of or relating to joints - **articular**
   To join together by causing adhesion – **agglutinate** (v.t.), adj. **agglutinated**, n. **agglutination**
      A substance that causes agglutination – **agglutinin**
   Joined by kinship or affinity – **affined**
   The congenital joining of two parts – **cohesion**
   Congenitally joined together – **adnate** (said of unlike parts), n. **adnation**
   Degenerative joint disease – **osteoarthritis**
   A connection or joint between bones; a degenerative process in a joint – **arthrosis**
   Closely joined – **coadunate**
   Surgical joining of one tubular or hollow organ to another – **anastomosis**
      To join by anastomosis – **anastomose** (v.t.)

The natural or artificial fusion of two organisms – **parabiosis**

The line of junction or an immovable joint between two bones, esp. of the skull – **suture**

Stiffening of a joint – **ankylosis**

Neuralgic pain in a joint – **arthralgia**

Inflammation of a joint or joints – **arthritis**

Any disease of a joint – **arthropathy**

A joint between bones or between movable parts of an outside shell; a joint between two separable parts, as a leaf and a stem – **articulation**

Any of several forms of bone articulation in which the bones are rigidly joined without an intervening cavity - **synarthrosis**

An immovable peg and rigid socket articulation, as of a tooth in its socket - **gomphosis**

A form of joining in which an elastic cartilage connects the bones and motion is limited – **amphiarthrosis**

Really or apparently having no joints – **anarthrous**

Joke – see Humor

Journal

To record in a journal; to keep a personal or financial journal – **journalize** (v.t./v.i.)

Journalism:

Very subjective journalism – **parajournalism**

A short news story that accompanies and presents sidelights of a major news story – **sidebar**

A free-lance reporter or photographer who doggedly searches for sensational stories about or takes candid pictures of celebrities – **paparazzo**, pl. **paparazzi**

A part-time or free-lance news correspondent for the electronic or print media; a newspaper reporter who serves another publication or news agency part time – **stringer**

Judaism (see also Hebrew):

A Jew who does not observe Jewish precepts – **goy**, pl. **goyim**

A Jewish marriage broker or a matchmaker – **schatchen**; **shadchan**; **shadchen**, pl. **schatchens** or **shadchans** or **shadchens** or **shadchonim**

An extreme dislike of Jews and Jewish culture – **anti-Semitism** (n. **anti-Semite**); **Judaeophobia**; **Judophobia**; **Judophobism**

Judge:

Judges as a whole – **judicature**; **judiciary**

Under judicial deliberation; before a judge – **sub judice**

Capable of being judged or liable to be judged – **judicable**

One who acts as a judge – **judicator**

In private with a judge instead of in open court – **in camera**

An incidental and collateral opinion uttered by a judge that is not material to his decision and not binding – **obiter dictum**

A judge's seat – **banc**

Judgment:

The quality or state of being correct in intellectual judgment - **rectitude**

Juice:

The acidic juice of sour and unripe fruit such as grapes or crab apples – **verjuice**

Juggler, the art or performance of a – **jugglery**

Jump – see Leap

Junior, the rank or condition of being a – **juniority**

Jury (see also Law):
    Of or relating to a jury or jurist – **juristic**
    The panel of prospective jurors from which a jury is chosen – **venire**
    A group of persons summoned to fill vacancies on a jury that has become deficient in number; a judge's writ or order summoning these persons – **tales**
        One summoned under a writ of tales – **talesman**
    The decision reached by a jury at the end of a trial - **verdict**
    A jury unable to agree on a verdict – **hung jury**
    A special jury selected from an original panel of 48 members from which each party strikes off names until the list is reduced to twelve – **struck jury**
    An attempt to corrupt a jury, as with bribery – **embracery**

Justice:
    Of or relating to the administration of justice – **judicatory; judicial**
    The administration of justice – **judicature**
    A system of courts of law for the administration of justice – **judiciary**
    A vindication of divine justice in the face of the existence of evil – **theodicy**

Justify, serving to – **justificative; justificatory**

K

Kangaroo:

    A male kangaroo – **boomer**; **buck**; **jack**

    A female kangaroo – **doe**; **flyer**; **jill**

    A young kangaroo – **joey**

    A group of kangaroos – **court**; **mob**; **troop**

Keel:

    Shaped like a keel; having a keel – **carinate** (Biol.); **carinated** (Biol.); **ridged**

Keenness or acuteness, as of thought or vision – **acuity**

Kennel – see Dog

Key:

    A key for opening more than one of a set of locks – **master key**

    The projecting ridge of a lock or keyhole that prevents the turning of a key other than the proper one; the notch cut into

        a key that correspond to such a ridge – **ward**

        Having notches or wards - **warded**

    The part of a key that enters the lock and engages the bolt or tumblers – **bit**

Kidnap:

    To kidnap (a man) for compulsory service aboard a ship – **shanghai** (v.t.), pret. **shanghaied**

Kidney:

    Of, relating to or near the kidneys – **adrenal**; **nephritic**; **renal**

    At or on the kidneys – **adrenal**

    Originating in the kidney; having the capacity to generate new kidney tissue - **nephrogenous**

    Inflammation of a kidney – **nephritis**, adj. **nephritic**

    Inflammation of both the kidney and its pelvis – **pyelonephritis**

    The surgical removal of a kidney – **nephrectomy**

    Surgical incision into the kidney – **nephrotomy**

    The science that deals with the kidney – **nephrology**

    Shaped like a kidney – **reniform**

Killing (see also under type of person or thing killed):

    A substance that is capable of destroying living organisms – **biocide**

    A chemical used to kill pests, esp. insects and rodents – **pesticide**

    A chemical used to kill plants, esp. weeds – **herbicide**

    The killing of animals for food – **slaughter**

    The killing of a large number of persons – **carnage**; **slaughter**

        A large-scale slaughter – **hecatomb**

    The act or an instance of intentionally killing oneself; one who kills oneself – **suicide**

        The study of suicide, suicidal behavior and suicide prevention – **suicidology**

    The killing of a wife by her husband; a man who kills his wife – **uxoricide**

    The killing of an infant; one who kills an infant – **infanticide**

    The act of killing one's father, mother or other close relative; one who commits such an act – **parricide**, adj. **parricidal**

    The killing of a woman; a person who kills a woman - **femicide**

    The act of killing one's spouse; one who kills his or her spouse - **mariticide**

    The killing of one person by another; one who kills another person – **homicide**

The killing of a son or daughter; a parent who commits such a murder - **filicide**

Systematic, planned killing of a racial, political or c ultural group – **genocide**

The killing of a tyrant; one who kills a tyrant – **tyrannicide**

To kill (cattle) by cutting the spinal cord – **pith** (v.t.)

A sudden quarrel resulting in an unpremeditated homicide – **chance-medley** (Law)

To kill as a sacrifice – **immolate** (v.t.)

To kill by suffocation or strangulation so as to leave the body intact and suitable for dissection – **burke** (v.t.)

To kill (a prominent person) – **assassinate** (v.t.), n. **assassin**

The intentional causing of a painless death to a person or lower animal, in order to avoid prolonged suffering – **euthanasia**

To kill or destroy by cutting off the oxygen supply – **asphyxiate** (n. **asphyxiant**); **suffocate**

To kill by squeezing the throat so as to choke or suffocate – **strangle** (v.t.)

   The act of strangling; the state of being strangled – **strangulation**

Execution by strangulation or by breaking the neck with an iron collar screwed tight; a collar used for this; to strangle in order to rob – **garrote**; **garrotte** (both n./v.t.)

To kill by lying upon – **overlie** (v.t.) (used esp. of animals)

Kindergarten:

   A child attending kindergarten; a kindergarten teacher – **kindergartner**

Kinds – see Form

King:

   The domain ruled by a king – **kingdom**; **kingship**

   Relating to or suitable for a king – **kingly**; **regal**

   The killing of a king; a person who kills a king or is responsible for his death – **regicide**

Kissing:

   The act of kissing – **osculation**, v.t. **osculate**

   Of, relating to or concerned with kissing - **oscular**

Knee:

   To bend the knee – **genuflect** (v.i.), n. **genuflection** or **genuflexion**

   A knock-kneed person – **valgus**

Kneel:

   Something, as a cushion, on which to kneel – **kneeler**

   To bend the knee in a kneeling or half-kneeling position, as in worship – **genuflect** (v.i.), n. **genuflection** or **genuflexion**

Knife:

   One who makes, repairs or sells cutting instruments such as knives – **cutler**

   A narrow dagger used in medieval times to deliver the death stroke to a seriously wounded knight – **misericord**; **misericorde**

   Shaped like a pruning knife - **cultrate**

Knight:

   Knights collectively; the rank, profession or dignity of a knight; behavior and qualities worthy of a knight – **knighthood**

   A wandering knight, esp. one traveling in search of adventures – **knight-errant**, pl. **knights-errant**, n. **knight-errantry**

   Medieval knighthood; the principles and customs of medieval knighthood; the qualities that were idealized by knighthood; a group of knights – **chivalry**

A paragon of chivalry – **paladin**

Knob:
    Having or resembling a knob or knoblike protuberance – **umbonate**
    Having the surface covered with rounded protuberances – **knobbed**; **torose**
    A small knob – **capitulum** (Anat.)

Knowledge (see also Learning):
    Of, relating to or involving knowledge or the act of knowing – **epistemic**
    Knowing everything; having total knowledge – **omniscient**
    Of or producing knowledge – **sciential**
    Relating to all branches of knowledge – **encyclopedic**
        Encyclopedic learning – **encyclopedism**; **pansophy**; **polymathy**
    The doctrine that all knowledge is derived from sense experience – **empiricism**, adj. **empirical**
    A knowable thing whose existence is theoretically problematic – **noumenon**, pl. **noumena**
    A doctrine or belief that ultimate or immaterial realities cannot be known through the rational processes of the mind –
        agnosticism; **nescience**
    The doctrine that knowledge is wholly or chiefly derived from pure reason – **intellectualism**, adj. **intellectualistic**
    The doctrine that objects of knowledge have no existence except in the mind of the perceiver – **mentalism**
    A person of exceptionally wide knowledge – **polyhistor**; **polymath**
    A universal wisdom or knowledge – **pansophy**
    A systematic view of all human knowledge – **pansophism**
    Superficial knowledge – **sciolism**
    A supposed knowledge of natural and supernatural forces –**sciosophy**
    The branch of philosophy that studies the origin, nature, methods, validity and limits of knowledge – **epistemology**,
        adj. **epistemic**; **epistemological**
    The preliminary body of knowledge and rules necessary for the study of some art or science – **propaedeutics**
    Without knowledge or education; displaying lack of knowledge or education – **ignorant**
        An ignorant person – **ignoramus**
    Known or understood by only a few – **arcane**; **esoteric**
    Divine communication of knowledge - **afflatus**
    To make known or familiar; to foster growing knowledge of, familiarity with, acceptance of – **propagate**; **publicize**
        (both v.t.)

L

Labor (see also Work):

   The industrial management of labor – **human engineering**
   Unpaid or partially paid labor - **corvée**

Labor Union:

   To organize into a labor union; to cause to join a labor union; to organize or join a labor union – **unionize** (v.t./v.i.)
   A business or industrial establishment whose employees are required to be union members or to agree to join the union within a specified time after being hired – **union shop**
   A union member elected to represent the union in its dealings with management – **shop steward**
   A labor union to which all the workers of a particular industry can belong, regardless of their trade – **industrial union**

Ladder, shaped like a – **scalariform**

Lake:

   Of, relating to or living or growing in lakes – **lacustrine**
   The bottom of a lake; the organisms living on lake bottoms – **benthos**, adj. **benthic** or **benthonic**
   Living or occurring in the deeper, open waters of lakes or ponds – **limnetic**
   The study of lakes, ponds and streams – **hydrobiology**; **limnology**
   A small mountain lake – **tarn**

Lamb:

   A lamb reared without the aid of its mother - **cosset**

Lance:

   To lower (a lance or spear) to an attack position – **couch** (v.t.)
   Shaped like a lance or lancet - **lanciform**

Land:

   The study of the configuration and evolution of landforms – **geomorphology**
   Detailed, precise description of a place or region; the technique of graphically representing the exact physical features of a place or region on a map; the physical features of a place or region – **topography**
      The topographic study of a given place in relation to its history – **topology**
   The geographical study of wet lands, as marshes or swamps – **telmatology**
   Pertaining to land or its products; attached to or arising from land or landed property – **praedial**; **predial**
   To or toward land – **landward**
   A large land area – **landmass**
      One of the principal landmasses of the earth – **continent**
      A large landmass that is separate to some degree but still part of a continent – **subcontinent**
      A hypothetical landmass that existed when all continents on earth were joined - **Pangaea**
      An actual or hypothetical landmass that might later be enlarged into a major continent or broken up into smaller ones – **protocontinent**
      A hypothetical protocontinent of the remote geologic past that rifted apart to form the continents of today – **supercontinent**
   A long projection of land into water – **peninsula**
   A narrow point of land extending into a body of water - **spit**
   A narrow strip of land connecting two larger landmasses – **isthmus**, adj. **isthmian**
   An increase of land along the shores of a body of water, as by alluvial deposit – **accretion**
   The lowest level to which a land surface can be reduced by the action of running water – **base level**
   A deep gully cut by an intermittent stream – **arroyo**

A flat-topped elevation with one or more clifflike sides – **mesa**
A land that is low in relation to the surrounding countryside – **lowland**
    A native or inhabitant of a lowland - **lowlander**
An extensive tract of open, uncultivated land covered with herbage and low shrubs – **heath**
Level and open country – **champaign** (n./adj.)
A point of land extending out into a body of water – **headland**; **promontory**
The higher parts of a region or tract of land; inland country – **upland**
Surrounded nearly or completely be dry land – **Mediterranean**
An area of low-lying land, as in the Netherlands, that has been reclaimed from a body of water and is protected by dikes – **polder**
A low-lying stretch of land, e.g., a small meadow or swamp or an elongated depression in land that is at least seasonally wet or marshy – **slough**; **swale**
An upland plain; a region without woods; an open hilly or rolling region; an unenclosed pastureland - **bent**; **moor**; **wold**
A boggy area of wasteland, esp. a high, poorly drained one covered by grasses and sedges growing in a thick layer of peat – **moor**
A flat, treeless grassland – **savanna**; **savannah**
The steep precipices forming the sides of a gorge or narrow – **dalles** (pl. only)
A treeless area that is located between the ice cap and the tree line of arctic regions, that has a permanently frozen subsoil and supports low-growing vegetation – **tundra**
A ridge of high land dividing two areas that are drained by different river systems; the region draining into a river, river system or body of water – **watershed**
Not productive owing to the results of excessive irrigation – **water-sick** (used of land)
Made up of both land and water – **terraqueous**
Derived from the land, esp. by erosion – **terrigenous** (used mainly of sediments)
To cover (land or a road surface) with loose material not worked in – **top-dress** (v.t.)
Removal of a piece of land from one property onto another as a result of a shift in the course of a boundary stream – **avulsion**
The addition to or increase in the value of land by means of improvements or naturally – **accession**
    Accession by the permanent recession of the water line – **dereliction**
To increase the productivity of (land) – **improve** (v.t.)
Those parts of one piece of land that abut on adjacent lands – **abuttals**; **boundaries**
A person who owns adjacent land – **abutter**
Of, relating to or growing on uncultivated land or open fields – **campestral**
A low mound or ridge of earth – **hammock**; **hummock** (adj. **hummocky**); **knoll**
Characterized by light annual rainfall and capable of sustaining only short grasses and shrubs – **semiarid**
A vast grass-covered semiarid plain – **steppe**
An area located between a desert and a grassland or woodland – **semidesert**
One who lives and works on land – **landsman**
An estate in land of which the inheritor has unqualified ownership and power of disposition – **fee simple**
Land owned independently, without any rent, payment, etc. – **allodium** (Law)
Legal possession of land; the act of taking legal possession of land – **seisin**; **seizin** (both Law)
    One who takes seisin – **seisor**; **seizor** (both Law)
Unlawful dispossession from real property – **disseisin**; **disseizin** (both Law)
To dispossess unlawfully of real property – **disseise**; **disseize** (both v.t., both Law)
The crops or products of the land legally belonging to a tenant – **emblements** (Law)
Legal possession and use of one's own land – **demesne** (Law; used chiefly in the phrase *to hold in demesne*)
The enclosed land surrounding a dwelling – **curtilage** (Law)

Landmark:
    A landmark visible from the sea – **seamark**

Landowners:

A social system that invests state authority and influence in the landowners – **territorialism**

Landscape:

A painter of – **landscapist**; **paysagist**

Of or marked by the clipping and trimming of live shrubs or trees into decorative shapes; such clipping and trimming - **topiary**

Landslide:

A landslide of wet volcanic debris on the side of a volcano; the deposit left by such a landslide - **lahar**

Language (see also Grammar, Speech, and Word):

Sign language - see Finger

The art of effective expression and the persuasive use of language – **rhetoric** (q.v.)

A language that is the recorded or hypothetical ancestor of another language or group of languages – **protolanguage**

A method of representing the sounds of language by literal symbols – **orthography**

The study of a language or languages at a specific stage of development – **descriptive linguistics**

The study of the interrelationship between language and other cultural behavioral phenomena – **metalinguistics**

The study of language as a systematically composed body of words with discernible regularity of structure and arrangement in sentences, etc.; the system of rules for generating sentences in a language; a book containing such rules – **grammar** (q.v.)

Considering or embracing phenomena (as the sounds of a language) as they occur, change or develop over time – **diachronic**; **diachronistic**; **diachronous**

Diachronic analysis or point of view – **diachrony**

The study of the time during which two or more languages have evolved separately from a common source; a technique for estimating such time by statistical comparison of vocabulary samples – **glottochronology**, adj. **glottochronological**

A stylized picture representing a word or idea – **hieroglyph**; **pictograph**

Of or relating to a system of writing, as that of ancient Egypt, in which pictorial symbos are used to represent words or sounds; written with such symbols; such writing; something resembling such a symbol or symbols - **hieroglyph**; **hieroglyphic**, adj. **hieroglyphic** or **hieroglyphical**

The oval or oblong figure used in ancient Egyptian hieroglyphics to enclose characters – **cartouch**; **cartouche**

The representation of things or sounds by means of their pictures instead of by symbols and words, as in hieroglyphics – **curiologics**, adj. **curiologic**; **curiological**

Curiological writing – **curiologics**

Any of various proposed international written languages using signs or symbols to represent ideas rather than words – **pasigraphy**, adj. **pasigraphic** or **pasigraphical**

The study or science of meaning in language forms – **semantics** (n. **semanticist**); **sematology**

To study or make critical comments on a language – **philologize** (v.i.)

Having no written language – **nonliterate**; **preliterate**

Of or relating to the ordinary, everyday, current form of a language – **demotic**; **vernacular**; **vulgar**

A vernacular word or expression; the use of the vernacular – **vernacularism**

An expression typical of or appropriate to the spoken language – **colloquialism**, adj. **colloquial**

Condemnatory language – **billingsgate**

Rude language arising from haughtiness and contempt - **contumely**

Defamatory language – **calumny**; **obloquy**; **slander**

A word, expression or mode of pronunciation peculiar to a province – **provincialism**

A word, phrase, pronunciation or manner of speaking that is peculiar to one locality – **localism**

A regional variety of a language distinguished by pronunciation, grammar, vocabulary, etc.; a variety of a language that with other varieties constitutes a single language of which no single variety is standard; the language peculiar to an occupational group or particular social class; the manner or style of expressing oneself in language - **dialect**

The study of dialects – **dialectology**

Using two dialects of the same language – **bidialectal**

A dialect other than the standard or literary dialect; illiterate or provincial speech - **patois**

A dialectical or regional pronuciation, esp. an Irish accent - **brogue**

A hybrid language or dialect – **jargon**; **pidgin**

    To speak in or use such a language or dialect – **jargon** (v.i.)

The speech of an individual, considered as a linguistic pattern unique among speakers of his or her language or dialect – **idiolect**

A language common to peoples of diverse speech that is used esp. for communication in commercial trade – **trade language**

A language or dialect of a region, country, or people that has become the common or standard language of a larger area and of other peoples - **koine**

A language used as a medium of communication between peoples who speak different languages; something similar to a common language – **lingua franca**

A human written or spoken language as opposed to machine language – **natural language**

To model (the meaning of a word) on that of an analogous word in another language – **calque** (v.t.)

A form of borrowing from one language to another whereby the semantic components of a given term are literally translated into their equivalents in the borrowing language – **calque**; **loan translation**

A specialized vocabulary used by a particular class or group – **argot**; **jargon**

Written in or making use of one language only – **monolingual**; **unilingual**

Able to use two languages; of or expressed in two languages – **bilingual**

Able to use three languages; of or expressed in three languages – **trilingual**

Of, including or depicted in several languages; using or able to use several languages – **multilingual** (n. **multilingualism**); **polyglot**, n. **polyglotism**

A fluent speaker of several languages – **linguist**

One with a reading, writing or speaking knowledge of several languages; a mixture or confusion of languages – **polyglot**

Composed of a mixture of languages – **macaronic**

A word-for-word translation; to manipulate the wording of (a text), esp. as a means of subtly altering the sense – **metaphrase** (n./v.t.)

To represent (letters or words) in the corresponding characters of another alphabet – **transliterate** (v.t.)

The use of terms or constructions felt by some to be undesirably foreign to the established customs of the language – **barbarism**

A speech form or expression of a language that is peculiar to itself grammatically or that cannot be understood from the individual meanings of its elements; the particular grammatical, syntactic and structural character of a given language – **idiom**, adj. **idiomatic**

Clear in meaning, expression or style - **pellucid**, n. **pellucidity** or **pellucidness**

A feeling for language; an ear for the idiomatically correct or appropriate – **sprachgefühl**

Agreeable sound, esp. in the phonetic quality of words – **euphony**, adj. **euphonic**

Harsh or unharmonious use of language, as opposed to euphony – **cacophony**

Loss or deficiency in the power to use or understand language caused by brain disease or injury - **dysphasia**

Loss of the ability to understand written or printed language – **alexia**; **word blindness**

Ambiguity in language - **amphibology**

All speakers of a particular language or dialect, whether located in one area or scattered – **speech community**

Of or relating to the origin of language – **glottogonic**

A character or symbol representing an idea or thing without expressing a particular word or phrase for it (as Chinese characters) - **ideogram**; **ideograph**

    The representation of ideas by ideograms or ideographs - **ideography**

Of, relating to or constituting the languages that developed from Latin – **Romance**

Neither Indo-European nor Semitic – **allophylian** (used of languages)

Not accented, as words or syllables – **atonic**, n. **atonicity** or **atony**

Larks, a group of – **ascension**; **bevy**; **exaltation**

Larva (pl. larvae):
    The breeding of larvae – **vermination**
    An insecticide for exterminating larval pests – **larvicide**

Larynx (voice box; pl. larynges or larynxes):
    Of, relating to, affecting or situated near the larynx; produced in or with the larynx; a sound produced in or with the larynx – **laryngal**; **laryngeal**
    Surgical removal of all or part of the larynx – **laryngectomy**
    Inflammation of the larynx – **laryngitis**
    The branch of medicine that deals with the study and treatment of the larynx - **laryngology**

Laser, to function as a – **lase** (v.i.)

Latin:
    Of, relating to or derived from Latin – **Latinate**
    To translate into Latin – **Latinize** (v.t.)
    An idiom, structure or word derived from Latin – **Latinism**
    A Latin scholar – **Latinist**
    The way that Latin is spoken or written – **Latinity**

Lattice:
    An object, structure or material resembling a lattice; a structure made of lattices – **latticework**

Laugh:
    Inclined to laugh or capable of laughing – **gelastic**; **risible**
    The ability or tendency to laugh – **risibility**
    To laugh loudly or convulsively – **cachinate** (v.i.)
    To laugh at contemptuously – **fleer**; **scoff** (both v.i.)

Lava (see also Volcano):
    A small solidified fragment of lava – **lapillus**
    A stream of molten lava; a sheet of solid lava – **coulee**

Law (see also Bail, Judge, Jury, Property, Trial, Will, etc.):
    Justice applied in circumstances not covered by law – **equity**
    Of, relating to, concerned with, authorized by, based on, permitted by, in conformity with or created by the law; enforced or recognized by law rather than by equity; applicable to or typical of lawyers or their profession - **legal**
    Forbidden by law; forbidden by official rules; not legal – **illegal**
        To declare illegal – **ban**; **outlaw** (both v.t.)
    Legally punishable - **statutable**
    Established by law – **legal**; **statutory**
    To pass a law or laws – **legislate** (v.i.)
    Of or relating to the law – **jural**; **juristic**
    Of or relating to law and its administration - **juridical**
    The act or process of outlawing; the state of being outlawed; defiance of the law – **outlawry**
    Strict, literal adherence to the law – **legalism**
    An officially selected body of persons with the power and responsibility to make laws for a nation or state – **legislature**
    A specialist in law – **legist**
    The collective or comprehensive body of all the laws of a nation or state – **corpus juris**

The philosophy of law – **jurisprudence**
   Of or relating to jurisprudence – **juristic**
The science of law and legislation – **jurisprudence**; **nomology**
Versed in the law – **jurisprudent**
A party engaged in a lawsuit; engaged in a lawsuit – **litigant**
To subject to or engage in legal proceedings – **litigate** (v.t./v.i.)
Of, relating to or characterized by litigation; tending to litigate – **litigious**
One who appeals, esp. to a higher court; of or relating to appeals – **appellant**
   A person appealed against – **appellee**
   A person who carries an appeal to a higher court – **appellor**
To lose a case by not appearing – **default** (v.i.)
One who impedes the passage of legislation – **obstructionist**
To make no longer criminal or illegal – **decriminalize** (v.t.)
Doing more than is strictly required by law – **supererogation**
The right or power of a state to enforce a law – **imperium**
Not governed or sanctioned by law – **extralegal**
To make void – **annul**; **vacate** (both v.t.)
A rendering null and void - **defeasance**
Law based on judicial decision and precedent rather that statute – **case law**
Utterance of defamatory statements injurious to the reputation or well-being of a person – **slander**
A written, printed or pictorial statement that defames one's character or reputation, or exposes one to public ridicule –
   libel
A law that protects journalists from being compelled to reveal confidential sources of information – **shield law**
Capable of managing one's own affairs – **sui juris**
By law or by right – **de jure**
Of or designating a mandatory act or duty admitting of no personal discretion or judgment in its performance –
   ministerial
The grounds for action in a suit – **gist**
Legally subject to a court suit – **suable**
The party that institutes a suit in a court - **plaintiff**
One against whom an action is brought – **defendant**
To clear (a defendant) of a charge – **acquit**; **purge** (both v.t.)
An acknowledgment by a defendant that all or part of a plaintiff's cause is just, whereupon the defendant permits
   judgment to be entered without trial – **cognovit**
The act of one who attempts to or acts so as to influence a court, jury, or other office or officer corruptly - **embracery**
Damages awarded by a court to a plaintiff as additional punishment of a defendant for a serious wrong – **punitive**
   damages
To punish by a monetary penalty that is left to the discretion of the court – **amerce** (v.t.)
The defendant's risk of conviction when put on trial – **jeopardy**
A defendant who refuses to plead when under arraignment – **mute**
A plaintiff's answer to a defendant's plea or counterclaim – **counterplea**
To agree respecting the conduct of legal proceedings – **stipulate** (v.t./v.i.) (used in the phrase *stipulate to*)
   That can be stipulated - **stipulable**
To deny formally (an allegation of fact by the opposition) in a lawsuit; formal denial of an allegation of fact in a lawsuit –
   traverse (v.t./n.)
The locality where an alleged crime or other cause of legal action occurs; the locality or political division from which a
   jury must be called and in which a trial must be held; the clause within a declaration naming the locality in which the
   trial is occurring or will occur - **venue**
To make known or public the terms of (a proposed law); to issue or give out (a law) by way of putting into execution –
   promulgate (v.t.)
A wrongful act, damage or injury done willfully, negligently, etc. – **tort**

The plea or fact that an accused person was elsewhere than at the scene of the offense with which he is charged – **alibi**

Maladministration of public office; neglect in preventing or reporting a crime – **misprision**

The improper and unlawful execution of an act that in itself is lawful and proper – **misfeasance**

    One guilty of misfeasance – **misfeasor**

The facts of a case that are admissible in evidence – **res gestae**

Documentary evidence by which a person can defend a title to property or a claim to rights – **muniment**

Evidence not bearing directly on the fact in dispute but on various attendant circumstances from which the judge or jury might infer the occurrence of the fact in dispute – **circumstantial evidence**

A judicial writ authorizing an officer to execute a judgment or make a search, seizure or arrest – **warrant**; **warranty**

To summon as a witness to give warranty of title – **vouch** (v.t.)

Unsupported or uncorroborated by authority, evidence or proof – **naked**

A written declaration made under oath before an official – **affidavit**

    One who makes an affidavit – **affiant**

A person who declares solemnly, but not under oath – **affirmant**

A person who testifies under oath, esp. in writing – **deponent**

Testimony under oath - **deposition**

Irrelevant matter in a legal pleading – **surplusage**

The transfer of title, right or claim to another; to renounce all claim to (a possession of right) – **quitclaim** (n./v.t.)

Inciting or stirring up groundless lawsuits – **barratry**, adj. **barratrous**

    One who commits barratry – **barrater**; **barrator**

A formal sealed contract or agreement; a suit to recover damages for violation of such a contract; to promise by such a contract or agreement; to enter into such an agreement – **covenant** (n./v.t./v.i.)

    The participant in a covenant to whom the promise is made - **covenantee**

    One who makes a covenant – **covenanter**

    Not bound, promised or guaranteed by a covenant – **uncovenanted**

Compensation for suffering, loss, or feelings injured – **solatium**

The performance of a legal contract as specified by its terms – **specific performance**

The right to utilize and enjoy the profits and advantages of something belonging to another so long as the property is not damaged or altered in any way - **usufruct**

    One who holds property by usufruct; of or of the nature of a usufruct – **usufructuary**

Session of a legislative body or court – **assize**

Subject to external or foreign laws or control - **heteronomous**

To send (one in custody) back to prison, to another court, or to another agency for further action; a person sent back thus; to send (a case) back to a lower court with orders about further action; an act or instance of this – **remand** (v.t./n.)

Important enough to affect the outcome of a case, the validity of a legal instrument, etc. – **material**

Without legal significance, through having been previously decided or settled – **moot**

The illegal encroachment upon or exercise of authority or privilege belonging to another – **usurpation**

A preliminary examination concerning the competence of a prospective witness or juror – **voir dire**

For the particular action or proceeding – **ad litem**

The absorption of a lesser estate, liability, right, action or offense into a greater one - **merger**

A party's strict legal rights, excluding jurisdictional or technical aspects; the factual substance of a case as distinguished from its form and procedural aspects – **merit**

The termination of a right or privilege through disuse, neglect or death – **lapse**

To make a formal accusation against by the findings of a jury – **indict** (v.t.), n. **indictment**

    One who indicts – **indicter**; **indicter**

    One who is indicted – **indictee**

    Any of the distinct charges in an indictment – **count**

An introductory or background statement explaining the allegations in a legal proceeding – **inducement**

A discrepancy between two statements in a legal proceeding – **variance**

A clause in some laws creating exemption because of conditions existing before encactment of legislation – **grandfather clause**

Postponement of the decision of a cause in civil law - **ampliation**

An illegal sharing in the proceeds of a lawsuit by an outside party that has promoted the litigation – **champarty**; **champerty**

To perform, execute or sign (a will or other legal instrument) – **make** (v.t.)

Evil intent – **malice**

A legal instrument authorizing one to act as another's attorney or agent – **power of attorney**

A minor or incompetent person placed under the care or protection of a guardian or court – **ward**

    The state of being a ward – **wardship**

To induce (a person) to commit an unlawful act or perjury; to procure (perjured testimony) – **suborn** (v.t.)

A law designed to regulate Sunday activities – **blue law**

A law designed to protect the public from buying fraudulent securities – **blue-sky law**

One who is neither privy nor party to a title, act or contract – **stranger**

Of or relating to both medicine and law – **medicolegal**

A law, decree or edict setting a time limit on legal action – **statute of limitations**

Lawyer:

    A petty, quibbling lawyer, esp. an unscrupulous one – **pettifogger**, v.i. **pettifog**

Layer:

    A horizontal layer of a material, esp. one of several parallel layers arranged one on top of another – **stratum**, pl. **strata** or **stratums**

        Of a stratum or strata - **stratal**

        Having the form of strata – **lamelliform**; **stratiform**

        To form, arrange or deposit in strata; to form strata – **stratify** (v.t./v.i.)

        Having thin strata – **straticulate**, n. **straticulation**

        The act or process of stratifying; a stratified configuration – **stratification**

    Lacking definite layers – **unstratified**

    To split into thin layers – **delaminate** (v.i.)

    To insert between layers; to arrange in alternate layers – **interlaminate**

    Having, composed of or arranged in thin layers – **lamellar**; **lamellate**; **lamellated**; **laminate**

    Having more than one layer – **multiplicate**

    Having concentric layers, as the bulb of an onion – **tunicate** (Bot.)

Lead (metal):

    Made of lead – **leaden**

    Containing lead – **leaden**; **plumbiferous**

    Chronic lead poisoning – **plumbism**

    Of or like lead; produced by lead absorption or lead poisoning – **saturnine**

Leader/Leadership:

    The foremost or leading position in a trend or movement; those occupying a foremost position – **vanguard**

    A leader who obtains power by means of impassioned appeals to the emotions and prejudices of the people – **demagog**; **demagogue**

    A leader of a passive group of followers - **bellwether**

Leaf (see also Biology: Physical Characteristics):

    Having or bearing a leaf or leaves; having a specified number or kind of leaves – **foliaceous**; **leaved**

    Of or relating to a leaf or leaves; shaped like a leaf – **foliate**

    Resembling a leaf – **phylloid**

Lacking leaves – **aphyllous**; **naked**
The state of being in leaf – **foliation**
Feeding on leaves – **phyllophagous**
Thriving on or parasitic to leaves – **foliicolous**
Of, relating to or resembling the leaf of a plant – **foliaceous**; **foliate**; **foliose**
Having leaflike structures – **foliaceous**
Plant leaves as a whole; a cluster of leaves – **foliage**
Having or composed of subdivided or compound leaflets – **decompound**
To deprive (a tree or plant) of leaves, or to cause the leaves to fall off; to lose foliage – **defoliate** (v.t./v.i.)
Having a single leaf – **unifoliate**
Having two leaves – **bifoliate**; **diphyllous**
Having two leaflets – **bifoliolate**
Having three leaves, leaflets or leaflike parts – **trifoliate**; **trifoliated**
Having five leaves, leaflets or leaflike parts – **quinquefoliate**
Bearing numerous leaves or leaflets – **foliose**; **frondescent**; **leafy**
A modified or rudimentary leaf – **cataphyll**
Having leaves of different forms on one plant – **heterophyllous**
Having or designating united leaves or leaflike parts – **gamophyllous**
Having leaflets or lobes radiating from one point – **palmate**
A circular cluster of leaves – **rosette**
Having opposite leaflets that are subdivided into opposite leaflets, as compound leaves – **tripinnate**
Heart-shaped, with the tapering end at the point of attachment – **obcordate** (used of leaves)
Having thick, fleshy leaves that conserve moisture – **succulent**
The leaf of a grass or similar plant – **blade**
The arrangement of folded leaves in a bud - **vernation**
The tendency of the leaves of some plants to change their position at nightfall - **nyctitropism**
The following biological terms are used esp. of leaves:
   Arranged in two vertical rows or ranks on opposite sides of an axis – **distichous**
   Growing in pairs or divided into two parts – **binate**
   Having veins – **nervate**
   Divided into two, almost to the base – **bipartite**
   Spreading or recurved at the tip – **squarrose**
   Ending with a sharp tip – **apiculate**
   Having a blunt or rounded tip – **hebetate**; **obtuse**
   Having a blunt or rounded tip with a shallow notch – **retuse**
   Heart-shaped – **cordate**
   Gradually tapering to a slender point – **attenuate**
   Having a rough and ridged surface – **rugose**
   Coming to a point and having the veins terminate at the tip – **acrodrome**; **acrodromous**
   Having irregularly saw-toothed divisions directed backward – **runcinate**
   Having a wavy, indented margin – **sinuate**; **sinuated**; **sinuous**
   Overlapping at the margins – **imbricate** (used esp. of leaves in the bud)
   Having a margin with rounded or scalloped projections – **crenate**; **crenated**
   Having tiny notches or scallops – **crenulate**; **crenulated**
   Having a somewhat waxy margin – **repand**
   Rolled inward at the edges – **involute**
   Rolled back on the undersurface from the tip or margins – **revolute**
   With the edges turned or folded inward but not overlapping – **induplicate**
   With edges cut deeply into narrow, fringelike segments or lobes – **laciniate**
   Having overlapping edges – **obvolute** (used of leaves and petals in a bud)
   Narrow and tapering at each end – **lanceolate**

Broad and rounded at the tip and tapering at the base – **oblanceolate**
Broad and rounded at the base and tapering toward the end - **ovate**
Egg-shaped, with the narrow end attached at the stalk – **obovate**

League, one who belongs to a - **leaguer**

Leak:
Something that escapes by leaking; an amount lost as the result of leaking – **leakage**

Leaping:
Of, relating to, adapted for or characterized by leaping – **saltatorial**; **salutatory**
To jump vertically with a forward leap, as practiced by springbok – **pronk** (v.i.)

Learning (see also Knowledge):
One who loves learning – **philolog**; **philologer**; **philologian**; **philologist**; **philologue**
To interpret or make available by philological investigation – **philologize** (v.t.)
One who is unduly concerned with book learning and formal rules without an understanding or experience of practical affairs; one who displays one's learning in such a way as to try to impress others – **pedant**, adj. **pedantic**
Pedantic attention to rules or detail; the outlook or manner characteristic of a pedant; an instance of pedantic behavior – **pedantry**

Lease:
A holder of a lease – **lessee**
One who lets property under a lease – **lessor**
To lease for less than the proper value – **underlet** (v.t.)
Possession by lease; property held by lease – **leasehold**

Leather:
Of or like leather in appearance, texture or quality – **coriaceous**
To convert (skin) into white leather by mineral tanning – **taw** (v.t.)

Left:
Left command (to an animal); to turn left – **haw** (n./v.i.)
Of or facing the left side; left-handed – **sinistral**

Leg:
Of or relating to the part of the leg behind the knee joint – **popliteal**
Having four legs or leglike appendages; an animal with four legs – **tetrapod**
Having six legs – **hexapod**; hexapodous

Legion:
Of, relating to or constituting a legion; a soldier of a legion – **legionary**
A member of a legion – **legionnaire**

Leisure, characterized by – **leisured**

Length:
Of or relating to length – **longitudinal**
At full length – **in extenso**
Capable of being drawn out in length – **ductile**; **tractile**

Lens (see also Optics and Surfaces, Curved)
    Of or relating to a lens; shaped like a biconvex lens - **lenticular**
    Behind a lens – **retrolental**
    A plano-convex lens used to concentrate light – **bull's eye**; **bull's-eye**
    A convex lens used to focus the sun's rays and produce heat – **burning glass**
    A concavo-convex lens – **meniscus**

Leopard:
    A female leopard – **leopardess**
    A group of leopards – **leap**

Leprosy:
    Of, relating to, resembling or having leprosy – **leprous**
    A hospital for treating leprosy – **leprosarium**

Letter:
    The development or design of the shape of an alphabetic letter – **letterform**
    A mark added to a letter to indicate a special phonetic value or to distinguish words otherwise graphically identical –
        diacritic; **diacritical mark**
    The writing of letters or epistles – **epistolography**
    Of or associated with letters or letter-writing; carried on or made up of letters, as a relationship – **epistolary**

Liberal:
    An instance of being liberal – **liberality**
    To make or become liberal – **liberalize** (v.t./v.i.)

Lice (sing. louse):
    Infested with lice – **lousy**
    Of, relating to or caused by lice – **pedicular**
    Infestation with lice – **pediculosis**; **phthiriasis**

License:
    One to whom a license is granted – **licensee**
    One who is licensed by an authorized body to practice a specified profession – **licentiate**

Lichen:
    Of, relating to or resembling lichen; covered with lichens – **lichenous**

Lies/Lying (see also Truth):
    An abnormal compulsion to lie or twist the truth – **mythomania**
    Calculated misrepresentation through concealment of the facts; an inference drawn from such a misrepresentation –
        subreption, adj. **subreptitious**

Life (see also Live):
    Plant and animal life – see Biology
    Of or characteristic of life; necessary to the continuation of life; life-sustaining – **vital**
    A way of life; a manner of living – **modus vivendi**, pl. **modi vivendi**
    An area of activity in which one is most expert, successful or happy – **forte**; **métier**
    The characteristic that distinguishes the living from the nonliving; the capacity to live, grow or develop – **vitality**
    To endow with life – **animate**; **vitalize**; **vivify** (all v.t.)
        Animating force – **animus**

The development of life from preexisting life – **biogenesis**
Representing real life accurately – **lifelike**
Continuing or not changing for a lifetime - **lifelong**
A long duration of life; length of life – **longevity**
    The theory or practice of promoting longevity – **macrobiotics**
Pertaining to life or specific life conditions – **biotic**
Characterized by the absence of life – **abiotic**, n. **abiosis**
Bringing back to life – **anabiosis**
A short-lived thing – **ephemeron**
The biological science of essential and characteristic life processes, activities and functions – **physiology**
The ascription of living characteristics to inanimate objects – **introjection**
A written account of a person's life – **biography**
The study of the decline of life, esp. as exhibited in biological groups nearing extinction – **geratology**
Data that record significant events and dates in human life, as births, deaths and marriage – **vital statistics**

Light:
    The scientific study of light and vision – **optics** (q.v.)
    Deflection of a light wave at the boundary between two mediums with different refractive indices or in passage through a medium of nonuniform density – **refraction**
    The study of the refraction of light – **dioptrics**
    Not capable of being refracted – **irrefrangible** (used of light and other radiations)
    Capable of responding to light photoelectrically or by chemical reaction – **photoactive**
    Depending on light for the continuance of life and growth – **photobiotic**
    Movement in response to light – **photokinesis; photopathy; phototaxis; photot-ropism; phototropy**
    The measurement of the properties of light, esp. of luminous intensity – **photometry**
    The fraction of radiant energy absorbed by the surface that it strikes – **absorptivity**
    Abnormal intolerance of or sensitivity to light; an abnormal fear of light - **photophobia**
    Adaptation of the eyes to light – **photopia**
    Sensitive to light – **photosensitive**
    Sensitivity to light – **phototonus**
    To make (an organism or substance) sensitive to light – **photosensitize** (v.t.)
    Something that emits light – **illuminant**
    Generating, transmitting or yielding light – **luminiferous**
    Emitting light, esp. self-generated light – **luminous**
    Transmitting, yielding or producing light – **luminiferous**
    Admitting maximum passage of light without diffusion or distortion – **pellucid**, n. **pellucidity** or **pellucidness**
    Without light – **aphotic**
    Avoiding light – **lucifugal; lucifugous**
    Reflecting light – **relucent**
    Impervious to the passage of light; not reflecting light – **opaque**
        The quality or state of being opaque – **opacity**
        A chemical agent added to a material to make it opaque - **opacifier**
    Surgical coagulation of tissue using intense light energy, as a laser beam – **photocoagulation**
    The treatment of disease, esp. certain skin conditions, with light – **phototherapy**
    Admitting and diffusing light so that objects beyond cannot be clearly perceived – **translucent**
    Capable of transmitting light so that objects or images beyond can be clearly perceived – **transparent**
    Emission of visible light by a hot object; the light so emitted – **incandescence**, adj. **incandescent**
        To become incandescent – **incandesce** (v.i.)
    The emission of light by processes that derive energy from essentially nonthermal sources, esp. as distinct from incandescence – **luminescence**, adj. **luminescent**
        To become luminescent – **luminesce** (v.i.)

The emission of light by living organisms, such as the firefly – **bioluminescence**; **phosphorescence**
    Phosphorescence developed in a previously excited substance (quartz, e.g.) upon gentle heating –
        thermoluminescence; thermophosphorescence
Persistent emission of light following exposure to and removal of incident radiation – **phosphorescence**, adj.
    phosphorescent
    To emit light in this way – **phosphoresce** (v.i.)
    A phosphorescent light hovering or flitting over swampy ground at night – **ignis fatuus**
The emission of electromagnetic radiation, esp. visible light, resulting from the absorption of incident radiation and
    persisting only as long as the stimulating radiation is continued – **fluorescence**
    To undergo, produce or exhibit fluorescence – **fluoresce** (v.i.)
Reflecting an iridescent light – **opalescent**, n. **opalescence**
A pathologic effect produced by light (e.g., swelling) – **photopathy**
Flickering lightly on or over a surface; characterized by effortless brilliance or lightness – **lambent**
Exhibiting a progressively larger lighted surface (as the moon) – **increscent; waxing**
More than half but less than fully illuminated – **gibbous** (used of the moon or a planet)
A faint, hazy cone of light often seen in the west after sunset or in the east before sunrise – **zodiacal light**
A hypothetical particle that travels faster than the speed of light – **tachyon**
Glowing with light – **lucent** (n. **lucency**); **luciform; luminous** (n. **luminosity**); **radiant**
Luminous at night – **noctilucent** (used esp. of high clouds)
A luminous area surrounding the sun or other bright light when seen through thin cloud, fog or mist – **areole; corona;**
    glory; halo; nimbus
A halo around an object's shadow cast by the sun on a cloud or bank of mist at high altitudes or in polar regions -
    anthelion
That property of ultraviolet light, x-rays, etc., by which chemical reactions are produced – **actinism**
Of or relating to an organism that is receptive to, seeks, or thrives in light – **photophilic; photophilous**
The response of an organism to the length of exposure to light in a 24-hour period – **photoperiodicity**;
    photoperiodism

Lightning:
    Flashing like lightning – **fulgurant**
    Emitting lightning flashes; emitting flashes resembling lightning – **fulgurous**
    Lightning that appears as a broad, sheetlike illumination of parts of a thundercloud – **sheet lightning**
    Extreme or irrational fear of thunder and lightning – **astraphobia**

Limbs, having well-formed – **clean-limbed**

Line:
    A distinctive line, shape or contour, esp. of the face – **lineament**
    Of, relating to or resembling a line – **linear**
    To project or put in a linear form – **linearize** (v.t.)
    The act of marking or outlining with lines; an arrangement of lines – **lineation**
    Marked with fine lines – **lineolate**
    Formed, bounded or characterized by curved lines – **curvilinear**
    Lying on the same line; containing a common line – **collinear**
    Relating to, having or bounded by three lines – **trilinear**
    A straight line segment passing through the center of a figure, esp. of a circle or sphere, and ending at the periphery;
        the length of such a segment – **diameter** (q.v.)
    A straight line cutting a curve at two or more points- **secant**
    One of the short lines used to shade or indicate slopes on maps – **hachure**
    A line that intersects a system of lines – **transversal; traverse**
    Having perpendicular lines – **orthographic**

Divination by lines and figures – **geomancy**

Linen:
  Household linen, esp. table linen – **napery**

Lion:
  A female lion – **lioness**
  A young lion – **cub**
  A group of lions – **flock**; **pride**; **troop**

Lips:
  Having lips or liplike parts – **labiate**; **labiated**; **lipped**
  Having gaping, liplike parts – **ringent** (Biol.)
  Of or relating to the lips or labia – **labial**
    To make labial – **labialize** (v.t.)
  A liplike structure – **labium** (Zool.)

Liquid (see also Fluid):
  Becoming or tending to become liquid – **liquescent**; **melting**
  To cause to become liquid – **liquefy**; **liquify** (both v.t.); n. **liquefaction**
  To plunge into or steep in a liquid – **souse** (v.t.)
  The amount of liquid within a container that is lost during shipment or storage – **ullage**
  To draw off (a liquid) by piercing a hole in a cask or other container – **broach** (v.t.)
  To clarify (a liquid) by removing a surface scum – **despumate** (v.t.)
  To transfer (liquid) by pouring from one container into another – **transfuse** (v.t.)
  Pouring on of liquid, as in baptism – **affusion**
  Made liquid by heat – **molten**
  To introduce (gas) into a liquid – **sparge** (v.t.)
  Of, relating to or operated by the force of a moving liquid – **hydrodynamic**; **hydrodynamical**
  A suspension of precipitated matter in a watery substance – **magma**

Literal, to make – **literalize** (v.t.)

Literature and Related Terms (see also Figures of Speech):
  Ordinary writing – **prose**, adj. **prosaic**
    A writer of prose - **prosaist**
  One who loves literature – **philolog**; **philologer**; **philologist**; **philologue**
  The literary intelligentsia – **clerisy**; **literati**
  The world of literary hacks – **grub street**; **Grub Street**
  A man of letters – **litterateur**
  A literary or dramatic form of discourse in which a character talks to himself or reveals his thoughts in the form of a monologue without addressing a listener – **soliloquy**
    To utter or put into a soliloquy – **soliloquize** (v.t./v.i.)
  A monologue representing a fictional character's thoughts and emotions – **interior monologue**
  Collected literary excerpts or fragments of writing – **analecta**; **analects**
  A brief literary quotation or quotable passage - **snippet**
  A selection of literary passages, used in studying literature or a language – **chrestomathy**
  A collection of literary pieces, such as poems, short stories or plays – **anthology**
    To compile or include in an anthology – **anthologize** (v.t.)
  A collection of writings on a topic – **symposium**, pl. **symposia** or **symposiums**
  A collection of diverse literary works – **miscellany**; **varia**

A printed anthology of the works of one author or of writings on related subjects – **omnibus**

A fictional prose narrative longer than a short story or novelette; the literary genre represented by such works – **novel**

    A short novel – **novelette**; **novella**

    A writer of novels – **novelist**

    A novel in which actual persons or places are depicted in fictional guise – **roman à clef**

A literary or dramatic work involving struggle, calamity, etc., esp. one that has an unhappy but meaningful end – **tragedy** (q.v.)

Of, belonging to or typical of a literary genre in which the rogue-hero's escapades are typically depicted in a context of a sharp social satire; of or involving clever rogues or adventurers – **picaresque**

A literary work openly imitating the previous work of another artist – **pastiche**

A literary or dramatic work in which each character, object and event symbolically illustrates an idea or moral or religious principle; an instance of this – **allegory**, adj. **allegorical**, n. **allegorist**, v.i./v.t. **allegorize**

    A short allegorical story with a lesson or moral – **apologue**; **fable**

A short conversational piece of writing – **causerie**

A formal written account treating a subject systematically and in detail – **treatise**

An adventure story – **conte**

A literary sketch or brief prose work – **pastel**; **vignette**

    A maker of or a specialist in vignettes – **vignetter**; **vignettist**

A collection of anecdotes, reminiscences, etc. – **ana**, pl. **ana** or **anas**

A long, elaborate tale of woe – **jeremiad**

An edition of the works of an author, with notes by various scholars or editors; an edition containing various versions of a text; designating or relating to such an edition or text – **variorum**

A group of three literary or dramatic works that are related in subject matter or theme – **trilogy**

A series of four related dramas, operas or literary works – **tetralogy**

The sacred literature of a given people – **hierology**

Literary works for children; written works produced in childhood or youth – **juvenilia**

A literary work in which human vice or folly is attacked through irony, derision or wit; the branch of literature that comprises such works – **satire**

    A writer of satirical works – **satirist**

    To ridicule by means of a satire – **satirize** (v.t.)

    A broad satirical piece that ridicules a person, group or institution; light, good-humored satire; to satirize (a person, group, etc.) in this way – **lampoon** (n./v.t.)

    A lampoon posted in a public place – **pasquinade**

A literary work that broadly mimics an author's characteristic style and holds it up to ridicule; to ridicule a literary work thus – **parody** (n./v.t.)

A sensational literary work of poor quality, produced quickly for profit – **potboiler**

A written memorial or tribute to a scholar, consisting of a volume of learned articles or essays by his or her colleagues or admirers – **festschrift**

A professional reciter of literary works - **reader**

The leading character or principal figure – **protagonist**

A simple story illustrating a moral or religious lesson – **parable**

A short story that illustrates a moral or makes a point in an argument – **exemplum**

A medieval collection of allegorical fable about real and imaginary animals – **bestiary**

A paper or pamphlet containing a declaration or appeal, esp. one distributed by a special interest group – **tract**

A peddler of devotional literature – **colporteur**

    The work of a colporteur – **colportage**

A character in a play, novel, etc., who voices the central theme or viewpoint of the work – **raisonneur**

An improbable character or a contrived device or event suddenly introduced to untangle a plot or resolve a situation – **deus ex machina**

An archaic word, phrase, style, etc. – **archaism**

    To use archaisms – **archaize** (v.i.)

Typical of or appropriate to writing that seeks the effect of speech – **colloquial**

The use of vivid description or figures of speech (q.v.) (in writing or speaking) to produce mental images – **imagery**

A similarity or repetition of terminal consonants in two or more syllables, words or lines – **consonance**

Repetition of a words or phrases at the start of several successive clauses, sentences, paragraphs or verses - **anaphora**

A partial rhyme in which the accented vowel sounds correspond but the consonants differ – **assonance**

A short literary work describing a picturesque episode or pleasant scene of country life – **idyl**; **idyll**

   A writer of idylls – **idyllist**

   Of, relating to or like an idyll – **idyllic**

A ludicrously abrupt transition from an elevated to a commonplace style – **bathos**, adj. **bathetic**

A satirical imitation or burlesque of the heroic manner or style – **mock-heroic**

   Having a mock-heroic style – **Hudibrastic**

To combine (e.g., two variant texts) into one whole – **conflate** (v.t.)

Witty writings and sayings – **facetiae**

A nonsense composition - **amphigory**

A writer of fiction, esp. a prolific writer of pulp fiction – **fictioneer**

Of or relating to the creation of fiction – **fictive**

The outcome of the plot of a play or novel – **denouement**; **dénouement**

A literary work consisting of two contrasting plots – **diptych**

A subordinate plot – **subplot**

To steal and use (the ideas or writings of another) as one's own – **plagiarize** (v.t./v.i.), n. **plagiarism** or **plagiary**

The use of misspellings to represent dialectal or nonstandard speech – **eye dialect**

The theory or practice of emphasizing the regional characteristics of locale or setting, as by stressing local speech - **regionalism**

The transposition of initial or other sounds of words – **spoonerism**

The practice of expressing ideas in a prose composition in single lines corresponding to natural cadences or sense divisions – **stichometry**

A verbal expression, as a word or phrase; the way in which something is worded; a phrase or sentence having little or no meaning; a use of words regarded as obscuring ideas or reality – **verbalism**

An expression possessing cleverness in perception and choice of words – **witticism**

The writing or telling of short narratives concerning an interesting, amusing or curious event – **anecdotalism**

A florid and deliberately obscure literary style – **Gongorism**

A bit of literary crudity – **gaucherie**

A small or petty work, as of literature – **opuscle**; **opuscule**; **opusculum**, adj. **opuscular**

Of or relating to style, esp. literary style - **stylistic**

A style in fictional literature characterized by gloomy settings; violent, grotesque or mysterious events; and a mood of decay and degeneration – **gothicism**, adj. **gothic**

A literary style characterized by haziness and lack of sharp definition – **obscurantism**, n. **obscurantist**

Literary style that reflects an adherence to that of ancient Greece or Rome – **classicism**

A concise, cleverly worded saying, esp. a paradoxical one – **epigram**

   Literary style characterized by the use of epigrams – **epigrammatism**

The style of writing characterized by derision – **sardonicism**

Literary interpretation that seeks to extract from language a spiritual significance – **anagoge** (pl. **anagoges**); **anagogy**, pl. **anagogies**

Literature regarded as a fine art; light and elegant literature, esp. that which is excessively refined – **belles-lettres**, adj. **belletristic**, n. **belletrist**

To edit (a written work) by removing or modifying passages considered vulgar or objectionable – **bowdlerize**; **expurgate** (both v.t.)

To correct a literary work, esp. by textual alterations – **emend** (v.t.)

A word or phrase used in place of another, supposedly less gentile term – **genteelism**

Subject matter or style producing or designed to produce startling or thrilling impressions, or to excite and please vulgar taste - **sensationalism**

A manuscript in which one or two earlier erased writings are found - **palimpsest**

Divination by interpretation of a literary passage chosen at random – **bibliomancy**

Live (see also Life):

To live in such a manner as to undo the effects of – **unlive** (v.t.)

To live longer than – **outlive**; **survive** (both v.t.)

Capable of living, developing or germinating under favorable conditions - **viable**

An abnormal desire to live alone – **agromania** (see also Alone)

A person who lives abroad on funds sent from home – **remittance man**

Liver:

Of, relating to, occurring in, or acting on the liver – **hepatic**

Inflammation of the liver – **hepatitis**

Originating in or produced by the liver – **hepatogenic**; **hepatogenous**

The quality or condition of being toxic to the liver – **hepatotoxicity**

Livestock (see also Animal and Pasture):

The raising of livestock – **stockbreeding**

One who owns or raises livestock; one who is in charge of livestock or works on a stock farm – **stockman**

To feed or pasture (livestock) for a fee – **agist** (v.t.)

To feed (livestock) when grazing is not possible – **winter-feed** (v.t.)

Feed for livestock - **fodder**

Fodder prepared by storing and fermenting green forage plants in a silo – **silage**

The dried stalks and leaves of a cereal crop, used as fodder after the grain has been harvested – **stover**

Seasonal movement of livestock and herders to different grazing grounds – **transhumance**

Loan:

A loan or advance of government funds for service to the government – **imprest**

A loan to be paid within or by a specified time – **time loan**

Lobe:

Having lobes – **lobate**; **lobated**; **lobed**

A small lobe; a subdivision or section of a lobe – **lobule**

Having or consisting of lobules – **lobulate**; **lobulated**

A part resembling a lobe; the state of being lobed – **lobation**

Divided into two lobes; having two lobes – **bilobate**; **bilobated**; **bilobed**; **bilobular**

Divided into two lobes by a median cleft – **bifid**

Having three lobes – **trilobated**; **trilobed**

Divided into three narrow lobes - **trifid**

Having ten lobes – **decalobate**

Cut into many lobes – **multifid**

Surgical removal of a lobe – **lobectomy**

Lobster:

A female lobster – **hen**

A young lobster – **chicken lobster**

Local:

To make local; to restrict, confine or attribute to a specific locality; to become local – **localize** (v.t./v.i.)

Not local – **azonic**
Excessive devotion to local interests and customs – **sectionalism**

Location (see also Place):
Located nearest the center of the body or the point of attachment – **proximal** (Biol.)
Located far from the origin or line of attachment – **distal** (Anat.)

Lock (see also Key):
One who makes or repairs locks – **locksmith**
A lock set to open at a specific time – **time lock**

Locusts, a group of – **plague**; **swarm**

Log:
To cause a floating log to spin rapidly by rotating with the feet; to participate in such activity – **birl** (v.t./v.i.)
A barrier composed of a chain of floating logs enclosing other free-floating logs – **boom**
A log of a size large enough for sawing into boards – **saw log**

Logic (see also Reason/Reasoning):
A practitioner of a system of logic – **logician**
The branch of logic dealing with the general principles of the formation of knowledge – **methodology**
To bring (isolated observations) together by an explanation or hypothesis that applies to them all – **colligate** (v.t.)
In the relation of a particular proposition to a universal with the same subject, predicate and quality; such a proposition
   – **subaltern**

Logos (logotypes):
The use of logos in printing and design – **logography**

Lots:
The casting or drawing of – **sortition**
Divination by drawing lots - **sortilege**

Love:
Love of mankind in general – **philanthropy**
Of or relating to the love of children – **philoprogenitive**
Excessive love or admiration of oneself – **narcissism**
Strongly attracted to or indicative of love, esp. sexual love – **amative**; **amatory**; **amorous**
A person much occupied with love and love-making – **amorist**
A love affair, esp. of an illicit or secret nature – **amour**
Magical or necromantic love – **pneumatology**
A man with whom one is in love or has an intimate relationship – **inamorato**
A woman with whom one is in love or has an intimate relationship – **inamorata**

Lowering:
Abnormal and permanent lowering of an organ – **ptosis**

Loyalty:
One who maintains loyalty to a lawful government, political party or sovereign, esp. during war or revolutionary change
   – **loyalist**

Luck:

Dependent upon chance, luck, or an uncertain outcome – **aleatory**

The faculty of making fortunate and unexpected discoveries by accident – **serendipity**, adj. **serendipitous**

Lungs:

Of or relating to the lungs – **pulmonary**; **pulmonic**

Having lungs or lunglike organs – **pulmonary**; **pulmonate**

The surgical removal of a lung or part of a lung – **pneumectomy**

Of or involving the lungs and the stomach – **pneumogastric**

Acute or chronic inflammation of the mucous membrane of the bronchial tubes – **bronchitis**

Deposition of coal dust within the lungs from inhalation of sooty air – **anthracosis**

Chronic dilation of the bronchial tubes, with cough and formation of mucopurulent matter – **bronchiectasis**

Chronic lung inflammation caused by prolonged inhalation of asbestos particles – **asbestosis**

Luster – see Gem

Lyre, shaped like a - **lyriform**

M

Machines:
The technology of the efficient use of machines by human beings – **human engineering**
The study of relationships between man and machines – **biotechnology**

Mackerel:
A group of mackerel – **shoal**
A young mackerel – **blinker**; **spike**; **tinker**

Magic:
A person who practices magic – **charmer**; **magician**; **sorcerer**; **thaumaturge**; **thaumaturgist**; **wizard** (q.v.)
A great magician – **archimage**
A conjurer or magician who creates illusions, as by slight of hand; an adherent of illusionism - **illusionist**
An object held to confer on its bearer supernatural powers or protection; something having apparently magical power –
talisman, adj. **talismanic**
The art or practice of casting spells; the ritual chanting or reciting of verses supposed to have magic or occult power –
charm; **incantation**; **mojo**; **rune**
A small object worn or carried to ward off evil or ensure good fortune – **amulet**; **charm**; **mojo**; **rune**
A sign, word or device of supposed occult power in magic or astrology – **sigil**

Magnetism:
The total flow of magnetism or magnetic lines of force through a magnetic circuit – **magnetic flux**
The power of a magnet to induce magnetism in a piece of iron, steel, etc., brought into its magnetic field – **magnetic
induction**
Designating or relating to points of equal magnetic induction – **isomagnetic**
The study of electrically conducting fluids in electric and magnetic fields – **hydromagnetics**;
magnetohydrodynamics
The study of magnetic characteristics associated with atmospheric conditions – **aeromagnetics**

Magpies, a group of – **tidings**

Male:
Of or relating to male offspring – **androgenous**
Related on the male or father's side; a relative on the male or father's side only – **agnate**, n. **agnation**
Derived from the male line – **agnate**; **patriclinous**; **patroclinous**
A society in which descent and succession are traced through the male line – **patriarchy**
Relating to, based on, or tracing descent through the male line - **patrilineal**
The domination of society and politics by males – **androcracy**

Mallards, a flight of – **sord**

Mammals:
The study of mammals – **mammalogy**
A mammal that lacks a placenta and has an external abdominal pouch (marsupium) containing the teats – **marsupial**

Man (see also Human):
In relation to man – **manward**; **manwards**
Resembling man; manlike – **anthropoid** (said of apes)
Of or having the characteristics of a man – **masculine** (n. **masculinity**); **virile**, n. **virility**
A male relative; a man sharing the same racial, cultural or national background as another – **kinsman**

Extreme or irrational fear of men – **androphobia**

Hatred of men – **androphobia**; **misandry**, n. **misandrist**

A dislike of males (in women) – **misandria**; **misandry**

The rule of a family or tribe of men – **patriarchy**

Emphasizing masculine points of view or interests; centering or centered on or in the male - **androcentric**

Management:

Of, like, or characteristic of a manager – **managerial**

The position, authority or duties of a manager – **managership**

Capable of managing one's own affairs – **sui juris** (Law)

One who manages the affairs of another - **procurator**

The procurement, maintenance, distribution and replacement of personnel and material – **logistics** (sing. or pl. in number)

Skilled management – **generalship**

The management of affairs; the management of a public or private institution – **administration**, v.i./v.t. **administer**

Maladministration of a public office – **misprision**

Mane, having a – **maned**

Mantle, having a – **chlamydate** (Zool.)

Manuscript:

The genealogy of the manuscripts of a literary work – **stemma**, pl. **stemmata** or **stemmas**

A room, as in a monastery, library, etc., where manuscripts are stored, read or copied – **scriptorium**

Manuscript notes:

Indication that a letter, word or other matter marked for omission is to be retained – **stet**

Indication that the word or passage occurs frequently in the work cited – **passim**

Indication that a term or idea is to be found throughout a cited work – **sic passim**

Above – **supra**

In the work cited – **op. cit.** (opera citato)

In the place cited – **loc. cit.** (loco citato)

In the same place – **ib.** or **ibid.** (ibidem)

Which see – **q.v.** (quod vide)

See – **v.** or **vide**

Compare – **cf.** (confer)

The same – **id.** (idem) (used to indicate a previously mentioned reference)

Maps/Mapping:

The art or technique of making maps – **cartography**

The technique of mapping a region or district – **chorography**

A book or bound collection of maps – **atlas**

A line on a map or chart connecting:

Points of equal atmospheric pressure – **isobar**; **isopiestic**

Points of equal magnetic dip – **isoclinic line**

Points of equal magnetic declination – **isogonic line**

Points of equal value – **isogram**; **isoline**

Points of equal atmospheric density - **isostere**

Points receiving equal sunlight – **isohel**

Points receiving equal rainfall – **isohyet**

Points having equal mean temperature for a specified period, or equal temperatures at a specific time – **isotherm**; **isothermal**

Points having the same property simultaneously, as requiring the same time to be reached by available transportation from a given center – **isochrone**

Points having the same amount of cloudiness – **isoneph**

Points having the same numerical value – **isopleth**

Points where ice starts to form at approximately the same period at the onset of winter – **isopectic**

Points where ice starts to melt at approximately the same period in spring - **isotac**

Marble:

To make, color, grain or streak in imitation of marble – **marbleize** (v.t.)

Of or like marble – **marbly**; **marmoreal**; **marmorean**

A marble to be used as a shooter; to shoot a marble – **taw** (n./v.i.)

Margin:

Of, relating to or comprising a margin; written or printed in the margin of a book – **marginal**

To provide with a margin – **marginate** (v.t.)

Having a distinct margin – **marginate**; **marginated**

Beneath a margin – **submarginal**

Marginal notes – **marginalia**

Marijuana (cannabis):

Addiction to marijuana **– cannabism**

Marriage:

Of or relating to marriage or the marital relationship – **conjugal**; **connubial**; **hymeneal**; **marital**; **matrimonial**; **nuptial**; **spousal**

The state of being married – **matrimony**; **wedlock**

Ready for marriage; of a marriageable age or condition – **nubile** (used of young women)

Of or relating to the wedding ceremony – **nuptial**

A nuptial song or poem in honor or praise of a bride and bridegroom – **epithalamion**; **epithalamium**; **epithalamy**, pl. **epithalamia** or **epithalamies** or **epithalamiums**

The personal possessions that a bride assembles for her marriage – **trousseau**, pl. **trousseaus** or **trousseaux**

Occurring or existing prior to marriage – **premarital**

An offer of marriage – **proposal**

A bridegroom's attendant at the former's wedding – **best man**; **groomsman**

The condition of being unmarried – **celibacy**

One who remains unmarried; of or relating to the condition of being unmarried or to one who has remained thus – **celibate**

The criminal offense of marrying one person while still legally married to another – **bigamy**

Remarriage after the death or divorce of one's own spouse – **digamy**

A second legal marriage after the death or divorce of a first spouse - **deuterogamy**

The practice of being married to more than one person at a time – **polygamy**, adj. **polygamous**

A marriage form or custom in which a woman has only one husband at a time – **monandry**, adj. **monandrous**

To marry a member of another group; to marry within one's family, tribe or clan – **intermarry** (v.i.)

Marriage within a particular group, class or tribe consistent with custom or law – **endogamy**

The practice of marrying outside one's own tribe, class, etc. – **exogamy**; **outbreeding**

Marriage with a person of inferior social position – **mésalliance** (pl. **mésalliances**); **misalliance**

Marriage to the widow of one's brother – **levirate**

Marriage of a man to his wife's sister, usually after the wife has died or proved sterile – **sororate**

Of or relating to a marriage between one of royal or noble birth and a partner of lower rank, in which no title or estates of the royal or noble partner may be claimed by the partner of inferior rank, nor by any of the offspring of the marriage – **morganatic**

Of, relating to or born of a morganatic marriage – **left-handed**

The legal status of a woman during marriage - **coverture**

A newly married man who was previously considered a confirmed bachelor – **benedict**

A man who first marries and then murders one wife after another – **bluebeard**

False and actionable pretension that one is married to someone – **jactitation of marriage**

Marriage or cohabitation between a white person and a member of another race - **miscegenation**

Hatred of marriage – **misogamy**

Martens, a group - **richness**

Martyr:

Like or in the manner of a martyr – **martyrly**

To put (a person) to death for adhering to a faith or belief – **martyrize** (v.t.)

A place where the relics of martyrs are preserved – **martyrium**, pl. **martyria**

A shrine built in honor of a martyr – **martyry**

A list of martyrs – **martyrology**

Mask:

Having masklike markings – **masked**

A person who wears a mask – **masker**

Masonry – see Stone

Mass:

Formed into a rounded, compact mass – **clustered**; **glomerate**

To make or form into a rounded mass; formed in this way – **agglomerate** (v.t./adj.)

The product of a body's mass and linear velocity – **momentum**

A solid mass of inorganic material formed in the human body – **calculus** (pl. **calculi** or **calculuses**); **concretion**

Relating to, caused by or having a calculus or calculi – **calculous**

The formation of calculi in the body – **lithiasis**

Preventing the formation or development of calculi – **antilithic**

Surgery to remove calculi – **lithotomy**

Surgical pulverization of calculi in the urethra or bladder – **lithotrity**

Massage:

The treatment of disease by massage – **massotherapy**

A man who gives massages professionally – **masseur**

A woman who gives massages professionally – **masseuse**

A massage in which finger pressure is applied to those areas of the body used in acupuncture – **shiatsu**

Master or magistrate, suitable for a – **magisterial**

Mastoid:

The surgical removal of part or all of a mastoid – **mastoidectomy**

Inflammation of the mastoid – **mastoiditis**

Matchbooks or matchboxes, one who collects – **phillumenist**

Matched, badly – **ill-sorted**

Mating:
    Of, relating to or occurring in the mating season – **nuptial**
    Random mating within a breeding population – **panmixis**, adj. **panmictic**

Matted or growing in dense tufts or turflike clumps – **caespitose**; **cespitose**

Matter:
    The theory that all matter has life, or that matter and life are inseparable – **hylozoism**, adj. **hylozoistic**
    The theory that regards matter and its motions as the only reality and all occurrences as due to material agencies –
        materialism
    The science of matter and energy, and of interactions between the two – **physics**
    The study of the deformation and flow of matter – **rheology**
    The quantity of matter in a body as measured in its relation to inertia – **mass**
    Of, relating to or existing in a state of matter intermediate between liquid and crystal – **mesomorphic**
    Of or relating to a body of matter as a whole, perceived apart from molecular or atomic properties - **molar**

Mature, the process of becoming – **maturation**

Maximum:
    Of, relating to or consisting of a maximum – **maximal**

Mayor, the office or term of office of a – **mayoralty**

Mealy in texture – **farinaceous**

Meaning:
    Having only one meaning - **univocal**
    Having or capable of two meanings - **amphibolous**

Measure:
    Of or relating to measure – **mensural**
    Of or relating to measurement – **metrical**
    The science that deals with measurement – **metrology**
    A standard of measurement – **metric**; **module**
    Of or exhibiting equality in measurements or dimensions; a line connecting points of equal measurements – **isometric**
    Equality of measure – **isometry**
    Of, relating to or characterized by equality of measure – **isometric** (adj./n); **isometrical**
    The official measurement of weight or contents – **metage**
    The study and technique of human body measurement for use in anthropological classification and comparison –
        anthropometry, n. **anthropometrist**
    Measurement of the depth of large bodies of water – **bathymetry**
    Having the contents made even with the top of a measuring device of container – **stricken**
    A dry measure having the contents leveled off – **struck measure**
    To check, adjust or systematically standardize the graduations of a quantitative measuring instrument – **calibrate** (v.t.)

Meat:
    Composed of, prepared with, or relating to meat or meat products – **fleishig**
    One who carves meat – **trencher**
    To cut (meat) into long strips and dry in the sun or cure by exposing to smoke – **jerk** (v.t.)

Meat cured in this way – **jerky**

Medals:

One who designs, makes or collects medals; a recipient of a medal – **medalist**

Medicine:

Relating to or having the properties of medicine – **medicinal**

Potentially responsive to treatment with medicine – **medicable**

A solid medication designed to melt within a body cavity other than the mouth – **suppository**

Substances used as or in preparing medical remedies – **materia medica**

A medicine or remedy of secret composition recommended by its preparer but usually lacking general repute or acceptance - **nostrum**

A roving hawker of nostrums who attracts customers with stories, jokes or tricks - **mountebank**

Of or applied to an isolated part of the body – **topical**

A soothing medication – **abirritant**

A medicine meant to be licked with the tongue - **linctus**

Doing neither harm nor good, as a medicine - **adiaphorous**

A person who assists a medical professional – **paramedic**

Medical treatment by mechanical methods, as massage – **mechanotherapy**

The study of medicine as it relates to biological systems – **biomedicine**

Tending to draw together or constrict tissue; a substance that does this – **astringent**; **styptic**

Medical study and treatment of nonsurgical diseases in adults – **internal medicine**

A physician specializing in internal medicine – **internist**

The degree to which a drug, nutrient or other agent becomes available at the physiological site of activity – **bioavailability**

The branch of medicine that deals with the use of specialized mechanical devices to support or supplement weakened joints or limbs – **orthotics**

The branch of medicine that deals with the diseases and injuries resulting from sports participation – **sports medicine**

The branch of medicine that deals with the biological, physiological and psychological effects of space flight on human beings – **space medicine**

Traditional medicine practiced by people who have no access to modern medical services – **folk medicine**

A system of medicine based on the use of small quantities of remedies that in large doses produce effects similar to those of the disease being treated – **homeopathy**

The science of medicine or healing; a treatise on medicine and physicians – **iatrology**

The science of medicinal dosage – **dosology**; **posology**

Meeting:

To call together or summon to meet – **convoke** (v.t.)

An agreement to meet at a certain time and place; a meeting or meeting place that has been agreed on; to keep such an agreement – **tryst** (n./v.i.)

Fully attended or constituted; including all entitled to be present – **plenary** (used esp. of meetings and conferences)

The minimum number of members of a constituted body who must be present for the valid transaction of business - **quorum**

A scheduled meeting of a small group of advanced college or graduate students engaged in special study or original research under the guidance of a professor; a meeting for an exchanged of ideas in a particular area - **seminar**

A group of people who meet regularly for a seminar in a specialized field - **workshop**

An unplanned meeting – **rencounter**

A conference typically held for the discussion of points in dispute - **parley**

Closed or secret session – **in camera**

A meeting or conference for discussion of some topic- **symposium**, pl. **symposia** or **symposiums**, adj. **symposiac**

Melon:
  A melon grower – **melonist**
  A place for growing melons – **melonry**

Melting:
  Formed by melting or casting – **fusile**
  Capable of being melted or fused by heating – **fusible**
  The temperature at which a solid becomes a liquid at standard atmospheric pressure – **melting point**
  The process or art of melting; the quantity or substance produced by a melting process – **meltage**

Member:
  The state of being a member; the total number of members in a group – **membership**
    The entire membership of a specific group - **plenum**
  A group of three closely related members - **trinity**
  A custom or usage regarded as a criterion for distinguishing members of one group from those of another - **shibboleth**

Membrane:
  Made of or similar to a membrane – **membranous**
  A membranous structure, as the fold under the tongue, that restrains movement or supports a part – **frenum**
  An enclosing membrane – **capsule**; **indusium**
  A thin membrane extending between the fore and hind limb to form a wing or winglike extension, as in bats and flying squirrels; an expandable, membranous fold of skin between the wing and body of a bird - **patagium**

Memoirs, a person who writes – **memorialist**

Memory (see also Forgetting):
  Related to or concerning memory – **mnestic**
  A recollection or recalling to mind; an act or process of recalling the past – **anamnesis**; **remembrance**; **reminiscence**
  The state of being remembered; the length of time spanned by one's memory – **remembrance**
    Remarkable things worthy of remembrance – **memorabilia**
  A thing remembered – **memory**; **reminiscence**
  Something serving to celebrate or honor the memory of a person or event – **memorial**; **remembrance**
  Memory of a supposed life before the present one - **anamnesis**
  Relating to, assisting, or designed to assist the memory; a device (such as a formula or rhyme) used as an aid in remembering – **mnemonic**
  A system to improve or develop the memory – **mnemonics**
  Unusually accurate or vivid memory – **hypermnesia**, adj. **hypermnesic**
  Total or partial loss of memory – **amnesia**, adj. **amnesic**
    Causing amnesia – **amnestic**
  A distortion of memory in which fantasy and experience are confused – **paramnesia**
  A filling in of gaps in memory by free fabrication - **confabulation**
  The act or process of becoming oblivious or forgetting – **oblivescence**
  The occurrence in consciousness of images not recognized as produced by the memory, but appearing as original creations – **cryptamnesia**; **cryptomnesia**
  The belief that every mental impression remains in the memory – **panmnesia**
  The illusion of having previously experienced something actually being encountered for the first time – **déjà vu**

Menstruation:
  To undergo menstruation – **menstruate** (v.i.)
  The first occurrence of menstruation – **menarche**

The physical contents of menstruation – **catamenia**; **menses**
Abnormally heavy menstrual flow – **menorrhagia**
Abnormal absence or suppression of menstruation – **amenorrhea**; **amenorrhoea**
A medicine that hastens or induces menstrual flow – **emmenagogue**
The period of cessation of menstruation – **menopause**

Mental illness (see also Behavior):
The study, diagnosis, treatment and prevention of mental illness – **psychiatry**
Severe mental disorder characterized by degeneration of normal intellectual and social functioning, and by partial or total withdrawal from reality – **psychosis**, pl. **psychoses**, adj. **psychotic**
One afflicted with psychosis – **psychotic**
Relating to or inducing psychotic symptoms – **psychotomimetic**
A psychotic reaction marked by withdrawal from reality with highly variable accompanying disturbances of mood, thought and behavior – **schizophrenia**, adj. **schizophrenic**
Characteristic of or resembling schizophrenia – **schizoid**
One afflicted with schizophrenia – **schizophrene**; **schizophrenic**
A schizophrenic disorder marked by plastic immobility of the limbs, stupor, negativism and the inability to speak – **catatonia**, adj. **catatonic**
One afflicted with catatonia – **catatonic**
A schizophrenic disorder marked by foolish mannerisms, delusions, hallucinations and regressive behavior – **hebephrenia**, adj. **hebephrenic**
A functional disorder of the mind or emotions without obvious organic lesion or change, and involving abnormal behavioral symptoms, as anxiety or phobia – **neurosis**, pl. **neuroses**, adj. **neurotic**
One afflicted with neurosis – **neurotic**
A neurosis marked by the presence of bodily symptoms with no physical cause or basis – **conversion reaction**
The scientific study of pathological mental conditions – **psychopathology**
The science or method of treating psychological abnormalities and disorders by psychological techniques, esp. by psychoanalysis, group therapy or consultation – **psychotherapy**
The method developed by Sigmund Freud and others to treat mental disorders (esp. neuroses) through free association, dream interpretation, etc. – **psychoanalysis**
One who is undergoing psychoanalysis - **analysand**
In psychoanalysis, awareness of and adjustment to environmental demands in a way that assures ultimate satisfaction of instinctual needs – **reality principle**
The branch of psychiatry that deals with incipient and borderline mental disorders, esp. in childhood and youth – **orthopsychiatry**
Of, relating to or being a theory holding that mental illness is related to chemical deficiencies and imbalances – **orthomolecular**
A type of manic-depressive psychosis, exemplified by rapidly changing ideas, extremes of emotion, and physical overactivity; violently abnormal behavior – **mania**, n. **maniac**
Pathological obsession with a single idea or subject – **monomania**
A mental disorder in which fantasies of power or wealth predominate – **megalomania**, n. **megalomaniac**
An attack of mental inertia and hopelessness – **psycholepsy**
A mental disorder of unknown origin or cause – **psychopathy**
Violently incurable insanity – **acromania**
Extreme or irrational fear of becoming insane - **lyssophobia**

Merchants or trade, of or relating to – **mercantile**

Mercury (the element):
To treat or combine with mercury or a mercury compound – **mercurate** (v.t.)
Poisoning cause by mercury or its compounds – **mercurialism**

Merge:
   To merge into each other through a series of stages, forms, or types – **intergrade** (v.i.)

Metal:
   Containing metal – **metaliferous**
   Of, resembling, or having the properties of a metal – **metalline**
   Having the appearance of a metal – **metalloid** (see also Chemistry)
   A metal that is a mixture of two or more metals, or of a metal and something else – **alloy** (q.v.)
   To combine with another metal – **amalgamate** (v.t.), adj. **amalgamative**
   To melt or fuse (ores), separating the metallic constituents – **smelt** (v.t.)
   To whiten (a metal) by soaking in acid or by coating with tin – **blanch** (v.t.)
   Consisting of or containing one metal – **monometallic**
   The use of metals or metal compounds in the treatment of disease – **metallotherapy**
   Gilded metal, such as silver, bronze or copper - **vermeil**
   The art of working metal, esp. by the use of embossing and chasing to form minute detailed reliefs – **torentics**
   To ornament (iron or steel, e.g.) with inlaid work of precious metals – **damascene** (v.t.)
   Shaped or decorated with patterns in relief made by hammering and pressing on the reverse side – **repoussé** (used esp. of metals)
   A thin disk of metal – **paten**; **patin**; **patine**
   A mass of metal shaped in a bar or block; a casting mold for metal – **ingot**
   The study of the structure of metals and their compounds, esp. with a microscope – **metallography**
   Of or relating to metalworking – **vulcanian**
   The science or procedures of extracting metals from their ores, of purifying metals and of creating useful objects from metals – **metallurgy**
   The technology of powdered metals – **powder metallurgy**

Meteor:
   A celestial body that appears as a meteor when entering the earth's atmosphere – **meteor**; **meteoroid**
   The glowing trail or streak that appears in the sky when a meteoroid is made luminous by friction with the earth's atmosphere – **meteor**
   The metallic or stony material of a meteoroid that survives passage through the atmosphere and reaches the earth's surface – **meteorite**
   Of or relating to a meteor or meteoroid; formed by a meteoroid; resembling a meteor in speed and brilliance – **meteoric**
   A group of meteors appearing together – **meteor shower**

Metric system:
   To convert to or adopt a metric system – **metrify** (v.i./v.t.)
   Conversion to the metric system of weights and measures – **metrication**; **metrification**

Mice:
   A group of mice – **nest**
   An animal that catches mice – **mouser**

Microscope:
   The study or use of microscopes – **microscopy**
   The representation, study or description of microscopic objects – **micrography**
   Too small to be seen through a microscope – **submicroscopic**

Middle:
   Relating to, situated in or extending toward the middle – **medial median**; **mesial**

Situated or occurring between two extremes or in a middle position or state; one who is situated thus – **intermediate**
 The state of being intermediate or of acting intermediately - **intermediacy**
 Intermediate in character - **osculant**
A middle way – **via media**
An element or factor intermediate between two groups – **tertium quid**

Middle Ages (the period in European history between antiquity and the Renaissance, often dated from A.D. 476 to 1453):
 Of, relating to or belonging to the Middle Ages – **medieval**; **mediaeval**, n. **medievalist** or **mediaevalist**
 A fondness or admiration for the culture, mores, etc., of the Middle Ages; the method or spirit of the Middle Ages; beliefs or practices of the Middle Ages - **medievalism**

Milk:
 To secrete or produce milk – **lactate** (v.i.), n. **lactation**
 Inducing lactation – **lactogenic**
 Of, relating to or derived from milk – **lactic**
 Becoming or appearing milky; yielding a milky juice, as a plant - **lactescent**
 Conveying milk – **lactiferous**
 Secreting milk – **lactescent**; **lactiferous**
 Concentrated, unsweetened milk – **evaporated milk**
 Sweetened evaporated milk – **condensed milk**
 Milk from which the cream has been removed – **skim milk**
 The first milk secreted by the mammary glands immediately after childbirth, lasting for a few days - **colostrum**
 Nonsecretion or dysfunctional secretion of milk following childbirth – **agalactia**
 Secretion and continued production of milk – **galactopoiesis**
 Giving milk – **milch**
 To withhold mother's milk from (the young of a mammal) and substitute other nourishment – **wean** (v.t.)
  A recently weaned child or animal – **weanling**
  Not yet weaned – **sucking**
  A young mammal that has not been weaned - **suckling**
 The watery part of milk that separates from curds, as in the process of making cheese – **whey**
 A drink made from the fermented milk of a mare or camel – **koumiss; kumiss; kumys; kumyss**

Mind/Mental Processes (see also Intellect and Understand):
 The scientific study of mental process and behavior – **psychology** (see Behavior)
 The scientific study of interactions between mental and biological processes – **psychobiology**
 The branch of psychology that studies the relationships between physical stimuli and sensory responses – **psychophysics**
 The science of laws of the mind – **nomology**
 The study of mind; the science of phenomena regarded as purely mental in origin - **noology**
 Any theory that emphasizes analysis of experience rather than the role of mental processes, or brain lesions rather than mental conflicts and maladjustments, or that emphasizes structure rather than function – **structuralism**
 Affecting the mind or mental processes – **psychoactive** (used of a drug or chemical)
  A psychoactive substance – **psychochemical**
 The description of someone's mental characteristics and their development – **psychography**; **psychological biography**
 Not easily perceived by the mind - **impalpable**
 The condition of being in the mind or experientially given - **immanence**
 The keeping of two contradictory ideas or opinions in one's mind at the same time and the conscious belief in both of them - **doublethink**

Mine (explosive device):
    A military engineer who lays, detects or disarms mines – **sapper**

Mineral:
    The study of minerals, including their distribution, identification and properties – **mineralogy**; **oryctognosy**; **oryctology**
    Structural alteration of a mineral without change of chemical composition – **metastasis**; **paramorphism**
    A mineral that has the crystalline form of another mineral rather than the form normally characteristic of its own composition - **pseudomorph**
    A mineral that encloses a different mineral – **perimorph**
    The successive order in which a formation of associated minerals is generated – **paragenesis**
    To convert to a mineral substance; to transform a metal into a mineral by oxidation; to impregnate with minerals – **mineralize** (v.t.)
    The property possessed by certain minerals of exhibiting three different colors when illuminated by white light and viewed from three different directions – **trichroism**, adj. **trichroic**
    The splitting or tendency to split of a crystallized substance along definite crystalline planes, yielding smooth surfaces – **cleavage**
        Having good cleavage – **spathic**
    A narrow vein or irregular filament of mineral traversing a rock mass of different material - **stringer**
    A glacial or alluvial deposit of gravel or sand containing eroded particles of valuable minerals; a place where such a deposit is washed to remove its mineral content – **placer**
    Of or relating to something that has survived, as structures or minerals after destructive processes - **relict**
    Unstable mechanically or chemically – **labile** (used of minerals, strata, etc.)
    Worthless material, as rock, in which valuable minerals are found – **gang**; **gangue**
    A lustrous reflection from certain planes in a mineral grain – **schiller**
    Designating minerals occurring in flaky layers – **platy**

Mining:
    To discover and open (a vein or deposit); to extract from a mine – **win** (v.t.)
    An inclined trough in which ore is separated from waste by washing with running water – **buddle**
    An almost horizontal entrance to a mine – **adit**
    An inclined vertical shaft or passage between levels in a mine - **winze**
    To dig a mine beneath – **undermine** (v.t.)

Minstrel:
    The art or profession of a minstrel – **minstrelsy**
    A wandering minstrel and storyteller in medieval France and England – **jongleur**

Miracle (theurgy):
    Of the nature of a miracle; caused by or as if by a miracle; having the power to work miracles – **miraculous**
    The study of or a discourse on miracles – **thaumatology**
    The working of miracles – **thaumaturgy**
    A performer of miracles – **thaumaturge**; **thaumaturgist**

Mirror:
    Of or relating to mirrors and reflected images – **catoptric**; **mirrory**
    Resembling a mirror - **mirrory**
    The branch of optics dealing with the formation of images by mirrors – **catoptrics**
    Of, resembling, or produced by a mirror or speculum (polished metal plate used as a reflector) – **specular**
    A long mirror mounted on swivels in a frame – **cheval glass**
    A large high mirror, esp. one designed to occupy the wall space between windows – **pier glass**

Missile:
    The art and science of making and using guided or ballistic missiles – **missilery; missilry**
    The study of the dynamics or the flight characteristics of projectiles – **ballistics**
    The simultaneous discharge of a number of missiles; the missiles thus discharged – **volley**

Mist, wind-driven – **scud**

Miter:
    Of, relating to or resembling a miter – **mitral**
    Shaped like the miter (tall pointed hat) of a bishop – **mitriform**

Mites/Ticks:
    The study of mites and ticks – **acarology**
    A symbiotic relationship to mites and ticks – **acarophily**
    A pathological belief that the skin is infested with mites or insects – **acarophobia**
    Infestation with mites – **acariasis**
    An agent that kills mites – **miticide**
    Transmitted by ticks – **tick-borne**

Mixing:
    Capable of being mixed in all proportions – **miscible**
    Incapable of mixing or blending – **immiscible**
    To mix so as to make a unified whole – **amalgamate**; **blend** (both v.t./v.i.)

Model:
    A model or pattern of excellence or perfection of a kind – **paragon**
    An original model or type after which other similar things are patterned – **archetype**

Module:
    Having or comprised of modules – **modularized**
    Of, relating to or based on a module – **modular**

Moisture:
    Relating to, marked by or requiring considerable moisture – **hydric**
    To drive moisture from – **dehydrate**; **dessicate**; **exsiccate** (all v.t.)
    To remove atmospheric moisture from – **dehumidify** (v.t.)
    Movement of an organism in response to moisture – **hydrotaxis**
    To moisten and rub (a part of the body) with a lotion – **embrocate** (v.t.)

Mold (frame or hollow form):
    Capable of being molded – **fabricable**; **fictile**
    Construction of a mold of a mark, as a footprint, for evidence in a criminal investigation; a mold used in such an investigation – **moulage**

Molecule:
    Within a molecule – **intramolecular**
    Consisting of more than one molecule; of greater complexity than a molecule – **supramolecular**
    Relating to, consisting of or affecting two molecules – **bimolecular**
    Relating to, consisting of or formed from three molecules - **trimolecular**

Mollusks:
> The study of mollusks – **malacology**
> Of or relating to mollusks – **molluscan**; **molluskan**
> An agent that kills mollusks – **molluscicide**

Monarch:
> Designating a specified year of a monarch's reign, calculated from the date of accession – **regnal**

Monastery:
> Of, relating to, typical of, or similar to monasteries or persons living in religious or contemplative seclusion – **monastic**; **monastical**
> The monastic system, condition, or mode of life – **monachism**; **monasticism**
> A member of a religious order living in a convent or community – **cenobite**; **coenobite**, n. **cenobitism**
> Modification of monastic rules; the room in a monastery used by monks granted such an exemption – **misericord**; **misericorde**

Money (see also Coin):
> Of or relating to money or its means of circulation – **monetary**
> To establish as legal tender – **monetize** (v.t.)
> A person authorized to coin or mint money – **moneyer**
> Producing wealth or profits – **lucrative**
> A yearly payment of money – **annuity**
> Money ventured by a bettor or speculator likely to have inside information; investments made by alert, experienced investors; well-informed bettors or speculators – **smart money**
> Money as an object of worship – **golden calf**; **Mammon**; **mammon**
> The greedy pursuit of wealth – **mammonism**, n. **mammonist** or **mammonite**
> Money due for payment of duties or customs – **devoirs**
> Money refunded as compensation (as for damages) or as a special favor or inducement - **drawback**
> An offer of money or service in payment of an obligation – **tender** (Law)
> Paper money issued for temporary emergency use – **scrip**
> Coined money – **coin**; **specie**
> A currency that is in circulation outside its own country – **xenocurrency**
> Monetary assistance granted by a government to a person or a private commercial enterprise; financial assistance given by one person or government to another – **subsidy**
> The collecting of coins, medals, paper money, etc. – **numismatics**; **numismatology**, n. **numismatist**
> To restore (silver, e.g.) to use as legal tender – **remonetize** (v.t.)
> To divest (a coin, e.g.) of monetary value; to stop using (a metal) as a monetary standard – **demonetize** (v.t.)
> Money advanced from government funds to enable a person to discharge his duties - **imprest**
> The granting of financial aid; financial aid granted to an individual or organization; a subsidy from a government or foundation; to provide with such aid or support – **subvention** (n./v.t.)
> Incapable of being readily converted into cash – **illiquid**
> Not redeemable for money in coin – **inconvertible**
> The act or practice of lending money at an exhorbitant or illegal rate of interest; such an excessive rate of interest – **usury**, n. **usurer**, adj. **usurious**
> A profit or revenue taken from the minting of coins – **seigniorage**
> The use of only one metal as a monetary standard or for coinage - **monometallism**
> The use of two metals jointly to form the standard of value - **bimetallism**
> To provide insufficient funding for – **underfund** (v.t.)
> Money or goods given in charity – **alms** (pl. in number)
>> Of or relating to alms or the giving of alms – **eleemosynary**

Monkey:
  A group of monkeys – **tribe**; **troop**
  Of, relating to, characteristic of or resembling a monkey – **simian** (adj./n.)

Monopoly – see Economics

Monster:
  Of or like a monster – **monstrous** (n. **monstrosity**, n. **monstrousness**); **teratoid**
  The study of the production, development, anatomy and classification of monsters – **teratology**
  Anomaly of organic form and structure; worship of monsters – **monstrosity**; **teratism**; **teratosis**
  Production of monstrous growths or fetuses - **teratogenesis**
  Something that causes fetal monstrosities or malformations – **teratogen**, adj. **teratogenic**
  Divination by monstrosities – **teratoscopy**

Month:
  Occurring monthly; having a monthly duration – **menstrual**
  In or of the month before the present one – **ultimo**
  Occurring every two months or twice a month – **bimonthly**
  Occurring or appearing two times during each three-month period of the year – **biquarterly**
  A period of three months – **trimester**
  Performed, occurring or appearing every three months – **quarterly**; **trimonthly**

Monument:
  A monument erected in honor of a dead person whose remains lie elsewhere – **cenotaph**
  A large stone used in various prehistoric monuments – **megalith**
  A prehistoric monument consisting of a single, tall, upright megalith – **menhir**
  A prehistoric monument of monoliths (large stone blocks) surrounding a mound - **cromlech**
  A monument in the form of an upright stone or slab with an inscribed or sculptured surface – **stela** (pl. **stelae** or
    stelai); **stele**, pl. **stelae** or **steles**, adj. **stelar**

Mood:
  A temperament characterized by cyclic alterations of mood between elation and depression – **cyclothymia**
    One afflicted with cyclothymia - **cyclothyme**

Moon (see also Light):
  Of, relating to or designating the moon – **selenian**
  Involving, caused by or affecting the moon; measured by the revolution of the moon – **lunar**
  An astronaut who explores the moon – **lunarnaut**
  The elapsed time between two successive new moons – **lunation**
  The mathematical study of the exact size and shape of the moon – **selenodesy**
  The study of the physical features of the moon – **selenography**
  The astronomical study of the moon – **selenology**
  A view or picture of the surface of the moon – **moonscape**
  Toward the moon – **moonward**
  Situated beyond the moon – **superlunar**; **superlunary**
  Situated beneath the moon – **sublunar**; **sublunary**
  Of or relating to the period between the old and new moon, when the moon is not visible – **interlunar**
  Between the earth and the moon – **cislunar**
  Revolving about or surrounding the moon – **circumlunar**
  The full moon nearest the time of the September equinox – **harvest moon**
  The full moon after the harvest moon – **hunter's moon**

A luminous spot on a lunar halo – **paraselene**
A moon valley – **rille**
Divination involving observation of the moon – **selenomancy**
Shaped like a half-moon – **semilunar**; **semilunate**

Moose:
A male moose – **bull**
A female moose – **cow**
A young moose – **calf**

Morals:
One who acts without moral restraint; morally unrestrained – **libertine**
The quality or state of being libertine; the behavior of a libertine – **libertinism**
The doctrine that moral values and duties can be perceived directly – **intuitionalism**; **intuitionism**
The theory or study of moral obligation - **deontology**
Contrary to accepted moral principles – **immoral**
The quality or state of being immoral; an immoral act or practice – **immorality**
An advocate of immorality – **immoralist**
Morally contaminated – **scrofulous**

Morning:
Of or relating to the morning – **matin**; **matinal**; **matutinal**

Morphine:
A condition produced by the habitual use of morphine – **morphinism**
One addicted to morphine – **morphinist**
An addiction to morphine – **morphinomania**; **morphiomania**; **morphomania**
To treat with or subject to the influence of morphine – **morphinize** (v.t.)

Mosaic:
To form into a mosaic pattern, as by using small squares of stone or glass – **tesselate**; **tessellate** (both v.t.)
Of, relating to or resembling a mosaic - **tesselated**; **tessellated**
One of the small squares of stone or glass used in making mosaic patterns; something that is likened to a piece of mosaic – **tessera**, pl. **tesserae**

Moslem – see Islam

Moss, overgrown with – **mossgrown**; **mossy**

Mother:
The killing of one's mother; one who kills one's mother – **matricide**
The mother of an illegitimate child – **grass widow**
Related on the mother's side; a relative of one's mother's side – **enate**; **enatic**
Gravitating toward or centering on the mother – **matricentric**
An excessive adoration of mothers by their children – **momism**
The emotional bond between mother and child – **silver cord**

Moths and butterflies, an entomologist specializing in the study of – **lepidopterist**

Motion/Movement:
Of, relating to or produced by motion - **kinetic**

The study of the motions of the human body – **kinesiology**

Involuntary movement in one part when another part is moved – **synkinesis**

Pathologically excessive motion – **hyperkinesia**; **hyperkinesis**

The production of motion, esp. in inanimate and remote objects, by the alleged exercise of psychic powers - **psychokinesis**

Movement of objects by scientifically inexplicable means – **telekinesis**; **teleportation**

The study of motion exclusive of the influences of mass and force – **cinematics**, **kinematics**, adj. **kinematic**, **kinematical**

The study of the relationship between motion and the forces affecting motion – **dynamics**

The study of all aspects of motion, comprising both kinematics and dynamics – **kinetics**

The study of body movements, gestures, facial expressions, etc., as a means of communication – **kinesics**; **pasimology**

Capable of moving or being moved from one place to another – **mobile**, n. **mobility**

Not moving; firmly in position – **immobile**, n. **immobility**

A sudden state of immobility, with loss of muscle tone – **cataplexy**

Immobility of an organism cause by chemicals such as carbon dioxide – **narcosis** (Biol.)

Loss or impairment of the ability to move or have sensation in a bodily part as a result of injury to or disease of its nerve supply – **paralysis**

Loss or impairment of the ability to execute movements without muscular paralysis - **apraxia**

Moving slowly – **tardigrade**

Moving at the same rate - **synchronous**

To make motionless, as with terror, amazement or awe – **transfix** (v.t.)

Having lost motion – **torpid**

A restriction on free activity or movement – **fetter**; **trammel**; **trammels**

Moving or having the power to move spontaneously – **motile** (Biol.)

Moving about; in motion – **astir**

The path of a moving body or particle, esp. such a path in three dimensions – **trajectory**

Moving in a circular or spiral path – **gyral**; **gyratory**

Movement of a limb such that its distal end delineates an arc - **circumduction**

To move with an irregular elliptical or spiral motion – **circumnutate** (v.i.)

Things that impede movement or progress – **impedimenta**

Moving aimlessly – **errant**

Moving in only one direction – **unidirectional**

Capable of moving freely in all directions – **versatile** (Biol.)

To move from one country or area and settle in another; to change location periodically – **migrate** (v.i.), adj. **migratory**

The act or process of migrating; a group migrating together – **migration**

Capable of being moved by entreaty – **exorable**

Motion pictures ("movies"):

Motion pictures as a whole; a motion picture theater - **cinema**, adj. **cinematic**

Employees of the movie industry – **filmdom**

The movie industry - **cinema**; **filmdom**

Of, relating to or resembling movies – **filmic**

A motion picture enthusiast – **cineast**; **cinéaste**

A person who produces or directs motion pictures – **filmmaker**

The art or technique of making movies – **cinema**; **cinematics**; **cinematography**

A film presenting factual events or circumstances – **documentary**

A film presenting a fictional story that incorporates many factual details or actual events – **semidocumentary**

A scene filmed or televised without interrupting the run of the camera – **take**

The concurrence in time of the picture image and the corresponding sound during projection on a motion picture or television screen - **synchronism**

Filmmaking emphasizing unbiased realism – **cinéma vérité**
A detailed shooting script consulted to avoid errors and discrepancies from shot to shot – **continuity**
A script for a motion picture – **screenplay**
  One who writes screenplays – **scenarist**; **screenwriter**
Writings about films or film figures – **filmography**

Mound:
  A moundlike or rounded structure – **torus** (Biol.), adj. **toric**

Mountain (see also Earth):
  The study of the physical geography or mountains and mountain ranges – **orography**; **orology**
  The process of mountain formation, esp. by a folding and faulting of the earth's crust – **orogeny**
  The measurement of mountains – **orometry**
  Of any mountainous region – **alpestrine**; **montane**
  Located under or at the base of a mountain or mountain range – **submontane**
  Of or relating to peoples or regions lying beyond the mountains, esp. south of the Alps – **ultramontane**
  On this side of the mountains – **cismontane**
  Living beyond or coming from the far side of the mountains; sweeping down from the mountains; one who lives beyond
    the mountains – **tramontane**; **transmontane**
  Relating to, living on or coming from the northern side of the Alps – **transalpine**; **tramontane**; **transmontane**
  Of or designating mountainous regions of the earth just below the timberline – **subalpine**
  Formed or lying at the foot of a mountain or mountain range – **piedmont**
  A spur of a range of mountains or hills – **offset**
  An isolated mountain peak that projects above surrounding ice – **nunatak**
  A transverse cleft or crevice in a mountain ridge through which a stream flows – **water gap**
  A long chain of mountains, esp. the main mountain system of a large land mass – **cordillera**
  A large mountain mass or compact group of connected mountains forming an independent portion of a range – **massif**
  A mountain climber – **alpinist**; **Alpinist**
  A method of descent in which the climber slides down a rope looped over or fastened to an overhead projection; to
    descend a mountain in this way – **abseil** (n./v.i.)
  A sharp, narrow mountain ridge or spur – **arête**
  The slope of one side of a mountain or mountain range – **versant**

Mourn:
  Mournful to an exaggerated or ludicrous degree – **lugubrious**

Mouth:
  Of or relating to the mouth – **oral**; **oscular**; **stomatic**
  Of or relating to the mouth cavity – **buccal**
  Administered by way of the mouth – **peroral**
  Toward the mouth or oral region – **orad**
  Opposite to or away from the mouth – **aboral**
  Having no mouth or stomata – **astomatous**
  Having a broad mouth – **eurystomatous**
  Inflammation of the mucous tissue of the mouth – **stomatitis**
  Dryness of the mouth caused by malfunction of salivary glands - **xerostomia**
  The expanse of an open mouth, a bird's beak, or similar structure – **rictus**
  The mouth of a voracious animal - **maw**
  The branch of medicine concerned with the mouth and its disorders – **stomatology**, adj. **stomatologic** or
    stomatological, n. **stomatologist**

Mucus:
   Of or relating to mucus – **mucous**
   Resembling mucus – **mucous**; **pituitous**
   Secreting or producing mucus – **muciferous**; **mucous**; **pituitous**
   Containing mucus and pus – **mucopurulent**
   Inflammation of mucous membranes – **catarrh**

Mud:
   To soil with mud – **bemire** (v.t.)
   To be or become wet and muddy – **drabble** (v.i./v.t.)
   Mud deposited by water – **silt**; **sullage**
   The therapeutic use of mud, esp. treatment by mud baths – **pelotherapy**
   Mud prepared and used for therapeutic purposes – **peloid**
   Dwelling in mud or muddy regions – **limicolous**

Mules:
   A group of mules – **barren**; **rake**
   A driver of mules – **muleskinner**

Multiply:
   Tending to multiply; capable of multiplying or increasing – **multiplicative**

Murder – see Killing

Muscle:
   Of, relating to or consisting of muscle – **sarcous**
   The scientific study of muscles – **myology**
   The study of muscles and their movements, esp. for physical conditioning – **kinesiology**
   The system of muscles of an animal or body part – **musculature**
   Giving rise to or forming muscle tissue; of muscular origin – **myogenic**
   Influencing the ability of muscles to contract – **inotropic**
   Within a muscle – **intramuscular**
   A muscle that raises a bodily part – **levator**
   A muscle that contracts or compresses a bodily part – **constrictor**
   A muscle that flexes a joint – **flexor**
   A muscle that contracts and is opposed by contraction in another muscle, the antagonist – **agonist**
   Insufficient muscular tone – **atony**, adj. **atonic**
   Muscular rheumatism; muscular pain – **myalgia**
   Muscular weakness or fatigue – **myasthenia**
   Loss or lack of muscular coordination – **ataxia**, adj. **ataxic**
   Inability of a ring muscle or sphincter to relax – **achalasia**
   Continuous muscular contraction – **tetanus**, adj. **tetanic**
      To produce or induce tetanus in – **tetanize** (v.t.)
   A sudden, involuntary muscular contraction – **spasm**
      Relieving or preventing spasms; a drug that has this effect – **antispasmodic**
   Temporary muscular contraction – **myotonia**; **tonic spasm**
   Twitching of individual segments of a muscle – **myokymia**
   An intense involuntary muscular contraction – **convulsion**, adj. **convulsive**
      A convulsion marked by rapidly alternating muscular contraction and relaxation – **clonus**, adj. **clonic**, n. **clonism**
      An abnormal tendency to convulsions, tetany or spasms - **spasmophilia**

Purposeless and uncontrollable muscular movement – **hyperkinesia** (pl. **hyper-kinesias**); **hyperkinesis**, pl. **hyperkinesises**

Muscular strength or power – **thews**

Of, relating to or involving the muscles and the skeleton - **musculoskeletal**

Museum:

The science or profession of museum organization, equipment and management – **museology**

Museum methods of classification and display - **museography**

Mushroom, shaped like a – **fungiform**; **fungoid** (see also Fungus)

Music (see also Hymns, Singing and Song):

Relating to music or its performance – **melophonic**

Marked by or suggestive of melody or song – **canorous**

Melodic material added above or below an existing melody – **counterpoint**

Of, relating to or using counterpoint – **contrapuntal**

A specialist in contrapuntal music – **contrapuntist**

A short melody or phrase that is constantly repeated at the same pitch – **ostinato**

Having a single melodic line – **monophonic**, n. **monophony**

A melodic ornament in which a principal note is rapidly alternated with a note a half or full stop below – **mordent**

To write a melody for (a song lyric) – **melodize** (v.t.)

Characterized by melody; like an aria – **ariose**

Music with two or more distinct melodies combined into a unified musical composition – **polyphony**, adj. **polyphonic**

The historical and scientific study of music – **musicology**

The study of music of various cultures – **ethnomusicology**

A musician with masterly ability, technique or personal style – **virtuoso**, pl. **virtuosi** or **virtuosos**

A woman who is a virtuoso – **virtuosa**

The skill or style exhibited by a virtuoso – **virtuosity**

Brilliant technique or style in performance – **bravura**

A smooth and connected manner of performance; a passage of music so performed - **legato**

An intense dislike of music – **musicophobia**

The set of syllables *do* through *ti*, used to represent the tones of the scale – **sol-fa**

The use of the sol-fa syllables to note the tones of the scale – **solfeggio**; **solmization**

The act or a system of using syllables to represent the tones of the scale – **solmization**

The symbol placed on a staff to indicate the meter – **time signature**

The group of sharps or flats placed to the right of the clef on a staff to identify the key – **key signature**

The principal part in a duet or ensemble composition – **primo**

The second part in a concert piece – **secondo**

A crescendo followed by a diminuendo (gradual decrease in force or volume); the sign indicating this – **swell**

Music characterized by ornate figuration; one who sings or has the ability to sing thus – **coloratura**

One skilled in musical harmony – **harmonist**

Having notes of a fixed rhythmic value – **mensural**

The unstressed note or notes introductory to a phrase or composition – **pickup**

A progression of chords moving to a harmonic close or point of rest – **cadence**

Having cadence or rhythm – **cadent**

A pause or breathing at a point of rhythmic division in a melody – **caesura**; **cesura**

A passage bringing a movement or composition to a formal close – **coda**

An uninterrupted transition between one musical section or composition and another – **segue** (n./v.i.)

An extended virtuosic section for the soloist near the end of a movement of a concerto – **cadenza**

A stress produced by rising pitch as distinguished from increased volume – **tonic accent**

A single tone repeated with different words or time values – **monotone**

A short rhythmic phrase repeated constantly – **riff**

A shift of accent in a passage or composition that occurs when a normally weak beat is stressed – **syncopation**

A vibrating or quivering effect created in an instrument or vocal tone by barely perceptible minute and rapid variations in pitch – **trill**; **vibrato**

> A vibrato effect used for emotional effect or symptomatic of poor vocal control; a vibrating effect produced by the rapid repetition of a single tone or by rapid alteration of two tones – **tremolo**

Fluctuation of speed within a musical phrase or measure typically against a rhythmically steady accompaniment – **rubato**, pl. **rubati** or **rubatos**

A series of rapid musical notes or tones inserted in a musical composition as ornamentation - **roulade**

An abrupt and disconnected manner of performance, as of a musical instrument; a passage of music so performed – **staccato**

Having but one theme – **monothematic**

To read or perform without preparation or prior acquaintance – **sight-read** (v.t./v.i.)

The playing of the tones of a chord in rapid succession rather than simultaneously – **arpeggio**

Played by plucking rather than bowing the strings of an instrument – **pizzicato**

Performed with a springing bow – **arco saltando**; **spiccato**

A smooth, constant glide in passing from one tone to another – **portamento**

Of, relating to or being music that blends classical music with jazz improvisation – **third-stream**

A musical work produced by borrowing fragments or motifs from various sources – **pasticcio**

A musical composition of heterogeneous recorded sounds randomly modified and arranged – **musique concrète**

A form of theatrical presentation in which a dramatic performance is set to music; a work of this type – **opera**

The text of an opera or other dramatic musical work – **libretto**

> The writer of a libretto – **librettist**

An opera or other vocal composition based on a rural theme or subject – **pastorale**

A drama with the complete text set to music – **grand opera**

A theatrical production having many of the musical elements of opera, but lighter in subject and style – **operetta**

An opera or operetta with an amusing plot, spoken dialogue, and usually happy ending – **comic opera**

> A male singer of comic opera roles – **buffo**

A suite of ballet numbers used as an interlude in a full-length ballet, opera or similar program – **divertissement**

A musical piece openly imitating the previous work of another artist – **pastiche**

A musical composition for voices and instruments, narrating a story without dramatic action or costumes – **oratorio**

A style used in opera or oratorio in which the text is delivered in the rhythm of natural speech with slight melodic variation; a passage performed in this style – **recitative**

> A passage performed in a recitative style – **recitative**; **recitativo**

To write or perform (a composition) in a key other than the original or given key; to write or perform music in a different key – **transpose** (v.t.), n. **transposition**

To reset (music) for other instruments or voices or for another style of performance – **arrange** (v.t.)

A light-spirited instrumental work, esp. one with an improvised style and a free form – **capriccio**; **humoresque**

Music played as an accompaniment to a dramatic work, as a play or film – **incidental music**

An anthem, psalm or musical composition sung alternatively by divisions of a choir or congregation – **antiphony**, adj. **antiphonic**

A free composition structured according to the composer's fancy; a medley of familiar themes, musical variations and interludes – **fantasia**

Music embodying the episodes of a known story – **program music**

> Program music based on an extramusical theme in a single, extended movement for a symphony orchestra – **symphonic poem**; **tone poem**

A person who composes symphonies - **symphonist**

A composition written in free style with elaborate runs and harmonies – **toccata**

A set of related instrumental pieces – **partita**

A group of notes or tones sung to one syllable in plainsong; melodic embellishment – **melisma**, adj. **melismatic**

An abnormal liking for music and melody – **melomania**

The entire range of an instrument or voice – **diapason**
An expert on recorded music – **discophile**
A maker of stringed instruments, as violins – **luthier**
Of or relating to the strings of a musical instrument - **chordal**

Mutation:

An agent that causes biological mutation – **mutagen**
An individual or organism differing from the parental strain or strains as a result of mutation - **mutant**

Myth:

To turn (a person or event) into myth; to interpret as myth – **mythicize** (v.t.)
One who creates myths or mythical situations – **mythmaker**
The artistic representation of mythical subjects – **mythography**
A recorder of myths – **mythographer**
A narrator of myths or legends – **mythologer**
To construct or relate a myth – **mythologize** (v.t./v.i.)
The formation or production of myths; the tendency to create myths or give mythical status to (a person or event) – **mythogenesis**
Productive of myths – **mythopeic**; **mythopoeic**
A recurrent pattern, event or theme in myths – **mythologem**
A student or interpreter of myths – **mythicist**
Interpretation of myths as traditional accounts of historical persons and events – **euhemerism**; **Euhemerism**
An advocate of euhemerism - **euhemerist**
To interpret (mythology) on the theory of euhemerism – **euhemerize** (v.t.)
An opponent of myths – **mythoclast**

N

Nail (unguis – body part):

Of, resembling or having a nail – **ungula**

Having nails; a mammal having nails – **unguiculate**

The border tissue surrounding the nail – **perionychium**

Inflammation of the tissue surrounding a nail – **paronychia**; **whitlow**

Name:

Of, relating to or consisting of a name or names – **nominal**; **onomastic**

Existing in name only and not in actuality – **nominal**

The study of personal names – **anthroponymy**

The study of place names – **toponymy**

A name derived from a place or region – **toponym**

The science, laws or principles of classification – **taxonomy**

A taxonomic designation in which the genus and species name are the same – **tantonym**

A taxonomic name consisting of a single word – **monomial**

A taxonomic name that is objectionable for linguistic reasons – **caconym**, adj. **caconymic**

Consisting of two names or terms - **binomial**

Consisting of or relating to three names; a three-part taxonomic designation – **trinomial**

A person whose name is or is thought to be the source of the name of something – **eponym**, adj. **eponymous**

Derivation of a proper name, as of a city or institution, from that of a real or fictitious person – **eponymy**

A first or given name – **praenomen**

A person's own name – **autonym**

A fictitious name adopted by a writer – **anonym**; **nom de plume**; **pseudonym**

A pseudonym consisting of the real name written backwards – **ananym**

The use of a female pseudonym by a male writer – **pseudogyny**

A pet name or term of endearment; the formation or use of pet names – **hypocorism**

Of, relating to or derived from the name of one's mother or female ancestor; a name derived thus – **metronymic**

A name derived from a paternal ancestor, esp. one formed by an affix (attachment); a patrilineal surname or family name - **patronymic**

The custom of naming the parent after the child - **teknonymy**

Having an unknown or unacknowledged name – **anonymous**

By or under that name – **eo nomine**

The name of a historical person assumed by a writer – **allonym**

A system of names used in an art or science – **nomenclature**, adj. **nomenclaturial**

The study of nomenclature – **terminology**

The system of classifying plants and animals by a double name, the first of which is the name of the genus and the second that of the species – **binomial nomenclature**

An error in naming (a person, place, thing, etc.) – **misnomer**

Having the same name – **homonymous**

Being different names but having correspondence or interrelationship, e.g., *aunt* and *uncle* - **heteronymous**

The use of an epithet or appellative for someone's name, as *his excellency*; the use of a proper name to designate others sharing a particular characteristic, as *a Solomon*; the making of a common noun or verb from a proper name – **antonomasia**

To enter (a name) on a list or in a register – **inscribe** (v.t.)

Divination involving the letters of a name – **onomancy**

A collection or listing of names, esp. in a specialized field – **lexicon**; **onomasticon**

A collection or listing of proper names of persons or places – **onomasticon**

The science or study of the origin and forms of words or of proper names of persons or places – **onomastics**

The use of various names for one thing – **polyonymy**

Narrowing:
A constriction or narrowing of a duct or passage – **stenosis**; **stricture**

Nation (see also Country and Political Terms):
The state of being a nation – **nationhood**
Throughout a whole nation – **nationwide**
Aspirations for national independence in a country under foreign domination – **nationalism**
Of, relating to or involving two nations – **binational**
Of, relating to or involving more than two nations – **multilateral**; **multinational**
Courteous and friendly agreement and interaction between nations - **comity**
A nation that controls another nation in international affairs but allows it domestic sovereignty – **suzerain**, n. **suzerainty**

Native:
One native or indigenous to an area – **indigen**; **indigene**
An indigenous plant or animal – **autochthon**, adj. **autochthonous**
Not native to the environment; a plant that is not native to the environment – **adventive**

Nature:
The study of the general features and constitution of nature – **cosmography**
The study of nature and the physical universe – **natural philosophy**
The representation of nature, esp. in art and literature – **mimesis**
Controlled use and systematic protection of natural resources – **conservation**, adj. **conservational**
An advocate of conservation – **conservationist**
The assignment of a humanlike soul to nature, or to something that governs natural processes - **anthropopsychism**
The worship of nature – **physiolatry**, n. **physiolater**
Treatment of disease emphasizing nature, as with herbs, vitamins, manipulation, electric treatment, etc. – **naturopathy**; **natureopathy**, adj. **naturopathic**
A practitioner of naturopathy – **naturopath**
Veneration of the physical powers of nature – **physitheism**
Produced by natural rather than divine or human forces – **physiurgic**

Navel (omphalos; umbilicus):
A small opening, mark or depression resembling a navel – **umbilicus**
Having such a mark or depression – **umbilicate**; **umbilicated**
Contemplation of the navel – **omphaloskepsis**
One who stares fixedly at his navel to induce a mystical trance - **omphalopsychite**

Near:
The state of being near in space or relationship – **proximity**; **vicinity**

Necessary – see Essential

Neck:
Of or relating to a neck – **cervical**
Of, relating to or situated in the region of the throat – **jugular**
The nape of the neck – **nucha**
Contracted neck muscles producing an unnatural position of the head – **torticollis**, adj. **torticollar**
A band of feathers, hair or coloration around the neck – **torques** (Zool.)
Having a torques – **torquate** (Zool.)

Needle:
A needlelike structure or part – **spicula** (pl. **spiculae**); **spicule** (pl. **spicules**); **spiculum** (pl. **spicula**), adj. **spicular** or **spiculate**
A needlelike bristle, spine or crystal – **acicula**; **aciculum**, pl. **aciculae**, adj. **acicular**
Having aciculae; having marks like scratches made by a needle – **aciculate**; **aciculated**
Needle-shaped, or pointed at one end – **acerate**; **acerated**; **acerose**; **aciform**
A small, stiff, needlelike process – **stylet** (Zool.)

Negotiate:
One who negotiates – **negotiant**
A negotiating strategy holding that progress on one issue is essential for progress on other issues – **linkage**

Negro:
An aesthetic and ideological concept affirming the independent validity of Negro culture – **negritude**
One who is friendly to Negroes and their interests – **negrophile**
One who feels intense aversion to or fear of Negroes – **negrophobe**
Extreme or irrational fear of Negroes – **negrophobia**
A person having one quarter Negro ancestry – **quadroon**
A person whose ancestry is one-eighth Negro – **octoroon**

Neighborhood:
The residents of a particular neighborhood; the state of living in a neighborhood – **vicinage**
Of, belonging to or restricted to a neighborhood or limited area – **vicinal**

Nerve:
A nerve cell – **neuron**; **neurone**
A neuron that stimulates motion – **motoneuron**; **motor nerve cell**
Of or relating to a nerve – **neural**
Of, relating to or designating nerves carrying impulses from the nerve centers to the muscles – **motor**
A bundle of nerve fibers with a common origin, termination and function - **tract**
Transmitting impulses from sense organs to nerve centers – **afferent**; **sensory**
A sensory nerve ending that is sensitive to pressure changes – **baroreceptor**
A nerve consisting of both sensory and motor fibers – **composite nerve**
A group of nerve cells, esp. one found outside the brain or spinal cord – **ganglion**, pl. **ganglia** or **ganglions**
Having ganglia – **gangliate**; **gangliated**; **ganglionated**
A club-shaped enlargement at the end of a nerve fiber – **bouton**
To supply (a bodily part) with nerves – **innervate** (v.t.)
Inflammation of a nerve – **neuritis**
Inflammation of more than one nerve at a time – **multiple neuritis**
A sharp, sudden pain along a nerve – **neuralgia**, adj. **neuralgic**
A tumor composed of nerve tissue – **neuroma**
The medical study of the nervous system and its disorders – **neurology**
The medical study of diseases of the nervous system – **neuropathology**
Disease or abnormality of the nervous system – **neuropathy**
The anatomical study of the nervous system; the structural makeup of nervous tissue and the nervous system – **neuroanatomy**
The medical study of both psychiatric and neurological disorders – **neuropsychiatry**
Surgery of the nervous system or any of its parts – **neurosurgery**
Surgical cutting or stretching of a nerve, as to relieve pain – **neurotomy**
Surgical removal of a nerve or part of a nerve – **neurectomy**

Nest:

  To build a nest – **nidificate**; **nidify** (both v.i.)
  Nest-making – **nidulation**
  A nest for the eggs of insects or spiders – **nidus**
  Remaining in the nest for a period after hatching – **nidicolous**
  Leaving the nest shortly after hatching – **nidifuguous**
  Building a hanging nest – **pensile** (used of birds)
  The nest of a predatory bird built on a crag or other high place – **aerie**; **aery**

Net:

  Of or resembling a net in appearance or structure; forming a net or web – **retiary**; **reticular**; **reticulate**; **reticulated**; **retiform**
  Resembling a net in operation or effect – **intricate**; **reticular**
  A netlike formation or structure – **network**; **reticulum**, pl. **reticula**

Network:

  Resembling or forming a network – **reticulated**
  An anatomical network or mesh, as of veins or nerves – **rete**

New:

  To start or introduce something new – **innovate** (v.i./v.t.)
  Strikingly new – **novel**
    The quality of being novel – **newness**; **novelty**
  A fear of or aversion to novelty – **neophobia**
  Hatred of innovation or change – **misocainea**; **misoneism**

Nickel:

  Of or relating to nickel – **nickelic**; **nickelous**
  Bearing or containing nickel – **nickelic**; **nickeliferous**; **nickelous**

Night:

  Overtaken by night – **benighted**
  Of, relating to or occurring in the night; active at night – **nocturnal**
  Comprising a sequence of day and night - **noctidiurnal**
  Night blindness - **nyctalopia**
  Extreme or irrational fear of the night – **noctiphobia**

Nightingales, a group of – **watch**

Nile River or Nile Valley, of or relating to the - **Nilotic**

Nine:

  Of, relating to or based on the number nine - **novenary**
  Consisting of nine members, parts or elements – **ninefold**; **nonuple**
  A group or set of nine – **ennead** (adj. **enneadic**); **nonet**
  A polygon with nine sides – **nonagon**

Nipples (mammillae):

  Having nipples – **mammillate**
  Shaped like a nipple – **mammillate**; **mastoid**
  A small nipplelike projection – **papilla**, pl. **papillae**, adj. **papillary** or **papillate** or **papillose**

Nitrogen:
Of, derived from or containing nitrogen – **nitric**; **nitrous**
To combine or treat with nitrogen – **nitrogenize** (v.t.)
To remove nitrogen from – **denitrify** (v.t.)

Nobility:
Of or relating to the nobility – **nobiliary**
Having a title, esp. of nobility – **titled**

Noise (see also Sound):
Acoustical or electrical noise in which the intensity is the same at all frequencies within a given band – **white noise**
A harsh, shrill or creaking noise – **stridor**
A nonverbal auditory hallucination - **acoasm**; **acouasm**; **acousma**
Extreme or irrational fear of noise – **acousticophobia**; **phonophobia**

Noon, before – **antemeridian**; **antemeridien**

Norm:
Of, relating to or prescribing a norm or standard – **normative**

North:
Of or relating to the north or north wind – **boreal**
Progress toward the north – **northing** (n.)

Nose:
Of or relating to the nose – **nasal**, adj. **nasality**
Relating to the nasal cavities - **mycteric**
Plastic surgery of the nose – **rhinoplasty**
Examination of the nasal passages – **rhinoscopy**
In a nasal manner; in the direction of nasalization – **nasally**
The ratio of nasal breadth to nasal height, multiplied by 100 – **nasal index**
An opening in the nasal cavity of a vertebrate – **naris**; **nostril**
Having a broad, flat nose – **platyrrhine**; **platyrrhinian**
Turned up at the end – **retroussé**; **retroussée** (both used esp. of the nose)
Inflammation of the nasal mucous membranes – **rhinitis**
Promoting nasal discharge – **errhine**
The study of the nose – **nasology**
The branch of medicine that deals with the nose and its diseases – **rhinology**

Notary public, of or relating to a – **notarial**

Notch:
Having notched, toothlike projections – **serrate**; **serrated**
    Minutely serrated – **crenulate**; **crenulated**; **serrulate**; **serrulated**
Having a notched tip, as a leaf – **emarginated**
Irregularly notched, toothed or indented – **erose**
Deeply notched or forked, as the tail of some birds – **forficate**; **swallow-tail**

Note:
A note, esp. one in the margin – **apostil**; **apostille**; **gloss**
To provide critical or explanatory notes for – **annotate** (v.t.)

A brief explanatory note or translation of a difficult or technical expression, esp. one inserted in the margin or between lines of a text or manuscript – **gloss**

    The writing or compilation of glosses – **glossography**

    A collection of glosses – **gloss**; **glossary**

Noticing or observing, the act of – **espial**

Nourishment (aliment; see also Nutrition):

    Something that nourishes – **nutrient**; **nutriment**

    The act or process of giving or receiving nourishment – **alimentation**

    Inadequate to nourish the body or relieve hunger – **jejune**

    To provide with insufficient quantity or quality of nourishment to sustain proper health and growth – **undernourish** (v.t.)

    Poor nourishment or nutrition – **innutrition**, (adj. **innutritious**); **malnutrition**; **undernourishment**; **undernutrition**

Novel (written work) – see Literature

Novice (beginner):

    A place where novices live; the period of being a novice – **noviciate**; **novitiate**

Nuclear:

    The study of the forces, reactions and internal structures of atomic nuclei – **nuclear physics**

    One who arms and otherwise prepares a nuclear weapon for release onto a target; one who designs or devises nuclear weapons – **weaponeer**

    To prohibit or remove nuclear arms from – **denuclearize** (v.t.)

Nucleus (pl. nuclei):

    Of, relating to or forming a nucleus; within a nucleus – **nuclear**

    An atomic nucleus specified by its atomic number, atomic mass and energy state - **nuclide**

    Having a nucleus or nuclei – **nucleate**

    Having one nucleus – **mononuclear**; **uninucleate**

    Having two nuclei – **binucleate**

    Having more than two nuclei – **multinuclear**; **multinucleate**; **multinucleated**

    Without a nucleus or nuclei – **anuclear**; **enucleate**

    To remove the nucleus of – **enucleate** (v.t.)

Nude:

    The belief in going nude - **nudism**

    The practice of going nude – **adamitism**; **naturism** (n. **naturist**); **nudism**

    A practitioner of nudism – **Adamite**; **nudist**

    The quality or state of being nude - **nudity**

    Of or relating to nudism – **nudist**

    A nude human figure – **nude**; **nudity**

Numb:

    To make numb, esp. by cold – **benumb** (v.t.)

Number:

    A mark or symbol that represents a number – **numeral**; **numeric**

    Of, relating to or expressing numbers – **numeral**; **numerary**

Of or relating to a number or series of numbers; denoting numbers or a number; expressed in or counted by numbers – **numerical**

Exceeding the usual, stated or prescribed number – **supernumerary**

A numerical datum – **statistic**

The mathematics of the collection, organization and interpretation of numerical data; a collection of numerical data – **statistics** (former meaning: used with sing. v.; latter meaning: pl. in number)

A specialist in statistics; one who compiles statistical data – **statistician**

The statistical study of biological data – **biometrics**; **biometry**

The study of the occult meanings of numbers – **numerology**

Divination by the use of numbers – **arithmancy**

A number, such as 7¼, equal to the sum of an integer (whole number) and a fraction – **mixed number**

An inability to perform simple arithmetic tasks – **acalculia**

Nursery (for plants) – see Plants

Nut:

The edible kernel of a nut – **nutmeat**

The shell enclosing the meat of a nut – **nutshell**

Shaped like a nut – **nuciform**

Nutrition:

Of or relating to nutrition – **alimentary**

Having nutritive value – **alible**; **alimental**; **nourishing**

The science of nutrition and diet – **sitology**

Characterized by or relating to excessive nutrition – **polytrophic**

A substance that in minute amounts is essential to life – **micronutrient**

O

Oat:
Of or like oats – **avenaceous**; **oaten**
Made of or containing oats, oatmeal or oat straw – **oaten**

Oath:
A person who testifies under oath – **deponent**
Testimony under oath – **deposition**
One who refuses to take an oath, as of allegiance – **nonjuror**

Obedience:
The practice or principle of complete obedience to authority, even if unjust or arbitrary – **nonresistance**
Stubbornly disobedient – **contumacious**; **rebellious**

Observation:
Close observation, esp. of one under suspicion; the art of observing or the state of being observed – **surveillance**
Exercising surveillance; one who exercises surveillance – **surveillant**
To keep under surveillance – **surveil** (v.t.)

Occasion, the present or a particular – **nonce**

Ocean (see also Sea):
Of or relating to the ocean – **oceanic**; **thalassic**
The study and exploration of the ocean and its phenomena – **oceanography**; **oceanology**
Oceanology relating to seas and gulfs – **thalassography**
Supremacy on the seas – **thalassocracy**
Located on the other side of the Atlantic; spanning or crossing the Atlantic – **transatlantic**
Located beyond or on the other side of the ocean; spanning or crossing the ocean – **transoceanic**
Formed, situated or occurring beneath the ocean or the ocean bed – **suboceanic**
Of, relating to or living in open oceans or seas rather than waters adjacent to land or inland waters – **pelagic**
Strictly pelagic – **autopelagic**
Living in deep water and coming to the surface rarely – **spanipelagic**
Of or relating to the part of the oceanic zone into which enough sunlight enters for photosynthesis – **epipelagic**
Of or relating to the deeper parts of the ocean, esp. between 100 and 1000 fathoms – **bathyal**; **bathyalic**
The realm of the ocean lacking higher plant life because of the absence of light – **abyssal zone**, adj. **abyssal**
Of, relating to or occurring in the open water of the abyssal zone – **abyssalpelagic**; **abyssopelagic**
The slope from the continental shelf at 100 fathoms to the abyssal zone at 1000 fathoms – **bathyal district**; **bathyal zone**
Of, relating to or occurring on the sea bottom or the abyssal zone – **abyssalbenthic**; **abyssobenthic**
Of, relating to or living in the depths of the ocean, esp. below 2000 feet (607 meters) – **bathypelagic**
Of or relating to the ocean depths below 20,000 feet (6067 meters) – **hadal**
Of, relating to or living in the deepest parts of the ocean – **bathybial**; **bathybic**
A vertical gradient in ocean salinity – **halocline**
A submarine mountain rising to more than 3000 feet above the ocean floor but having a summit at least 1000 feet below sea level – **seamount**
Wind-blown sea spray – **spindrift**
Measurement of the depths of water in oceans, seas, or other large bodies of water; the information derived from such measurements – **bathymetry**

Odor:
 Having an odor – **odoriferous**; **odorous**
 A bad odor – **malodor**; **stench**
 Having a bad odor – **fetid**; **malodorous**; **rank**; **stinking**
 A distinctive odor, esp. a pleasant one – **aroma**, adj. **aromatic**
 To make aromatic or fragrant – **aromatize** (v.t.)
 The study of the detection and identification of odors – **olfactronics**

Offspring (see also Birth and Childbirth):
 Tending to produce offspring – **philoprogenitive**; **prolific**
 The condition of having borne offspring – **parity**
 Having produced offspring - **parous**
 Capable of producing offspring – **fecund**, n. **fecundity**
 Producing only one offspring at a time; having produced only one offspring – **uniparous**
 Producing two offspring in a single birth – **biparous**
 Producing more than one offspring at one time – **multiparous**
 Giving birth to living offspring that develop inside the body of the mother - **viviparous**
 A first-born offspring – **firstling**
 One of three offspring born at one birth – **triplet**
 A female who has not borne offspring – **nullipara**
 A female who has borne only one offspring – **primipara**, pl. **primiparae** or **primiparas**
 Of or relating to the production of male offspring – **androgenous**
 Producing many offspring at a single time – **polytocous**
 To transmit to offspring; to pass along to succeeding generations – **propagate** (v.t.)
 The study of the operation of factors producing degeneration in offspring – **cacogenics**; **dysgenics**

Oil:
 Derived from oil – **oleic**
 Of or relating to oil – **oleaginous**; **oleic**; **oily**
 Having the quality or characteristics of oil – **unctuous**
 A rapidly evaporating oil that does not leave a stain – **volatile oil**
 To pour or rub oil on – **anele**; **anoint** (both v.t.)
 Oil obtained esp. from the blubber of a whale – **train oil**
 A peculiar form or figure assumed by a drop of oil when placed on water or some other immiscible liquid – **oleograph**

Ointment:
 The process of applying ointment – **inunction**
 Having the characteristics of an ointment – **unctuous**
 To rub ointment on – **anele**; **anoint** (both v.t.)

Old (see also Aging):
 Old-fashioned; out of date – **antiquated**; **obsolete**
  Being in the process of becoming obsolete – **obsolescent**
  To become obsolescent – **obsolesce** (v.i.)
 Belonging to a much earlier time – **ancient**; **archaic**
 The use of obsolete or old-fashioned diction, idiom or style in writing or speaking; an outmoded or inefficient custom, standard, behavior, method, or way of thinking that survives from a past era; the preference for such customs, standards, etc.; an archaic word, phrase, expression or idiom – **archaicism**; **archaism**
  The worship of archaism – **archaeolatry**
  To make archaic; to express by archaisms – **archaize** (v.t./v.i.)
  One who archaizes – **archaist**, adj. **archaistic**

The quality of being old or ancient – **(of) antiquity**
Made, evolved or developed a long time ago – **antediluvial**; **antediluvian**; **antiquated**

Olive, shaped like an – **olivary**

Omitted, capable of being – **omissible**

Opening:
    A windowlike opening – **fenestra** (Anat.)
    An opening that gapes as if with voracious appetite - **maw**
    An opening in a bone or through a membranous anatomical structure – **foramen**
    Having two openings – **biforate**
    Having no opening – **imperforate**
    An opening or passage that can serve as an outlet, as for troops - **débouché**

Open spaces, extreme or irrational fear of – **agoraphobia**

Opera – see Music

Opinion (see also Survey):
    One who changes his or her opinions to suit the needs of the moment – **trimmer**
    Popular opinion or sentiment – **vox populi**

Opposite:
    A direct opposite – **antipode**
    One that is the exact opposite of another – **antipodes** (sing./pl.)

Optics (see also Vision):
    One who makes lenses and eyeglasses; one who sells optical instruments and articles – **optician**
    Having the same focus or foci – **confocal**
    Having two different focal lengths – **bifocal**
    Having three different focal lengths – **trifocal**
    Including everything visible in one view – **panoptic**; **panoptical**
    The failure of light rays from one point to converge to a single focus; an error in a lens or mirror causing such failure –
        aberration
    Deflection of a light wave at the boundary between two mediums with different refractive indices or in passage through
        a medium of nonuniform density – **refraction**
        Of, caused by or causing refraction – **anaclastic**; **refractional**; **refractive**; **refringent**
        Capable of being refracted – **refrangible**
        Refractive power – **refringence**
    Corrected for distortion, lack of sharpness, etc. (as in a lens) – **aplanatic**
    Corrected for both chromatic and spherical aberration – **apochromatic**
    To adjust the line of sight of (an optical device) – **collimate** (v.t.)
    The branch of optics dealing with the formation of images by mirrors - **catoptrics**

Orange:
    A place where orange trees are cultivated – **orangery**

Orbit:
    The point nearest the earth in the orbit of the moon or a satellite – **perigee**
    The point most distant from the earth in the orbit of the moon or a satellite – **apogee**

Orchid:
  Of, relating to or characteristic of the orchid family of plants – **orchidaceous**
  The study of orchids – **orchidology**

Order (command):
  An authoritative order having legal force – **decree** (q.v.)

Order (sequence):
  The next to last item in a series – **penult**; **penultima**; **penultimate**
  Next to last – **penultimate** (adj.)
  Third from the end in a series – **antepenultimate** (adj.)

Organ (body part):
  The origin and development of biological organs – **organogenesis**
  The study of the structure and functions of plant and animal organs – **organology**
  The scientific description of the organs of animals and plants – **organography**
  The treatment of disease with animal organs or extracts – **organotherapy**
  The wall of an organ – **paries**, pl. **parietes**
  Within the wall of an organ or cavity – **intramural**
  The cavity of a hollow organ – **antrum**
  The inner open space of a tubular organ – **lumen**
  The inner surface of an organ farthest away from the opening – **fundus**
  The innermost layer of an organ or part – **intima**
  An outgrowth of an organ – **appendix** (q.v.)
  A subordinate or external organ – **appendage** (q.v.)
    A small appendage – **appendicle**
  The internal organs of an animal, esp. the heart, liver and lungs – **purtenance**
  The internal organs of a human being or nonhuman animal – **entrails**; **viscera**, adj. **splanchnic**, **visceral**
    To remove the viscera of – **disembowel**; **eviscerate** (both v.t.)
  A sac, membrane or envelope that encloses an organ or part – **capsule**
  The natural covering of an organ or part - **tunic**
  The external covering of an organ – **adventitia**
  A displacing of an organ, esp. the uterus, in which its axis is inclined farther forward than is normal – **anteversion**
    To cause anteversion – **antevert** (v.t.) (Pathol.)
  The protrusion of an organ or other bodily structure through the wall that usually contains it – **hernia**; **rupture**
    To protrude so as to form a hernia – **herniate** (v.i.), n. **herniation**
  Forward displacement of an organ – **proptosis**
  The modification of the orientation of an organ as a result of wounding – **traumatropism**, adj. **traumatropic**
  Directed toward a central organ - **afferent** (used esp. of nerves)

Origin:
  An origin – **provenience**
  Place of origin – **provenance**; **provenience**; **source**
  Of recent origin – **neoteric**
  The study of origins – **etiology**
  The doctrine of origins – **archeology**
  Having an origin from something outside – **adscititious**
  Of mixed origin – **mongrel**
    To make mongrel in race, nature or character – **mongrelize** (v.t.)

Ostrich:

Of, relating to or resembling an ostrich or related bird - **struthious**

Otter:

A male otter – **dog**
A female otter – **bitch**

Outburst:

Marked by or given to sudden flare-ups or outbursts – **vesuvian**

Outdoors:

Taking place outdoors - **alfresco**

Outline:

A brief outline or summary of a topic – **abstract**; **epitome**; **précis**; **synopsis**
    To present or write a synopsis of – **synopsize** (v.t.)
    Of or consisting of a synopsis; presenting an account from the same point of view – **synoptic**
An outline of the main points of a text, speech, or course of study - **syllabus**

Outlook:

The taste or outlook characteristic of a period or generation – **Zeitgeist**

Outside (see also External):

Lying outside; of or relating to the outside - **extrinsic**

Ova – see Egg

Ovary:

Surgical removal of an ovary – **oophorectomy**; **ovariectomy**; **ovariotomy**
Surgical incision into an ovary – **ovariotomy**
The surgical removal of both ovaries – **oophorectomy**
To remove the ovaries of (a female animal) – **castrate**; **spay** (both v.t.)
    An animal whose ovaries have been removed - **spay**
Ovarian inflammation – **oophoritis**; **ovaritis**

Overlap:

To overlap and even (chamfered or beveled plank edges) so as to form a flush surface – **sypher** (v.t.)

Owl:

A group of owls – **parliament**
A young owl – **owlet**

Owner/Ownership:

Befitting an owner – **proprietary**
Perpetual ownership of real estate by institutions such as churches that cannot transfer or sell them – **mortmain**

Ox – see Cattle

Oxygen:

To treat or infuse with oxygen – **oxygenate**; **oxygenize** (both v.t.)
The combination of a substance with oxygen – **oxidation**

To combine with oxygen – **oxygenate** (v.t.); **oxygenize** (v.t.); **oxidize** (v.i. or v.t.)

A chemical reagent that oxidizes – **oxidant**

To remove oxygen from – **deoxidize**; **deoxygenate** (both v.t.)

Unconsciousness or death caused by lack of oxygen – **asphyxia**

To cause or undergo asphyxia – **asphyxiate** (v.t./v.i.)

Causing or tending to cause asphyxia; a substance or condition that causes asphyxia – **asphyxiant**

Deficiency in the amount of oxygen reaching bodily tissues – **anoxia**; **hypoxia**

Absence of oxygen – **anoxia**

Lacking in plant nutrients and abundantly supplied with dissolved oxygen throughout, as a body of water – **oligotrophic**

Living or occurring only in the presence of oxygen – **aerobic**, n. **aerobe** or **aerobium**

Oysters:

One who cultivates or sells oysters – **oysterman**

P

Page:
Of, relating to or consisting of pages; page for page – **paginal**
To number the pages of – **paginate** (v.t.)
Having no page numbers – **unpaged**

Pain:
Total or partial loss of the sense of pain – **anesthesia**
To make insensible to pain – **anaesthetize**; **anesthetize** (both v.t.)
A person trained to administer anesthetics – **anesthetist**
The study of anesthesia and anesthetics – **anesthesiology**
Being unable to feel pain (although conscious) – **analgesia**
　Anything that produces analgesia; of or causing analgesia – **analgesic**
Anything that relieves or lessens pain – **anodyne**; **nepenthe**
Capable of easing pain or discomfort; a medicine that does this – **lenitive**
Producing pain – **algogenic**
Sudden pain along a nerve – **neuralgia**
Pain concentrated in the head region – **cephalalgia** (see also Headache)
Pain affecting half of the human body – **hemialgia**
Pleasure derived from inflicting pain on others – **sadism**, n. **sadist**
Pleasure derived from being subjected to physical pain inflicted by oneself or others – **masochism**, n. **masochist**
Pleasure derived from simultaneous sadism and masochism – **sadomasochism**
Sexual pleasure derived from inflicting or suffering pain – **algolagnia**
The unconscious desire for pain or destruction – **pain principle**
The tendency to reduce pain and seek immediate gratification of instinctual needs – **pleasure principle**
An indifference to pleasure or pain – **stoicism**, n. **stoic**, adj. **stoic** or **stoical**
Extreme or irrational fear of pain - **algophobia**

Painting – see Art

Pairs:
Occurring in pairs – **bigeminal**; **didymous**; **twinned**
To arrange or occur in pairs; to double – **geminate** (v.t./v.i.)
Joined in or forming a pair or pairs – **jugate**

Palace:
Of, suitable for or of the nature of a palace – **palatial**

Pamphlets:
A writer of pamphlets or other short works taking a partisan stand on an issue – **pamphleteer**

Pan:
Shaped like a pan, dish or cup – **patelliform**

Pancreas:
Inflammation of the pancreas – **pancreatitis**
Surgical removal of the pancreas – **pancreatectomy**

Panel, a member of a – **panelist**

Pantomime:
   One who acts or plays in a pantomime – **mummer**
      A performance by mummers - **mummery**

Paper:
   Resembling paper – **chartaceous**
   A number of sheets of paper put together for binding or bound loosely together to form a notebook or pamphlet - **cahier**
   The art or process of folding paper into a flower, bird, etc. – **origami**
   The art of making ornamental designs by cutting and folding paper – **kirigami**
   Paper made from the pith or stems of the papyrus (a tall aquatic sedge), used as a writing material in ancient times – **papyrus**
      The study of papyrus manuscripts - **papyrology**
   Paper with fine parallel and cross lines produced in manufacturing - **laid paper**
   Paper that exhibits a fine mesh pattern when held up to the light – **wove paper**
   Small pieces of paper resulting from the formation of holes in punched tape or data cards – **chad**

Parachute:
   The delivery of supplies to a place by parachute – **paradrop**

Parallel:
   Characterized by parallel arrangement in a vertical row – **orthostichous**
   Arrangement in opposite and parallel rows – **enfilade**

Paralysis:
   Slight or partial paralysis – **paresis**
   Paralysis of a single limb or part of the body, such as one side of the face – **monoplegia**, adj. **monoplegic**
   Paralysis of one side of the body – **hemiplegia**, adj. **hemiplegic**
   Paralysis of corresponding parts on both sides of the body – **diplegia**
   Complete paralysis of the lower half of the body, caused by damage to the spinal cord – **paraplegia**, adj./n. **paraplegic**
   Complete paralysis of the body from the neck down – **quadriplegia**, adj./n. **quadriplegic**

Parasite:
   A substance used to destroy parasites – **parasiticide**
   The scientific study of parasites – **parasitology**
   The typical mode of existence or behavior of a parasite; a diseased condition caused by parasitic infestation - **parasitism**
      A disease that results from parasitism – **parasitosis**
   A partially parasitic organism – **hemiparasite**
   An organism living parasitically within another organism – **endoparasite**
   A parasite living on the exterior of another organism – **ectoparasite**
   Spending alternative stages of a life cycle on different unrelated hosts – **heterecious**; **heteroecious**
   Parasitic within a cell – **cytozoic**, n. **cytozoon**
   Free of parasites – **axenic**

Parathyroid glands, surgical removal of – **parathyroidectomy**

Pardon:
   A general pardon, esp. for political offenses against a government – **amnesty**
   Easily excused or forgiven – **pardonable**; **venial**

Parent:

In the place or position of a parent – **in loco parentis**

Having the same parents or having the same grandparents on one side – **german** (e.g. cousin-german)

Parish:

Of, relating to, supported by or located in a parish – **parochial**

Parotid gland:

Inflammation of the parotid glands – **parotiditis**; **parotitis**

Surgical removal of a parotid gland – **parotidectomy**

Parrot:

Of, relating to or characteristic of parrots – **psittaceous**; **psittacine**

A group of parrots – **flock**

Particles:

Of, relating to or formed of separate particles – **particulate**

Partridge:

A group of partridges – **covey**

A young partridge - **squeaker**

Parts:

Divided into parts – **parted**; **partite**

Serving to divide something into parts – **partitive**

Consisting of two parts – **binate**; **bipartite**; **dimeric**

Having two distinct main parts – **bicorporeal**

Of or divided into three parts – **threefold**; **tripartite**; **triple**

Having or consisting of four parts – **quadripartite**; **tetramerous**

Consisting of numerous parts – **multipartite**; **polymerous**

Cleft into several or many parts – **multifid**

To break or separate into parts – **diffract** (v.t./v.i.)

The innermost or secret parts – **penetralia**

Capable of being parted – **partible**

Pass:

To pass across, over or through – **traverse** (v.t.)

Passing through from one place to another; one who does this - **transient**

Passengers:

The number of passengers who ride a particular public transit system – **ridership**

Passion:

Of or relating to passion – **passional**

Having or capable of intense feelings; showing or expressing strong emotion; arising from or marked by passion – **ardent**; **passionate**

Past:

To understand or interpret in terms of past perceptions – **apperceive** (v.t.), n. **apperception**

Explanation of past events through the laws of causation – **palaetiology**; **paletiology**

The (often oppressive) influence of the past upon the present – **mortmain**

Paste, to make into a – **impaste** (v.t.)

Pasture:
    The right to graze animals on land suitable therefor – **pasturage**
        The pasturage of a cow, horse or sheep for a year - **collop**
    The right to pasture animals on common land – **commonage**

Patent:
    One who has been granted a patent – **patentee**
    One who grants a patent – **patentor**

Patient:
    A patient who receives treatment at a hospital or clinic without being hospitalized – **outpatient**
    A patient admitted to a hospital – **inpatient**

Patio, a roofed – **lanai**

Paving:
    One who paves; materials or tools used for paving – **pavior**

Paw:
    Of, relating to or corresponding to an animal's paw – **palmar**

Pay/Payment:
    Payment of wages in goods rather than by money – **truck system**
    An amount owed in payment – **arrearage**
    A draft or bill payable upon presentation – **sight draft**
    Authorizing delay in payment – **moratory**
    A payment made for protection; money or other valuables paid by one ruler or nation to another as acknowledgment of submission or as the price of protection by that other nation – **tribute**, adj. **tributary**
    The annual payment of an allowance or income; the right to receive or the obligation to make such payment – **annuity**
        One who is entitled to receive an annuity – **annuitant**
    A regular fixed payment, as a salary or allowance – **stipend**
        Compensated by or receiving a stipend – **stipendiary**
    To pay insufficiently or less than deserved – **underpay** (v.t.)
    To make repayment or return for – **requite** (v.t.)
    To attach (a debtor's pay, e.g.) so that money or property due or belonging to another can be applied to the payment of the debt – **garnish**; **garnishee** (both v.t.), n. **garnishment**
        A debtor who is the subject of a garnishment – **garnishee**

Pea, shaped like a – **pisiform**

Peace:
    To end war or violence in peace – **pacify** (v.t.)
        To pacify by giving in to the demands of – **appease** (v.t.), n. **appeasement**
    Peace of mind; emotional tranquility – **ataraxia**
    Promoting or conducive to peace and conciliation rather than contention and partisanship – **eirenic**; **irenic**, adj. **irenical**

Peafowl:
    Male – **peacock**

Female – **peahen**
A group of peafowl – **muster**
Of or like a peacock; resembling a peacock's tail – **pavonine**

Pear, shaped like a – **pyriform**

Pearl:
Resembling pearls – **pearly**
Having a pearly gloss or shine – **pearlescent**
A person who dives in search of pearl-bearing mollusks – **pearl diver**; **pearler**
A boat whose crew is engaged in seeking or trading pearls – **pearler**
To form into or adorn with pearls – **impearl** (v.t.)

Penis (pl. penises or penes; or phallus, pl. phalluses or phalli):
Having the penis erect – **ithyphallic** (used of graphic and sculptural representations)
Persistent erection of the penis, esp. due to disease – **priapism**, adj. **priapic** or **priapean**
A representation of the penis and testes as an embodiment of generative power – **phallus**, adj. **phallic**

Pension, constituting a – **pensionary**

People (see also Population):
Of or relating to the common people – **demotic**
Between living people – **inter vivos**
A person who has suddenly risen above his social and economic class without the background or qualifications for his new status – **parvenu**
A person of superior knowledge or taste – **cognoscente** (pl. **cognoscenti**); **connoisseur**
Of, relating to or involving relations between persons – **interpersonal**
A person serving no apparent function – **supernumerary**
A champion of the people - **tribune**

Perception (see also Senses):
Capable of being perceived – **perceptible**
An object perceived – **percept**
Beyond or above perception by the senses – **supersensible**
Of, based on or involving perception – **perceptual**
Below the threshold of conscious perception – **subliminal**
An image or sensation that stays or comes back after the external stimulus has been withdrawn – **afterimage**
An afterimage of peripheral origin – **aftersensation**
Perception by means other than normal sense perceptions – **extrasensory perception**
Perception of or response to distant stimuli by extrasensory means – **telaesthesia**; **telesthesia**
A subjective sensation or image of sense other than the one being stimulated – **synaesthesia**; **synesthesia**, adj. **synesthetic**
  A synthesthetic visual sensation – **photism**
  A synesthetic auditory sensation - **phonism**
The tendency to interpret a vague stimulus as something known to the viewer - **pareidolia**
The supposed ability to discern objects hidden from sight or at a great distance – **clairvoyance**; **clairvoyancy**; **cryptaesthesia**; **cryptesthesia**
The perception of color in response to nonchromatic stimuli – **chromesthesia**; **color hearing**
The sensory experience derived from the muscle senses – **kinaesthesia**; **kinesthesia**; **kinaesthesis**, pl. **kinesthesias** or **kinestheses**

An optical phenomenon creating the illusion of water, resulting from light distortion by alternate layers of hot and cool air – **fata morgana** (pl. **fata morganas**); **mirage**

Perching or adapted for perching – **insessorial**

Perfume:
    A maker or seller of perfumes – **perfumer**
    The art of making perfumes – **perfumery**
    A vessel for perfumes, esp. one in which incense is burned – **censer**; **thurible**
        One who carries a thurible – **thurifer**
    One who censes (perfumes with odors, or burns or offers incense to) – **censer**

Period:
    Having identical periods; having identical period or phase – **synchronous**
        A synchronous occurrence, movement or arrangement – **synchrony**

Personality - see Behavior

Perspiration (sweating; sudation):
    Perspiration in excessive or abnormal amounts – **hidrosis**
    Perspiration when copious and induced by a perspiration-inducing agent – **diaphoresis**
    Inducing perspiration; an agent that induces perspiration – **diaphoretic**; **sudorific**
    Foul-smelling perspiration – **bromidrosis**
    Absence or reduction of perspiration – **adiaphoresis**
    Of or relating to sweat prevention; a drug to inhibit sweating - **adiaphoretic**
    To exude or pass through pores or interstices, as perspiration does – **transude** (v.i.)
    Causing or increasing perspiration; something that does this – **sudatory**; **sudorific**; **sudoriparous**
    Producing or secreting perspiration – **sudoriferous**; **sudoriparous**
    The study of sweat and sweat glands – **eccrinology**

Persuasion:
    The art of effective expression and the persuasive use of language – **rhetoric** (q.v.)
    Capable of being persuaded – **persuasible**

Petroleum:
    Derived from petroleum – **petrolic**
    A chemical derived from petroleum – **petrochemical**
    The chemistry of petroleum and its derivatives – **petrochemistry**
    The strategic practice of controlling petroleum sales in order to achieve international political and economic goals – **petropolitics**

Pewter:
    One who makes pewter objects - **pewterer**

Phantoms or specters, extreme or irrational fear of – **spectrophobia**

Pharynx:
    Of, relating to, located in or coming from the pharynx – **pharyngeal**
    Inflammation of the pharynx – **pharyngitis**
    Surgical removal of the pharynx – **pharyngotomy**

Phases:
    Having two phases – **diphase**

Pheasant:
    A group of pheasants (on the ground) – **brood**; **covey**; **nide**
    A group of pheasants (rising) – **bouquet**
    A young pheasant – **poult**

Philosophy (selected terms):
    The philosophical study of:
        The nature of values and value judgments – **axiology**
        The general nature of morals and the specific moral choices an individual makes in relating to others – **deontology**; **ethics**
        The nature and sources of knowledge – **epistemology**
        The principles of reasoning – **logic** (q.v.)
        The ultimate nature of reality – **metaphysics**; **ontology**
        Design or purpose in natural phenomena - **teleology**
    Combining or drawing upon various philosophical or theological doctrines – **eclecticism**
    A doctrine that all values are worthless; rejection of all distinctions in moral value - **nihilism**
    The doctrine that considers utility as the criterion of action and the useful as good or worthwhile; the ethical theory that social and political action should be directed toward achieving the greatest good for the greatest number – **utilitarianism**
    The theory that the world is neither completely good nor completely evil; the belief that society tends toward improvement and that human effort can further its improvement – **meliorism**
    The theory that concrete experience, whether perceptual, intuitive, activistic, axiological or mystical, is the source of truth – **experientialism**
    The idea that the welfare and happiness of mankind in this life is the highest goal – **humanism**
    The theory that all things and events come to be by chance – **casualism**
    The tendency to approach philosophical problems from the standpoint of psychology – **psychologism**
    The theory that the self is the only thing that can be known and verified, or that the self is the only reality – **solipsism**
    The theory that the phenomena of life possess a unique character by virtue of which they differ radically from physico-chemical phenomena – **vitalism**
    The theory that the will is the ultimate constituent of reality, and is central to all moral questions and superior to all other moral criteria – **voluntarism**
    The theory that all knowledge is derived from original divine revelation and is transmitted by tradition – **traditionalism**
    A theory that stresses the external elements of reality to the relative neglect of the mental – **objectivism**
    (For the many additional philosophical theories, the reader is advised to consult specialized works on philosophy.)

Phobias – see under thing feared

Phonograph records:
    The study and cataloguing of phonograph records – **discography**
    One who is devoted to the study and collecting of phonograph records – **discophile**
    A phonograph needle – **stylus** (pl. **styli**); **style**

Photography:
    To expose (film) to light for too short a time to produce normal image contrast – **underexpose** (v.t.), n. **underexposure**
    To expose (film) too long or with too much light – **overexpose** (v.t.)
    A photograph made with a telephoto lens; to photograph with such a lens – **telephotograph** (n./v.t.)
    A photograph made through a microscope – **photomicrograph**

A shadowy image produced without a camera by placing an object in contact with film or photosensitive paper and exposing it to light – **photogram**

Of or using a technique for filming a naturally slow process by photographing it at intervals so that the continuous projection of the frames gives an accelerated view of it – **time-lapse**

A blurring or spreading of light around bright objects or areas on a photographic image – **halation**

Astronomical photography – **astrophotography**

A free-lance photographer or reporter who doggedly searches for sensational stories about or takes candid pictures of celebrities – **paparazzo**, pl. **paparazzi**

Physical:

Exceeding or beyond the purely physical – **superphysical**

Preoccupied with or motivation by sensual, physical or carnal appetites rather than moral, spiritual or intellectual forces – **animalism**

The property of returning to an initial physical state or form following deformation; the degree to which this property is exhibited – **elasticity**

Capable of being drawn into wire or hammered thin – **ductile**, n. **ductility**

Piano:

Of or relating to the piano – **pianistic**

The art or principles of piano playing – **pianistics**

Pig:

Of or resembling a pig or swine – **porcine**

A male pig – **boar**

A female pig – **sow**

A young pig – **farrow**; **pig**

A young pig just after weaning – **shoat**; **shote**

A fattened young pig – **porker**

A litter of pigs; to give birth to a litter of pigs; to produce a litter of pigs – **farrow** (n./v.t./v.i.)

A young sow that has not yet farrowed – **gilt**

A pig that has been castrated before reaching sexual maturity – **barrow**

A place where pigs are kept – **piggery**; **pigpen**; **sty**, pl. **sties**

Pigeon:

A young pigeon – **squab**; **squeaker** (usu. used of racing pigeons); **squealer**

A group of pigeons – **flight**; **flock**

A pigeon coop – **loft**

Pilot (aviator):

A female pilot – **aviatrix**

Pineapples, a hothouse or plantation for growing – **pinery**

Pine cone, shaped like a – **pineal**

Pipes:

The transmission of liquids through pipes; the charge for such transmission – **pipeage**

Pirate:

To act as a pirate watching or searching for a prize or victim – **picaroon** (v.i.)

Pistol, one armed with a – **pistoleer**

Pitch (sticky substance), of or relating to – **piceous**

Pitted with cavities or cells – **faveolate**

Place:
    In the original place – **in situ**
    Nearness in place – **propinquity**; **proximity**
    To place side by side or next to something – **collocate**; **subjoin** (both v.t.)
    To place side by side, esp. for contrast or comparison – **juxtapose** (v.t.)
        To juxtapose in opposition; to place counter to – **counterpose** (v.t.)

Placenta, having no – **aplacental**

Plan:
    A person or thing that mars or spoils some plan by officious interference – **marplot**

Plane (level or flat surface):
    Of, relating to or situated on a plane – **planar**
    Situated or occurring in one plane – **uniplanar**
    Situated or occurring in the same plane - **coplanar**

Planet:
    Between planets – **interplanetary**
    A planet whose mean distance from the sun is greater than that of the Earth – **superior planet**

Plants - General Terms (see also Leaves):
    Of, relating to or characteristic of a plant – **vegetal**
    The plants of an area or region; plant life collectively – **vegetation**
    To uproot and replant (a growing plant); to engage in this; something replanted thus – **transplant** (v.t./v.i./n.)
    A place where plants are grown for sale, transplanting or experimentation - **nursery**
        One who owns or works in a nursery – **nurseryman**
    Difficult to raise except under perfect conditions – **miffy** (used of certain plants)
    The study of plants – **botany**, (adj. **botanical**, n. **botanist**); **phytology**
    The study of the distribution of plants - **phytogeography**
    The scientific study of the distribution of plants – **geobotany**; **phytogeography**
    The science of plant growth and nutrition – **agrobiology**
    The science of plant description – **phytography**
    The science of plant diseases – **phytopathology**
    The study of plant fossils and ancient vegetation - **paleobotany**
    The chemistry of plants – **phytochemistry**
    The origin and evolutionary development of plants – **phytogenesis**; **phytogeny**
    A race or fixed variety of plants – **stirps**, pl. **stirpes**
    Having a plant origin, as coal – **phytogenic**; **phytogenous**
    The branch of ecology that deals with the characteristics, relationships and distribution of associated plants – **phytosociology**
    To examine plants scientifically – **botanize** (v.i.)
    The cultivation of plants in water containing dissolved inorganic nutrients – **aquiculture**; **hydroponics**
    A substance used to destroy plants – **herbicide**
    Plant injury caused by insect or other toxin – **toxaemia**; **toxemia**

A necrotic area in a plant surrounded by healthy wood or bark – **canker**

Poisonous to plants – **phytotoxic**

An organism that is pathogenic to a plant – **phytopathogen**

The tendency of certain plants or their parts to become oriented at right angles to the line of force of a stimulus – **diatropism**

The process of rooting branches, twigs or stems still attached to a parent plant – **layerage**; **layering**

An abnormal swelling of plant tissue caused by insects, microorganisms or external injury – **gall**

    The study of galls produced on plants and trees by fungi, insects or mites – **cecidiology**; **cecidology**

The study of the numerical distribution of plants and plant groups – **floristics**

Plants that are cut and dried for fodder – **hay** (q.v.)

The occurrence of two distinct forms of the same parts in a single plant or in plants of the same kind – **dimorphism**

Of, relating to or characterized by a tendency in plants to grow or change in response to internal cell pressures as distinguished from environmental influences - **nastic**

An organic substance consisting of decayed vegetable matter that provides nutrients for plants and increases the water-retention of soil – **humus**

    Of, relating to or derived from humus – **humic**

    Forest humus – **mor**

Plant Parts (see also Flower):

The process by which plant parts, as leaves, are shed – **abscission**

Toward the stem – **adverse**

Having a woody stem or base – **suffrutescent**; **suffruticose**

Having no stem, or having only a very short stem – **acaulescent**; **acaulous**

Clasping or encircling the stems, as the base of some leaves – **amlexicaul**

Having slender, prostrate stems that root at intervals – **sarmentose**

Having thick, fleshy stems that conserve moisture – **succulent**

A swollen stem, bearing buds from which new plant shoots arise – **tuber**

    Resembling a tuber; producing or bearing tubers – **tuberose**; **tuberous**

Hardened tissue that develops over a wound or the cut end of a woody stem – **callosity**; **callus**

    Having calluses - **callous**

A part of a plant cut or broken off for grafting or planting – **cutting**; **scion**; **slip**

A plant duct containing latex – **laticifer**

A pitcherlike leaf or structure – **ascidium**

A (plant) structure shaped like a globe, cup or disk – **ascocarp**

A long, slender, coiling extension – **tendril**

A space filled with air that helps in flotation – **air vesicle**

A bundlelike cluster of fibers, leaves or flowers - **fascicle**

    Growing in a fascicle – **fascicled**; **fasciculate**; **fasciculated**

    Made up of fascicles – **fascicular**

A reproductive plant part that is modified for dispersal – **disseminule**

A branch arising from the stem base of a plant – **bottom break**

A covering of short hairs – **pubescence**, adj. **pubescent**

    Without pubescence; unprotected by scales; without leaves; not enclosed in ovaries - **naked**

Without seed leaves – **acotyledonous**

Bearing bulbs or growing from a bulb – **bulbous**

Having two lips, as a flower or corolla – **bilabiate**

Having two axes or branches – **biparous**

A main axis of a plant, such as the trunk of certain conifers, that maintains a single line of growth, giving off lateral branches – **monopodium**

Having a single, undivided trunk with lateral branches – **excurrent**

A downward bending of plant parts, caused by excessive growth on the upper side - **epinasty**

An upward bending of plant parts, caused by excessive growth of the lower side – **hyponasty**

Falling or disappearing before the usual time – **fugaceous**; **fugacious** (both used mainly of plant parts other than floral organs)

Plant Reproduction (see also Pollen):

Requiring fertilization in reproduction – **gamic**

Having male and female organs in the same structure – **synecious**; **synoecious**

The development of a plant without the union of sexual organs or cells – **apogamy**; **apomixes**

Characterized by self-fertilization in an unopened, budlike state – **cleistogamous**

The production of fruit without fertilization – **parthenocarpy**

Fertilization by the wind – **anemophily**, adj. **anemophilous**

Plant Types:

A plant whose life cycle is one year or season – **annual**

A plant that lasts or is active through the year or through many years, or has a life span of more than two years - **perennial**

A cultivated plant of a kind not known to have a wild or uncultivated counterpart – **cultigen**

A plant bearing flowers that retain their color when dried – **immortelle**

A nonparasitic plant that grows on an aerial part or another plant – **aerophyte**

Any plant that has the seeds enclosed in an ovary – **angiosperm**

Any plant that produces seeds not enclosed in a seed case or ovary – **gymnosperm**

A plant that grows in and is adapted to an aquatic or very wet environment – **hydrophyte**, adj. **hydrophytic**, n. **hydrophytism**

A plant that grows in and is adapted to an environment deficient in moisture – **xerophyte**, n. **xerophytism**, adj. **xerophilous** or **xerophytic**

A plant having, fleshy leaves that conserve moisture – **succulent**

Of or relating to plants growing wild in fields and uncultivated areas - **agrestal**

A plant that grows in rubbish, poor land or waste – **ruderal** (n/adj.)

A plant that grows on another plant on which it depends for mechanical support but not for nutrients – **epiphyte**

A desert plant – **eremophyte**

A plant growing in saline soil – **halophyte**, adj. **halophytic**

A plant that grows best in full sunlight – **heliophyte**

A plant that derives its nourishment from living or dead organic sources – **heterophyte**

A plant that grows on rock or stone – **lithophyte**, adj. **lithophytic**

A plant growing under conditions of well-balanced moisture supply – **mesophyte**

A plant of microscopic size – **microphyte**, adj. **microphytic**

A fossil plant – **phytolite**; **phytolith**

A plant suited to arctic or alpine conditions – **psychrophyte**

A plant that derives its nourishment from dead or decaying organic matter – **saprobe**; **saprophyte**

A plant adapted to climatic conditions in which periods of heavy rainfall alternate with periods of drought - **tropophyte**

A plant that thrives in soil rich in lime – **calcicole**

A plant that does not thrive in soil rich in lime – **calcifuge**

A plant that is not native to the environment – **adventive** (n./adj.)

A plant dispersed by animals – **zoochore**

A young plant that is grown from seed – **seedling**

A plant that produces flowers and true seeds – **phanerogam**

A cultivated plant growing from self-sown or accidentally dropped seed; growing in this way – **volunteer**

Plants that float on the surface of bodies of fresh water – **pleuston**

Low-growing plants that form a dense, extensive growth and tend to prevent weeds and soil erosion – **ground cover**

Marine vegetation growing at the bottom of the ocean – **bottom fauna**

Plaster:
  To coat with plaster, esp. to apply ornamental plasterwork to – **parge**; **parget** (both v.t.)
  A thin coat of plaster or mortar for giving a relatively smooth surface to rough masonry or for sealing it against moisture
    - **parging**

Plastic, to make – **plasticize** (v.t.)

Plates:
  Having, composed of or arranged in thin plates or scales – **lamellar**; **lamellate**; **lamellated**; **laminate**
  A horny, chitinous or bony external plate or scale, such as one of those on the shell of a turtle – **scute**; **scutum** (pl.
    scuta)
  A protective covering of bony plates or scales – **cuirass**
  A shieldlike bony plate or scale – **scutellum**, pl. **scutella**
  Covered with bony plates or scales – **sclerodermatous**; **scutate**; **scutellate**; **scutellated** (all Zool.)
  Platelike, as the scales of sharks and rays – **placoid**
  Shaped like a thin plate or scale – **lamelliform**

Platinum, of or like – **platinoid**

Platitudes (see also Proverbs):
  One who habitually uses platitudes – **platitudinarian**
  To use platitudes in speaking or writing – **platitudinize** (v.i.)

Platter, shaped like a – **scutellate**; **scutellated** (Biol.)

Play (as in Drama) – see Drama and Theater

Pleasure:
  One who holds that pleasure is the chief good – **hedonist**, n. **hedonism**
  Of, relating to or characterized by pleasure; of hedonism or hedonists – **hedonic**
  Pleasure derived from the misfortunes of others – **schadenfreude**
  Merrymaking involving unrestrained, esp. sexual, indulgence – **orgy**, adj. **orgiastic**
  One whose life is devoted to luxury and sensual pleasures – **sensualist**; **voluptuary**
  Apparently indifferent to or unaffected by pleasure or pain – **impassive**; **stoic**

Plentiful or abundant, but only apparently – **Barmecidal**

Pleura:
  Inflammation of the pleura – **pleurisy**
  Surgical removal of the pleura – **pleurotomy**

Plovers, a group of – **congregation**

Plowing – see Agriculture

Plume – see Feather

Poetry (verse) – General Terms:
  Of or relating to poetry – **Parnassian**
  The making of verses - **versification**

To change from prose into metrical form; to treat or tell in verse; to write a poem about (someone or something); to write verses – **versify** (v.t./v.i.)

One who converts (prose, e.g.) into verse; one who makes verses – **versificator**; **versifier**

Literary criticism that deals with the nature, forms and laws of poetry – **poetics**

An outdated or trite poem or expression – **poeticism**

A person who composes rhyming verse – **rhymer**; **rhymester**; **rimer**; **rimester**

A woman who writes poems – **poetess**

An inferior or pretended poet – **poetaster**; **versifier**

A professional reciter of epic poems – **rhapsodist**, adj. **rhapsodic**

An abnormal compulsion for writing poetry – **metromania**

Ineffectual, fatuous or second-rate rhyming - **crambo**

A line of poetry – **stich**

A four-line stanza – **quatrain**

A five-line stanza – **cinquain**; **pentastich**

An eight-line stanza – **octave**

Rhyming of vowel sounds – **assonance**

Continuation of a sentence from one line or couplet of a poem to the next so that closely related words fall on different lines – **enjambment**; **enjambement**

The arrangement of rhymes in a poem or stanza – **rhyme scheme**

A rhyme created by the use of two different words, or groups of words, of which both the stressed syllables and any following syllable are identical, but with variation in the preceding consonant, as in *knighted* and *delighted* – **identical rhyme**; **perfect rhyme**; **rich rhyme, rime riche**, pl. **rimes riches**

Rhyme using words or parts of words that are pronounced identically but have different meanings – **identical rhyme**; **rime riche**

A false rhyme that appears to have identical vowel sounds from similarity of spelling (as *move* and *love*), or that arises from a former similarity of vowel sound – **eye rhyme**

Rhyme between a word within a line and another word at the end of that line or between two words within two different lines – **internal rhyme**

A rhyme of only a single stressed syllable – **masculine rhyme**; **single rhyme**

A rhyme with a final unstressed syllable – **feminine rhyme**

Poetry in which the end of the line rhymes with a sound occurring in the middle of the line – **leonine rhyme**; **leonines**
Internal rhyme used in leonine poetry – **leonine rhyme**

Poetry – Meter:

Of, relating to or composed of rhythmic meter – **metrical**

Metrical structure; a particular metrical structure or style – **versification**

The systematic study of metrical structure – **metrics**; **prosody**

The analysis of poetry into metrical patterns – **scansion**

A metrical foot consisting of a short or unstressed syllable followed by a long or stressed one – **iamb**; **iambus**, pl. **iambi** or **iambs** or **iambuses**, adj. **iambic**

A metrical foot consisting of one long or stressed syllable followed by one short or unstressed one – **trochee**, adj. **trochaic**

A metrical foot consisting of a trochee followed by an iamb – **choriamb**

A metrical foot consisting of two long or stressed syllables – **spondee**, adj. **spondaic**

A metrical foot consisting of one long or stressed syllable followed by two short or unstressed ones – **dactyl**, adj. **dactylic**

A dactylic line including five dactyls and a trochee or spondee – **hexameter**

Dactylic hexameter in Greek or Latin; iambic pentameter in English – **heroic meter**; **heroic verse**

A metrical foot consisting of two short or unstressed syllables followed by a long or stressed one – **anapaest** (adj. **anapaestic**); **anapest**, adj. **anapestic**

A metrical foot consisting of one long or stressed syllable between two short or unstressed ones – **amphibrach**

A metrical foot consisting of one short or unstressed syllable between two long or stressed ones – **amphimacer**

A metrical foot consisting of one long or stressed syllable and three short or unstressed ones occurring in random order – **paeon**

A metrical foot consisting of three short or unstressed syllables - **tribrach**

Having a metrical rhythm marked by the mixture of several meters - **logaoedic**

Balanced, rhythmic flow – **cadence**; **cadency**

The accented or longer part of a foot or verse – **arsis**

The unstressed part of a foot (in prosody) - **thesis**

A line of poetry having four metrical feet; a verse consisting of such lines – **tetrameter**

A line of poetry having two metrical feet – **dimeter**; **dipody**

A line of poetry having five metrical feet – **pentameter**

A unit of poetry having seven metrical feet – **heptameter**

A stanza or strophe of seven lines – **heptastich**

Having eight measures or metrical feet to a line of poetry – **octameter**

A line of poetry containing eight syllables; a poem with eight syllables in each line – **octosyllable**

A poem composed of eleven syllables – **hendecasyllable**

A pause in a line of poetry dictated by sense or natural speech rhythm rather than by meter – **caesura**; **cesura**

Half a line of poetry, esp. when divided rhythmically from the rest of the line by a caesura – **hemistich**

A verse having two rhymed lines in iambic pentameter – **heroic couplet**

A stanza consisting of eight lines of eleven syllables each in iambic pentameter and having a rhyme pattern abababcc – **ottava rima**

The addition of one or more syllables more than the normal number in a poem or metric line – **hypercatalexis**; **hypermeter**

One or more unstressed syllables added to the beginning of a line of poetry which would ordinarily begin with a stressed syllable - **anacrusis**

Designating a verse that lacks part of the last foot – **catalectic**

Having the full number of syllables in the last foot; a line of poetry having the full number of syllables in the last foot – **acatalectic**

Rhythm in which the stress regularly falls on the first syllable of each foot – **falling rhythm**

A forcefully accented verse rhythm in which a stressed syllable is followed by an irregular number of unstressed or slack syllables to form a foot having a metric value equal to that of the other feet in the line – **sprung rhythm**

Termination of a line of poetry in an unaccented syllable – **feminine ending**

Having each succeeding word or line longer by one element (as a syllable or metric foot) than its predecessor – **rhopalic**; **ropalic**

A rhopalic line, verse or stanza – **rhopalic**, n. **rhopalism**

Poetry – Types:

A humerous or nonsensical verse of five anapestic lines, usually with the rhyme scheme aabba – **limerick**

A short poem that can be set to music; a medieval short lyric poem – **madrigal**, adj. **madrigalesque** or **madrigalian**

A composer of madrigals – **madrigaler**; **madrigalist**; **madrigaller**

A fixed form of poetry running on two rhymes and typically having 15 lines of eight or ten syllables divided into three stanzas, with the beginning of the first line of the first stanza serving as the refrain of the second and third stanzas – **rondeau** (pl. **rondeaux**); **rondel**

Poetry not following a conventional metrical or stanzaic pattern and having either an irregular rhyme or no rhyme at all – **free verse**; **vers libre**

Poetry consisting of unrhymed lines – **blank verse**

Poetry that is written mainly to amuse and entertain – **light verse**

Loose, irregular poetry, esp. of an inferior or trivial nature – **doggerel**

A poem with a regularly recurring refrain – **roundelay**

A short poem tersely and wittily expressing a single thought or observation – **epigram**

A piece of nonsense poetry – **amphigory**

A poem expressing grief – **elegy**; **lament**; **threnody**

A poem in which the poet retracts something said in a previous poem – **palinode**

A lyric poem in which a long line of verse is followed by a short one – **epode**

Poetry that visually conveys the poet's meaning through the graphic arrangement of letters, words or symbols on the page – **concrete poetry**

An unrhymed lyric poem of Japanese origin having three lines containing five, seven, and five syllables respectively – **haiku** (sing./pl.); **hokku** (sing./pl.)

A Japanese verse form in five lines, the first and third composed of five syllables and the rest of seven – **tanka**

Of or relating to poetry composed of homogeneous and recurrent lines, as in recitative poetry – **stichic**

A poem in which the consecutive final letters of the lines spell a name - **telestich**

Poetry composed of dactyls and trochees, or of anapests and iambs, producing a movement somewhat suggestive of prose; a verse of this type – **logaoedic**

A personal, direct, intense style of poetry – **lyricism**

A long narrative poem celebrating the feats of a traditional or legendary hero – **epic**

    Epic poetry as a literary genre – **epopee**

    Epic poetry handed down by word of mouth – **epos**

A poem in a wild, irregular strain - **dithyramb**

An obscene piece of verse - **ithyphallic**

A long verse narrative in which the characters are animals with human feelings and motives – **beast epic**

A poem about agriculture or rural life – **georgic**, adj. **georgic** or **georgical**

A poem in the form of a pastoral dialogue – **eclogue**

A unit of poetry consisting of two successive lines, rhyming and having the same meter – **couplet**

A group of three lines of poetry – **triplet**

A poem having four lines – **quatrain**

A poem having five lines – **pentastich**

A verse form that is comprised of quatrains in which the second and fourth lines are repeated as the first and third lines of the following quatrain, and in which the final line of the poem repeats the opening line – **pantoum**

A verse form consisting of a series of triplets having ten-syllable or eleven-syllable lines of which the middle line of one triplet rhymes with the first and third lines of the following triplet – **terza rima**, pl. **terse rime**

A poetic triplet of lines that rhyme or are connected with adjacent rhymes; one of the three-line stanzas linked by rhyme in terza rima – **tercet**

A humorous quatrain about a person who is generally named in the first line – **clerihew**

A poem or stanza of eight lines withh a rhyme scheme ABaAabAB in which the fourth and seventh lines are the same as the first, and the eighth line is the same as the second - **triolet**

A 14-line poem usually made up of an octave and a sestet embodying the statement and the resolution of a single theme – **sonnet**

    A composer of sonnets – **sonneteer**

    A stanza constituting the last six lines of a sonnet – **sestet**

    A sonnet form comprising an octave with the rhyme pattern abbaabba, and a sestet of various rhyme patterns such as cdccdc or cdecde - **Italian sonnet**; **Petrarchan sonnet**

    A sonnet form composed of three quatrains and a terminal couplet with the rhyme pattern abab cdcd efef gg – **Shakespearean sonnet**

    A sonnet form comprising three interlocking quatrains and a terminal couplet with the rhyme pattern abab bcbc cdcd ee - **Spenserian sonnet**

A 19-line poem of fixed form consisting of five tercets and a final quatrain on two rhymes, with the first and third lines of the first tercet repeated alternately as a refrain closing the succeeding stanzas and joined as the final couplet of the quatrain – **villanelle**

Point:

    Having the form or character of a point - **punctiform**

    Terminating in or tipped with a sharp point – **acuate**; **cuspidate**; **cuspidated**

Marked by or composed of points or dots – **punctate**; **punctiform**
Tapering to a point - **acuminate** (adj.) (n. **acumination**); **fastigiate**; **fastigiated**
To taper to a point – **acuminate** (v.i.)
Slender and pointed – **acerose**; **styloid**
Sharp-edged and pointed – **cultrate**; **cultrated**
Not sharp or pointed in form – **obtuse**
Having a narrower base than top – **inverse** (Bot.); **obverse**
Having two points – **bicuspid**; **bicuspidate**
Having three points – **tricuspid**; **tricuspidal**
A pointed instrument – **style**; **stylet**; **stylus**
   Having one style – **monostylous**
   Shaped like a style – **styliform**
   Of or relating to a style or stylus – **stylar**
Extreme or irrational fear of sharply pointed objects – **belonephobia**
The highest point of anything - **apex** (pl. **apexes** or **apices**, adj. **apical**); **peak**; **tip**

Poison:
   The quality or state of being poisonous (toxic); the degree to which a poison is toxic – **toxicity**
   Producing poison or toxic substances; derived from toxic matter – **toxicogenic**; **toxigenic**
   The study of the nature, effects and detection of poisons and the treatment of poisoning – **toxicology**
   Producing toxins (poisons secreted by organisms) - **toxigenic**
   Producing or conveying poison – **toxiferous**
   Something that poisons (intoxicates) – **intoxicant**
   Extremely poisonous – **virulent**
      To make less virulent – **attenuate** (v.t.)
   A serum containing toxin – **antitoxin**
      Of, containing or acting as an antitoxin – **antitoxic**
   A poisonous secretion of an animal, such as a snake or spider – **venom**, adj. **venomous**
   To make poisonous or noxious; to impregnate with venom – **envenom** (v.t.)
   An antitoxin for venom; a serum containing such an antitoxin – **antivenin**
   A remedy to counteract poison – **alexipharmic**; **antidote**
   A poison that acts on the organism in which it is generated – **autotoxin**
   Expelling or counteracting poison – **alexipharmic**; **alexipharmical**; **antidotal**
   The course or process of being poisoned – **venenation**
   The presence of pathogenic organisms or their toxins in the blood or tissues – **sepsis**, adj. **septic**
   A substance that is held to be an antidote against poison – **mithridate**
   The production of immunity against the action of a poison by consuming it in gradually larger doses – **mithridatism**
   Extreme or irrational fear of being poisoned – **toxiphobia**

Poland:
   To cause to acquire Polish customs or attitudes – **polonize** (v.t.)
   A quality or trait held to be distinctive of Poles or Polish culture; a characteristic feature of Polish occurring in another
      language – **polonism**
   A specialist in Polish language, literature or culture – **polonist**

Pole:
   Having, acting by means of or produced by a single pole – **unipolar**
   Having, acting by means of or produced by two poles - **bipolar**

Political terms (see also Government):
   The people collectively of a politically organized nation or state – **body politic**

One of a very few dominant nations in an era when the world is divided politically into these nations and their satellites; an extremely powerful nation; an international governing body able to enforce its will upon the most powerful nations – **superpower**

A place where political speeches are made – **hustings**

A group of persons, parties or nations united for common action – **bloc**

A candidate for office whose chances of winning are slight but who may garner enough votes to prevent one of the leading candidates from winning – **spoiler**

A candidate who is unexpectedly nominated at a political convention – **dark horse**

To abstain from using, buying or dealing with to express protest or to coerce – **boycott** (v.t./n.)

A false or slanderous story used for political advantage - **roorback**

Devoted to or biased in support of a single party or cause – **partisan**

Consisting of or supported by members of two political parties – **bipartisan**

The study of political elections - **psephology**

A political party organized as opposition to the existing parties in a two-party system – **third party**

To break away from a political party or its policies – **bolt** (v.t./v.i.)

One who withdraws his support from a political group or organization; a regular member who bolts a party and adopts an independent position – **mugwump**, n. **mugwumpery** or **mugwumpism**, adj. **mugwumpian** or **mugwumpish**

The domination of a political organization by a political boss – **bossism**

The nonclerical control or administration of a political system or social function – **laicism**

The body of voters represented by an elected legislator or executive – **constituency**

The right or privilege of voting – **franchise**; **suffrage**

A woman advocate of suffrage for women – **suffragette**, n. **suffragettism**

An advocate of the extension of political voting rights, esp. to women – **suffragist**

Having no vote, esp. denied a political vote – **disenfranchised**; **disfranchised**; **voteless**

To deprive (an individual or group) of the right to vote – **disfranchise**; **disenfranchise** (both v.t.)

An election district having only a few voters but the same voting power as other, more populous districts – **rotten borough**

Voting the straight party ticket with no variation – **brass-collar** (adj.)

An unofficial vote or poll indicating the trend of opinion on a candidate or issue – **straw vote**

A vote or decree of the people, typically on some measure submitted to them by some person or body having the initiative; a consultation whereby a population exercises the right of national self-determination – **plebescite**; **plebiscite**

The theory or practice of forming coalitions, esp. of political factions – **fusionism**

A sham candidate put forward to conceal the candidacy of another or divide the opposition – **stalking-horse**

The use of obstructionist tactics, esp. prolonged speechmaking, to delay legislative action – **filibuster** (n./v.i./v.t.)

A conspiratorial group of plotters or intriguers – **cabal**

One who advocates direct revolutionary action to secure social and political gains - **maximalist**

The disposition in politics to preserve the status quo; the principles and practices of persons or groups so disposed - **conservatism**

Conservative to an extreme – **ultraconservative**

The practice of publicizing accusations of disloyalty or subversion with insufficient regard to evidence – **McCarthyism**

A doctrine that denies the relevance of morality in political affairs and holds that deceit is justified in pursuing and retaining political power – **Machiavellianism**; **Machiavellism**

An advocate of equal political, economic and legal rights for all persons – **egalitarian**, n. **egalitarianism**

A political philosophy directed to the needs of the common people and advocating a more equitable distribution of wealth and power – **populist**, n. **populism**

Someone who obtains power by means of impassioned appeals to the emotions and prejudices of the people – **demagog**; **demagogue**, n. **demagoguery** or **demagogism**

A political movement that advocates bringing industry and government under the control of labor unions by means of direct action, e.g., general strikes and sabotage – **anarchosyndicalism**; **syndicalism**

Favoring or resulting in extreme or revolutionary changes; an advocate of such changes – **extremist** (n. **extremism**), **radical**, n. **radicalism**, n. **ultraism**

One who resorts to extreme measures – **extremist**

A political extremist or radical who believes in violence to attain an end – **sansculotte**, adj. **sanscullotic**, n. **sansculotism** or **sansulotterie**, v.t./v.i. **sansculottize**

Promoting or favoring political reform; one who favors or strives for such reform - **progressive**, **progressivism**

One who cooperates treasonously with an enemy occupier of one's country – **collaborationist**; **collaborator**, n. **collaborationism**

One who advocates political separation – **separatist**, n. **separatism**

Any of various theories or social and political movements advocating collective or government ownership and administration of the means of production and control of the distribution of goods – **socialism**, n. **socialist**, adj. **socialist** or **socialistic**

Defeatist activities and propaganda favoring an enemy country – **boloism**

The study of the relationships between politics and geography – **geopolitics**

The influence of one nation over others – **hegemony**

To cede back (a territory or jurisdiction) – **retrocede** (v.t.)

An arrangement between two nations or groups that effects a workable compromise on issues in despute without permanently settling them – **modus vivendi**

Subject to external or foreign laws or control – **heteronomous**

A relationship of protection and partial control assumed by a superior power over a dependent country or region; the country or region thus protected and controlled – **protectorate**

A nation that controls another nation in international affairs but allows it domestic sovereignty – **suzerain**

The power or domain of a suzerain – **suzerainty**

A policy or practice of noninvolvement or nonalignment with conflicting alliances – **neutralism**; **neutrality**

The belief that nations would benefit from acting independently rather than collectively, emphasizing national rather than international goals; aspirations for national independence in a country under foreign domination - **nationalism**

Extreme nationalism, esp. when opposed to international cooperation – **ultranationalism**

A national practice or policy of territorial or economic expansion – **expansionism**, n. **expansionist**

A national policy of abstaining from economic or political entanglements with other countries – **isolationism**

The policy or practice of intervening in the affairs of another sovereign state – **interventionism**

The policy of extending a nation's authority by the acquisition of territory or by the establishment of economic and political influence over other countries - **imperialism**

An advocate of the recovery of territory of which one nation has been deprived or of territory historically or culturally related to one's nation but now subject to a foreign government – **irredentist**, n. **irredentism**

A foreign policy motivated by a desire to regain territory lost earlier to an enemy – **revanche**; **revanchism**

Of, relating to or marked by a policy of revanche; one who advocates a policy of revanche - **revanchist**

One who supports a belligerent foreign policy – **chauvinist**; **jingo**

The practice, esp. in international politics, of seeking advantage by creating the impression that one is willing and able to pass the brink of nuclear war rather than concede – **brinkmanship**

Reestablishment of cordial relations, as between two governments or factions - **rapprochement**

To annex (a lesser state) to a greater state as a means of permitting the ruler of the lesser power to retain his title and part of his former authority – **mediatize** (v.t.)

A diplomatic policy based on the aggressive pursuit of national interests without regard for ethical or philosophical considerations – **realpolitik**

Designating diplomatic language or action in which two or more governments agree to use the same forms in their relations with other governments – **identic**

An agreement between two or more governments or powers for cooperative policy or action – **entente**

A relaxation or reduction of tension between nations – **détente**

Extreme or irrational fear of politicians – **politicophobia**

Pollen:
  Of or relating to pollen – **pollinic**
  To transfer or convey pollen from an anther to a stigma of (a plant or flower) in the process of fertilization – **pollenate**;
    pollinate; **pollinize** (all v.t.)
  Pollination of one plant by another – **cross-pollination**; **geitonogamy** (adj. **geitonogamous**); **xenogamy**
  Fertilization of a flower by its own pollen – **antogamy** (adj. **antogamous**); **self-fertilization**; **self-pollination**
  Fertilization by pollen from another flower – **allogamy**; **cross-fertilization**
  Producing, yielding or adapted for carrying pollen – **polleniferous**; **polliniferous**
  An adhesive mass of agglutinated pollen grains – **pollinium**
  Allergic reaction to pollen – **pollenosis**; **pollinosis**
  Normally wind-pollinated – **anemophilous**
  Pollinated by animals – **zoophilous**
  Pollinated by birds – **ornithophilous**
  The scientific study of pollen and spores - **palynology**

Pond – see Lake

Ponies, a group of – **string**

Population:
  A sudden sharp increase in the relative numbers of a natural population – **irruption**, adj. **irruptive**
  The tendency of population to encroach upon the means of subsistence – **Law of Population**
  The study of vital and social statistics, as of the deaths, births, marriages, etc., of populations – **demography**

Pores, having – **poriferous**; **porous**

Porpoises, a group of – **school**

Portraits, a person who makes – **portraitist**

Position:
  Lying with the front or face downward – **prone**; **prostrate**
  Lying on the back with the face upward – **supine**
  Having a horizontal position; lying down – **recumbent**
  A position assumed in lying down – **decubitus**, pl. **decubiti**
  To return or spring back to a prior or original position – **recede**; **recoil**; **resile**; **retract** (all v.i.)
  A position advantageous for action or observation – **coign of vantage**
  Lower in position or rank – **subaltern** (adj./n.)
  Someone who is lower in position or rank – **subaltern**; **subordinate**

Possession:
  The act of restoring possession to a former owner – **recession**
  To deprive of possession – **expropriate** (v.t.)
  To claim or seize as one's right; to make undue claims to the possession of – **arrogate** (v.t.)

Postcards, the collecting of – **deltiology**

Potential, the complete development of one's own – **self-realization**

Pottery/Ceramics:
  One who makes pottery – **potter**

One who engages in ceramic arts, manufacturing or technology – **ceramist**
The description or study of ceramics – **ceramography**
A piece of broken pottery – **potsherd**; **shard**; **sherd**
An outer coat of glaze on a piece of pottery – **overglaze**

Pouch:
Shaped like a pouch or sac – **bursiform**; **saccate**

Pound sign (#), the – **octothorpe**

Pound (striking blow):
To shape into a leaf or plate by pounding – **malleate** (v.t.)

Poverty:
The quality or state of being a pauper – **pauperism**
The condition of being a pauper – **pauperage**
To make poor – **depauperate** (v.t.), (n. **depauperation**); **depauperize** (v.t.), (n. **depauperization**);   **impoverish** (v.t.)
To free from pauperism or from paupers – **dispauperize** (v.t.)
Extreme poverty – **penury**; **privation**
To deprive of the claim of a pauper to public support – **dispauper** (v.t.)
Extreme or irrational fear of poverty – **peniaphobia**

Powder:
Powdery in texture – **farinaceous**
To crush, pound or grind into a powder – **pulverize**; **triturate** (both v.t.)
    Capable of being pulverized – **pulverable**
Made of, covered with or crumbling to fine powder or dust – **farinose** (Biol.); **pulverulent**
To become covered with a powdery crust – **effloresce** (v.i.), n. **efflorescence**
To grind to a fine smooth powder while in moist condition – **levigate** (v.t.)
A powdery substance, as a medicine, taken by inhaling – **snuff**
    One who uses snuff – **snuffer**

Power:
Having unlimited power or universal power, authority or force – **omnipotent**, n. **omnipotence**

Praise:
Of, relating to or giving praise – **laudative**; **laudatory**
    A laudatory tribute, either oral or written – **accolade**; **eulogy**, adj. **eulogistic**
A formal eulogistic composition intended as a public compliment; elaborate praise – **encomium** (pl. **encomia** or **encomiums**); **panegyric**
One who praises – **encomiast** (adj. **encomiastic** or **encomiastical**); **panegyrist**, adj. **panegyrical**
To praise lavishly – **extol**; **extoll** (both v.t.)
To praise excessively or fawningly – **adulate** (v.t.)

Preaching:
Of, relating to or characteristic of preaching or a preacher – **predictatory**
The art of preaching – **homiletics**

Prediction – see Future; see also under thing or type of phenomenon used (for prediction)

Pregnancy (cyesis; gravidity):

To make pregnant (enceinte) – **impregnate**; **inseminate** (both v.t.)

Capable of being impregnated – **impregnable**; **pregnable**

A woman who is pregnant for the first time – **primipara**

A woman's pregnancy status, often followed or preceded by a number indicating the number of times she has been pregnant; a pregnant woman – **gravida**, pl. **gravidae** or **gravidas**

The period of preparation for pregnancy that immediately precedes estrus in female mammals – **proestrus**

Passing through the placenta – **transplacental**

Narrowing of blood vessels in a pregnant woman - **preeclampsia**

To carry (unborn young) within the uterus for a period following conception – **gestate** (v.t.), adj. **gestatory** or **gestational**, n. **gestation**

Pressure:

Characterized by or registering equal pressure – **isobaric**; **isopiestic**

Of or exhibiting equal osmotic pressure – **isosmotic**; **isotonic**

Of, relating to, producing, operating at or occurring at pressures higher than normal atmospheric pressure – **hyperbaric**

Below normal pressure – **hypobaric**, n. **hypobarism**

Pretend:

To pretend to be sick or injured in order to avoid responsibilities or work – **malinger** (v.i.), n. **malingerer**

Prevent:

To prevent or counteract by anticipating – **obviate** (v.t.)

Prey:

Living by seizing or taking prey – **predaceous**; **predacious**; **predatory**; **rapacious**

The capturing of prey as a means of maintaining life – **predation**

Subsisting by seizing prey; adapted for the seizing of prey; of, relating to or characteristic of birds of prey – **raptorial**

Price (see also Economics):

The lowest price at which merchandise or property will be auctioned or sold at public sale – **upset price**

To establish and maintain the price of (a commodity) by governmental action – **valorize** (v.t.)

A sharp and continuing increase in price levels – **inflation**

One who advocates a policy of inflation – **inflationist**

Very high inflation – **hyperinflation**

A condition in which a high rate of price and wage inflation is accompanied by stagnant consumer demand and a high rate of unemployment – **stagflation**

Downward movement of inflated prices to a more normal level - **disinflation**

Restoration of deflated prices to a desirable level by the use of monetary powers - **reflation**

Prickle (aculeus, pl. aculei):

Having an aculeus or aculei – **aculeate**

Priest:

Of or relating to priests or the priesthood – **priestly**; **sacerdotal**

Primitive in structure or form – **protomorphic**

Principles:

The science of first principles – **archelogy**

Abandoning of what one believed (e.g., principles, political beliefs, etc.) – **apostasy**
>A person guilty of apostasy – **apostate**
To abandon principles – **apostatize** (v.i.)

Printing:
>Composition of printed material from movable type – **typography**
>A single piece of type bearing two or more elements; the name, trademark or symbol of a company or publication, borne on one printing plate or piece of type – **logotype**
>>The use of logotypes in printing and design – **logography**
>A type-setting error – **corrigendum**, pl. **corrigenda**
>To shade (a section of a photograph) during the printing process to blunt or reduce intensity – **dodge** (v.t.)
>An apprentice in a printing establishment – **printer's devil**
>The part of a newspaper or magazine stating the publishers, owners and editors, the location of the business, editorial offices, etc. – **masthead**
>A title printed at the top of every page or every other page – **running head**
>The space between two paragraphs – **break**
>To blot or blurr, or to print blurred or doubled; to become blurred – **mackle** (v.t./v.i.)
>Printing from engraved or carved wooden linoleum blocks – **block printing**
>The part of a block of type underlying the impression surface – **body**
>Printing from a plane surface on which the image to be printed is ink-receptive and the blank area ink-repellent – **lithography**
>>A lithographic process that uses an aluminum plate instead of a stone – **algraphy**
>Printing from a smooth surface by indirect image transfer, as from photomechanical plates – **offset**; **offset printing**
>A process of printing involving the use of heat – **thermography**, n. **thermographer**
>The presence or emergence of earlier images, forms or strokes that have been changed or painted over – **pentimento**

Prism:
>Of, relating to or resembling a prism – **prismatic**; **prismatical**

Prison/Prisoner:
>Held as a prisoner - **captive**
>The theory and practice of prison management and criminal rehabilitation – **penology**; **poenology**
>A dark cell or chamber for confining prisoners – **dungeon**
>>A dungeon having a trap door in the ceiling as its only means of access or communication – **oubliette**
>A file of prisoners chained together in transit - **coffle**

Prizewinner:
>Of or relating to a prizewinner; one honored for achievements esp. in the arts or sciences - **laureate**

Probable:
>The state of being probable or likely – **likelihood**; **probability**

Problem:
>Of or relating to a formulation, esp. a speculative one, serving as a guide in the study or solution of a problem – **heuristic**

Professor:
>The office or rank of a professor; university or college professors as a group – **professoriat**; **professoriate**

Profits:
>A share of profits received by a stockholder or policy holder – **dividend**

Concerned exclusively with profits and costs – **bottom-line**

Progress intelligently planned and directed – **telesis**, pl. **teleses**

Projectiles, the study of the flight characteristics of – **ballistics**

Projection:
    Having an upper part projecting beyond the lower – **overshot**
    To cause to project or protrude – **exsert** (v.t.)
    Capable of being exserted (e.g., the tongue of a snake) – **exsertile**

Property:
    One's most valued personal or household effects – **lares and penates**
    An arrangement by which a husband sets aside property to be used for the support of his wife after his death -
      jointure
    A legal title to property held by one party for the benefit of another – **trust**
    A person who transfers ownership of property to another – **alienor; transferor**
    A person to whom ownership of property is transferred – **alienee; assignee**
      A person who makes an assignment - **assignor**
    A government's right to take private property for public use – **eminent domain**
    The right to take and sell or hold the property of a debtor as security or payment for a debt - **lien**
    A lien or claim on property - **encumbrance**
    Transfer of title to property from one person to another – **conveyance**
    To guarantee clear title to (real property) – **warrant** (v.t.)
    Joint ownership of inherited property – **coparcenary**
    Property that can be inherited – **hereditament**
    Reversion of property to the state in the absence of legal heirs or claimants – **escheat**
      The state's right to acquire property by escheat – **escheatage**
    The nature and extent of an owner's rights with respect to his or her property – **estate**
    An action to recover personal property said or claimed to be unlawfully taken – **replevin**
      Capable of being recovered by replevin – **repleviable**
      To regain possession of by a writ of replevin – **replevy** (v.t.)
    The right of a person who survives a partner or joint owner to the entire ownership of something that was previously
      owned jointly – **survivorship**
    The doctrine of an equal division or equitable redistribution of landed property; a social or political movement designed
      to bring about land reforms or to improve the economic status of the farmer – **agrarianism**
    Protracted or permanent absence from their property by owners – **absenteeism**
    To dispossess unlawfully of real property – **disseise; disseize** (both v.t.)
    A right that grants use of another's property – **servitude**
    An abstract of all of the documents affecting the title of real property – **brief**
    Permanent property, as land, rents or franchises, that may be held by one person for another – **tenement**
    A person who holds property under a deed made without valuable consideration – **volunteer**

Prophet:
    The inspired utterance of a prophet – **prophecy; vaticination**
    Of, relating to or having the nature of a prophet – **oracular; prophetic; prophetical; vatic**
    Relating to, marked by or having the nature of prophecy – **fatidic; fatidical; prophetic; prophetical**
    To speak as a prophet; to reveal by divine inspiration – **prophesy; vaticinate** (v.t./v.i.)
    To be a prophet – **vaticinate** (v.i.)
    A female prophet – **prophetess; pythoness; sibyl**
    One regarded as a source of prophetic statements; an authoritative declaration from such a source – **oracle**

Divination by the responses of oracles supposed to be divinely inspired – **theomancy**

The killing of a prophet; the killer of a prophet – **vaticide**

Prostate:

Inflammation of the prostate – **prostatitis**

Surgical removal of all or part of the prostate – **prostatectomy**

Prostitute:

Relating to or resembling a prostitute – **meretricious**

A young woman combining part-time prostitution with some other occupation - **grisette**

A worn-out prostitute - **harridan**

Protest:

To say in protest; to protest – **remonstrate** (v.t./v.i.)

To protest angrily – **inveigh**; **rail** (both v.i.)

Proverbs (see also Platitudes):

A terse saying embodying general truths – **aphorism**; **maxim**

A person who composes or repeats maxims – **maximist**

A terse aphorism – **apopthegm**; **apothegm**

A rhetorical proverb – **paroemia**

One who makes, collects or uses proverbs – **proverbialist**

The study of proverbs – **paroemiology**

A student of proverbs - **paroemiologist**

Publicity:

One who publicizes, esp. a press agent or public relations consultant – **publicist**

To publicize with circulars – **circularize** (v.t.)

Methodical publicizing of a particular doctrine or of allegations reflecting its views and interests – **propaganda**, n. **propagandist**, n. **propagandism**

To spread (a doctrine or opinion) by propaganda; to subject (a person or group of persons) to propaganda; to spread propaganda – **propagandize** (v.t./v.i.)

A liking or talent for publicity - **réclame**

Publishing:

A manual giving rules and examples of usage, punctuation and typography, used esp. in the preparation of copy for publication – **style book**

A press that publishes a book at the author's expense – **vanity press**

A publisher's emblem or trademark; an inscription typically placed at the end of a book giving facts relating to its publication - **colophon**

To publish the name of (a person) as outlawed – **proscribe** (v.t.)

Pull:

The act of pulling, as a load over a surface by motor power; the state of being pulled – **traction**, adj. **tractional**

Exerting traction – **tractive**

Pulse (Physiol.):

Of or relating to the pulse – **sphygmic**

Resembling a pulse – **pulselike**; **sphygmoid**

Absence or imperceptibility of the pulse – **acrotism**

Abnormally slow heartbeat – **bradycardia**

A condition in which the pulse occurs in groups of two rapid beats with a pause following each pair of beats – **bigeminy**

Having a double beat (of the pulse) – **dicrotal**; **dicrotic**

A pathological doubling of the pulse with each heartbeat - **dicrotism**

Pun (calembour; paronomasia):

The act or practice of punning – **paronomasia**, adj. **paronomastic**

Puncture:

The surgical puncture of a membrane or body cavity – **centesis**

Punishment/Penalty:

Of, relating to, prescribing or subject to punishment – **penal**

To punish by imposing an arbitrary penalty – **amerce** (v.t.), n. **amercement**

Exemption from punishment or penalty – **impunity**

To pay the penalty for – **expiate** (v.t.), n. **expiation**

Legally punishable – **statutable**

The act or motive of punishing another in payment for an injury or wrong he or she has committed – **retaliation**; **retribution**; **revenge**; **vengeance**

An act or attitude motivated by vengeance – **vendetta**

Desiring vengeance; inflicting or serving to inflict vengeance – **vengeful**; **vindictive**

To seek or take vengeance for (oneself or another); an act of taking vengeance – **revenge** (v.t./n.)

Desiring or disposed to seek revenge – **vengeful**; **vindictive**

Pupil (student):

The state or period of being a pupil – **pupilage**; **pupillage**

Puppet:

One thought to resemble a short fat puppet – **Punchinello**

Pure:

The quality or state of being pure - **purity**

Of exceeding purity – **ultrapure**

To free from impurities – **purge**; **purify** (both v.t.)

Something that purifies, refines or changes – **alembic**

To remove (impurities and other elements) by or as if by cleansing; to become clean or pure – **purge** (v.t./v.i.)

Purging or tending to purge; a medicine that purges – **cathartic**; **purgative**

Purple:

To make or become purple – **empurple** (v.t./v.i.)

Deep purple in color – **amaranthine**

Pus:

To form or discharge pus – **suppurate** (v.i.)

The condition of secreting or containing pus – **purulence**

A discharge of pus – **pyorrhea**; **pyorrhoea**

The formation of pus – **pyosis**

Pus in a bodily cavity – **empyema**

Slight, inflamed elevations of the skin filled with pus – **pustules**

Of, relating to or having pustules - **pustular**

Puzzles:
    Of or like an enigma (one that is puzzling) – **enigmatic**; **puzzling**
    To make enigmatic – **enigmatize** (v.t.)
    The investigation or analysis of enigmas – **enigmatology**
    A word puzzle – **logogriph**
    A puzzle composed of words or syllables that appear in the form of pictures – **rebus**

Pygmy, resembling or characteristic of a – **pygmoid**

Python:
    Of, relating to or resembling a python – **pythonic**

Q

Quail:
  A group of quail – **bevy**; **covey**

Quantity:
  Capable of containing a large quantity – **capacious**

Quartz:
  Containing quartz – **quartziferous**

Queen:
  The domain ruled by a queen – **kingdom**; **kingship**
  The husband of a reigning monarch, such as a queen – **prince consort**

Question:
  To question (a government official) formally about a government policy or action, or about personal behavior –
    interpellate (v.t.), n. **interpellation**
    One who interpellates - **interpellator**
  To question formally – **interrogate** (v.t.)
  Of the nature of a question; used to ask a question – **interrogative**
  A written question, as to a witness – **interrogatory** (Law)
  To call into question – **oppugn** (v.t.)

Quote:
  To bring forward and quote for formal consideration – **adduce** (v.t.)

R

Rabbit:

A group of rabbits – **nest**

Of or typical of rabbits or hares – **leporine**

An area where rabbits live in burrows; a colony of rabbits - **warren**

A person who keeps a rabbit or rabbit warren – **warrener**

The fur of a rabbit – **coney**; **cony**; **rabbit**

Rabbit fur, esp. when sheared and dyed; a castrated male rabbit – **lapin**

To hunt rabbits – **rabbit** (v.i.)

Rabies (hydrophobia):

Of, relating to or afflicted with rabies – **hydrophobic**; **lyssic**; **rabid**

Races (human types):

Of, for, or consisting of members of two races – **biracial**

Existing between or involving two or more races or members of different races; of, relating to or designed for two or more races or members of different races – **interrace**; **interracial**

The policy or practice of imposing the social separation of races, as in schools, housing, etc. – **segregation**

One who advocates or practices a policy of racial segregation – **segregationist**

Racial prejudice or discrimination – **racialism**; **racism**

The theory or doctrine that the white race, and esp. the Germanic race, is the superior one – **gobinism**

A mixture of races, esp. cohabitation or marriage between a white person and a member of another race – **miscegenation**

The study of the geographical distribution of races or peoples, and their relationships with their environments - **ethnogeography**

The psychology of races and peoples – **ethnopsychology**; **folk psychology**

The study of the evolution of races – **ethnogeny**

Radar – see Radio

Radial:

Having radial form – **actiniform**

Radiation:

The use of radiation for the scientific examination of material structures – **radiology**; **radioscopy**

The study of the effects of radiation on living organisms – **radiobiology**

The treatment of disease with radiation – **radiotherapy**

To expose to or treat with radiation – **irradiate** (v.t.), n. **irradiation**

The ratio of absorbed to incident radiation – **absorptance**

Photochemically active radiation (as of the sun) – **actinic ray**

Not allowing the penetration of light (as x-rays) – **radiopaque**

Sensitive to radiation – **radiosensitive**

Radio:

Designating or being a simultaneous communication of two or more messages on the same wire or radio channel – **radio**

A method of detecting distant objects or phenomena and determine their velocity, position, etc., by analysis of very high frequency radio waves reflected through their surfaces – **radar**

Detection of distant objects by radar – **radiolocation**

Radio frequencies:
  10,000- 30,000 hertz (cycles per second) – **very low frequency** (VLF or vlf)
  30–300 kilohertz (thousand cycles per second) – **low frequency** (LF or lf)
  300-3,000 kilohertz – **medium frequency** (HF or hf)
  3,000-30,000 kilohertz - **high frequency** (HF or hf)
  30-300 megahertz (million cycles per second) - **very high frequency** (VHF or vhf)
  300-3,000 megahertz – **ultrahigh frequency** (UHF or uhf)
  3,000-30,000 megahertz - **superhigh frequency** (SHF or shf)
  30,000-300,000 megahertz – **extremely high frequency** (EHF or ehf)

Radioactive/radioactivity:
  The chemistry of radioactive materials – **radiochemistry**
  Caused by radioactivity – **radiogenic**
  A radioactive element - **actinogen**; **radioelement**

Radiography – see X-rays

Radium:
  Containing radium – **radiferous**

Rags, a seller of – **ragman**; **ragpicker**

Rail (marsh bird), relating to or resembling the – **ralliform**

Railroad:
  The right of one railroad company to use the track system of another; the charge for such use – **trackage**
  A worker employed to repair or inspect railroad tracks – **trackman**; **trackwalker**
  A crew member on a railroad train – **trainman**
  A railroad supervisor of a division of a rail line – **trainmaster**
  A work crew assigned to a section of railroad track – **section gang**
  A laborer assigned to a section gang – **section hand**
  A railroad track that is 56½ inches wide; a railroad or railroad car that meets this specification – **standard gauge**
  An area where railroad cars are switched and trains assembled – **switchyard**
  One who operates railroad switches – **switchman**
  A railroad sleeping car – **Pullman**; **wagon-lit**, pl. **wagons-lits** or **wagon-lits**
  The farthest point on a railroad to which rails have been laid – **railhead**
  The pulling power of a railroad engine – **traction**, adj. **tractional** or **tractive**

Rain:
  Of or relating to rain – **hyetal**; **pluvial**; **pluviose**; **pluvious**; **rainy**
  Caused by rain – **pluvial**
  Characterized by heavy rainfall – **pluvious**
  The study of the geographical distribution of rainfall – **hyetography**
  The branch of meteorology that studies rain - **ombrology**
  The branch of meteorology that deals with the automatical registration of precipitation – **pluviography**
  The branch of meteorology that deals with the measurement of rainfall – **pluviometry**
  The process of seeding a cloud with a chemical or chemicals to produce rainfall – **nucleation**
  Capable of withstanding or thriving in the presence of much rain – **ombrophilic**; **ombrophilous** (both Bot.)
  Incapable of withstanding long-continued rain - **ombrophobous**, n. **ombrophobe**; n. **ombrophoby**
  Wind-driven rain – **scud**

Range:
   The extreme range of a fluctuating quality – **amplitude**
   A range of values of a quantity or set of related quantities; a broad range of related quantities, ideas or activities - **spectrum**, adj. **spectral**

Rare:
   A rare person or thing – **rara avis** (pl. **rara avises** or **rarae aves**); **rarity**
   To make rare – **rarefy**; **rarify** (both v.t.)

Rate:
   Moving or operating at the same rate – **synchronous**

Ratio:
   Maintaining the ratio of parts – **homolographic**

Rats, one that catches or kills – **ratter**

Raven:
   A group of ravens – **unkindness**
   Of, resembling or typical of birds such as ravens and crows – **corvine**

Ray:
   Having rays or raylike parts – **radiate** (Biol.)

Read/Reading:
   Capable of being read or deciphered – **legible**
   Not read, studied or perused – **unread**
   Unable to read and write; one who is unable to read and write – **illiterate**, n. **illiteracy**
   Impairment of the ability to read – **dyslexia**, adj. **dyslexic**
   A slowness of reading not attributable to lack of intelligence – **bradylexia**
   Inability to read, caused by brain lesions – **alexia**
   A reading difficulty characterized by confusion between similar but oppositely oriented letters (b-d, etc.) and a tendency to reverse direction in reading - **strephosymbolia**
   Having attained an elementary level of reading and writing ability – **semiliterate**
   The use of selected reading materials as aids in medical and psychiatric treatment; guidance in the solution of personal problems through directed reading – **bibliotherapy**

Realism in art and literature – **verism**

Reality:
   Something in the world of reality as distinguished from its eternal and ideal archetype or prototype - **ectype**

Rear:
   Located behind a part or toward the rear of a structure – **posterior**

Reason/Reasoning (see also Argument and Logic):
   To reach (a conclusion) by reasoning – **deduce** (v.t.)
   To deduce by logical methods; to reason discursively – **ratiocinate** (v.i.)
   Deductive reasoning consisting of a major premise, a minor premise, and a conclusion; subtle or specious reasoning – **syllogism**, adj. **syllogistic** or **syllogistical**
   The branch of logic dealing with syllogisms – **syllogistics**

To reason or argue by syllogisms; to deduce by syllogism – **syllogize** (v.i./v.t.)

A truncated syllogism in which one of the propositions is understood but not stated - **enthymeme**

A refutation cast in syllogistic form - **elenchus**

Reasoning from the general to the specific – **deduction**; **syllogism**

Fallacious or illogical reasoning, esp. a faulty argument of whose fallacy the reasoner is unaware – **formal fallacy**; **paralogism**, n. **paralogist**, adj. **fallacious** or **paralogistic**

To reason falsely – **paralogize** (v.i.)

Hatred of reason, enlightenment or argument – **misology**

Rebound:

To rebound at least once from a surface – **ricochet** (v.i./n.)

A collision followed by a rebound; to make such a collision and rebound; to collide with and rebound; to cause to rebound thus – **carom** (n./v.i./v.t.)

Recluse, the condition of being a – **reclusion** (see also Hermit)

Record:

A chronological record of the events of successive years; a periodical compiling the records and reports of an organization or a scholarly field – **annals**; **chronicles**

Rectum:

The branch of medicine concerned with the physiology and pathology of the rectal area – **proctology**

Inflammation of the rectum or anus – **proctitis**

Red:

Bright red in color – **rutilant**

Growing or becoming red – **rubescent** (n. **rubescence**); **erubescent**; **flushing**; **reddening**

Unusual redness of pigmentation, as of hair or plumage – **erythrism**

Morbid avoidance of the color red – **erythrophobia**

Producing redness – **rubefacient**

Tinged with red – **reddish**; **rufescent**, n. **rufescence**

Having the color of red wine - **vinaceous**

Reduce:

To reduce to particles that are only a few microns in diameter – **micronize** (v.t.)

Reeds or canes, bearing – **baculiferous**

Refer:

The act of referring; one that is referred to – **reference**

Something that refers; something referred to – **referent**

Relating to an act of reference – **referential**

Refine - see Pure

Reflex:

The reflex component of the function of a body part or system or of a particular kind of activity – **reflexology**, n. **reflexologist**, adj. **reflexologic**

Refute:

Incapable of being refuted – **indisputable**; **irrefragable**; **irrefutable**

Region:
   Occurring in or inhabiting two or more regions – **polydemic**
   A subdivision of a region, esp. of an ecological region – **subregion**

Reign:
   The period of time between the end of a sovereign's reign and the accession of a successor – **interregnum**
   To reign between other reigns – **interreign** (v.i.)

Relationship:
   Joined or connected in some way – **affined**; **related**
   Relationship by marriage – **affinity**
   Nearness of blood – **kinship**; **propinquity**
   Relationship by descent from the same ancestor; blood relationship – **consanguinity**
   The formation of close, specialized human relationships in populations, esp. the study and measurement of
      preferences – **sociometry**
   A relationship in which two or more organisms live in close association and in which one may derive some benefit but
      in which neither harms or is parasitic on the other - **commensalism**

Religion:
   A mixture of religious forms and deities by worshipers – **theocracy**
   Excessive or affected religious zeal – **religionism**; **religiosity**
   Overly religious, esp. in a conspicuous or sentimental manner – **religiose**
   An affectedly or excessively religious person – **pietist**, n. **pietism**
   A hypocritical pretender to religion – **tartufe**; **tartuffe**
   Renewed interest in religion; a meeting or series of meetings in order to reawaken religious faith – **revival**; n.
      revivalist
      The spirit or activities typical of religious revivals – **revivalism**
   Hostility or indifference to religion – **impiety** (adj. **impious**); **irreligion**, adj. **irreligious** or **irreverent** or **sacriligious**
   A renunciation of religious faith - **apostasy**
   The belief that all religions are of like validity – **indifferentism**
   The doctrine or practice of destroying religious images – **iconoclasm**, adj. **iconoclastic**, n. **iconoclast**
   The raising of a person or thing to divine standing – **apotheosis**; **deification**
   A collection of money taken at a religious service - **offertory**
   To convert from one faith or belief to another – **proselytize** (v.t.)
   A new convert to a religion – **neophyte**; **proselyte**
   The practice of proselytizing; the state of being a proselyte – **proselytism**
   One who prepares candidates for initiation into religious mysteries or a mystery cult- **mystagogue**, n. **mystagogy**, n.
      mystagoguery

Remedy:
   The study of remedies and their sources, preparation and use – **material medica**
   A remedy for all diseases, evils or difficulties – **panacea**

Remembrance - see Memory

Remove:
   To remove before publication or presentation of obscene or otherwise objectionable or erroneous parts – **expurgate**
      (v.t.)

Rent:
   Exhorbitant rent – **rack-rent**

One who pays rent to use or occupy land, a building or other property owned by another – **tenant**

One who rents property from a tenant – **subtenant**

A contract granting occupation or use of property during a certain period in exchange for a specified rent; the term or duration of such contract; property occupied or used under the terms of such a contract; to occupy or use under such a contract – **lease** (n./v.t.)

One who holds a lease – **lessee**

One who lets property under a lease - **lessor**

Repair:

The act or process of repairing; the state of being repaired – **reparation**

The act or process of making amends, as for an injury, wrong, sin, etc. – **atonement**; **expiation**; **reparation**, adj. **reparative** or **reparatory**

To make amends – **atone** (v.i.); **expiate** (v.t./v.i.)

Something done or paid as amends – **compensation**; **reparation**

Repeat/Repetition:

Repeating a word or phrase at the beginning of successive clauses or sentences – **anaphora**

The repetition of a key word, esp. the last one, at the beginning of the next sentence or clause – **anadiplosis**

Excessive repetition or lack of variation in movements, ideas or patterns of speech – **stereotypy**

Wearisome repetition of words or phrases just uttered by others – **echolalia**

The uncontrollable repetition of a gesture, word, phrase or expression - **perseveration**

Replace/Replacement:

To replace or supplant; to cause to be replaced by another – **supercede**; **supersede** (both v.t.)

The act or process of superseding - **supersedure**

Artificial replacement of a limb, tooth or other part of the body; a device used for this purpose – **prosthesis**, adj. **prosthetic**

Prosthetic surgery – **prosthetics**

Prosthetic dentistry – **prosthodontics**

Reproduction (see also Biology: Reproduction, and Childbirth)

The impregnation of more than one ovum within a single menstrual cycle by separate acts of coitus – **superfecundation**

Reproducing itself – **self-replicating**

Reptiles:

The study of reptiles and amphibians – **herpetology**

Of, relating to, typical of or similar to a reptile – **reptilian**

Of or relating to limbless reptiles – **ophidian**

A flying reptile – **pterosaur**

Resemblance – see Similarity

Residue (see also Sediment):

The pulpy residue left after the juice has been pressed from fruits – **marc**

The unmelted residue left after animal fat or tallow has been rendered – **greaves**

The residue left in a still after the process of distillation - **vinasse**

Resin:

To impregnate, permeate or flavor with resin – **resinate** (v.t.)

Yielding resin – **resiniferous**

Of, relating to, characteristic of or containing resin – **resinoid**

Resource:
A key resource to be used at the opportune moment - **trump**

Respect:
Worthy of respect or reverence by virtue of dignity, character, position or age; com-manding respect or reverence – **respectable**; **venerable**, v.t. **venerate**, n. **veneration**
Conferring or showing respect – **honorific**

Respiration – see Breathing

Response:
The capacity to respond to stimuli – **irritability**
The threshold of a physiological or psychological response – **limen**, pl. **limens** or **limina**, adj. **liminal**
Of or being a motor response to an ideational rather than a sensory stimulus – **ideomotor**
Designating an involuntary action or response; involuntary response to a stimulus – **reflex** (q.v.)

Responsibility:
To assume financial responsibility for – **underwrite** (v.t.)

Restaurant, the manager or owner of a – **restauranteur**; **restaurateur**

Restlessness:
Extreme restlessness or tossing in bed during illness – **jactitation**

Retire:
To allow to retire on a pension because of age or infirmity – **superannuate** (v.t.)

Return:
One who returns to a former place after prolonged absence; of, relating to or typical of one who does this - **revenant**

Revelation:
Of, like or conveying a revelation – **apocalyptic**; **apocalyptical**

Revenge – see Punishment/Penalty

Reverse:
To reverse the order or place of – **interchange**; **transpose** (both v.t.)
Capable of being reversed – **reversible**
A reversal of policy or opinion – **tergiversation** (v.i. **tergiversate**); **volte-face**

Revision:
A critical revision of a text incorporating the most plausible elements from varying sources; a text thus revised - **recension**

Revolt:
A military revolt – **pronunciamento**, pl. **pronunciamentoes** or **pronunciamentos**

Revolve:
To revolve around or on a center or axis – **gyrate** (v.i.)

Rhetoric (see also Figures of Speech):

   Strained use of a word or phrase, as for rhetorical effect – **catachresis**

   Mentioning something by saying that it will not be mentioned – **apophasis**

   A sudden transition from one point to another - **metastasis**

   The anticipation and answering of an objection or argument in advance of its being put forward by one's opponent – **prolepsis**

   The suggestion, by deliberately concise mention of a topic, that little of significance is being omitted - **paraleipsis**; **paralepsis**; **paralipsis**; **preterition**

   The repetition of a word in different cases or inflections in the same sentence - **polyptoton**

   The repetition of a word or phrase with intervening words setting off the repetition - **opanalepsis**

   The repetition of a word or words at the end of two or more successive verses, clauses or sentences – **epiphora**; **epistrophe**

Rhinoceros (pl. rhinoceros or rhinoceroses):

   A group of rhinos – **crash**

Rhyme – see Poetry

Rhythm:

   The study of rhythm – **rhythmics**

   One who is expert in, has a keen sense of, studies or produces rhythm – **rhythmist**

   Lacking rhythm – **arrhythmic**; **arrhythmical**

Rib:

   Ribs collectively – **ribbing**

   A rib or riblike part or segment – **costa**, pl. **costae**

   Having a single rib or riblike part – **unicostate**

   Having two principal longitudinal ribs – **bicostate** (Bot.)

   Having three costae or riblike ridges – **tricostate**

   Situated or occurring between the ribs – **intercostals**

   On the inner surface of a rib or ribs - **intracostal**

Ribbon:

   A ribbonlike anatomical structure – **taenia** (pl. **taeniae** or **taenias**); **tenia**, pl. **teniae** or **tenias**

Rickets (rachitis):

   That cures or prevents rickets; a remedy or preventive for rickets - **antirachitic**

Riddle:

   To solve or explain (a riddle or mystery) – **unriddle** (v.t.)

Ridge:

   A keel-shaped ridge – **carina**, pl. **carinae**

Ridicule – see Literature

Right (direction):

   Of or situated on the right side – **dexter**

   Of, relating to or situated on the right – **dextral**

Right (privilege):
   To violate the rights, esp. the trade rights, of others – **interlope** (v.i.), n. **interloper**
   To deprive of a statutory or constitutional right – **disfranchise** (v.t.)

Ring:
   Provided with or made up of rings – **annulate; annulated; annulose; ringed**
   Any ring or ringlike part – **annulus**
   A formation of rings – **annulation**
   Shaped like a ring – **circinate**
   A ring made of two narrower rings interlocked - **gimmal**

Rip:
   To rip away or tear off forcibly – **avulse** (v.t.), n. **avulsion**

Ripe/Ripen:
   To bring to ripeness or maturity; to cause to ripen – **maturate** (v.t./v.i.)
   Ripening early; a fruit or vegetable that ripens early – **rareripe**

Rising:
   A rising again into life, activity or prominence – **resurgence**
      One who experiences resurgence - **resurgent**
   Rising or tending to rise – **assurgent**
   Rising upward – **anabatic**

Ritual:
   An authority on or student of rituals; a person who practices or advocates the obser-vance of rituals – **ritualist**

River:
   Of, relating to or living in a river – **fluvial; riverine**
   The study of rivers – **potamology**, n. **potamologist**
   Inhabiting the banks of a river – **riverine**
   One who lives or has property on the bank of a river - **riparian**
   The land area drained by a river and its tributaries – **river basin**
   The source of a river – **riverhead**
   The water from which a river rises - **headwater**
   Toward a river – **riverward**
   The wide lower course of a river where its current is met by the tides – **estuary**, adj. **estuarial, estuarine**
   Relating to deposits, esp. near the mouth of a river, formed by the joint action of the ocean and a river – **fluviomarine**
   The rapids of a river – **dells**
   A river or stream flowing into a larger river or stream – **tributary**
   A river branch that flows away from the main stream – **distributary**
   A river branch that re-enters the main stream – **anabranch**
   A long, narrow inlet of a river that gradually decreases in depth from mouth to head - **ria**
   The residue that is deposited in a channel as a river or stream runs its natural course – **channel-lag deposit**
   Low-lying land along a river – **bottomland**
   Toward or near the source of a river; a region so located – **upriver**
   The plankton of rivers - **potamoplankton**
   A U-shaped bend in a river – **oxbow**

Road:
   A side road taken to avoid the tollgates on a major highway; to travel on such a road – **shunpike** (n./v.i.)

A road, roadbed or trail that ascends a steep incline in a winding course – **switchback**

A road built along the edge of an overhanging precipice or along the face of a cliff – **corniche; corniche road**

Indicating a local road instead of a highway - **vicinal**

Robots, the study and application of the technology of – **robotics**

Rock (see also Minerals and Stone):

Of, relating to or resembling rock – **petrous**

Hemmed in by or bordered with rocks – **rock-bound**

A high rock or pile of rocks on the top of a hill – **tor**

An isolated rock that juts out – **scar**

A rock fragment - **clast**

Loose fragments, particles or grains that have been formed by the disintegration of rocks – **detritus**

Loose rock debris – **scree**

A loose deposit of rock debris accumulated at the base of a cliff or slope – **colluvium**

Rock debris transported downhill by rain – **rain-wash**

A rock composed of pebbles and gravel embedded in a loosely cemented material; composed of loosely cemented heterogeneous material – **conglomerate**

Pulverized rock produced by glacial abrasion – **rock flour**

Rock composed of fine fragments, as of clay, quartz particles or rock flour – **pelite**

Made up of microscopic fragments – **cryptoclastic** (used of rocks)

Having rocks or rock outcroppings – **rock-ribbed**

A steeply projecting mass of rock forming part of a rugged cliff or headland – **crag**

A peak of rock shaped like a needle – **aiguille**

Inhabiting or growing among rocks – **rupicolous; saxicole; saxicolous**

A polished and striated rock surface cause by one rock mass sliding over another – **slickenside**

A layer of rock having the same composition throughout; a formation containing a number of layers of rock having the same composition throughout – **stratum**, pl. **strata**

A thin stratum occurring esp. in metamorphic rocks – **folium**

A smooth crack at which rock strata have moved on each other; a small fault – **slip**

To insert (a sheet of lava, e.g.) between layers or beds of other rock – **intercalate; interstratify** (both v.t.)

To lie in interposed or alternate strata – **interstratify** (v.i.)

Marked by breaches of continuity or abrupt transitions or variations in geological structure – **transilient** (used esp. of rocks)

The character of a rock formation or of the rock found in a geological area or stratum expressed in terms of its structure, mineral composition, color and texture; the branch of geology that studies the mineral composition and structure of rocks – **lithology**

Designating strata parallel to each other without interruption – **conformable**

An older rock formation completely surrounded by newer strata – **inlier**

A portion of stratified rock separated from a main formation by erosion – **outlier**

An area of land in which the rock strata are tilted toward a common center – **basin**

To make into a hard rock mass by the action of heat, pressure or cementation; to harden thus – **indurate** (v.t./v.i.)

A fragment removed from a rock surface by weathering – **spall; spawl**

Burrowing in rock – **lithodomous** (Biol.)

A bend in a stratum of rock – **fold**

A fold with layers sloping downward on both sides from a common crest – **anticline**

A recumbent anticline or fold of strata; a mass of rock moved from its original position by an anticline – **nappe**

The branch of geology that studies the classification, correlation and interpretation of stratified rocks – **stratigraphy**, n. **stratigrapher**

Of or relating to the shape, structure and arrangement of the rock masses forming the earth's crust - **geotectonic**

An upward displacement of rock on one side of a fault - **upthrow**

A series of scars on a glaciated rock surface – **chatter marks**; **chattermarks**

An alteration in composition, texture or structure of rock masses caused by great heat or pressure – **metamorphism**, adj. **metamorphic**

> Metamorphism in which chemical and physical changes occur as a result of reaction with external material – **metasomatism**; **metasomatosis**

> Metamorphism that changes simple minerals into complex ones - **anamorphism**

Rock composed of sharp-angled fragments cemented in a fine matrix – **breccia**, v.t. **brecciate**

A rock fissure filled with a metalliferous ore; a vein of mineral ore deposited between clearly demarcated nonmetallic rock layers – **lode**

The direction of a horizontal line in the plane of an inclined structural feature such as a rock bed or vein – **strike**

Of or relating to rocks, such as flint or obsidian, having shell-like surfaces when frac-tured – **conchoidal**

Molten rock deep in the earth – **magma**, adj. **magmatic**

> Derived from magma – **extrusive**

Molten rock that issues from a volcano or fissure in the earth's surface; the rock formed by the cooling and solidifying of such molten rock – **lava** (q.v.)

To thrust (molten rock) into a stratum – **intrude** (v.t.), adj. **intrusive**, n. **intrusion**

Formed by solidification from a molten or partially molten state – **igneous**; **pyrogenic** (both used of rocks)

> Igneous rock formed beneath the surface of the earth by consolidation of magma – **pluton**

> A mass of igneous rock intruded between layers of sedimentary rock, causing uplift - **laccolith**

> The mineral composition of a specific sample of igneous rock – **mode**

> Relating to igneous rocks containing large amounts of silica and alumina - **salic**

> A relatively thin sheet of igneous rock intruded between beds of other rock – **sill**

> Thin, round crystals forming a beadlike design in glassy igneous rock – **margarite**

Designating rocks and minerals having a granular structure similar to that of loaf sugar – **saccharoid**

The solid rock underlying the soil, clay, gravel, etc., on the earth's surface - **bedrock**

A portion of bedrock or other stratum protruding through the soil level – **outcrop**

The layer of loose rock material resting on bedrock, constituting the surface of most land – **regolith**

A cliff or escarpment resulting from the erosion of soft rock that has been brought against hard rock by faulting – **faultline scarp**

Of or relating to rocks formed from sediment or from fragments of other rocks deposited in water – **sedimentary**

> The science that deals with the description, classification and origin of sedimentary rock – **sedimentology**

The description and classification of rocks – **petrography**

The study of the origin, composition, structure and alteration of rocks – **petrology**

> The branch of petrology that deals with the origin of rocks – **petrogenesis**

The act or operation of carving figures or inscriptions on rock – **petroglyphy**

A carving or line drawing, esp. an ancient one, on a rock – **petroglyph**

Rocket:

> A person who designs, launches, studies or pilots rockets – **rocketeer**

> The science and technology of rocket design, construction and flight - **rocketry**

Rod:

> Rod-shaped – **bacillar**; **bacillary**; **bacilliform**; **baculiform**; **virgate**

> Shaped like a small rod – **virgulate**

> Divination by means of a rod or wand, esp. for locating underground water or ores - **rhabdomancy**

Rodents, an agent used to kill – **rodenticide**

Rolled:

> Rolled up from the tip, as a young fern frond – **circinate**

Rolled or folded together, with one part over another – **coiled**; **convolute**

Roof:
Someone employed to lay slate roofs – **slater**
A porch roof projecting over a driveway at the entrance to a building, providing shelter for those getting in and out of vehicles – **porte-cochère**; **porte-cochere**
A domed roof or ceiling; a small, typically domed structure on a roof – **cupola**
A rooflike anatomical structure – **tectum**

Root:
Resembling a root - **rhizoid**
Of, relating to or growing from the root – **radical** (Bot.)
Having the form of a root – **rhizomorphous** (Bot.)
Feeding on roots – **rhizophagous**
Living on or in roots – **radicicolous**
Giving rise to roots – **rhizogenetic**; **rhizogenic** (both Bot.)
To pull out by or as if by the roots – **deracinate**; **uproot** (both v.t)

Rope:
A long rope with a running noose for catching livestock – **lariat**; **lasso**; **reata**; **riata**
To pass (a rope or rod) through a hole, ring, pulley or block – **reeve** (v.t.)
A performer on a tightrope or a slack rope – **funambulist**, n. **funambulism**
Made from strands of old rope – **twice-laid**
The untwisted end of a rope – **fag end**
Constructed of three ropes of three strands each, twisted together counterclockwise – **cable-laid**
    A cable-laid rope with a circumference of less than ten inches (25.4cm) – **cablet**

Rose – see Flower

Rotation:
Of, relating to, causing or characterized by rotation – **rotary**; **rotative**
Capable of rotation around a central axis – **trochoid**; **trochoidal**
A rotation to the right – **dextrorotation**
To rotate along with another body – **corotate** (v.i.)
The point in the orbit of a revolving body nearest the center of gravity about which the body moves - **pericenter**
Not rotating – **irrotational**

Rough to the touch – **scabby**; **scabrous**; **scaly**

Routine:
To establish a routine for; to reduce to a routine – **routinize** (v.t.)

Rows:
Arranged or occurring in a series of rows – **seriate**
Arranged in regular rows – **ordinate**
Arranged in two or more series of rows – **polystichous**
Arranged in four vertical rows – **tetrastichous**

Royalty:
The emblems, symbols, rights and privileges of royalty – **regalia**

Rubber:
   To coat, treat or impregnate with rubber – **rubberize** (v.t.)

Ruby, of the color of a – **rubious**

Rulers:
   A succession of rulers from the same line or family – **dynasty**

Rumors, a person who spreads – **rumormonger**

Running, adapted to or specialized for – **cursorial**

Russia:
   Interest in or enthusiasm for Russia and its people, culture, etc. – **Russophilia**
   An extreme fear or dislike of Russians – **Russophobia**

Rust:
   Something that prevents rust or that cannot rust – **antirust** (n./adj.)
   Rust-colored – **rubiginous**

S

S, shaped like the letter – **sigmate**; **sigmoid**; **sigmoidal**

Sac:
    A saclike bodily cavity, esp. one located between joints or at points of friction between moving structures – **bursa**, pl.
        bursae or **bursas**, adj. **bursal**
    Formed of or divided into a series of saclike dilations or pouches – **saccular**; **sacculate**; **sacculated**
    A sac that encloses an organ or part – **capsule**
    A small sac – **saccule** (pl. **saccules**); **sacculus**, pl. **sacculi**
    A bodily sac, esp. an abnormal membranous one containing a gaseous, liquid or semi-solid substance – **cyst** (q.v.)

Sacred:
    A sacred or holy place – **sanctum**
        The sanctum in an ancient temple – **adytum**
    The desecration, profanation, misuse or theft of something sacred – **sacrilege**
    Relating to sacred rites or observances - **sacral**
    A receptacle for sacred relics – **reliquary**; **shrine** (q.v.)
    The learning or literature concerning sacred things – **hierology**, n. **hierologist**
    The worship of sacred things – **hierolatry**

Sacrifice:
    A large-scale sacrifice – **hecatomb**
    The deliberate sacrifice of oneself – **self-immolation**

Saints:
    A biography of saints – **hagiography**
    The worship of saints – **hagiolatry**; **hierolatry**; n. **hagiolater**

Saliva (adj. salivary):
    To secrete or produce saliva – **salivate** (v.i.)
    Excessive flow of saliva – **ptyalism**
    Saliva dribbling from the mouth – **slaver**
    Any substance chewed to increase saliva flow – **masticatory**
    An agent that increases the flow of saliva – **sialagogue**
    Inflammation of a salivary gland – **sialadenitis**

Salmon:
    Resembling or characteristic of a salmon – **salmonid**; **salmonoid**
    A young salmon – **parr**; **smolt**

Salt:
    Of or relating to salt – **saline**; **salty**
    Containing salt – **saliferous**; **saline**; **salty**
    Yielding salt – **saliferous**
    A land area encrusted with salt – **salina**
    To remove (salts and other chemicals) from saline water, esp. sea water – **desalinate**; **desalinize**; **desalt** (all v.t.)
    One who manufactures or sells salt; one who treats food with salt – **salter**
    A building or place of salt manufacture – **saltern**; **saltworks**
    Salt water used for preserving and pickling foods – **brine**
    Capable of tolerating a wide range of saltwater concentrations – **euryhaline**

An organism existing or growing in a saline environment – **halobiont**
An organism requiring a saline environment – **halophile**, adj. **halophilic** or **halophilous**
Of or relating to organism that is able to live only within a limited range of water salinity – **stenohaline**

Same:
    Having the same substance, nature or essence – **consubstantial**
    Of or exhibiting equality in measurements or dimensions – **isometric**
        Not isometric – **anisometric**
    Always the same; being the same as another or others; consistent in appearance – **uniform**
        Uniform throughout in structure or composition – **homogeneous**; **homogenous**

Sand:
    Sandlike in appearance or qualities; growing in sandy areas – **arenaceous**
    Growing or living in sand – **arenicolous**

Sandals, winged – **talaria**

Sandpipers, a group of – **murmuration**

Sapphire, of or resembling – **sapphirine**

Sarcastic, bitingly – **mordant**

Satisfied, incapable of being – **insatiable**

Saturate, a substance used to – **saturant**

Sausage, shaped like a – **allantoid**

Saved or salvaged, capable of being – **salvable**

Sawing, one employed at – **wood-sawyer**

Scabies, of or relating to – **scabious**

Scabs, having – **scabious**

Scale (see also Plate):
    A scale or scalelike structure – **lamina** (Zool.; pl. **laminae** or **laminas**); **squama**, pl. **squamae**
    An arrangement of scales, as on a fish – **squamation**
    Covered with or formed of scales; resembling a scale or scales – **scaly**; **squamose**; **squamous**
    Having or consisting of minute scales – **squamulose**
    Having rough or spreading scalelike processes – **squarrose** (Biol.)
    Having or consisting of loose, flaky scales – **leprose**; **leprous**; **scurfy**
    A covering of small scales, as on a bird's leg – **scutellation**
    Covered with small, flaky scales – **lepidote**
    Made of or covered with scaly particles, as dandruff – **furfuraceous**

Scar:
    Tissue scarring resulting from trauma or surgical incision – **keloid**
    A scar left where a leaf or a branch has been detached – **cicatrix**, pl. **cicatrices**

Scarlet fever:
>Resembling scarlet fever or its rash – **scarlatinoid**

Scene (see also Drama and Theater):
>A short scene or incident, as from a movie – **vignette**
>>A maker of or specialist in vignettes – **vignetter**; **vignettist**
>A place behind the scenes – **coulisse**

Scheme:
>To form into a scheme – **schematize** (v.t.), n. **schematism**
>A furtive scheme; to engage in such a scheme; to effect (a desired result) by such a scheme – **intrigue**; **plot** (both v.i./v.t.)
>>One who intrigues – **intrigant**; **intriguant**; **intriguer**

School:
>Of or relating to schools – **academic**; **scholastic**
>Occurring or conducted between or among schools – **interscholastic**
>Carried on or existing within the bounds of a school or other institution – **intramural**
>One who attends school or studies with a teacher – **philomath**; **pupil**; **scholar**
>The methods, discipline and achievements of a scholar – **scholarship**
>Close adherence to the methods, traditions and teachings of a particular school or sect; pedantic adherence to scholarly methodology – **scholasticism**
>A school that trains persons with special abilities for qualifications in trades – **vocational school**
>A secondary school; a school for training priests, ministers or rabbis; a private school for girls – **seminary**
>>A seminary student – **seminarian**

Scimitar, shaped like a – **acinaciform**

Scorpion:
>Of, relating to or resembling a scorpion; curved or curled like the tail of a scorpion – **scorpioid**

Scotland:
>Of, relating to or characteristic of Scotland or its people or language; the people of Scotland – **Scots**; **Scottish**
>The dialect of English used in Scotland - **Scots**
>A word or expression characteristic of Scottish English – **Scotticism**
>A native or resident of Scotland – **Scot**; **Scotsman**; **Scottie**

Scratch:
>Characteristically scratching the ground for food – **rasorial**

Sculpture:
>A person who sculptures (sculpts) – **sculptor**
>A woman who sculptures – **sculptress**
>Sculptured relief in which the forms project from the background by at least half their depth – **alto-relievo**; **alto-rilievo**; **high relief**
>Sculptured relief that projects very little from the background – **bas-relief**; **relief**

Scurvy:
>Of, relating to, resembling or afflicted with scurvy – **scorbutic**
>Something that cures or prevents scurvy – **antiscorbutic** (n./adj.)

Sea (see also Ocean):
   Of or relating to seas; situated around inland seas – **maritime**; **thalassic**
   At or toward the sea – **seaward**
   Inhabiting the sea – **maricolous**
   Conveyed by sea; carried on or over the sea – **seaborne**
   An arm of the sea that extends inland to meet the mouth of a river – **estuary**, adj., **estuarial**, **estuarine**
   Sea spray – **spindrift**; **spoondrift**
   Surrounded by the sea – **seagirt**
   A choppy sea – **pople**; **popple**
   A permanently or commonly used sea route – **sealane**
   The bottom of a sea or lake; the organisms living on sea or lake bottoms – **benthos**, adj. **benthic** or **benthonic**
   Of or from some place beyond the sea – **ultramarine**
   Crossing the sea; located beyond or coming from across the sea – **transmarine**
   Near or living near the sea – **maritime**
   Relating to, existing or created for use beneath the sea – **undersea**
   A sea open to all nations – **mare liberum**
   A navigable body of water that is under the jurisdiction of one nation or is shared by two or more nations – **mare nostrum**
   A sea under the jurisdiction of a single nation and not open to all others – **mare clausum**
   Oceanography relating to seas and gulfs – **thalassography**

Seal (the mammal):
   A young seal – **cub**
   An adult male Alaskan fur seal – **seecatch**
   A group of female seals – **harem**
   A group of seals – **crash**; **herd**; **pod**

Seal (to close tightly):
   A sealing agent – **sealant**

Seal (as a sign, emblem, etc.):
   Impression of or by a seal – **sigillation**
   To close by or as if by a seal; having markings like seals – **sigillate** (v.t./adj.)
   The official public seal of a state or nation – **broad seal**
   The study of seals and signets – **sigillography**; **sphragistics**

Search:
   To search with intent to steal – **rifle** (v.t.)

Seasons – see under the specific season (winter, spring, etc.)

Seat:
   A seat on the back of an elephant or camel – **houdah**; **howdah**

Seaweed:
   The botanical study of seaweeds and algae – **phycology**

Sebaceous glands, overaction of the – **steatorrhea**; **steatorrhoea**

Seclusion:
   Of, fond of or seeking seclusion – **seclusive**

Second (unit of time):
  One thousandth of a second – **millisecond**; **sigma**
  One millionth of a second – **microsecond**
  One billionth of a second – **nanosecond**
  One trillionth of a second – **picosecond**
  One quadrillionth of a second – **femtosecond**

Secret:
  A profound secret or mystery – **arcanum**, pl. **arcana** or **arcanums**
  The innermost or most secret parts – **penetralia**
  To frustrate or combat by secret measures – **countermine** (v.t.)

Secretary:
  One employed to take dictation or to copy manuscript – **amanuensis**, pl. **amanuenses**

Secretion:
  An agent that stimulates secretion – **secretagogue**
  Relating to or performing the function of secretion – **secretory**
  Secreting externally – **eccrine**
  Secreting internally; the internal secretion of a gland – **endocrine**; **endocrinic**; **endocrinous**
  Secretion of an endocrine gland discharged directly into the blood – **internal secretion**
  The study of secretory organs and eccrine secretions – **eccrinology**

Sediment (see also Residue):
  Sediment settling during fermentation, esp. in wine – **dregs**; **lees**

Seed:
  Of, relating to or containing seed – **seminal**
  The dispersal or production of seed – **semination**
  Bearing seed – **seminiferous**
  Feeding on seeds – **graminivorous**
  Having a single seed – **monospermous** (Bot.)
  The act of scattering seed; to scatter (seed) – **broadcast** (n./v.t.)
  The outer coat of a seed – **testa** (Bot.)

Segment:
  Made up of segments (as some worms) – **meristic**
  One of a series of homologous segments, as in worms and lobsters – **metamere**, n. **metamerism**
  An arthropod, such as the centipede, having a segmented body and many legs – **myriapod**
  Having three similar segments or parts – **trimerous** (Biol.)
  A segment composing part of the body of a radially symmetrical animal – **actinomere**

Seize:
  The act or policy of seizing people or property for public service or use – **impressment**

Selenium:
  Of, relating to or containing selenium – **selenic**
  Bearing selenium – **seleniferous**
  Selenium poisoning - **selenosis**

Self:
  Second self; another of the same kind – **alter idem**
  Another self; another aspect of oneself – **alter ego**
  All that is not part of the ego or the conscious self – **nonego**
  Self-denying – **ascetic**; **austere**
  Self-generated; self-produced – **antogenous**; **autogenic**
  Lack of self control – **acrasia**
  A self-taught person – **autodidact**
  To concentrate (one's interests) on oneself; a person who does this; to exhibit such behavior – **introvert** (v.t./v.i.), n. **introversion**
  Someone whose interests are selfless and lie in others or the environment – **extravert**; **extrovert**, n. **extraversion** or **extroversion**

Sell:
  To sell goods; to sell by means of a vending machine; to have a market – **vend** (v.t./v.i.), adj. **vendable** or **vendible**
  Capable of being sold; suitable for sale – **vendable**; **vendible**
  One who sells or vends; a sales representative – **vender**; **vendor**
    A buyer - **vendee**
  A small-scale wholesaler - **jobber**
  A miscellaneous collection of goods for sale as a lot – **job lot**

Semen:
  Of, relating to or containing semen – **seminal**
  Conveying or producing semen – **seminiferous**
  To introduce semen into the uterus of – **inseminate** (v.t.)

Semitic:
  The study of Semitic history, languages and cultures – **Semitics**
  Semitic characteristics, esp. the ways, ideas, influence, etc., of the Jewish people; a word or idiom peculiar to, derived from or characteristic of a Semitic language, esp. of Hebrew – **Semitism**, n. **Semitist**

Senator:
  Of, relating to or befitting a senator or a senate – **senatorial**

Sensation (see also Feeling):
  Of or relating to sensation - **sensational**
  The study of pleasant and unpleasant sensations – **hedonics**
  Above the threshold of sensation – **supraliminal**
  Partial loss of sensation – **hypesthesia**; **hypoesthesia**
  Use of sensational material or methods in order to shock, excite, etc.; sensational subject matter; interest in the effect of sensational subject matter – **sensationalism**

Senses:
  Of or relating to the senses – **sensorial**; **sensory**
  Perceived by the senses – **sensate**
  Perception by the senses – **sense perception**
  Abnormal sensitivity of the senses – **hyperaesthesia**; **hyperesthesia**, adj. **hyperesthetic**
  Relating to or making use of several bodily senses – **multisensory**
  Relating to or affecting a sense or sense organ – **sensual**
    To make sensual – **sensualize** (v.t.)
  Of or relating to the sensory reception of a chemical stimulus - **chemosensory**

The reaction of a sense organ to a chemical stimulus – **chemoreception**
Relating to or perceived by a sensory organ – **organoleptic**
Pathological loss of auditory, sensory or visual comprehension – **agnosia**

Sensitivity:
Excessive sensitivity to stimuli – **hyperirritability**, adj. **hyperirritable**
Sensitivity to emotional stimuli - **affectivity**
The sensory experience derived from the muscle senses – **kinaesthesia; kinesthesia; kinaesthesis**, pl. **kinestheses** or **kinesthesias**
Excessive or abnormal sensitivity – **hypersensitivity**, adj. **hypersensitive**
Hypersensitivity to proteins or other substances – **anaphylaxis**
To make sensitive – **sensitize** (v.t.)
Less than normal sensitivity – **hyposensitivity**, adj. **hyposensitive**
To make less sensitive – **hyposensitize** (v.t.)

Sentence (grammatical sense):
To break (a sentence) down into component parts of speech with an analysis of the form, function and syntactical relationship of each part – **parse** (v.t.)
A sentence with two or more coordinate independent clauses – **compound sentence**
A sentence with two or more independent clauses and one or more dependent clauses – **compound-complex sentence**
A sentence that expresses a condition or supposition – **conditional sentence; conditional complex**
A subordinate clause, esp. in a conditional sentence – **protasis**
A sentence in which the principal clause comes last or which has no subordinate or trailing elements following full grammatical statement of the essential idea – **periodic sentence**
A sentence in which the principal clause comes first and the latter part of which contains subordinate modifiers or trailing elements – **loose sentence**
Inversion of the order of syntactical elements in the second of two juxtaposed and syntactically parallel phrases or clauses – **chiasmus**, pl. **chiasmi**
The clause stating the conclusion or consequence of a conditional sentence – **apodosis**
Coordinating ranging of clauses, phrases or words one after the other without coordinating connections - **parataxis**
Syntactical inconsistency or incoherence within a sentence - **anacluthon**

Separable into parts or having removable sections – **clastic**

Serial:
To write or publish in serial form – **serialize** (v.t.)

Series:
One after the other, in a series – **seriatim**
A closely linked series – **catena**, pl. **catenae** or **catenas**
To connect in a series; connected or linked in a series – **concatenate** (v.t.), n. **concatenation**

Serious:
Both serious and comic – **seriocomic**

Serum:
Containing, secreting or resembling serum – **serous**
Consisting of serum and pus – **seropurulent**
The treatment of disease by administration of a serum or antitoxin – **serotherapy**
A serum containing antibodies – **antiserum**

The study of serums – **serology**

Servant:
A colonial immigrant from Europe to America who paid for the voyage by serving as an indentured servant for a specified period – **redemptioner**

Settlements:
The science of human settlements – **ekistics**

Seven:
A group of seven – **hebdomad**; **heptad**; **septet**; **septette**
A series of seven – **heptad**
Seven-sided – **septilateral**
Consisting of or containing seven; multiplied by seven; to multiply by seven – **septuple** (adj./v.t.)

Sewers:
A system of sewers; the removal of waste materials by means of a sewer system – **sewerage**

Sex, biological – see Biology: Reproduction

Sexuality, human:
Responsive to sexual stimulation – **erogenic**; **erogenous**
A person who has not experienced sexual intercourse – **virgin**, adj. **virginal**
Composed of or intended for individuals of one sex – **monosexual**
Of or relating to both sexes – **bisexual**
Belonging to or with the characteristics of both sexes; lacking the typical characteristics of either sex – **epicene**
Having characteristics typical of the other sex – **epicene**; **intersexual**
Having both male and female characteristics – **androgynous**; **hermaphroditic**
Of or relating to sexual intercourse; transmitted by sexual intercourse – **venereal**
The study of venereal disease – **venereology**
To make sexual in character or quality – **sexualize** (v.t.)
The study of human sexual behavior – **sexology**
Excessively interested or involved in sexual activity – **hypersexual**
An abnormality of sexual desire – **erotopathy**, n. **erotopath**
Excessive sexual desire, esp. as a symptom of mental disorder - **erotomania**
Excessive or abnormal sexual desire in a male – **satyriasis**; **satyrism**
Excessive or abnormal sexual desire in a female – **nymphomania**, adj. **nymphomaniac** or **nymphomaniacal**, n. **nymphomaniac**
Abstinence from sexual intercourse – **celibacy**
  One who abstains from sexual intercourse; being in such a state of abstention – **celibate**
The absence or impairment of sexual desire - **anaphrodesia**
Something that lessens sexual desire – **anaphrodisiac** (n./adj.)
The arousal or the attempt to arouse sexual feeling by means of suggestion, symbolism, or allusion to an art form; a state of sexual arousal or anticipation; a sexual impulse or desire; abnormally insistent sexual passion – **eroticism**; **erotism**
  Of, devoted to or tending to arouse sexual love or desire – **erotic**
Literary or artistic items having an erotic theme - **erotica**
One who finds violent adventures erotic – **hybristophiliac**
One given to sensual, esp. sexual, pleasures – **carnalist**
Fleshy lust or its indulgence – **carnality**
The arousal and satisfaction of sexual desires within or by oneself – **autoeroticism**; **autoerotism**

Sexual attraction to the elderly – **gerontophilia**, adj. **gerontophilic**, n. **gerontophile**

Temporary or continued sexual relations outside wedlock – **hetaerism**; **hetairism**

The use of feces or filth for sexual excitement – **coprophilia**

The displacement of erotic or libidinal interest and satisfaction to a fetish (as an object) – **fetichism**; **fetishism**

One disposed to become a member of the opposite sex; one whose sex has been changed – **transsexual**

The practice of adapting the dress of the other sex - **transvestism**

Arousing or appealing to an obsessive interest in sex; obsessively interested in sexual matters; marked by an obsessive interest in sex – **prurient**

Sexual intercourse between persons who are so closely related that their marriage is illegal or forbidden by custom – **incest**, adj. **incestuous**

To induce to have sexual intercourse – **seduce** (v.t.), adj. **seductive**, n. **seduction** or **seducement**

    A woman who seduces – **seductress**

Excitation of the genital organs by manual contact or means other than sexual intercourse – **masturbation**; **onanism**

Sexual intercourse purposely interrupted by withdrawal of the male before ejaculation – **coitus interruptus**; **onanism**

Incapable of sexual intercourse – **impotent**, n. **impotence** or **impotency**

Involuntary seminal discharge without orgasm – **spermatorrhea**; **spermatorrhoea**

One who derives sexual gratification from observing the sex organs or sexual acts of others, esp. from a secret vantage point – **peeping Tom**; **voyeur**, n. **voyeurism**

Anal copulation of one male with another; anal or oral copulation with a member of the opposite sex; copulation with an animal – **sodomy**

    One who engages in sodomy – **sodomite**

One who engages in anal intercourse, esp. with a boy – **paederast**; **pederast**, n. **paederasty** or **pederasty**

    A boy kept by a pederast – **catamite**

Sexual desire in an adult for a child – **paedophilia**; **pedophilia**, adj. **pedophiliac** or **pedophilic**, n. **pedophile** (Note: the last term is not found in all dictionaries, but has come into common usage.)

The development of male secondary sexual characteristics in a woman – **virilism**

Sexually appealing or stimulating – **lascivious**; **salacious**

Sexual gratification derived from inflicting or experiencing pain – **algolagnia**

Sexual desire for others of one's own sex; sexual activity with another member of the same sex – **homoeroticism**; **homoerotism**; **homosexuality** (adj. **homosexual**); **uranism**; n. **homosexual** or **uranist**

    Being actively concerned with the welfare and rights of homosexuals; one actively concerned with such welfare and rights – **homophile**

    The practice of homosexual relations between women - **lesbianism**

        One who practices lesbianism – **lesbian** (n./adj.)

        Of or relating to lesbianism – **sapphic**; **Sapphic**

        Lesbianism involving the simulation of heterosexual intercourse – **tribadism**

            A woman who practices **tribadism** – **tribade**, adj. **tribadic**

    A male homosexual - **urning**

    Male homosexuality - **urningism**

Sexual gratification derived from viewing nude bodies, erotic photos, etc. – **scopophilia**; **scoptophilia**

The practice of getting sexual stimulation and satisfaction by rubbing against something, esp. another person – **frottage**

    One who practices frottage - **frotteur**

An erotic fixation on animals – **zoophilia**; **zoophilism**, n. **zoophile** or **zoophilist**, adj. **zoophilic** or **zoophilous**

A go-between or liaison in sexual intrigues – **pander**; **panderer** (n. **panderism**); **procurer**

    To act as such a go-between; to act as such a go-between for (someone) – **pander** (v.i./v.t.)

The practice of, indulgence in or addiction to unusual sexual activities – **paraphilia**, adj. **paraphilic**

An emphasis of sexual interest upon one part of the body – **partialism**

The pervasion of all conduct and experience with sexual emotions; the theory that regards all desire and interest as derived from sex instinct – **pansexualism**; **pansexuality**

Shade/Shadow:
    Affording or forming shade – **shady**; **umbrageous**
    A dark area, esp. the darkest part of a shadow from which all light is cut off – **umbra**
    In shadow – **adumbral**
    A partial shadow between regions of complete shadow and complete illumination – **penumbra**
    An object, as the style of a sundial, that makes a shadow used as an indicator – **gnomon**
    A picture or photograph made up of shadows or outlines – **skiagram**; **skiagraph**
        The art or technique of making skiagrams – **skiagraphy**
    A fighting with a shadow - **sciamachy**

Shafts:
    A system of shafts for transmitting motion or power; material from which shafts are made - **shafting**

Shakespeare, a collection of items by or relating to – **Shakespeareana**; **Shakespeariana**

Shaking:
    The act or process of shaking violently; the condition of being shaken violently – **succession**

Shape:
    Easily shaped or molded – **ductile**, n. **ductility** (both said esp. of metals)
    Capable of being shaped or formed, as by pressure or hammering – **malleable** (n. **malleability**); **plastic**, n. **plasticity**
    To shape (metal or plastic) by forcing it through a die – **extrude** (v.t.)
    Distortion of shape - **anamorphism**

Shark – see Hide

Shave:
    To shave or cut off the surface of (leather or rubber) – **skive** (v.t.), n. **skiver**
    Fine metallic filings or shavings removed by a cutting tool – **swarf**

Sheath:
    A sheathlike structure or part – **vagina** (q.v.), adj. **vaginal**
    Forming or enclosed in a sheath – **vaginate**; **vaginated**
    To enclose in or as if in a sheath – **invaginate** (v.t.) (n. **invagination**); **intussuscept**, n. **intussusception**
    Having a sheath – **thecate**

Sheep:
    Of or characteristic of a sheep – **ovine** (adj./n.)
    A group of sheep – **flock**
    A male sheep – **ram**
    A castrated male sheep – **wether**
    A female sheep – **ewe**
    A young sheep – **lamb**; **yeanling**
    A wild sheep – **moufflon**; **mouflon**
    A pen for sheep – **sheepfold**
    A driver of sheep – **drover**
    One who herds and tends sheep – **shepherd**
    Of or characteristic of shepherds or flocks – **bucolic**; **pastoral**
    The meat of fully grown sheep – **mutton**
    Sheepskin sheared and processed to look like beaver or seal – **mouton**

Sheik, the area ruled by a - **sheikdom**

Shell:
    Of or relating to a shell or shell-like outer covering – **testaceous**
    Bearing or forming a shell – **conchiferous**
    To remove from or as if from a shell – **unshell** (v.t.)
    Having a shell – **conchiferous**; **crustaceous**; **testaceous**
    Shaped like a shell or like half of a bivalve shell – **conchiform**
    Resembling or being a shell or hard crust – **crustaceous**
    A shell-like structure – **concha**
    Having a shell consisting of two hinged parts; a mollusk that has such a shell – **bivalve**
    The study of shells and mollusks; a treatise on shells – **conchology**, n. **conchologist**

Sheriff, of or relating to a – **shrieval**

Shield:
    A shield-shaped object – **scutcheon**
    A shieldlike structure – **clypeus**; **scutellum** (both Biol.)
    A shieldlike bony plate or scale – **scutellum** (Biol.)
    Shaped like a shield – **scutate**; **scutellate** (Biol); **scutellated** (Biol.) **scutiform**
    Shaped like a round shield – **clypeate**; **clypeated**

Ships, boats and nautical terms (see also Steamboat):
    The arrangement of sails, masts and spars on a sailing vessel – **gear**; **rigging**
    To equip (a ship) with shrouds, sails and spars – **rig** (v.t.)
    At or toward the upper rigging – **aloft**
    To remove or break off the mast of – **dismast** (v.t.)
    To haul down (a mast or sail); to lower (a flag or sail) in salute or surrender – **strike** (v.t.)
    To lower or take in (a sail, mast, or the like) suddenly – **douse** (v.t.)
    Rigged with three or more masts and square sails – **ship-rigged**
    Unusually tall – **taunt** (used of masts)
    The front section of a ship – **bow**; **prow**
        The forward part of a ship's bow – **cutwater**
    The curved, scroll-like ornamentation at the top of a ship's bow that resembles the neck of a violin – **fiddlehead**
    The rear part of a ship – **stern**
        Toward the stern – **abaft**; **astern**
        Farthest astern – **aftermost**; **sternmost**
        The stern area of an open boat – **stern sheets**
        The part of a ship's stern from the water line to the extreme outward swell - **counter**
    Halfway between the bow and the stern – **amidships**; **midships**
    Of, relating to or located in the middle of a ship – **midship**
    On or to the left side – **aport**; **larboard**
    The right-hand side of a ship as one faces forward – **starboard**
    The steering gear of a ship – **helm**
    To turn or shift (the helm of a vessel) to the left – **port** (v.t.)
    The left-hand side of a ship as one faces forward - **larboard**; **port**
    The principal deck of a ship – **main deck**
    The forward part of a ship's deck – **foredeck**
    The stern portion of the upper deck of a sailing ship – **quarter-deck**
    The aftermost deck of a ship – **poop deck**
    The part of a ship's deck past amidships toward the stern – **afterdeck**

The lowest deck of a ship – **orlop**

The space in a ship between decks used a storeroom – **lazaret**; **lazaretto**

The lower interior part of a ship in which cargo is stored - **hold**

The side of a ship above the water line; all the guns on one side of a warship; the simultaneous discharge of all of the guns on one side of a warship – **broadside**

Located outside the hull of a vessel; being away from the center line of a vessel – **outboard**

The upper edge of a ship's side – **gunnel**; **gunwale**; **wale**

At right angles to a ship's keel – **abeam**

The depth of a vessel's keel below the water line, esp. when loaded – **draft**

The distance between the water line and the uppermost full deck – **freeboard**

To sink beneath the water – **founder** (v.i.) (used esp. of ships, boats, etc.)

A docking place for a ship – **pier**; **slip**

A space for a ship between two docks or wharves; the difference between a vessel's actual speed through water and the speed at which the vessel would move if the screw were propelling against a solid - **slip**

Wreckage of a ship cast ashore - **wrack**

The spaces at either end of an open boat in front of and behind the seats – **sheets**

A boat race or organized series of boat races – **regatta**

A boat that plies a regular route carrying passengers, freight and mail – **packet**

A flat-bottomed boat with squared ends; to convey in such a boat; to travel or hunt in such a boat – **punt** (n./v.t./v.i.)

The raised frame along the sides of the cockpit of a boat – **coaming**

To propel (a boat) by working an oar from side to side over the stern; to use this technique to propel a boat – **scull** (v.t./v.i.)

The act of turning (an oar blade) horizontal between strokes; to turn (an oar blade) in this way; the wake of a submarine's periscope – **feather** (n./v.t.)

The member of a rowing crew who sits nearest the coxswain or the stern and sets the tempo for the oarsmen; the position of this crew member occupies; to set the pace for (a rowing crew) – **stroke** (n./v.t.)

A seat across a boat for an oarsman – **thwart**

Shaped like a boat – **cymbiform**; **navicular**; **scaphoid**

The thick planks on a ship's side – **bends**

A ship's lantern - **pharos**

The portable ladder or stairway hung from the side of a ship – **accommodation ladder**

The upward curve or amount of upward curve of the lines of a ship's hull as viewed from the side; the position in which a ship is placed so that it remains clear of a single bow anchor; a swerving or veering course; to swerve or cause to swerve from a course – **sheer** (n./v.i./v.t.)

An opening in the side of a ship that allows water to run off – **scupper**

Across the course, line or length of – **athwart**

A rope or chain attached to one or both of the lower corners of a sail, serving to move or extend it; to extend (such ropes or chains) in a particular direction – **sheet**

To secure or make fast (a rope, e.g.) by winding on a cleat or pin – **belay** (v.t.)

A rope handrail on a ladder or gangplank – **manrope**

A thick post on a ship or wharf, used for securing ropes and hawsers – **bollard**

A knot that joins a rope to a rope or to another object – **bend**

To loosen or untie (a rope or sail) – **unbend** (v.t.)

A rope used to raise or lower a sail – **halliard**; **halyard**

A rope attached to the bow of a boat, used esp. for tying up - **painter**

A cable or rope used in mooring or towing a ship – **hawser**

An opening in the bow through which a hawser is passed – **hawse**; **hawse-hole**

A short rope or gasket (cord or canvas strap) used on a ship as a fastener or for securing rigging – **laniard**; **lanyard**

A span of chain, rope or wire securable at both ends to an object and slung from its center point – **bridle**

Hanging just clear of the bottom – **aweigh** (used of an anchor)

A small anchor – **kelleg**; **kellock**; **killick**; **killock**

Of, relating to or located on the side sheltered from the wind - **lee**

The drift of a ship or aircraft to leeward of true course – **leeway**

Situated or moving toward the side toward which the wind is blowing – **leeward**

    At, on or to the leeward side – **alee**

    To drift to leeward – **sag** (v.i.)

    To turn or cause to turn to leeward; to coat or cover (e.g. seams of a ship) with waterproof materials – **pay** (v.i.)

Of or moving toward the quarter from which the wind blows; of or on the side exposed to the wind; in a direction from which the wind blows – **windward**

    To windward – **aweather**

    To pass to windward of, despite bad weather; of or relating to the windward side of a ship – **weather** (v.t./adj.)

The direction or course of wind or water – **set**

The rate of flow of a water current – **drift**

The position of a vessel relative to the trim of its sails; the act of changing from one such position to another; to change (the course of a vessel) from one position to another; to bring (a sailboat) into the wind in order to change its position relative to the trim of its sails; to change the direction or course of a vessel – **tack** (n./v.t./v.i.)

To progress against the wind by tacking – **beat** (v.i.)

The bulging part of a sail – **bag**

To hoist and secure (a sail, e.g.) – **lash**; **trice** (both v.t.)

The change the course of (a ship) by turning away from the direction of the wind – **veer**

To shift or cause to shift a fore-and-aft sail from one side of a vessel to another while sailing before the wind – **jib**; **jibe** (both v.t./v.i.)

To make (a sailing vessel) come about with the wind aft; to come about with the stern to windward – **wear** (v.t./v.i.)

With sails trimmed flat for sailing as close to the wind as possible – **close-hauled**

Capable of sailing close to the wind with little drift to leeward – **weatherly**

To overhaul and go ahead of (a ship) when close-hauled; to gain ground on a sailing vessel – **forereach** (v.t./v.i.)

The act of sailing closer into the wind; the forward side of a fore-and-aft sail; the fullest part of the bow of a ship; to steer a sailing vessel nearer into the wind; to flap while losing wind (used of a sail) – **luff** (n./v.i.)

To sail quietly with or as if with no apparent wind – **ghost** (v.i.)

To run before a gale with little or no sail set - **scud** (v.i.)

With sails extended on both sides – **wing and wing**

The zigzag route of a vessel forced by contrary winds to sail on different courses – **traverse**

The distance sailed by a ship on a westerly course – **westing**

The act or art of great-circle sailing – **orthodromic**; **orthodromy**

The path of a ship that maintains a fixed compass direction, shown on a map as a line crossing all meridians at the same angle – **loxodromic curve**; **rhumb line**

    Relating to sailing on a rhumb line – **loxodromic**; **loxodromical**

The backward movement of a vessel – **sternway**

At such a distance that only the superstructure is visible; with main deck awash (washed by or floating on waves) – **hull down** (used of ships)

Flowing or blowing with little speed; cessation of movement in a current of water or air – **slack**

To deviate from the intended course; to cause to deviate thus; an act of such deviation – **yaw** (v.i./v.t./n.)

The act of changing course by less than 90 degrees – **oblique**

Stranded in shallow water or on a reef, shoal, etc. – **aground**

To cause (a ship) to tilt to one side; an inclination to one side – **heel** (v.t./n.)

To tilt to one side – **heel**; **list** (both v.i.)

Tilting, as a ship – **alist**

Heeling over little in spite of great wind or the press of the sail – **stiff**

The visible track of turbulence left by something moving through the water – **wake**

Skill in managing or navigating a boat or ship – **seamanship**

Wide or deep enough for passage – **navigable**

Space at sea adequate for maneuvering a ship – **sea room**

Transported by ship – **seaborne**

An established or frequently used sea route – **sea-lane**

A sea-lane used by trading ships – **trade route**

Trade or navigation in coastal waters – **cabotage**

The amount a ship carries or is able to carry – **shipload**

Heavy material put into a ship's hold to enhance stability – **ballast**

Cargo, equipment or part of a ship thrown overboard to lighten a ship in distress – **jetsam**

One of a specific number of days in port allowed the lessee of a ship without charge; a day of delay spent in port – **lay day**

Clearance granted to a ship to proceed into port after compliance with quarantine or health regulations – **pratique**

To move (a vessel) by hauling on a line that is fastened to or around an anchor, piling or pier – **warp** (v.i./v.t.)

Passage of a ship through a lock; the toll for using a lock; a system of locks – **lockage**

To leave, as a port or harbor – **put out** (v.i.)

Built with the hull planks lying flush or edge to edge, rather than overlapping – **carvel-built**

The number of tons of water a ship displaces afloat; a duty or charge per ton on cargo – **tonnage**

A sheltered offshore anchorage for ships – **roadstead**

The minimum rate of motion required for the helm of a ship to have effect – **steerageway**

To clean and coat (the bottom of a wooden ship) with pitch – **grave** (v.t.)

To clean (a wooden ship's hull) by applying heat to soften the pitch and then scraping – **bream** (v.t.)

In a vertical or nearly vertical position – **apeak**

Rigging not immediately necessary and stored either aloft or on the upper decks – **top-hamper**; **top hamper**

To make secure by lashing – **frap** (v.t.)

A warship large enough to take a position in the line of battle – **ship of the line**

A ship privately owned and crewed but authorized by a government during wartime to attack and capture enemy vessels; the commander or a crew member of such a ship – **privateer**

A vessel capable of operating or remaining under water – **submersible**

A ship used on lakes – **laker**

A number of warships operating together under one command – **argosy**; **armada**; **fleet**

　A small fleet of ships; a fleet of small ships – **flotilla**

The carrying of boats and supplies overland between two waterways, as during a canoe trip; any place or route over which this is done - **portage**

A floating structure used for closing off the entrance to a dock or canal lock – **caisson**

A person employed in the loading or unloading of ships – **longshoreman**; **lumper**; **stevedore**

To load or unload the cargo of (a ship); to load or unload a ship – **stevedore** (v.i./v.t.)

Navigation of a ship or airplane by observation of landmarks directly or by means of radar; the charting or steering of a course (as for a ship) - **pilotage**

A carpenter employed in the construction or maintenance of ships – **shipwright**

An unlawful breach of duty on the part of a ship's master or crew resulting in injury to the ship's owner – **barratry**

Shoes:

Not having or wearing shoes – **unshod**

A person who cleans and polishes shoes for a living – **bootblack**

Shoot/Shooting:

One who shoots, esp. a marksman – **shootist**

To shoot at in a random manner; to shoot at randomly selected targets – **plink** (v.t./v.i.)

The practice of shooting at clay pigeons – **trapshooting**

Shore (see also Surf):

Of or relating to the waters and deposits of a shoreline – **neritic**

Of, relating to or existing on a shore; a shore or coastal region – **littoral**

Near the seashore – **sublittoral**

On shore – **ashore**

Toward the shore – **ashore**; **shoreward**; **shorewards**

Close to a shore; coming toward a shore – **inshore**

The seaward pull of receding waves breaking on a shore – **undertow**

A shore toward which the wind is blowing and toward which a ship is likely to be driven – **lee shore**

The part of a shore covered at high tide; the part of a shore between the water and inhabited or cultivated land –
   foreshore

The period at high or low tide when there is no visible flow of water – **slack water**

Material cast ashore, esp. seaweed – **sea wrack**
   Sea wrack used as fertilizer – **seaware**

A long narrow shoal extending from the shore – **spit**

The sound of surf breaking on the shore - **rote**

A structure projecting out from a shoreline into the water as protection against beach erosion; to build or equip with
   such structures – **groin; groyne** (both n./v.t.)

A shoreline above the present water level - **strandline**

Shorthand – see Writing

Shrine (see also Sacred):

   A small structure used as a shrine – **aedicula** (pl. **aediculae**); **aedicule** (pl. **aedicules**); **edicule**, pl. **edicules**, adj.
      aedicular

   A shrine consecrated to a prophetic deity; one who serves as a deity at such a shrine – **oracle**

Shrinking, the process of – **shrinkage**

Shrub:

   Relating to, like or assuming the form of a shrub - **frutescent**

   Shrublike, esp. in form – **fruticose**

Sick/Sickness:

   Very sick – **à la mort**

   A condition of prolonged ill health - **invalidism**

   To pretend to be sick or injured (in order to avoid work or duty) – **malinger** (v.i.), n. **malingerer**

   To regress after partial recovery from an illness – **relapse** (v.i.)

   Not responsive to treatment – **refractory** (used of an illness)

   A sickly or weak person, esp. one who is constantly and morbidly concerned with his health – **valetudinarian**, adj.
      valetudinary

   The persistent conviction that one is or is likely to become ill, when illness is neither present nor likely –
      hypochondria; **hypochondriasis**, n. **hypochondriac**, adj. **hypochondriac** or **hypochondriacal**

Sickle:

   A sickle-shaped structure – **falx**, pl. **falces**

   Sickle-shaped – **falcate**; **falcated**; **falciform**; **falculate**

Side:

   To place side by side, esp. for contrast or comparison – **juxtapose** (v.t.), n. **juxtaposition**

   Side by side; adjoining – **approximal** (Anat.)

   Of, relating to, on, having, involving or affecting only one side; obligating only one of two or more parties, nations or
      persons – **unilateral**

   Of, relating to or having two sides – **bilateral**; **two-sided**

Having two equal sides – **isosceles**
Of, relating to or having three sides – **trilateral**
Having three unequal sides – **scalene**
Having sides of unequal length or form – **oblique** (Bot.)
Of, relating to or having many sides – **multilateral**

Sieve:
Having perforations like a sieve – **cribriform**
Material removed or separated with or as if with a sieve – **siftings**
Not sifted – **unbolted** (used of flour)

Sight (see also Vision):
Serving, resulting from or relating to the sense of sight; done or maintained by sight only – **ocular**; **visual**
Capable of being seen; obvious or perceptible to the eye – **visible**, n. **visibility**
Of, relating to or designed to assist sight – **optical**
Sharp-sighted – **lyncean**

Sign:
Capable of being depicted as a sign – **signifiable**
The process in which something functions as a sign – **semiosis**
A sign or image considered magical – **sigil**
The science dealing with signs and sign language – **semiology**
The study of relationships between signs and symbols and what they represent to their interpreters – **semasiology**;
semeiotics; **semiotics**
The branch of semiotics that deals with the relationships between signs and expressions and their users –
pragmatics
The branch of semiotics that deals with the formal properties of signs and symbols – **syntactics**

Signal:
To send (a signal), as by wire or radio; to send out a signal – **transmit** (v.t./v.i.), n. **transmission**
Able to be transmitted - **transmissible**
Capable of transmitting or receiving signals in all directions – **omnidirectional**
A system for signaling using two flags that are held one in each hand – **semaphore**
The use of signs in signaling – **semiology**
A drum or trumpet signal for a conference with the enemy - **chamade**

Signature:
Bound by signed agreement; one who has signed a treaty or other document – **signatory**
A flourish made after or below a signature – **paraph**
A petition or protest on which the signatures are arranged in a circle in order to conceal the order of signing – **round robin**
To sign one's name at the bottom of (a letter or document) – **undersign** (v.t.)

Silent:
Gloomily silent – **sullen**; **taciturn**

Silica:
Bearing or containing silica – **siliceous**; **silicic**; **siliciferous**
Resembling or derived from silica – **siliceous**; **silicic**
Producing or in partial combination with silica – **siliciferous**
To convert or become converted into silica – **silicify** (v.t./v.i.)

Silicon:
Containing, resembling or derived from silicon – **siliceous**; **silicic**

Silk:
Of, relating to or consisting of silk – **sericeous**; **silky**
The production of raw silk and the raising of silkworms for this purpose – **sericulture**
A print made by the silk-screen process – **serigraph**

Silver:
Of or relating to silver – **argentic**; **lunar**
Containing silver – **argentic**
Bearing or producing silver – **argentiferous**
Adorned with silver – **clinquant**
An alloy of 92.5% silver with copper or another metal; objects made of such alloy – **sterling silver**
The free coinage of silver, esp. at a fixed ratio to gold – **free silver**
One who makes, repairs or replates articles of silver – **silversmith**

Similar/Similarity:
Of the same or similar nature or kind – **homogeneous**; **homogenous**
Similarity in some respects between things otherwise unlike; similarity in function between parts dissimilar in origin and structure – **analogy**, adj. **analogous**
Consisting of the same elements in varying proportions – **heterologous**
Correspondence between parts or organs, possibly of dissimilar function, related by common descent – **homogeny**, adj. **homogenous** (Biol.)
Similar in structure and evolutionary origin – **homologic**; **homological**; **homologous**
    The quality or state of being homologous – **homology**
    A homologous organ or part – **homolog**; **homologue**
The quality or state of being similar in external appearance, size or form – **homomorphism**
Resemblance caused by common ancestry – **homophyly**
Superficial structural similarity arising from convergence or parallel evolution – **homoplasy**
A relationship of characteristic similarity, equivalence or identity among constituents of a system or between different systems; similarity of form and arrangement of parts on opposite sides of a boundary – **symmetry**, adj. **symmetric** or **symmetrical**
    To make symmetric – **symmetrize** (v.t.)
    Symmetric arrangement of constituents, esp. of radiating parts, about a central point – **radial symmetry**
        Having radial symmetry – **actinomorphic**; **actinomorphous**; **radiate**
    Bilaterally symmetric so as to be capable of being symmetrically divided only along a single longitudinal plane – **zygomorphic**; **zygomorphous**, n. **zygomorphism**
    Both bilaterally and radially symmetric – **biradial**
    Displaying only half the faces needed for total symmetry – **hemihedral**
    Lack of symmetry – **asymmetry** (adj. **asymmetric** or **asymmetrical**); **dissymmetry**
    Asymmetric at the axial ends – **hemimorphic**
    Having asymmetric parts – **anisometric**
The resemblance, through natural selection, of one organism to another or to a natural object, as an aid to concealment – **mimicry**

Sin:
The study or science of the doctrine of sin – **hamartiology**
Capable of sinning – **peccable**, n. **peccability**

Singing (see also Song):
    Types of voice parts and singing voices:
        Female, highest to lowest pitch:
            soprano
            mezzosoprano
            alto or **contralto**
        Male, highest to lowest pitch:
            alto or **countertenor**
            tenor
            baritone or **barytone**
            bass
            basso profundo

    A woman singer, esp. an opera singer – **cantatrice**; **chanteuse**
    To sing with trills, runs or quavers – **warble** (v.i./v.t.)
    To sing so that the voice fluctuates between the normal chest voice and a falsetto; to sing (a song) thus – **yodel** (v.i./v.t.)
    The art of ornate vocalization – **melismatics**
    An ode (classical poem) sung by one voice – **monody**

Sinus membrane, inflammation of a – **sinusitis**

Sister:
    Of, relating to or like a sister – **sisterly**; **sororal**
    The killing of a sister; one who kills his own sister – **sororicide**

Sitting:
    Characterized by or requiring much sitting; accustomed to sitting or taking little exercise – **sedentary**

Six:
    Composed of or divided into six parts – **senary**; **sexpartite**; **sextuple**
    A group of six persons or things – **sextet**
    Of, based upon or characterized by six; compounded of six things – **senary**; **sextuple**
    Six times as many or as much – **sextuplicate**; **sixfold**
    A series or group of six – **hexad**
    Relating to six hundred – **sexcentenary**

Sixty:
    Of, relating to or based on the number 60 – **sexagesimal**

Size:
    Being of the same size as an original – **life-size**; **life-sized**
    Of different sizes – **varisized**

Skeleton:
    Of or relating to the skeleton – **osteal**; **skeletal**
    The surgical or manipulative treatment of disorders of the skeletal system and associated motor organs – **orthopaedics**; **orthopedics**

Sketch:
    To sketch or outline in a shadowy way – **adumbrate** (v.t.), n. **adumbration**

Ski/Skiing:
    Skiing along a zigzag course; a race along such a course, laid out with flag-marked poles – **slalom**
    A cross-country ski run or race – **langlauf**
    A cross-country ski race of approximately 35 miles – **dauerlauf**, pl. **dauerlaufs** or **dauerläufe**
    A turn or stop performed by shifting the weight forward on the ski that will be on the outside of the turn and pulling its tip gradually inward – **telemark**; **Telemark**
    To make a fast, straight run in skiing; a straight, steep course for skiing – **schuss** (v.i./n.)
        One who schusses very proficiently – **schussboomer**
    A hollow made in the snow by a skier falling backward – **sitzmark**
    To ski across rather than down (a hill); to descend a slope in a zigzag way; the zigzag course of a skier moving down a steep slope – **traverse** (v.t./v.i./n.)
    A posture assumed in skiing in which the skier leans forward from the ankles – **vorlage**
    A jump made from a crouching position with the use of both poles – **geländesprung**
    To point (skis) inward; to point skis inward in order to slow down or turn – **stem** (v.t./v.i.)
    A skiing turn made by stemming the downhill ski and placing one's weight upon it while bringing the other ski into a parallel position – **stem turn**
    A skiing turn made by lifting a ski, putting it down again pointed in the direction of the turn, and placing one's weight on it while bringing the other ski into a parallel position – **step turn**

Skin:
    Of or relating to the skin – **cutaneous**; **dermal**; **dermic**
    Resembling skin – **dermatoid**
    Having a thin skin or rind – **thin-skinned**
    Inflammation of the skin – **dermatitis**
    The medical study of skin physiology, pathology, etc. – **dermatology**
    The use of skin grafts in plastic surgery to replace skin loss or correct defects – **dermatoplasty**
    The patterns of ridges of skin on the fingers, the palm, and the bottom of the feet; the science dealing with the study of these patterns – **dermatoglyphics**
    The anatomical description of the skin – **dermatography**
    The protective outer layer of the skin – **epidermis; epithelium**
        Of, relating to or having the characteristics of the epidermis – **epidermoid**
    The layer of skin beneath the epithelium – **corium**; **derma**; **dermis**
    Located or found just beneath the skin – **subcutaneous**
    Passed, done or effected through or by means of the skin - **percutaneous**
    Within the skin – **intracutaneous**
    A skin eruption – **exanthem**; **exanthema**
    A ridge or bump raised on the skin by a lash, blow, or allergic disorder; to mark (the skin) with such ridges or bumps – **wale**; **welt** (n./v.t.)
    A localized thickening and enlargement of the horny layer of the skin – **callosity**; **callus**
        Having calluses – **callous**
        The state of being calloused – **callosity**
    Pathological thickening and hardening of the skin – **scleroderma**, adj. **sclerodermatous**
    To wear off or tear the skin of – **abrade**; **excoriate** (both v.t.)
    An excessive sensitivity of skin – **hyperaesthesia**; **hyperesthesia**
    Abnormal or impaired skin sensation (e.g. burning, prickling, itching or tingling) – **paraesthesia**; **paresthesia**
    Having a light complexion and light hair; an individual with these features – **xanthocroid**
    The skin of an animal – **hide** (q.v.)
    A person who flays, dresses or sells animal skins – **skinner**

To strip the skin or blubber from (a whale, e.g.) – **flense** (v.t.)

To shed, peel or scale off – **desquamate** (v.i.) (used of skin)

A membranous covering, skin or coat – **velamen**; **velum** (both Anat.)
    Having or covered by a velum – **velate**

An outer covering or coat (of an organism, part or organ) – **integument**

Acting medicinally by absorption through the skin – **endermic**

Within the dermis of the skin – **intradermal**

A skin disease – **dermatosis**

A disease of the skin marked by overgrowth of horny tissue – **keratosis**, pl. **keratoses**, adj. **keratotic**

Injected beneath the skin – **hypodermic**

Abnormal dryness of the skin – **xeroderma**

The shedding of an outer layer of skin – **ecdysis**

The dead outer skin shed by a snake or amphibian – **slough**

A hereditary or congenital mark or growth on the skin – **nevus**

Skin discoloration of a patchy brown or black nature – **chloasma**, pl. **chloasmata**

Darkness of complexion – **nigrescence**, adj. **nigrescent**

Scaly or shredded dry skin – **scurf**

The feeling of insects creeping on or in the skin – **formication**

A spreading skin eruption or lesion – **serpigo**

Premature aging of the skin – **geroderma**; **gerodermia**

A rose-colored skin rash – **roseola**

Bluish discoloration of the skin, caused by inadequate oxygenation of the blood – **cyanosis**

A discolored spot on the skin – **macula**, adj. **macular**

Having a swarthy or black complexion and black hair – **melanous**

Abnormally dark pigmentation of the skin or other tissues – **melanosis**

Having light brown or yellowish skin – **xanthous**

Partial or total lack of skin pigmentation – **leucoderma**; **leukoderma**

A condition in which pressure or friction on the skin causes raised marks – **dermatographia**; **dermographia**

Extreme or irrational fear of touching the skin or fur of an animal – **doraphobia**

Skull (cranium, pl. craniums or crania; see also Head):

Of or relating to the skull – **cranial**

Having a skull – **craniate**

Within the skull – **intracranial**

The highest point of the skull - **vertex**

Congenital separation of the skull – **cranioschisis**

Congenital separation of the skull and spine – **craniorachischisis**

The act of cutting or crushing the human skull to facilitate birth; surgical cutting or removal of part of the skull –
    craniotomy

The surgical correction of skull defects – **cranioplasty**

Involving both the cranium and the brain – **craniocerebral**

Having a ratio of skull height to skull length of less than 75% - **orthocephalic**; **orthocephalous**

An abnormality in which the skull is pointed – **acrocephaly**

The back of the skull – **occiput**

The superior portion of the skull that lacks the lower jaw and facial parts – **calvarium**

The scientific study of the skull, esp. in humans – **craniology**

The study of the shape, protuberances, etc., of the skull, based on a belief that it is indicative of character and mental
    capacity – **phrenology**, n. **phrenologist**

Surgical removal of part of the cranium – **craniectomy**

The science of measuring skulls – **craniometry**, n. **craniometrist**

The observation or examination of the human skull – **cranioscopy**, n. **cranioscopist**

Sky:
 Of or relating to the sky – **celestial**; **empyreal**; **empyrean**
 At or toward the sky – **skyward**
 Open to the sky – **hypaethral**
 A sky covered with rows of small, fleecy clouds, suggesting the streaks on a mackerel's back – **mackerel sky**

Slant:
 At a slant – **aslant**; **obliquely**
 Having a slanting or sloping direction, course or situation – **inclined**; **oblique**
  The quality or state of being oblique – **obliquity**

Slate:
 Slates collectively – **slating**
 Someone employed to repair or install slate roofs – **slater**

Slave:
 Bondage to a master or household; a mode of production in which slaves constitute the principal work force – **slavery**
 Against slavery – **antislavery**
 A file of slaves chained together in transit – **coffle**
 Advocacy of the abolition of slavery – **abolitionism**, n. **abolitionist**
 A ship engaged in slave traffic; a person who traffics in slaves – **slaver**
 A U.S. territory in which slavery was prohibited before the Civil War – **free soil**

Sleep:
 Of, suggestive of or resembling sleep – **hypnoid**; **hypnoidal**; **slumberous**; **slumbery**; **slumberous**; **soporific**
 Causing or inducing sleep; tending to produce sleep – **hypnagogic**; **hypnogogic**; **hypnotic**; **sleepy**; **slumberous**;
  slumbery; **slumbrous**; **somnolent**; **somnifacient**; **somniferous**; **somnific**; **soporiferous**; **soporific**
 A sleep-inducing drug – **hypnotic**; **soporific**
 Of or relating to the period or state of drowsiness preceding sleep – **hypnagogic**; **hypnogogic**
 Of or relating to the semiconscious period or state preceding complete awakening – **hypnopompic**
 Chronic inability to sleep – **agrypnia**; **insomnia**; **sleeplessness**
 An abnormally deep sleep – **sopor**; **stupor**
 Deep unconsciousness produced by a drug – **narcosis**
 A condition characterized by sudden and uncontrollable attacks of deep sleep – **narcolepsy**
 One who talks while asleep – **somniloquist**, n. **somniloquy**
 Walking while asleep or in a sleeplike condition – **noctambulation**; **noctambulism**; (adj. **noctambulant** or
  noctambulous); **somnambulism**
 To walk while asleep – **somnambulate** (v.i.), n. **noctambule** or **somnambulist**
 Abnormal fear of sleep – **hypnophobia**; **hypnophoby**
 To pass the winter in a dormant or torpid state – **hibernate** (v.i.), n. **hibernation**
  A case, covering or structure in which an organism remains dormant for the winter; the shelter of a hibernating
   animal – **hibernaculum**
 To pass the summer, esp. in a state of dormancy – **aestivate** (v.i.) (n. **aestivation**); **estivate** (v.i.) (n. **estivation**) (both
  Zool.)
 The science dealing with sleep and hypnotic phenomena – **hypnology**

Slender:
 To become slender or more slender; to make slender; to cause to appear slender – **slenderize** (v.i./v.t.)

Slipper, shaped like a – **calceiform**; **calceolate** (both Bot.); **soleiform**

Slogans:
   One who invents or uses slogans – **sloganeer**
   To express in slogan form – **sloganize** (v.t.)

Slope:
   At a slope – **aslope**
   The general slope of a region – **versant**
   A steep slope resulting from erosion or faulting, and separating two relatively level areas of differing elevations –
      escarpment
   Sloping downward from opposite directions to meet in a common point – **synclinal**
   Sloping upward – **acclivous**
   An upward slope – **acclivity**
   Moderately steep – **declivitous**
   A gentle slope – **glacis**, pl. **glacis** or **glacises**
   A descending slope – **declivity**
   Having the same dip or inclination – **isoclinal**; **isoclinic**
   Sloped to allow water to run off – **weathered** (Archit.)
   A slope, as of the outer side of a wall, that recedes from bottom to top – **batter**

Slow:
   To slow the progress of - **delay**; **retard** (both v.t.)
   A substance used or intended to retard an undesirable reaction – **inhibiter**; **inhibitor**

Slug (animal):
   Of, relating to or like a slug – **limacine**

Small:
   Smallest in amount or degree – **minimal**
   Too small to be seen by the naked eye but large enough to be seen under a microscope – **microscopic**
   Too small to be seen with an ordinary microscope – **submicroscopic**; **ultramicroscopic**
   A copy or model that reproduces or represents something in greatly reduced size; something small of its class –
      miniature
   Smaller than miniature; extremely small – **subminiature**; **ultraminiature**
   To make subminiature – **subminiaturize** (v.t.)
   A very small person, esp. one afflicted with dwarfism; an unusually small animal or plant; to cause to appear small by
      comparison; to grow smaller or become stunted – **dwarf**, pl. **dwarfs** or **dwarves** (n./v.t./v.i.)
      The condition of being a dwarf – **dwarfishness**; **nanism**, adj. **nanitic**
      Artificial dwarfing, as of trees by a horticulturist – **nanization**

Smallpox (variola):
   Having pustules or marks like those of smallpox; to inoculate with smallpox – **variolate** (n./v.t.)

Smell (see also Odor):
   Of, relating to or contributing to the sense of smell – **olfactive**; **olfactory**; **osphretic**
   The sense of smell or the act of smelling – **olfaction**; **osphresis**
   Having or characterized by a sense of smell – **osmatic**
   Depending chiefly on the sense of smell for orientation – **osmatic**; **osmic**
   Capable of being smelled – **osphretic**
   Total or partial loss of the sense of smell – **anosmia**; **anosphrasia**; **anosphresia**
   The study of smells or the sense of smell – **olfactology**
   The testing and measurement of the sensitivity of the sense of smell – **olfactometry**

An exhalation or smell, esp. when unpleasant – **effluvium**; **effluvia**, pl. **effluvia** or **effuviums** or **effluvias**

Smoke:
Of or relating to smoke or fumigating – **fumatory**

Smooth:
Having a smooth or slippery quality – **lubricious**, n. **lubricity**

Snail:
Shaped like a snail shell; spirally twisted – **cochleate**; **cochleated**

Snake (see also Python and Viper):
A group of snakes – **bed**
Of or like a snake – **anguine**; **ophidian**; **serpentine**
Having the form of a snake - **anguiform**
Feeding on snakes – **ophiophagous**
A venomous or presumably venomous snake – **viper** (q.v.)
Suggestive of a venomous snake – **viperous**
The study of snakes – **ophiology**, n. **ophiologist**
The figure of the sacred serpent depicted on the headdress of ancient Egyptian rulers and deities as an emblem of sovereignty – **uraeus**
The worship of snakes or attribution of divine or sacred nature to them – **ophiolatry**

Sneeze:
The act of sneezing – **sternutation**
Of, relating to or marked by sneezing – **errhine**; **sternutative**; **sternutatory**
Causing or tending to cause sneezing – **errhine**; **sternutative**; **stertunator**; **sternutatory**
An agent that causes sneezing – **errhine**; **stertunator**

Snipe (wading bird), a group of – **walk**; **wisp**

Snore:
The act or an instance of producing a snoring or rasping sound in breathing because of obstruction of air passages - **stertor**
Marked by snoring; characterized by a harsh snoring or gasping sound - **stertorous**

Snow:
Of or relating to snow; resembling snow – **niveous**; **snowy**
Of or growing in or under snow – **nival**
Partially consolidated by thawing and freezing but not yet converted to glacial ice – **firn**
Rough, granular melted and refrozen snow – **corn snow**; **spring corn**; **spring snow**
A long, wavelike ridge of snow found on the polar plains, formed by the wind – **sastruga**
Precipitation consisting of snow pellets – **graupel**

Soak/Soaking:
The process of soaking; the condition of being soaked; the amount of liquid that soaks into, through, or out of an object – **soakage**
To soften by soaking in liquid; to separate parts by soaking; to become softened thus – **macerate** (v.t./v.i.), n. **maceration**
To soak or moisten (flax, e.g.) in order to soften and separate fibers by partial rotting – **ret** (v.t.)

Soap:
   Resembling or having the qualities of soap – **saponaceous**
   To convert into soap – **saponify** (v.i./v.t.), adj. **saponifiable**
   Combined or treated with a soap – **saponated**

Society (see also Class):
   Avoiding the society of others – **asocial**
   Opposed to the basic principles or the established order of society – **antisocial**
   An individual with asocial or antisocial behavior or character traits – **sociopath**
   The quantitative study of preferred relationships in a social group – **sociometry**
   Both social and cultural – **sociocultural**
   Both social and economic – **socioeconomic**
   Both social and political – **sociopolitical**
   Both social and religious – **socioreligious**
   The study of human society and human social behavior and institutions; analysis of a social institution or societal
      segment – **sociology**; n. **sociologist**
   The totality of socially transmitted behavior patterns, arts, beliefs, institutions and all other products of human work and
      thought typical of a population or community at a given time – **culture** (q.v.)
   A diagram representing interpersonal relations among individuals in a group – **sociogram**
   The theory that the natural interdependence of members of a society offers a basis for social organization based on
      solidarity of interests – **solidarism**
   The belief that society has an innate tendency toward improvement and that this tendency may be furthered through
      conscious human effort – **meliorism**
   A condition of society in which various ethnic, racial or religious groups coexist – **pluralism**
   Abnormal fear of people, esp. in groups – **anthropophobia**

Socket:
   Of or like a socket - **alveolar**; **socketlike**

Soil:
   Of or relating to soil, esp. as it affects living organisms – **edaphic**
   The study of the origins, characteristics and uses of soils – **pedology**
   The study of the soil conditions of past ages – **paleopedology**
   The applied science of soils in relation to crop production – **agrology**, n. **agrologist**
   The process of soil formation – **pedogenesis**
   A specific layer of soil in a cross section of land – **horizon**
   The soil zone of increased microbial growth and activity that surrounds the roots of a plant – **rhizosphere**
   The maximum amount of water that a particular kind of soil can hold – **field capacity**
   The process.by which soils are depleted of bases and become acidic – **podzolization**
   The surface layer of soil; to remove the surface layer of soil from (land) – **topsoil** (n./v.t.)
   The layer or bed of earth beneath the surface soil – **subsoil**; **undersoil**
   To plow or turn up the layer beneath the surface soil – **subsoil** (v.t.)
   The washing away of the lighter or finer particles in a soil – **elutriation**, v.t. **elutriate**
   Permanently frozen subsoil – **permafrost**
   To cause (soil) to form lumps or masses; to form such masses – **flocculate** (v.t./v.i.)
   Of or relating to a soil that is composed of particles that do not hold together – **cohesionless**
   Designating soil occurring in flaky layers – **platy**
   Feeding on soil - **geophagous**

Soldier:
  Of, relating to or befitting a soldier – **soldierly**
  Soldiers collectively – **soldiery**
  A soldier armed with a spear – **spearman**
  A soldier who has spent his life away from battle – **carpet knight**
  The quartering of troops; a group of temporary structures for housing troops - **cantonment**

Solve:
  Capable of being solved or explained – **soluble**

Son:
  The fact or relationship of being a son – **sonship**
  A younger son – **cadet**
  The killing of a son; a parent who kills his or her son – **filicide**

Song (see also Music):
  A writer of song lyrics – **lyricist**; **lyrist**
  A song sung in celebration of a wedding – **epithalamium**; **prothalamion**
  A popular sentimental song of unrequited love – **torch song**
  A song expressing grief – **elegy**; **lament**; **threnody**
  A funeral song – see Funeral
  To celebrate in song; to sing joyously – **carol** (v.t./v.i.)
  A song or ode recanting or retracting something in a former one - **palinode**
  A song of praise or thanksgiving; to praise, glorify or worship in or as if in such a song; to sing such songs – **hymn** (n./v.t./v.i.)
    A book or collection of hymns – **hymnal**; **hymnbook**
    The singing or composition of hymns; the hymns of a particular place, time or church – **hymnody**; **hymnology**
    A hymn, esp. a short one, expressing praise to God - **doxology**

Soot:
  Colored by or as if by soot; of, relating to or containing soot – **fuliginous**; **sooty**

Soul:
  The belief that the soul is inherited from the parents along with the body – **traducianism**, n. **traducianist**
  The transmigration of souls – **metempsychosis**
  The belief that natural objects and phenomena, and the universe itself, possess souls and consciousness – **animism**, adj. **animistic**, n. **animist**

Sound (see also Noise):
  Of or relating to audible sound – **sonic**
  Of, relating to or having the nature of sound, esp. speech sounds – **phonic**
  Producing or conducting sound – **soniferous**
  The act or process of producing sound - **sonification**
  The study or science of sound – **acoustics**; **phonics**
  Perception of or response to sound waves – **phonoreception**
  Of, producing or using waves with frequencies below that of audible sound – **infrasonic**; **subsonic**
  Of or relating to acoustic frequencies above the range audible to the human ear – **ultrasonic**
  The diagnostic use of ultrasonic waves – **ultrasonography**
  The acoustics of ultrasound (ultrasonic sound); a technology using ultrasound – **ultrasonics**
  Having or producing sound; having or producing a full, deep, or rich sound – **sonorous**
  A low roar; a deep murmur or humming – **brool**

Striking with a deep, reverberating sound, as waves against the shore - **plangent**

Characterized by or resembling a resonant sound produced by the nose – **nasal**

A soft, whispering or rustling sound – **murmur**; **sough**; **susurration**; **susurrus**

A gentle, murmuring sound - **purl**

Harsh, unpleasant sound – **cacophony** (adj. **cacophonous**); **discordance**; **discordancy**; **dissonance**

To cause to ring or sound loudly; to make a harsh ringing sound – **tang** (v.t./v.i.)

A course, rattling sound somewhat like snoring – **rhonchus**

A ringing sound in the head – **acoasm**; **acouasm**; **acousma**

A sound in the ears, such as buzzing, ringing or whistling, cause by a defect in the auditory nerve - **tinnitus**

Agreeable sound – **euphony** (adj. **euphonious**); **harmoniousness**

   To make euphonious – **euphonize** (v.t.)

To produce a shrill grating or creaking sound – **gride**; **stridulate**, adj. **stridulatory**, n. **stridulation**

To scrape, graze, or rub against something so as to produce a harsh, rasping sound; a griding or grating sound – **gride** (v.i./n.)

A dull, heavy sound, as of a fall; a movement producing such a sound - **flump**

Designating sound reception by one ear - **monaural**

Diagnostic monitoring of the sounds made by internal organs or an internal body part – **auscultation**, v.t. **auscultate**

Sour:

  Sour or bitter in taste – **acerb**

  A sour or bitter taste; sharpness, bitterness or sharpness of temper, etc. – **acerbity**

  Slightly sour; turning sour – **acescent**

South:

  Of, relating to or coming from the south – **austral**

  Situated toward or from the south – **southerly**

  Progress toward the south; the difference in latitude between two positions as a result of a movement to the south – **southing**

  Farthest south – **southernmost**

  At or toward the south – **southward**

Southeast:

  Toward, in or from the southeast – **southeasterly**

  At or toward the southeast – **southeastward**

Southwest:

  Toward, in or from the southwest – **southwesterly**

  At or toward the southwest – **southwestward**

Soviet:

  To cause to come under Soviet control; to cause to conform to Soviet political, social and cultural policy – **sovietize**; **Sovietize** (both v.t.)

  The study of the policies and strategy of the (former) Soviet government – **Kremlinology**

Space:

  Toward outer space – **spaceward**

  Space at or near the earth's surface, esp. space beneath the sea – **inner space**

  One trained to pilot, navigate, or otherwise take part in the flight of a spacecraft - **astronaut**

  The science of space travel – **astronautics**

  Navigation of spacecraft – **astrogation** (v.i. **astrogate**, n. **astrogator**); **astro-navigation**, n. **astronavigator**

  The study of the medical and biological effects of space flight – **bioastronautics**

The science of the biological, physiological and psychological effects of space flight on human beings – **space medicine**

Operating in or involving equipment operating in outer space - **spaceborne**

A scientific discipline that studies phenomena occurring in the upper atmosphere or in space; a discipline relating to or dealing with the problems of space flight – **space science**

An installation for testing and launching spacecraft – **spaceport**

A spacecraft carrying instruments designed to explore the physical properties of outer space or of celestial bodies other than Earth – **space probe**

A space vehicle designed to transport astronauts between Earth and space or an orbiting space station – **space shuttle**

Of, relating to or existing in both space and time – **spatiotemporal**

A space, esp. a small or narrow one, between things or parts – **interstice**, adj. **interstitial**

An extreme or irrational fear of being in or crossing open spaces – **agoraphobia**

An extreme or irrational fear of confined spaces – **claustrophobia**

Sparks:
　Capable of emitting sparks – **ignescent**
　Producing sparks by friction - **pyrophoric**

Sparrows, a group of – **host**

Spasm – see Muscle

Spatula, shaped like a – **spatulate**

Spearhead, shaped like a – **hastate**

Special:
　A devotion or restriction to a particular field of study or occupation – **specialism**, n. **specialist**
　Understood by or designed for the specially initiated alone; confined or limited to a small circle – **esoteric**
　　Esoteric doctrines or practices – **esotericism**; **esoterism**, n. **esoterist**
　　Esoteric items – **esoterica**

Species:
　Arising between species – **interspecific**
　Of the same species – **conspecific**
　Occurring between members of the same species – **intraspecific**

Speech (see also Figures of Speech, Language, Rhetoric, and Word):
　The study of the nature and structure of speech – **glottology**; **linguistics**; **philology**
　A specialist in linguistics – **linguist**; **linguistician**
　The study of the interaction between behavioral factors and linguistic behavior – **psycholinguistics**
　The study of linguistic behavior as influenced by social and cultural factors - **sociolinguistics**
　The study of regional speech – **linguistic geography**
　The study of speech sounds and their production, description, combination and representation by written symbols; the system of sounds of a particular language – **phonetics**, adj. **phonetic**
　　A specialist in phonetics – **phonetician**; **phoneticist**
　The practice of transcribing speech sounds by means of phonetic symbols – **phonotypy**
　A minimal linguistic feature, as phonetics in a word – **taxeme**
　The smallest unit of speech in a given language – **phoneme**, adj. **phonemic**
　The study and description of phonemes of a language – **phonemics**

Transposition of two phonemes in a word – **metathesis**, pl. **metatheses**

Any of the variant forms (in terms of pronunciation) of a phoneme - **allophone**

The sum of letters and letter combinations that represent a single phoneme – **grapheme**, adj. **graphemic**

The study of graphemes – **graphemics** (used with sing. or pl. verb)

A linguistic form that links a subject with its predicate - **copula**

A meaningful linguistic unit consisting of a word or word element that cannot be divided into smaller meaningful parts – **morpheme**; **semantime**

> Of or relating to the morphemes of a language – **lexical**

> The study of morphemes as a branch of linguistic analysis – **morphemics**

> Any of the variant forms (in terms of pronunciation) of a morpheme – **allomorph**

Modification of the sound of a morpheme conditioned by the context in which it is uttered - **sandhi**

Linguistic structure in terms of the phonological patterning of morphemes, as through variations that determine the different forms of morphemically related words – **morphophonemics**

The study of speech sounds, including phonetics and phonemics – **phonology**

The phonetic assimilation of a following to a preceding sound - **echoism**

A symbol or character representing a word or phoneme in speech – **phonogram**

> Representation of speech or speech sounds by means of phonograms – **phonography**

Standard pronunciation in a language; the study of pronunciation of a language – **orthoepy**, adj. **orthoepic** or **orthoepical**, n. **orthoepist**

The origin and historical development of a linguistic form – **etymology**

Of or relating to linguistic phenomena as they occur or change through time – **diachronic**

The use of a speech form that lacks a final or initial sound that a variant speech form has, as in the use of *'s* instead of *is* in *there's* - **elision**

Balanced, rhythmic flow (in speech) – **cadence**; **cadency**

A pair of letters representing a single speech sound – **digraph**

A voiced consonant regarded as a syllabic sound, as the last sound in the word *sudden* – **sonorant**

A speech sound produced by the relatively free passage of breath through the larynx (voice box) and mouth; a letter that represents this sound – **vowel**, adj. **vocalic**

> A system of vowels, as within a specific language; a vowel or vocalic sound – **vocalism**

> Preceding a vowel – **prevocalic**

> Designating a consonant or consonantal sound directly following a vowel – **post-vocalic**

> Immediately preceded and followed by a vowel – **intervocalic**

> Having more than one vowel – **plurivocalic**

> Two written vowels representing a single sound – **monophthong**

> A symbol placed over a vowel to show that it has a short sound - **breve**

Pronunciation of the usually silent final consonant of a word when followed by a word starting with a vowel – **liaison**

A letter or vocal sound having the sound of a vowel but used as a consonant – **semivowel**

A speech sound beginning with one vowel sound and moving to another vowel or semivowel position within the same syllable – **diphthong**

The change of a simple vowel to a diphthong – **breaking**

The drawing together into one syllable of two consecutive vowels ordinarily pronounced separately – **synaeresis** (pl. **synaereses**); **syneresis**, pl. **synereses**

The contraction of two syllables into one by joining in pronunciation two adjacent vowels – **synezesis**; **synizesis**

Patterned change of the root vowels in verbal forms, expressing changes of tense, etc. - **ablaut**

A change in a vowel sound caused by partial assimilation to a vowel or semivowel occurring in the following syllable; a diacritical mark, as the dots over a *ü*, to indicate such a change – **umlaut**

Pronounced with one lip - **labial**

Pronounced with both lips – **labial**; **bilabial**

Pronounced with the lip and teeth; a sound of this type – **labiodental**

Pronounced with the back of the tongue on or near the soft palate; a sound formed thus – **velar**

To articulate (a sound) by retracting the back of the tongue toward the soft palate – **velarize** (v.t.)

Being simultaneously labial and velar – **labiovelar**

Pronounced palatally – **mouillé**

Pronounced by vibration of the uvula or with the back of the tongue near or touching the uvula (q.v.) – **uvular**

Pronounced with the tip of the tongue turned back against the roof of the mouth – **retroflex**

Pronounced with the tip of the tongue; relating to consonants pronounced with the tip of the tongue – **apical**

Of or relating to a speech sound marked by stoppage or obstruction of the flow of air from the lungs – **obstruent**

A consonant marked by an articulation in which the air passage is completely closed (e.g., the *p* in *stop*) - **stop**

Boldness of speech – **parrhesia**

High-flown diction – **euphuism**

To speak in a grandiloquent style; to conclude or sum up a speech; to speak at length – **perorate** (v.i.), n. **peroration**

A pompous, rhetorical speech – **oration**

By word of mouth – **viva voce**

A roundabout or indirect way of speaking – **circumlocution** (adj. **circumlocutory**); **periphrasis**, pl. **periphrases**, adj. **periphrastic**

Of, characterized by or producing a hissing sound; a speech sound that suggests hissing; having, containing or producing the sound of an *s* or *sh* – **sibilant**

    A faulty pronunciation of sibilant sounds - **sigmatism**

    To utter or pronounce with a hiss – **sibilate** (v.t./v.i.)

The quality or state of being nasal – **nasality**

    Nasality in speech – **nasalism**

To speak in a nasal tone; the sound made thereby – **snuffle** (v.i./n.)

Spoken with little or no aspiration – **lenis**

A voiceless sound in speech – **surd**

Not sounded or pronounced – **aphonic**; silent

The study and treatment of speech defects – **logopedia**; **logopedics**, adj. **logopedic**

To make involuntary pauses or repetition of sounds while speaking; to utter (words or sounds) thus; the act or habit of speaking thus – **stammer**; **stutter** (v.i./n.)

    Stammering or stuttering speech – **traulism**

A disorder of speech – **lalopathy**

To repeat a word or sentence endlessly and meaninglessly – **verbigerate** (v.i.), n. **verbigeration**

Mispronunciation of the sound *r* or the substitution of another sound for it; replacement of the sound *z* by *r*, as in the evolution of a language – **rhotacism**; **rhotacismus**; **rotacism**

    To undergo or produce rhotacism – **rhotacize** (v.i.)

Mispronunciation of the letter *l*; the substitution of *l* for another sound; the substitution of another sound for *l* – **lallation**; **lambdacism**

Excessive use of the letter (or sound of) *l* - **lambdacism**

Pronounced without stress when in combination with a preceding sound - **enclitic**

Ambiguity of speech, esp. from uncertainty of the grammatical construction rather than of the meaning of the words – **amphibology**; **amphiboly**

Employing or involving speech for the purpose of revealing or sharing feelings or establishing an atmosphere of sociability rather than for communicating ideas - **phatic**

Bad speaking or pronunciation – **cacology**

Abnormally slow speech – **bradylogia**

Difficulty in speaking – **dysphonia**

Difficulty in expressing ideas through speech as a result of a mental disorder – **dyslogia**

A defect in the ability to make sounds, caused by neurological disorders involving the organs of speech – **dyslalia**

Difficulty in pronouncing words due to disease of the central nervous system – **dysarthria**

Inability to speak – **alogia**; **mutism**

Paralysis of the muscles involved in speech – **laloplegia**

Partial or total loss of the ability to speak or comprehend speech, as a result of brain damage – **aphasia**, adj. **aphasic**

    One afflicted with aphasia – **aphasiac**; **aphasic**

Aphasia in which the patient uses wrong words or words in senseless combinations - **paraphasia**

Infantile speech – **lallation**

Frivolous bantering talk – **persiflage**, v.i. **persiflate**

    One who indulges in persiflage - **persifleur**

Automatic speech without thought of the meaning of the words spoken - **psittacism**

Confused or unintelligible speech – **baragouin**; **galimatias**; **glossolalia**; **neolalia**

The involuntary repetition of sounds and words just uttered by others – **echolalia**

Pathologically incoherent, repetitious speech; incessant or compulsive talkativeness – **logomania**; **logorrhea**, adj. **logorrheic**

Capable of being spoken or voiced – **vocable**

Not to be spoken – **ineffable**

Sudden breaking off of a thought in the middle of a sentence, as if one were unwilling or unable to continue – **aposiopesis**, pl. **aposiopeses**

The act of speaking to oneself – **monology**; **soliloquy**

    To utter or put into a soliloquy – **soliloquize** (v.t./v.i.), n. **soliloquist** or **soliloquizer**

The act or practice of producing vocal sounds so that they seem to come from a source other than the speaker – **ventriloquism**; **ventriloquy**

    To practice ventriloquism – **ventriloquize** (v.i.)

The common, esp. nonstandard or substandard everyday speech of a country or region – **vernacular**; **vulgate**

    A vernacular word, phrase or expression – **vernacularism**

A person skilled in table talk - **deipnosophist**

A geographic boundary delimiting the area in which a given linguistic form occurs – **isogloss**

A person's individual speech pattern – **idiolect**

One who speaks, pleads or interprets for another – **prolocutor**; **spokesman**

A long speech made by one person – **monolog**; **monologue**

To make a speech – **speechify** (v.i.)

A farewell speech, esp. one delivered by a valedictorian at commencement exercises - **valedictory**

Tending to speak at great length – **prolix**, n. **prolixity**

A talk illustrated by impromptu pictures; a talk designed to brief a group for concerted action – **chalk-talk**

A long, angry speech – **diatribe**; **harangue**; **obloquy**; **tirade**

To launch a thunderous verbal attack – **fulminate** (v.i.), n. **fulmination**

Speech of lavish self-praise – **vaunt**

A bragging speech – **rhodomontade**; **rodomontade**; **rodomontado**

To declare solemnly – **affirm** (v.i./v.t.); **asseverate** (v.t.)

The introductory part of a speech – **preface**

An opening speech, as at a convention, that outlines the issues under discussion – **keynote address**

    One who gives a keynote address – **keynoter**

A lecture or discourse on a religious or moral theme – **homily** (v.i./v.t. **homilize**; **preach**); **sermon**, v.i./v.t. **sermonize**

    One who prepares or delivers a homily – **homilist**; **homilete** (adj. **homiletic** or **homiletical**); **sermonist** (adj. **sermonic** or **sermonical** or **sermonish**); **sermonizer**

    The branch of theology that deals with sermons – **homiletics**

    A collection of sermons – **sermonary**

    A short sermon – **sermonette**

    Knowledge or study of sermons; the preaching of sermons – **sermonology**

Speed:

To increase the speed of; to move or act faster – **accelerate** (v.t./v.i.)

A vector quantity whose magnitude is a body's speed and whose direction is the body's direction or motion – **velocity**

At top speed; top speed – **tantivy**, pl. **tantivies** (adv./n.)

Having a speed approaching or being that of sound in air (approximately 738 mph at sea level) – **sonic**

Having a speed less than that of sound in a designated medium – **subsonic**

Of or relating to aerodynamic flow or flight conditions at speeds close to the speed of sound – **transonic**

Having, caused by or related to a speed greater than the speed of sound in a designated medium – **supersonic**

The study of phenomena produced by the motion of a body through a medium at velocities greater than that of sound – **supersonics**

Of speed equal to or exceeding five times the speed of sound – **hypersonic**

One nautical mile (1,852 meters) per hour – **knot**

Spell (in the magical sense) – see Magic

Spelling:

The art or technique of correct spelling according to established usage – **orthography**, adj. **orthographic** or **orthographical**

Spelled correctly – **orthographic**; **orthographical**

Incorrect or bad spelling – **cacography**

The practice of spelling in a way contrary to standard usage; spelling in which the same letters represent different sounds in different words or syllables – **heterography**

Spend/Expend:

The act or process of spending; an amount spent or expended – **expenditure**

Relating to expenditure, esp. on food and clothing; regulating or limiting expenses – **sumptuary**

To write off (expenditures) by prorating over a certain period – **amortize** (v.t.)

Spending of public funds obtained by borrowing – **deficit spending**

Sperm:

Of or relating to sperm – **spermatic**; **spermous**

An agent that kills sperm – **spermatocide**; **spermicide**

The generation of sperm – **spermatogenesis**

Resembling sperm – **spermatic**; **spermatoid**; **spermous**

The entry of several sperms into an ovum during fertilization – **polyspermy**

Sphere:

Of or relating to a sphere – **spherical**

Having the shape of a sphere or globe – **globate**; **globoid**; **globose**; **globous**; **globular**; **spheral**; **spherical**; **spheriform**

The quality or state of being spherical – **sphericity**

Varying slightly from sphericity – **aspheric**; **aspherical**

A miniature sphere – **spherule**

A small spherical mass – **globule**

Composed of or producing globules – **globuliferous**

A figure resembling but not identical to a sphere – **spheroid**, adj. **spheroid** or **spheroidal**

To enclose in or as if in a sphere – **ensphere** (v.t.)

A representation of a sphere or part of a sphere on a plane surface – **planisphere**

The geometry of figures on a sphere – **spherical geometry**

Spices as a group; the aromatic or pungent quality of spices – **spicery**

Spider (class: Arachnida):

Resembling a spider's web – **arachnoid**

Having the texture of a spider's web - **arachnean**

The zoological study of spiders and other arachnids – **arachnidology**; **arachnology**, n. **arachnologist**

Feeding on spiders – **arachnophagous**

Extreme or irrational fear of spiders – **arachnophobia**

Of, relating to or resembling arachnids (spiders, scorpions, mites, ticks, etc.) – **arachnoid**; **arachnoidal**; **arachnoidean**

A substance that kills arachnids – **arachnicide**

Poisoning caused by the bite or sting of an arachnid – **arachnidism**; **arachnoidism**

Spike, borne in or forming a – **spicate**

Spindle:

Shaped like a spindle (tapering at each end) – **fusiform**

Spine (pointed projection):

Having a spine or spines - **echinate**; **spinescent**; **spiniferous**; **spinose**; **spinous**; **spiny**

Tending toward the form of a spine – **spinescent**

Covered with spines – **echinate**

Resembling a spine – **acanthoid**; **spinous**

A small spine or thorn – **spinule**

    Shaped like a spinule – **spinulose**

    Having spinules – **spinulose**; **spinulous**

A needlelike spine, prickle or crystal – **acicula**, pl. **aciculae**, adj. **acicular**

Having aciculae – **aciculate**; **aciculated**

Having a roughened surface because of many short spines – **muricate**; **muricated**

Having no spines or thorns – **anacanthous**

Spine (the spinal column or rachis; see also Vertebra):

Of or relating to the spinal cord – **myeloid**

Having a backbone or spinal column – **vertebrate** (adj./n.)

Surgical severance of spinal nerve roots to relieve pain or hypertension – **rhizotomy**

Abnormal forward curvature of the spine; the state of one thus affected – **lordosis**

Abnormal rearward curvature of the spine; the state of one thus affected – **kyphosis**

Excessive inward or downward curvature of the spine – **swayback**

Abnormal lateral curvature of the spine – **scoliosis**

The primitive backbone in some lower vertebrates – **notochord**

Spinning:

Spinning like a top – **turbinate**; **turbinated**

Having or appearing to have a spinning motion - **strobic**

Spiral:

A spiral form or structure – **helix** (pl. **helices** or **helixes**) adj. **helical** or **helicoid** or **spiriferous**

A spiral or twisted formation, such as one of the whorls of a gastropod shell – **volute**

Resembling a spiral – **helical**; **spiroid**

Arranged in or having a shape resembling that of a flattened spiral – **helicoids**

Rolled up or curled in a spiral – **involute**

Having spiral parts – **spiriferous**

Spire, a slender – **flèche**

Spirit:

A doctrine that holds that all that exists is spirit; the doctrines and practices of spiritualists; the quality or state of being spiritual – **spiritualism**

An individual through whom other persons seek to communicate with the spirits of the dead – **medium**
A supposed noisy, mischievous spirit or ghost – **poltergeist**
The production of images of spirits on film without the use of a camera – **psychography**
Divination by communicating with spirits of the dead – **necromancy**

Splash:
  The sound of a splash of liquid – **swash**

Spleen:
  Of or relating to the spleen – **lineal**; **splenetic**; **splenic**
  In or near the spleen – **splenic**
  Inflammation of the spleen – **splenitis**
  Enlargement of the spleen – **splenomegaly**
  The surgical removal of the spleen – **splenectomy**

Split:
  Capable of being split – **fissile**
  Splitting or opening along a transverse circular line – **circumscissile** (Bot.)

Spore:
  The study of spores and pollen – **palynology**
  Producing spores of one kind only – **homosporous**
  A spore-bearing structure - **sporophore**
  A spore-bearing cell or mass of cells – **archespore**
  A large spore – **macrospore**
  An agent used to kill spores – **sporicide**
  Producing spores – **sporiferous**
  The production or formation of spores – **sporogenesis**
  A leaf or leaflike organ that bears spores – **sporophyll**
  To produce or release spores – **sporulate** (v.i.)

Spot:
  A transparent spot or marking – **fenestra**, pl. **fenestrae** (Biol.)
  A colored spot - **mottle**
  The pattern of spots on a plant or animal – **maculation**
  A bright, iridescent or transparent spot on the wing of a bird, butterfly or moth – **speculum**, pl. **specula** or **speculums**, adj. **specular**
  Having tiny spots, points or depressions – **punctate**; **punctated**
  Having variegated markings, esp. spotted in black and white – **piebald**

Spreading or expanded, as tree branches – **patulent**; **patulous** (both Bot.)

Spring (motion) – see Position

Spring (season):
  Of, relating to, occurring in, characteristic of or resembling spring – **vernal**

Spur:
  Wearing spurs; having a spur or spurs – **spurred**
  One who makes spurs – **spurrier**
  A spur or spurlike projection – **calcar**, pl. **calcaria** (Anat.)

Spy:
    Spying or using spies to obtain secret intelligence – **espionage**
    A secret agent who infiltrates an organization in order to incite its members to commit punishable acts – **agent provocateur**, (pl. **agents provocateurs**); **provocateur**

Squire:
    The collective body of squires or landed gentry of a country; the social, economic and political class formed by the landed gentry – **squirarchy**; **squirearchy**; n. **squirearch**

Squirrels, a group of – **dray**

Stables collectively – **stabling**

Stain:
    Capable of being stained readily with dyes – **chromophil**
    Easily stained with basic dye – **basichromatic**
    A tendency to stain with dyes – **basophilia**
    The section of a cell nucleus that is relatively uncolored by stains or dyes – **achromatin**
    Staining readily with acid dyes – **acidophilic** (Biol.)
    Discolored with yellowish-brown stains, as an old book or print – **foxed**; **foxy**

Stair/Staircase:
    The vertical support at the center of a circular staircase; a post that supports a handrail at the bottom or at the landing of a staircase – **newel**
    The horizontal part of a step in a staircase – **tread**
    The vertical part of a step in a staircase – **riser**

Stalactite:
    Having the form or position of a stalactite – **stalactiform**; **stalactitic**
    Of or covered with stalactites – **stalactitic**; **stalactitical**

Stalagmite:
    Having the form or position of a stalagmite; of or covered with stalagmites – **stalagmitic**; **stalagmitical**

Stalk (stipe):
    A stalklike part – **scape**; **stipe** (Bot.); **stipes**, pl. **stipites**
    Resembling or consisting of a scape; bearing scapes – **scapose**
    Having or supported on a stalk – **stipitate**
    Shaped like a plant stalk – **stipiform**; **stipitiform**
    A stalklike support or structure – **stipes**, pl. **stipites**

Stamp:
    The collection and study of postage stamps, postmarks and related materials – **philately**
      A collector of such materials - **philatelist**
    A postage stamp the price of which goes partly to pay postage and partly to the support of some public expense project – **semipostal**; **semipostal stamp**
    The collection of airmail stamps – **aerophilately**
    A book of postage stamps – **carnet**
    Of, relating to or characteristic of postage stamps printed upside-down in relation to one another – **tête-bêche**

Stand:
　　Standing with hands on hips and elbows bent outward – **akimbo**
　　Inability to stand due to muscular incoordination – **astasia**
　　One using standing room – **standee**

Star:
　　Stars collectively – **stardom**
　　Of, relating to or consisting of stars - **stellar**
　　　　A quasi-stellar object - **quasar**
　　　　The physics of stellar phenomena – **astrophysics**
　　Arranged like a star; radiating from a center – **tellaste**
　　Shaped like a star – **asteroid**; **asteroidal**; **astral**; **stellate**; **stellated**; **stelliform**
　　Shaped like a small star; radiating like a star – **stellular**
　　To stud with or as if with stars – **instar** (v.t.)
　　The surface of a star – **photosphere**
　　The rising of a star above the horizon – **ascension**
　　A cluster of stars – **asterism**
　　A five-pointed star (plane figure) – **pentacle**
　　A six-pointed star (as the Jewish Star of David) - **hexagram**
　　A seismological occurrence on a star – **starquake**
　　Of, relating to or designating a star that from a given observer's latitude does not go below the horizon – **circumpolar**
　　A variable star that suddenly increases greatly in brightness and then returns to its original appearance – **nova**
　　Three or more stars that appear as one to the naked eye – **multiple star**
　　The branch of astronomy that deals with the fixed stars – **astrognosy**
　　One fond of star lore – **astrophile**

Starch:
　　Made from, rich in or composed of starch – **farinaceous**
　　Of or like starch – **amylaceous**; **amyloid**

Starlings, a group of – **chattering**; **murmuration**

Starve:
　　One who is starving or is being starved - **starveling**

State:
　　Existing or occurring within a state's borders – **intrastate**
　　Relating to, existing between or connecting two or more states – **interstate**
　　Of, relating to or involving two states – **bistate**

Statement:
　　A formal or written statement testifying to a particular truth or fact – **affidavit**; **testimonial**
　　A statement that expresses or implies the threat of serious penalties if the terms are not accepted – **ultimatum**
　　A restatement of a text or passage in another form or other words; the making of such restatements; to express in or compose such a restatement – **paraphrase** (n./v.i./v.t.), adj. **paraphrastic** or **paraphrastical**, adj. **paraphrasable**, n. **paraphraser**
　　A statement indicating inability to do a particular thing – **non possumus**

Stationery, one who sells – **stationer**

Statue:

Statues collectively; the art of making statues; of, relating to or suitable for a statue – **statuary**

A small statue – **statuette**

A statue with a stone head, hands and feet, and a wooden trunk – **acrolith**

A niche for a statue - **aedicula** (pl. **aediculae**); **aedicule** (pl. **aedicules**); **edicule**, pl. **edicules**, adj. **aedicular**

Stealing (larceny; theft):

One who commits larceny – **larcenist**

To rob of goods by force, esp. in time of war – **pillage** (v.i./v.t.); **plunder** (v.i./v.t.)

Property or goods stolen by fraud or force – **booty**; **loot**; **pillage**; **plunder**; **spoils**

One who plunders and robs – **bandit**; **brigand** (n. **brigandism** or **brigandage**); **plunderer**

To act as a brigand waiting or searching for a prize or victim – **picaroon** (v.i.)

An obsessive desire to steal, esp. in the absence of economic necessity – **kleptomania**, n. **kleptomaniac**

Steamboat:

A steamboat propelled by a paddle wheel at the stern – **stern-wheeler**

A steamboat with a paddle wheel on each side – **side-wheeler**, adj. **side-wheel**

Steel:

One who makes steel plate engravings – **siderographer**

The art of engraving steel - **siderography**

Steel shaped for use in construction – **structural steel**

Steeples:

A worker on steeples or other very high structures – **steeplejack**

Steering:

The steering of a course (as for a ship) – **pilotage**

Capable of being steered – **navigable** (used of vessels and aircraft)

To steer a sailing vessel nearer into the wind – **luff** (v.i.)

Stems, one who removes – **stemmer**

Step:

A set or series of steps for crossing a fence or wall – **stile**

One of a series of steps or tiered seats, as in an amphitheater – **gradin**; **gradine**

A broad flight of steps down to the bank of a river – **ghat**; **ghaut**

Stepmother:

Of, relating to or characteristic of a stepmother – **novercal**

Steroids, the production of – **steroidogenesis**

Still (for distillation):

A person who owns or manages a still or distillery; a person who operates a distillation apparatus - **stillman**

Stimulation:

Something causing or viewed as causing a response; an agent, action or state that elicits or accelerates physiological or psychological activity – **stimulant**; **stimulus**, pl. **stimuli**, adj. **stimulative** or **stimulatory**, v.i./v.t. **stimulate**, n. **stimulater** or **stimulator**, n. **stimulation**

The intensity below which a mental or physical stimulus cannot be perceived and can produce no response –
threshold
Reception of stimuli originating within the organism – **proprioception**
Uneasiness or distress resulting from lack of environmental stimulation – **cabin fever**
Abnormal irritability or responsiveness to stimulation - **erethism**
A phenomenon in which one type of stimulation evokes the sensation of another – **synaesthesia**; **synesthesia**

Sting (aculeus, pl. aculei):
Having an aculeus or aculei – **aculeate** (Zool.)
Causing stinging; a substance that causes stinging – **urticant**
To sting with or as if with nettles – **urticate** (v.t.)
The stinging organ in various coelenterates – **nematocyst**

Stir:
To make (a liquid) muddy or cloudy by stirring up sediment; to be in a state of agitation or turbulence – **roil** (v.t./v.i.)

Stock (capital raised through sale of shares):
Stock or capital funds of a company held in common by its owners – **joint stock**
The buying of stocks, bills of exchange, etc., in one market and selling them again at a higher price in another market
– **arbitrage**
The illegal buying of stock by a seller's agents to give the impression of an active market – **wash sale**
A sharp decline in stock prices on a heavy volume of trading followed by a rally – **selling climax**
To agree to buy (stock not yet offered publicly) at a fixed time and price – **underwrite** (v.t.)
A rise or increase, as in the price of a stock market security – **uptick**

Stomach:
Of or relating to the stomach – **gastric**; **stomachic**
Of or relating to the stomach and intestines - **gastrointestinal**
A medicine or other agent that strengthens or stimulates the stomach – **stomachic**
Surgical removal of all or part of the stomach – **gastrectomy**
Inflammation of the stomach – **gastritis**
Inflammation of the mucous membrane of the stomach and intestines – **gastroenteritis**
The medical study of the stomach and its diseases – **gastrology**
Surgical incision into the stomach – **gastrotomy**
Surgical construction of a permanent opening from the external surface of the body into the stomach – **gastrostomy**
Relating to, marked by or experiencing gastric distress caused by sluggishness of the liver or gallbladder - **bilious**
Introduction of material into the stomach via a tube – **gavage**
The burning sensation in the stomach caused by stomach hyperacidity – **cardialgia**; **heartburn**; **pyrosis**
The stomach of a voracious animal – **maw**

Stone (see also Rock):
Of the nature of stone – **lapideous**; **petrous**; **stony**
Resembling a stone - **lithoid**
Living under a stone – **lapidocolous** (used esp. of an insect)
Engraved in stone; suitable for inscription in stone – **lapidary**
Cut in or inscribed in stone – **lapidarian**
A mound of stones erected as a landmark or memorial – **cairn**
A large stone used in a prehistoric monument – **megalith**
A large stone block, esp. one used in sculpture or architecture – **monolith**
A freestanding, three-stone structure of two uprights capped by a lintel (horizontal architectural member), as found at
Stonehenge - **trilithon**

An upright stone or slab with an inscribed or sculptured surface, used as a monument or as a commemorative tablet in the face of a building – **stele**, pl. **stelae** or **steles**

A stone monument or edifice erected for religious or ceremonial purposes – **hagiolith**, adj. **hagiolithic**

A large, loose residual mass of stone left after the erosion of a once continuous bed or layer, specifically one of the large sandstone blocks scattered over the English chalk downs – **Druid stone**; **sarsen**

A foundation or sustaining wall of stones thrown together without order, e.g., to prevent erosion; stone used for this purpose; to form such a foundation or wall – **riprap** (n./v.t.)

To convert (wood or other organic matter) into a stony replica or stony substance by mineral replacement of organic matter – **petrify** (v.i./v.t.)

One who works with stone or brick – **mason**; **stonecutter**

To build of or strengthen with stone or brick- **mason** (v.t.)

    The trade of or work done by a mason; stonework or brickwork – **masonry**

      Masonry made with rubble - **rubblework**

      A supporting bed for masonry - **palliasse**

To remove the outer surface of (masonry) so as to freshen in appearance – **regrate** (v.t.)

A person who prepares and lays stones in building – **stonemason**

To work or dress (stone) to a stage prior to that of fine tooling – **scabble** (v.t.)

The art or practice of painting on stone – **lithochromy**

A dowel for joining two adjacent blocks of masonry – **joggle**

An act of pelting with stones; the penalty of stoning to death - **lapidation**

Divination by stones or other charms or talismans of stone – **lithomancy**

Of, relating to or typical of the Stone Age – **eolithic**; **protolithic**

Storehouse, a public – **étape**

Storks, a group of – **mustering**

Storm:

    A storm in which precipitation freezes on contact – **ice storm**

    A storm or gale blowing from the southeast – **southeaster**

    A storm or wind from the south – **southerly**

    A storm or wind from the southwest – **southwester**

    A storm or wind from the north – **northerly**

    A storm or wind from the west – **wester**; **westerly**

Story (see also Fable, and Literature and Related Terms):

    An unfounded, false, deliberately misleading story – **canard**

    One who tells or writes stories – **storyteller**

      A witty and accomplished storyteller – **raconteur**

    The plot of a story – **story line**

    A book containing a collection of stories; suggestive of the style of such a book – **storybook**

    A story that causes or expresses grief - **jeremiad**

    An entertainment consisting of the telling of a story by means of the shadows of miniature figures thrown on a wall or screen – **galanty show**

Stout, to make or become – **stouten** (v.t./v.i.)

Straight:

    Moving in, consisting of, bounded by or characterized by a straight line or lines – **rectilinear**

    Not in a straight line – **nonlinear**

Stranger:
   Extreme or irrational fear of strangers or foreigners – **xenophobia**

Strangle – see Killing

Strap:
   A strap-shaped or straplike structure – **ligula**; **ligule**
      Having a ligule; strap-shaped – **ligulate**
   A passenger, as on a bus or subway, who grips a hanging strap for support – **straphanger**

Strategy:
   The art of strategy – **strategics**
   A person who is skilled in strategy – **strategist**
   The technique or science of securing the objectives designated by strategy, esp. the art of deploying and directing troops, ships and aircraft in coordinated maneuvers against the enemy; the skill or art of using available means to achieve an end – **tactics**, adj. **tactical**, n. **tactician**

Straw:
   Of or like straw; straw-colored – **stramineous**
   A cone-shaped pile of straw or hay; to arrange (straw or hay) in this way – **cock** (n./v.t.)

Stream:
   In, at, or toward the source of a stream or current – **upstream**
   A flowing together of two or more streams; the point of juncture of such streams – **confluence**
   The channel through which a natural stream of water runs or once ran – **streambed**
   A gorge with a stream running through - **flume**

Strength:
   Having strength or force – **isodynamic**; **strong**
   Lack or loss of bodily strength and energy – **asthenia** (adj. **asthenic**); **weakness**
   The strength required to resist or withstand disease, fatigue, etc. – **endurance**; **stamina**, adj. **staminal**
   Restoring strength or vigor; something that restores strength or vigor – **roborant**
   To strengthen, gird or support from beneath – **undergrid** (v.t.)

Stress:
   The branch of medicine dealing with the ability of humans to survive in and cope with abnormally stressful environments – **biomedicine**

Stretch:
   Able to be stretched and extended – **ductile**; **tensile**

Stretcher:
   One who helps carry a stretcher or litter – **stretcher-bearer**

Strike (work stoppage):
   One who strikes; an employee who is on strike against his or her employer – **striker**
   Closed, immobilized or slowed down by a strike – **strikebound**
   One who works or provides an employer with workers during a strike – **scab**; **strike-breaker**

Structure:
   Abnormal structural arrangement – **heterotaxia**; **heterotaxis**; **heterotaxy**

Study:
   A small group of advanced students engaged in a special study or original research under the guidance of a professor;
      a course of study pursued thus – **seminar**
   An academic seminar on a broad field of study, typically led by a different lecturer at each meeting - **colloquium**

Stunt:
   The performance of stunts with an airplane or glider – **aerobatics**

Stupor:
   A drug that induces stupor – **narcotic**; **stupefacient**
   Inducing stupor – **narcotic**; **stupefacient**; **stupefying**
   The act of stupefying; the state of being stupefied – **stupefaction**

Style (pointed writing instrument; see also Point):
   The art or method of etching, engraving or writing with a style – **stylography**

Submarine:
   A group of submarines that attack a single vessel or convoy – **wolf pack**
   The wake of a submarine's periscope – **feather**

Subordinate and auxiliary – **ancillary**

Substance:
   Made up of a variety of substances – **farraginous**
   Having the same substance, nature or essence – **consubstantial**

Substitute:
   Serving or capable of serving as a substitute – **substitutive**
   To substitute one person for another – **subrogate** (v.t.)
   Done or endured by one person substituting for another; acting in place of someone or something else – **vicarious**
   A substance containing no medication and given merely to humor a patient – **placebo**

Subtle:
   To render subtle – **subtilize** (v.t.)
   The quality or state of being subtle; something subtle – **subtlety**

Suburb:
   One who lives in a suburb – **suburbanite**
      Suburbanites as a group or cultural class – **suburbia**
   To render suburban or impart a suburban character to – **suburbanize** (v.t.)

Success:
   A critical but not popular success – **succès d'estime**

Suck/Suction:
   Of, relating to or suited for suction – **aspiratory**
   A sucker – **acetabulum** (Zool.)
   Adapted for sucking or clinging by suction; having sucking parts – **suctorial**
   Having or producing suckers – **surculose** (Bot.)
   Having one oral sucker only, as certain flatworms – **monostome**; **monostomous**
   An organism having one oral sucker only – **monostome**

Sugar:

    To convert (starch, e.g.) into sugar – **saccharify** (v.t.)

    An abnormally low level of glucose in the blood; low blood sugar – **hypoglycemia**

        Hypoglycemia caused by excessive insulin in the blood – **insulin shock**

    An abnormally high level of glucose in the blood – **hyperglycemia**

    The dry pulp remaining from sugar cane after the juice has been extracted – **bagasse**

Sulfur (also sulphur):

    Of or relating to sulfur – **sulfureous**; **sulfurous**; **thionic**

    Similar to or suggesting sulfur – **sulfury**

    Containing or derived from sulfur – **thionic**

    To treat or react with sulfur – **sulfurate** (v.t.)

    To remove sulfur from – **desulfurize** (v.t.)

Summer:

    Of, relating to or appearing in summer – **aestival**; **estival**

    Of or relating to the latter part of the summer; occurring in the latter half of summer – **serotinal**; **serotinous**

    To spend the summer – **aestivate** (v.i.), n. **aestivation**

Sun:

    Of or relating to the sun – **heliacal**; **helical**; **solar**

    Near the sun - **heliacal**

    Rising and setting with the sun – **helical**

    Relative or referred to the sun; having the sun as a center – **heliocentric**

    To expose to sunlight, as for bleaching – **insolate** (v.t.), n. **insolation**

    To affect by exposing to the sun's rays; to convert (a building) to solar heat – **solarize** (v.t.), n. **solarization**

    Proceeding from the sun – **solar**

    Situated directly beneath the sun – **subsolar**

    Revolving around or surrounding the sun – **circumsolar**

    At or toward the sun – **sunward**

    Worship of the sun – **heliolatry**, n. **heliolator**

    The point farthest from the sun in the orbit of a planet or other celestial body – **aphelion**, pl. **aphelia**

    The point nearest the sun in the orbit of a planet or other celestial body – **perihelion**, adj. **perihelial**

    The point nearest the sun in the orbit of the moon or a satellite – **perigee**, adj. **perigeal** or **perigean**

    From left to right, like the sun's course as viewed in the Northern Hemisphere – **sunwise**

    Movement of an organism in response to sunlight – **heliotaxis**

    Therapy involving exposure to sunlight – **heliotherapy**

    Growth or movement of an organism toward or away from the sun – **heliotropism**

    A tendency for certain plants to turn away from the sun – **apheliotropism**

    A spot on the sun – **macula**, adj. **macular**

    A glassed-in room, porch, etc., exposed to the sun – **solarium**

    A device for absorbing solar radiation to be used in producing electricity or in heating buildings or water – **solar collector**

    A house equipped with glass areas and so planned as to utilize the sun's rays extensively in heating – **solar house**

    Radio noise emitted by the sun and its atmosphere – **solar noise**

    Any motion of the sun as a member of the galaxy – **solar motion**

    An interpretation of folk stories and ancient legends as primitive concepts of the nature and action of the sun – **solarism**

    A traditional story (as a folk tale, legend, etc.) that is interpreted as a primitive explanation of the course, motion or influence of the sun – **solar myth**

    One attracted to or adapted to sunlight – **heliophile**, adj. **heliophilous**

Avoiding the sun – **heliophobic**; **heliophobous**
One who is abnormally sensitive to the effects of sunlight – **heliophobe**

Superiority:
Prejudiced belief in the superiority of one's own group – **chauvinism**, adj. **chauvinistic**, n. **chauvinist**

Supernatural:
The impersonal supernatural force to which certain primitive people attribute good fortune, magical powers, etc. – **mana**
Supernatural intervention in human affairs – **theurgy**, n. **theurgist**
Of or relating to supernatural influences or phenomena – **occult** (n./adj.)
Occult learning – **gramary**; **gramarye**

Support:
To support from below – **sustain**; **underpin** (both v.t.)
Serving to support – **sustentacular** (Anat.)

Supposition:
Of the nature of, including or involving a supposition – **suppositive**

Surf – see Shore

Surface (see also Surfaces, curved):
Having upper and lower surfaces that are distinct and dissimilar – **bifacial**
The surface of an area or body – **superficies**
Floating on the surface – **supernatant**
Designating a substance capable of reducing the surface tension of a liquid in which it is dissolved – **surface-active**
A surface-active substance – **surfactant**
A front or principal surface; the more conspicuous of two sides - **obverse**
The surface on which a plant or animal grows or is attached – **substrate**
Having distinct upper and lower surfaces – **dorsiventral**
Assimilation of gas, vapor or dissolved matter by the surface of a solid or liquid – **adsorption**
To take up by adsorption – **adsorb** (v.t.)
An adsorbed substance – **adsorbate**
Capable of adsorption; an adsorptive material – **adsorbent**
A surface appearance, as a coloring or mellowing, of something grown beautiful, esp. with age or use - **patina**

Surfaces, curved:
Shaped like the inner surface of a ball – **concave**
Concave on both sides or surfaces – **biconcave**; **concavo-concave**
Having a surface or boundary that curves or bulges outward, as the exterior of a sphere – **convex**
Convex on both sides or surfaces – **biconvex**; **convexo-convex**
With greater convex than concave curvature – **convexo-concave** (used of lenses)
Concave on one side and convex on the other; having greater concave than convex curvature – **concavo-convex**
Flat or plane on one side and concave on the other – **planoconcave**
Flat or plane on one side and convex on the other – **planoconvex**
Having a round side and a flat side – **semiround**

Surgery:
A physician specializing in surgery – **surgeon**
The position, office, rank and duties of a surgeon – **surgeoncy**

Occurring prior to surgery – **preoperative**
Occurring after surgery – **postoperative**
The surgical removal of part of an organ or structure – **resection**
To protrude through an incision after an operation; to remove the entrails of – **eviscerate** (v.i./v.t.)
Surgical removal or amputation of any part of the body – **ablation**
Surgical removal of dead, devitalized or contaminated tissue from a wound - **débridement**
Surgery to remodel, repair or restore lost, injured or defective body parts or areas – **anaplasty**; **plastic surgery**
Surgery to relieve pressure - **fasciotomy**
Surgery on minute living structures or cells by means of a micromanipulator – **microsurgery**
Brain surgery when used to treat mental disorders – **psychosurgery**
The selective destruction of tissue by means of chemicals – **chemosurgery**
Left within a bodily organ or passage, esp. to facilitate drainage - **indwelling**

Surprise (also surprize):
The act of surprising; the condition of being surprised – **surprisal**

Surround (see also Barrier/Barricade):
Surrounding; encircling – **ambient**, n. **ambiance** or **ambience**
Something that surrounds or encompasses; an act of encircling; to encompass or gird – **cincture** (n./v.t.)

Survey:
A person who takes public-opinion surveys – **pollster**

Survive:
The power to survive – **vitality**
One that survives or persists – **survivor**
    The condition of being a survivor – **survivorship**
Usefulness in the struggle for survival – **survival value**
Incapable of surviving - **inviable**

Suspense:
Characterized by or causing suspense – **suspensive**

Suspicion:
A tendency toward suspiciousness and distrustfulness of others that is not based on objective reality – **paranoia**, adj. **paranoid**
    One afflicted with paranoia – **paranoiac**; **paranoic**; **paranoid**

Sustain:
The act of sustaining; the condition of being sustained – **sustenance**

Swallow (bird):
A group of swallows – **flight**

Swallow (Physiol.):
The act or process of swallowing – **deglutition**
To take in by or as if by swallowing – **ingest** (v.t.)
Difficulty in swallowing – **dysphagia**
Loss of the ability to swallow - **aphagia**
Painful swallowing – **odynophagia**

Swamp:

Of or relating to a swamp or swamps – **paludal**

A person who lives in or near a swamp; a person who clears a swamp - **swamper**

A swamp or bog formed by an accumulation of sphagnum moss, leaves, stunted trees, etc. – **muskeg**

Swan:

A group of swans – **herd**; **wedge**

A male swan – **cob**

A female swan – **pen**

A young swan – **cygnet**

A place where swans are raised – **swannery**

Curved like the neck of a swan – **cygneous**

The soft down of a swan – **swan's-down**; **swansdown**

Sway:

To sway from side to side – **oscillate**; **vacillate** (both v.i.)

Sweat – see Perspiration

Swelling:

The process of swelling; the condition of being swollen – **intumescence** (v.i. **intumesce**); **tumefaction**; **turgescence**

To swell or cause to swell – **tumefy** (v.i./v.t.)

Somewhat swollen - **tumescent**

A localized swelling – **nodule** (Anat.)

Causing unusual swelling – **varicose**

A varicose distention or swelling – **varicosity**

Capable of being swollen or distended – **distensible**

A bulging or rounded swelling or projection – **protuberance**; **protuberancy**; **torus**

The protuberance formed by the pubic bones – **mons**, pl. **montes**

The male mons – **mons pubis**

The female mons – **mons veneris**

To swell or bulge out – **protuberate** (v.i.), adj. **protuberant**

Swelling out on one side – **ventricose**; **ventricous**, n. **ventricosity**

Somewhat ventricose – **ventriculose**

Swim/Swimming:

Of, relating to or adapted for swimming – **natatorial**; **natatory**

Swimming or floating in the water - **natant**

An indoor swimming pool – **natatorium**

Capable of swimming freely – **free-swimming** (Biol.)

An aquatic exhibition consisting of swimming, diving, etc. – **aquacade**

Swine (sing./pl.):

A group of swine – **sounder**

A male swine – **boar**

A female swine – **sow**

Resembling or befitting swine – **swinish**

A keeper or tender of swine - **swineherd**

Sword:

A sword with only one cutting edge – **backsword**

Shaped like a sword – **ensiform**; **gladiate**; **xiphoid**

Syllable (see also Word):
A list of syllables, esp. a list or set of written characters, each one representing a syllable – **syllabary**
To form or divide into syllables – **syllabicate**; **syllabize** (both v.t.)
The use of written characters that represent syllables; division into syllables – **syllabism**
Having only one syllable – **monosyllabic**
A one-syllable word or utterance – **monosyllable**
A word having more than one syllable - **plurisyllable**
Having two syllables – **disyllabic**
A word having two syllables – **dissyllable**; **disyllable**
A word having three syllables – **trisyllable**
Having three or more syllables; marked by words having more than three syllables – **polysyllabic**; **polysyllabical**
Having many syllables - **sesquipedalian**
The last syllable of a word – **ultima**
Lacking a syllable at the end - **catalectic**
Elimination of the first syllable or letter of a word – **aphaeresis**; **apheresis**
Loss of a short unaccented syllable at the beginning of a word – **aphesis**, adj. **aphetic**
The blending into one syllable of two successive vowels of adjacent syllables – **synalepha**; **synaloepha**

Symbol (see also Logo):
Capable of being depicted by a symbol – **signifiable**
One who uses symbols or symbolism; one who interprets or represents conditions or truths by the use of symbolism –
    symbolist
The study or interpretation of symbols or symbolism – **symbology**
To describe or portray in symbols – **limn** (v.t.)
A graphic symbol, e.g. &, $, @, etc. – **ideogram**; **ideograph**
A symbol or letter representing an entire word, as ¢ for cents – **logogram**; **logograph**
A symbol or combination of symbols representing a sound, word or phrase, esp. in shorthand - **stenotype**
A bright or glorious symbol or ensign - **oriflamme**
The study of relationships between signs and symbols, and what they represent – **semantics**; **semasiology**;
    sematology; **semeiotics**; **semiotics**

Symphony – see Music

Symptoms:
The complex of symptoms of a disease; the medical science of disease – **semeiotics**; **semiology**; **semiotics**;
    symptomatology
Neither causing nor exhibiting symptoms – **asymptomatic**
A complex of four symptoms – **tetralogy**

Syphilis:
Of or relating to syphilis – **syphilitic**; **syphilologic**
Afflicted with syphilis; one afflicted with syphilis – **syphilitic**
Resembling syphilis – **syphiloid**
The medical study of syphilis – **syphilology**, n. **syphilologist**
One who writes scientifically about syphilis – **syphilographer**
The scientific description of syphilis – **syphilography**
The treatment of syphilis – **syphilotherapy**
The condition of being infected with syphilis – **syphilization**
To inoculate with syphilis or introduce syphilis among – **syphilize** (v.t.)

Extreme or irrational fear of becoming infected with syphilis – **syphilophobia**, n. **syphilophobe**

System:
   To formulate into or reduce to a system – **systematize**; **systemize** (both v.t.)
   Of or relating to a system or systems – **systemic**
   One who adheres to or formulates a system – **systematist**

T

Table (item of furniture):
   Belonging to or used at the table – **mensal**

Table (diagram):
   Organized as a table or list; calculated by means of a table – **tabular**
   To condense and list in tabular form – **tabulate** (v.t.), n. **tabulator**

Tail:
   Toward the tail or posterior part of the body; of, at, or near the tail or hind parts – **caudal**
   Having a tail – **caudate**
   Having two tails – **bicaudal**
   Having no tail – **acaudal**; **acaudate**; **anurous**; **excaudate**
   Relating to, designating or marked by a tail fin having two symmetrical lobes extending from the end of the vertebral
      column, as in bony fishes – **homocercal**
   Relating to, designating or marked by a tail fin having two unequal lobes, with the vertebral column extending into the
      upper lobe, as in sharks – **heterocercal**
   Having a tail as wide as or wider than the body – **rhopalocercous**
   A stubby, erect tail – **scut** (Zool.)

Tailor:
   Of or relating to a tailor, tailoring or tailored clothing – **sartorial**

Talc:
   Made of or containing talc – **talcose**

Tank:
   The capacity or contents of a tank; the act or process of putting or storing in a tank; the fee for storing in a tank –
      tankage

Tanning:
   The act, process or skill of tanning; something tanned – **tannage**
   One who tans hides – **tanner**
   A place where hides are tanned – **tannery**
   A chemical substance capable of promoting tanning – **tannin**, adj. **tannic**

Tapering sharply from one large end to a smaller end or part, as a sleeve – **leg-of-mutton** (adj.)

Tapeworms:
   An agent that destroys tapeworms – **taeniacide**; **teniacide**
   Infestation with tapeworms – **taeniasis**; **teniasis**

Tar:
   Of, suggesting or coated with tar – **tarry**

Taste:
   Of or relating to the sense of taste – **gustatory**
   The act or faculty of tasting – **gestation**
   A quality perceptible to the sense of taste – **flavor**; **sapor**
   Loss or impairment of the sense of taste – **ageusia**

Something having the effect of a sharp taste in the mouth – **tang**

Tax:
  Subject to import tax – **dutiable**
  A tax levied on persons who ultimately pass on the burden of the tax to others – **indirect tax**
  Of or denoting a tax system in which the rate of taxation increases as the taxable amount increases – **progressive**
  Of or denoting a tax system in which the rate of taxation decreases as the taxable amount increases - **regressive**
  A tenth part of one's annual income, either in kind or money, contributed voluntarily or due as a tax – **tithe**
    The act of levying or paying tithes - **tithing**
  A public record, survey or map of the value, extent and ownership of land as a basis for taxation – **cadaster**; **cadastre**

Tea:
  An establishment serving tea and other refreshments – **teahouse**; **tearoom**; **teashop**
  The articles used in serving tea – **tea service**
  A small table on wheels for serving tea or holding dishes – **teacart**; **tea wagon**
  A public garden where tea and light refreshments may be consumed – **tea garden**

Teaching/Instruction:
  Of, relating to or characteristic of teaching – **pedagogic**
  The art, science or profession of teaching – **didactics**; **pedagogics**; **pedagogy**
  A specialist in the theory and methods of education – **educationalist**; **educationist**
  A fee for instruction – **tuition**
  To teach to accept a system of thought uncritically; to instruct in a body of doctrine – **indoctrinate** (v.t.), n. **indoctrination**
    To try to counteract the effects of an indoctrination – **deprogram** (v.t.)
  Relating to or of the nature of preliminary instruction – **propaedeutic**
  Objects or activities used by a teacher to relate classroom teaching to real life – **realia**
  One who is being instructed in a subject at an elementary level – **catechumen**
    Instruction of catechumens – **catechesis**, pl. **catecheses**
  A private teacher; a provider of additional, specialized or remedial instruction; a college teacher or teaching assistant ranking below an instructor; to function as a private teacher; to instruct privately – **tutor** (n./v.i./v.t.)
    One who is being tutored – **tutee**
    The act or capacity of being a tutor; the state of being under the control or guidance of a tutor or guardian – **tutelage**

Tear (rip or pull apart):
  To tear apart or in pieces – **dilacerate** (v.t.)

Tears (eye lubricants; see also Eyes and Weeping):
  Of or relating to tears – **lachrymal**; **lacrimal**
  Excessive secretion of tears – **lacrimation**

Technical:
  Technical details, rules or methods – **technics** (sing./pl.)
  The quality or state of being technical – **technicality**
  To make technological – **technologize** (v.t.)

Tedious, the quality or state of being – **tedium**

Telephone:
  Of or relating to a telephone; transmitted by telephone – **telephonic**

The technology and manufacture of telephone equipment – **telephony**

Telescope:
The art or study of making or operating telescopes – **telescopy**, n. **telescopist**

Television:
A telecast by cable television – **cablecast**
A play written or adapted for television – **teleplay**
To broadcast by television; to broadcast (a program) by television – **telecast**; **televise** (both v.t.)
A television broadcast – **telecast**
A television transmitter – **televisor**
A course of televised lectures – **telecourse**
A motion picture produced for television – **telefilm**
Presenting a pleasing appearance on television – **telegenic**
An enthusiast of television, video recording, video equipment, etc. – **videophile**
A graphic that is digitally superimposed over the lower portion of a broadcast television image or a video frame - **chyron**

Temperature:
Measurement of temperature; the technology of temperature measurement – **thermometry**
The effect of rhythmic fluctuations of temperature on an organism – **thermoperiodicity**; **thermoperiodism**
Becoming soft when heated and hard when cooled – **thermoplastic**
Maintenance of a constant internal body temperature regardless of environmental temperature – **thermoregulation**
Maintaining a relatively constant and warm body temperature regardless of environmental temperature – **hemathermal**; **hematothermal**; **homoeothermic**; **homoiothermal**; **homoiothermous**; **warm-blooded**
Having a body temperature that varies with the external environment – **cold-blooded**; **poikilothermal**; **poikilothermous**
Normal regulation or adjustment of body temperature – **thermotaxis**, adj. **thermotactic**
Of or relating to an organism that is able to live only within a limited temperature range – **stenothermal**
Of, relating to or registering equal temperatures – **isothermal**
Abnormally low body temperature – **hypothermia**, adj. **hypothermic**
Adaptable to a wide range of temperatures – **eurythermal**; **eurythermic**; **eurythermous** (all Biol.)
Material, as a metal, resistant to high temperatures - **refractory**
Thriving at relatively low temperatures (e.g., at or below +15° C.) – **psychrophilic**

Ten:
A group or series of ten – **decade**
In groups of ten – **decuple**
Ten times as great – **decuple**; **denary**; **tenfold**
A number system using the base ten – **algorism**; **decimal system**

Tenant:
Tenants as a group; the state of being a tenant – **tenantry**

Tendon:
Of, having or resembling a tendon; made up of tendons – **tendinous**
Inflammation of a tendon – **tendinitis**; **tendonitis**
Inflammation of a tendon sheath – **tenosynovitis**
Surgical union of divided tendons with sutures – **tenorraphy**
Surgical division of a tendon for the relief of deformities caused by the shortening of a muscle – **tenotomy**

Tendril:
    A tendril or similar part – **cirrus**, pl. **cirri** (Bot.)
        Having or of the nature of a cirrus or cirri – **cirrate**
    Having or resembling tendrils – **capreolate** (Biol.)

Tennis:
    Tennis played on a grass court – **lawn tennis**

Tension:
    Having extreme arterial or muscular tension – **hypertonic**, n. **hypertonia**
    Extremely or abnormally tense, excitable, etc. – **hypertense**

Tent:
    Tents as a whole; a supply of tents available for accommodation; tent equipment – **tentage**
    Covered with tents; sheltered in or by tents; suggestive of a tent – **tented**

Territory:
    The status of a territory – **territoriality**
    To add to by the acquisition of territory; to reduce to the status of a territory; to distribute among territories –
        territorialize (v.t.)

Test:
    Having a limited number of correct and nearly correct answers – **structured** (used of a test)
    A difficult or critical test of ability for one who is inexperienced or lacking in knowledge – **pons asinorum**
    A test or criterion for determining the quality or genuineness of a thing - **touchstone**

Testicle (testis, pl. testes):
    Shaped like a testicle – **ovoid**; **testicular**; **testiculate**
    Failure of the testes to descend into the scrotum – **cryptorchidism**; **cryptorchism**
    To remove the testicles of – **castrate**; **emasculate**; **geld** (all v.t.)

Text (see also Book):
    Based on or conforming to a text – **textual**
    Of, relating to or contained in a text – **textual**; **textuary**
    To combine (e.g., two variant texts) into one whole – **conflate** (v.t.)
    A critical revision of a text incorporating the most plausible elements from varying sources; a version of a text
        established by critical revision – **recension**

Texture:
    Having a particular kind of texture; having marked texture – **textured**

Theater (see also Drama):
    One who often attends the theater – **theatergoer**
    Of, relating to or suitable for the theater – **theatric**; **theatrical**
    The art of the theater; theatrical mannerisms calculated for effect – **theatrics**
    The theater district of a town – **rialto**
    A summer theater – **strawhat**; **strawhat theater**
    Theatrical arts – **histrionics**
    The art of the theater - **dramaturgy**
    A loud whisper by an actor that is audible to the audience but is supposed for dramatic effect not to be heard by one or
        more of the actors – **stage whisper**

To speak in a stage whisper – **stage-whisper** (v.i.)

Skill in the use of theatrical techniques or devices – **stagecraft**

A member of a theatrical cast who can play any of the smaller roles on short notice – **utility man**

A theatrical composition in which highly improbable plots and humorous characterizations are used for effect – **farce**
>   One who writes or acts in a farce – **farceur**

The arrangement of performers and properties on a stage for a theatrical production; a stage setting – **mise en scène**

The stock of songs, plays, operas, readings, or other pieces that a player or company is prepared to perform -
repertoire
>   A theater in which a resident company presents plays from a specified repertoire – **repertory**

A section of moderately priced seats in a theater – **family circle**

The seats in a theater between the orchestra pit and the rear balcony – **parquet**

The seats in a theater directly below the rear balcony – **parquet circle**

A stage surrounded by seats – **arena theater**

To remove (theatrical properties) from the stage - **strike** (v.t.)

Theft – see Stealing and Thieving

Theme:
>   Of, relating to or constituting a theme – **thematic**

Theory:
>   Of, relating to or based on a theory – **theoretic**; **theoretical**
>   One who formulates, studies, or is expert in the theory of a science or art – **theoretician**; **theorist**
>   The theoretical aspect of a science or art – **theoretics**
>   To formulate or analyze theories; to analyze by way of theory – **theorize** (v.i.)

Therapy:
>   A specialist in therapy – **therapist**
>   Therapy that relies exclusively on natural remedies, such as sunlight supplemented by diet and massage, to treat illness – **naturopathy**
>   A system of therapy in which disease is considered the result of neural malfunction, and manipulation of the spinal column and related structures is the preferred method of treatment – **chiropractic**, n. **chiropractor**
>   Therapy with remedies that produce effects differing from those of the disease treated – **allopathy**, adj. **allopathic**
>   Therapy based on the use of minute quantities of substances that in large doses produce effects similar to those of the disease treated – **homeopathy**, adj. **homeopathic**

Thicken:
>   To thicken by evaporation – **condense**; **inspissate** (both v.t.)

Thieving, the practice of – **thievery**, adj. **thievish**

Thin:
>   To make or become thin, fine or small – **attenuate** (v.t./v.i.)
>   Having a thin or slender form – **tenuous**, n. **tenuity**
>   To become or cause to become very thin, esp. due to starvation – **emaciate** (v.t.)

Thinking (thought, cogitation, rumination):
>   Deep in thought; suggesting or expressing deep thought – **pensive**
>   Pensive contemplation – **melancholy**, adj. **melancholic**
>   Inclined to melancholy – **atrabiliar**; **atrabilious**
>   To examine mentally with thoroughness and care – **excogitate** (v.t.)

A person whose mental imagery consists of his own bodily motion – **motile**
Thinking directed away from reality and not following ordinary rules of logic – **dereism**, adj. **dereistic**
The capacity for, process of, or result of thinking proceeding to a conclusion through reason – **dianoia**, adj. **dianoetic**
The study of the circumstances under which mental processes occur – **psychostatics**
A place for thinking or study – **phrontistery**
Irrational thought – **irrationalism**

Thirteen, extreme or irrational fear of the number – **triskaidekaphobia**

Thorn – see Spine

Thousand:
　　Of or relating to a thousand – **millenarian**; **millenary**
　　A group that contains one thousand elements – **chiliad**
　　Relating to or consisting of a thousandth – **millesimal**
　　By the thousand; per thousand – **per mil**; **per mill**; **per mille**

Thread:
　　Threadlike – **filose**
　　A slender, threadlike appendage, part or structure – **filament** (q.v.); **filum**
　　Fitted with or involving the use of two threads – **bifilar**
　　Of or relating to thread – **filar**
　　Consisting of or resembling thread – **filamentous**; **thready**
　　Having the shape or form of a thread – **filiform**

Threat:
　　Of a threatening or menacing character – **minacious**; **minatory**

Three/Third:
　　Consisting of three parts – **ternary**; **threefold**; **trifold**; **trinal**; **trinary**; **trine**; **tripartitite**; **triple**; **triplex**
　　A group of three persons or things – **triad**; **trine**; **trio**
　　A set of three, esp. a set of three animals – **leash**
　　A set of three, esp. a combination of three numbers that wins a lottery prize – **tern**
　　Based on three; proceeding by threes – **ternary**
　　A group or set of three of one kind – **triplet**
　　Something consisting of three parts – **triplex**
　　Proceeding by threes – **ternary**; **trinary**
　　Made up of or arranged in threes – **ternary**; **ternate**
　　Consisting of sets or groups of three – **ternate**
　　One of a set of three identical things; three identical copies; to make threefold; to make three identical copies of –
　　　　triplicate (n./v.t.)
　　A group of three closely related members – **trinity**
　　The quality or state of being triple; three times as many or as much – **triplicity**
　　To divide into three – **trisect** (v.t.), n. **trisector**
　　Division into three parts – **trichotomy**
　　Three times – **thrice**
　　Being third in position, order, degree or rank – **tertiary**

Throat:
　　Of or relating to the throat – **gular**; **guttural**
　　Produced in the throat – **guttural**

Located in the throat – **gular**
Uttered or sounding as if uttered deep in the throat – **throaty**, n. **throatiness**

Throne, a claimant to the – **pretender**

Thrust:
    To thrust or force down, out or away – **detrude** (v.t.)
    To thrust forth or out – **exsert** (v.t.), (adj. **exsertile**); **extrude**; **obtrude** (both v.t.)
    Capable of being thrust outward, as a tongue, tentacle, etc. – **protrusible**; **protrusile**

Thumb:
    Of or relating to the thumb – **pollical**
    A print made by the thumb – **thumbprint**

Thunder:
    Extreme or irrational fear of thunder – **brontophobia**
    Extreme or irrational fear of thunder and lightning – **astraphobia**

Thyroid:
    Pathologically excessive production of thyroid hormones – **hyperthyroidism**, adj. **hyperthyroid**
        Poisoning from hyperthyroidism - **thyrotoxicosis**
    Surgical removal of the thyroid gland – **thyroidectomy**

Tickets:
    A book of bus or subway tickets – **carnet**
    A special offer of two tickets, as for a play or show, for the price of one – **two-fer**; **twofer**

Ticks – see Mites/Ticks

Tide:
    Of or relating to tidal phenomena caused by the moon – **lunitidal**
    The science or theory of tides – **tidology**
    Of, relating to or being the region between the extremes of high and low tide - **intertidal**
    Coastal land under water during high tide and exposed at low tide – **mud flat**; **tideland**
    A line or artificial indicator marking the high-water or low-water limit of the tide – **tidemark**
    Water that inundates land at flood tide; water affected by the tide; low coastal land drained by tidal streams –
        tidewater
    A tidal flood or flow – **aegir**; **eager**; **eagre**; **bore**
    A channel in which a tidal current runs – **tideway**
    A narrow channel through which tides flow – **swash**
    A tide of lowest range, occurring when the sun and moon are in quadrature (the angular separation of the sun and
        moon is 90°, as measured from the earth) – **neap tide**

Tie:
    To tie or bind with a ligature (cord, wire or thread) – **ligate** (v.t.), n. **ligation**

Tiger:
    A female tiger – **tigress**
    A young tiger – **cub**

Tile:

Relating to or resembling tile – **tegular**

A decorative design or picture made by setting small colored pieces, as tile, in mortar; something resembling such a design or picture; to make such a design or picture; to adorn with or as if with such a design or picture – **mosaic** (n./v.t.)

One of the small squares or stones used in making mosaic patterns – **tessera**, pl. **tesserae**

Tilt:

A tilting backward; the state of being tilted back – **retroversion**

Time:

Relating to, concerned with or limited by time – **temporal**

Independent of time – **atemporal**

Lasting only a short or limited time – **ephemeral**; **temporary**; **transient**; **transitory**

Existing or enduring for a limited time only – **finite**

　Surpassing the finite – **transfinite**

The state of being temporary – **temporality**

To postpone until a later time – **delay**; **defer** (both (v.t.)

To put off doing something until a later time – **delay**; **procrastinate** (both v.i.)

The time interval between two events – **cunctation** (adj. **cunctatory** or **cunctative**); **delay**

The latter or remaining part of a period of time; the early or best part of a period of time – **shank**

The arrangement of events in time – **chronology**, adj. **chronological**

A chronological listing of historical personages or events so as to indicate parallel existence or occurrence; a representation in the same picture of two or more events that occurred at different times – **synchronism**

Occurring at the same time or time period – **contemporaneous**; **synchronous**, n. **synchroneity** or **synchronism**

　A synchronous occurrence, movement or arrangement – **synchrony**

　Lack of synchronism – **asynchronism**

Equal in duration; marked by or occurring at equal intervals – **isochronal**; **isochronous**

　To make isochronal – **isochronize** (v.t.)

An error in time – **anachronism**, adj. **anachronistic** or **anachronous**

Discontinuity or distortion thought to occur in the flow of time – **time warp**

An indefinitely long time period – **age**; **eon**

The longest division of geologic time, having two or more eras – **eon**

Occurring or observed once in an age or century; lasting from century to century – **secular**

Of or relating to geologic periods that preceded the appearance of life – **azoic**

Of or relating to phenomena, esp. of language, as they occur or change through time – **diachronic**

The length of time, established by custom and varying among nations, that is allowed for payment of a foreign bill of exchange – **usance**

To place or define in time relations – **temporalize** (v.t.)

Nearness in time – **propinquity**

An instant of time - **punctilio**

One who keeps time or is concerned with time – **timist**

The science of measuring time; the art of making timekeeping instruments – **horology**

A timekeeping device, esp. an early or primitive one (e.g., a sundial) - **horologe**

The scientific measurement of time – **chronometry**

Tin:

Of or relating to tin – **stannic**; **stannous**

Containing tin – **stannic**

To coat with tin – **tin-plate**

One who makes and repairs tin articles – **tinsmith**

Tissue (Anat.):

    The formation and development of bodily tissues – **histogenesis**

    The anatomical study of the microscopic structure of plant and animal tissues; the microscopic structure of tissues -
        histology

    The disintegration of organic tissues – **histolysis**

    The pathology of diseased tissue – **histopathology**

    The physiology of the microscopic functioning of bodily tissues – **histophysiology**

    The study of tissue taken from a living person or organism, esp. in examination for the presence of disease – **biopsy**,
        adj. **biopsic**

    The chemistry of tissues and cells – **histochemistry**

    The regeneration of tissue – **neogenesis**

    Dead tissue separated from a living structure – **slough**

    Tissue characteristic of an organ – **parenchyma**

Titanium, of or containing – **titaniferous**

Title:

    One who holds a title, esp. for a championship - **titleholder**

    Having, relating to having the nature of or constituting a title – **titular**

    Use of a title in place of a name (e.g. "his honor") – **autonomasia**

    A theme, argument or subject indicated in a title (of a book, article, etc.) – **lemma**

Toads, a group of – **knot**

Tobacco:

    A dealer in tobacco – **tobacconist**

    A mixture of finely pulverized tobacco that can be inhaled; to use or inhale this substance – **snuff** (n./v.i.)

        The quantity of snuff inhaled at a single time – **pinch**; **snuff**

        One who uses snuff – **snuffer**

    A bundle of tobacco leaves sliced lengthwise – **book**

Toe:

    Without toes – **adactylous**

    Having more than the normal number of toes - **polydactyl**; **polydactylous**

    One having more than the normal number of toes – **polydactyl**, n. **polydactylism** or **polydactyly**

    Having two toes projecting forward and two projecting backward – **zygodactyl**; **zygodactylous** (both Zool.)

        A bird with such an arrangement of toes – **zygodactyl**

    Having three toes, claws or similar parts – **tridactyl**; **tridactylous**

    Having five toes on each hand or foot – **pendactyl**; **pendactylate**

    Having an odd number of toes – **perissodactyl**; **perissodactylous**

    Having abnormally short toes – **brachydactylic**

    A toe congenitally bent downward – **hammertoe**

    Having webbed toes – **palmate**; **web-footed**, n. **webfoot**

    Having lobed or partially webbed separated toes – **fissipalmate**

    Having the toes separated from one another; a carnivorous animal having separated toes – **fissiped**

    Having partial or reduced webbing between the toes - **semipalmate**; **semipalmated**

    Having webs connecting each of the four anterior toes – **totipalmate**

Token:

    A collector of transportation tokens – **vecturist**

Tone (Physiol.):
   Having less than normal tone or tension – **hypotonic**, n. **hypotonicity**

Tone (as in sound):
   The comparative or historical science of tones or speech intonations – **tonology**

Tongue:
   Of or relating to the tongue – **glossal**; **lingual**
   A tongue or tonguelike organ - **lingua**
   Of or relating to a tongue or tonguelike organ – **lingual**
   Something resembling a tongue in form or function – **languet**; **languette**
   Shaped like a tongue – **lingulate**
   Situated beneath or on the underside of the tongue – **sublingual**

Tonsil:
   Surgical removal of the tonsils – **tonsillectomy**
   Inflammation of the tonsils – **tonsillitis**
   Surgical incision of a tonsil – **tonsillotomy**

Tooth:
   Of, relating to or for the teeth or dentistry – **dental**
   The diagnosis, prevention and treatment of diseases of the teeth, gums and related structures – **dentistry**
      The dentistry of children's teeth – **pedodontia**; **pedodontics**
   Resembling a tooth – **dentoid**; **odontoid**
   Having the form of a tooth or teeth – **dentiform**
   Having teeth – **dentate**; **dentigerous**; **dentulous**
   The type, number and arrangement of teeth, esp. in animals – **dentition**
   Lacking teeth – **edentate**; **edentulous**; **toothless**
   Having toothlike projections – **dentate**
   Having two teeth or toothlike projections – **bidentate**
   A toothlike projection or part – **dentation**
   A small tooth or toothlike projection – **denticle**
      Having denticles – **denticulate**; **denticulated**
   A prominence or projection on the chewing surface of a tooth – **cusp**
      Having a cusp – **cuspate**; **cuspated**; **cuspidate**; **cuspidated**
      Shaped like a cusp – **cuspate**; **cuspated**
      A tooth having one cusp – **canine tooth**; **cuspid**
      A tooth having two cusps – **bicuspid**, adj. **bicuspid** or **bicuspidate**
      A tooth having three cusps - **tricuspid**, adj. **tricuspid** or **tricuspidal**
   Having a complete set of teeth – **full-mouthed** (used of livestock)
   Having the teeth all alike – **isodont**
   Having large teeth – **macrodont**
   Having two successive sets of teeth – **diphyodont**
   Having the teeth attached by their sides to the inner sides of the jaw – **pleurodont** (Zool.)
   An irregular, broken or projecting tooth – **snaggletooth**, adj. **snaggletoothed**
   To cut teeth (have a new tooth or teeth grow through the gums) – **teethe** (v.i.)
   Located between the teeth – **interdental**
   Adapted for tearing flesh apart – **carnassial** (used of teeth)
   The study of the anatomy, growth, diseases, etc., of teeth – **odontology**, adj. **odontological**, n. **odontologist**
   Of or designating tissue and structures surrounding and supporting the teeth – **periodontal**
      The dental specialty of periodontal disease – **periodontics**

The dental specialty and practice of correcting abnormally aligned or positioned teeth – **orthodontia**; **orthodontics**
The branch of dentistry concerned with tooth pulp diseases – **endodontics**
The branch of dentistry specializing in extraction of teeth – **exodontia**
The operation of cutting into a tooth – **odontotomy**
An abnormally large space between teeth – **diastema**
To bring the upper and lower teeth together – **occlude** (v.t./v.i.)
Of or relating to occlusions of the teeth – **occlusal**
Faulty occlusion – **malocclusion**
The habit of unconsciously gritting or grinding one's teeth – **bruxism**; **bruxomania**
Tooth decay – **caries** (sing./pl.)
   Relating to or afflicted with caries - **carious**
A pain in a tooth – **odontalgia**; **toothache**
A hard yellowish deposit on the teeth – **tartar**
   Of or relating to tartar - **tartaric**
   Consisting of or similar to tartar – **tartareous**
   Derived from tartar – **tartaric**; **tartarous**
   Made up of or containing tartar - **tartarous**
A film of mucus harboring bacteria on a tooth - **plaque**
Having or edged with notched, toothlike projections – **serrate**; **serrated**, n. **serration**
   Serrated on both sides; having serrations that are themselves serrated – **biserrate**

Top (object):
   Shaped like a top; spinning like a top – **turbinate**; **turbinated**
   A top with four lettered sides - **teetotum**

Top (location/direction):
   On or at the top – **atop**

Tortoise/Turtle:
   Of or relating to a tortoise– **testudinal**; **testudinarious**; **testudinate** (adj./n.)
   Resembling a tortoise – **chelonian**; **testudinal**; **testudinarious**
   Having the characteristics of or being a tortoise or turtle – **chelonian**
   Of, relating to or resembling a tortoise shell – **testudinal**; **testudinarious**
   Of or relating to a turtle – **testudinate** (adj./n.)
   A group of turtles – **bale**

Torture:
   A torture in which the victim's hands are tied behind his back and attached to a pulley by means of which he is pulled up off the ground and then dropped halfway down with a jerk – **strappado**, pl. **strappadoes**

Touch:
   Of or relating to the sense of touch – **haptic**; **haptical**; **tactile**; **tactual**
   The act of touching – **taction**
   Perceptible to the touch; used for feeling – **tactile**
   Proceeding from the sense of touch – **tactile**; **tactual**
   Capable of being touched, handled or felt – **palpable**; **tangible**
   Not perceptible to the touch – **impalpable**; **intangible**
   A person or thing not to be touched or meddled with – **noli me tangere**, pl. **noli me tangeres**
   To examine or explore by touching (an organ or area of the body) as a diagnostic aid – **palpate** (v.t.)
   Movement of an organism in response to direct tactile stimulation – **stereotaxis**; **stereotaxy** (adj. **stereotactic** or **stereotactical**); **thigmotaxis**, adj. **thigmotactic**

Movement of an organism in response to direct contact with a surface or object – **stereotropism**; **thigmotropism**
Extreme or irrational fear of touching or being touched – **aphephobia**; **haphephobia**; **haptephobia**

Towing:
    The act or service of towing; a towing charge – **towage**

Town:
    A resident of a town; a fellow resident on one's town – **townsman**
    A woman resident of a town or of one's town - **townswoman**
    The inhabitants or citizens of a town – **townspeople**
    Of or relating to town as opposed to country - **oppidan**

Track:
    The track or trail of an animal – **slot**; **spoor**
    To track or trail persistently – **dog** (v.t.)

Traction, exerting – **tractive**, adj. **tractional**

Tradition, adherence to – **traditionalism**

Tragedy:
    A writer of tragedies; a performer of tragic roles – **tragedian**
    An actress who performs tragic roles – **tragedienne**
    Relating to, being in the style of or having the nature of a tragedy; writing or performing in tragedy – **tragic**; **tragical**
    A flaw in the character of the protagonist of a dramatic or literary tragedy that causes his ruin – **tragic flaw**

Train (see also Railroad):
    The load that a train can carry – **trainload**

Trainee, the status or position of a – **traineeship**

Traitor:
    Having the character of a traitor – **traitorous**
    A woman who is a traitor – **traitoress**; **traitress**
    A traitor who serves as the puppet of the enemy occupying his country – **quisling**

Tranquil:
    To make or become tranquil – **tranquillise**; **tranquilize**; **tranquillize** (all v.t.)
    The quality or state of being tranquil – **tranquility**; **tranquility**
    Something that tranquilizes – **tranquilizer**

Transfer:
    To transfer from one vessel or vehicle to another; to transfer cargo from one vessel or vehicle to another – **tranship**; **transship** (both v.t./v.i.)
    Not capable of being transferred to another – **inalienable**

Transport/Transportation:
    Commercial transportation of goods; the charge for such transportation – **freightage**
    Of or designating a route of transportation carrying a main flow with many branches – **arterial**
    Relating to, involving or carried by two or more transportation lines - **interline**
    Designed to operate on land, water or in the air; a craft so designed – **triphibian**

An extreme or irrational fear of being in or riding in vehicles – **amaxophobia**

Trap:
   One who traps animals for their furs – **trapper**
      A trapper who uses wire traps to snare game – **wirer**

Travel:
   To enter and settle in a country or region to which one is not native – **immigrate** (v.i.), n. **immigration**
   Impossible to travel over or across – **impassible**
   A strong or irresistible impulse to travel – **wanderlust**
   Wearied from traveling – **wayworn**
   Traveling for pleasure – **tourism**
   The condition of traveling about, esp. in search of adventure – **errantry**

Treason, relating to or involving – **treasonous**

Tree:
   Of, relating to or resembling trees; living in trees – **arboraceous**; **arboreal**
   Having the form, structure, duration or life of a tree - **arboraceous**
   Having many trees – **arboreous**; **wooded**
   The cultivation of trees for study or for the protection of timber - **arboriculture**
   A treelike shape or arrangement – **arborization**
   Of or characterized by the clipping or trimming of live trees or shrubs into decorative shapes; work or art of this type – **topiary**
   A tree that has been cut back to the trunk to promote the growth of a dense head of foliage; to remove the crown of (a tree) – **pollard** (n./v.t.)
   A young tree – **sapling**
   The trees or forests of a region or country; a written work on this subject – **silva** (pl. **silvae** or **silvas**); **sylva** , adj. **silvan** or **sylvan**
   Care and cultivation of forest trees – **forestry**; **silviculture**
   Trees or wooded land regarded as a source of wood – **timber**
      Built of or covered with timber – **timbered**
      Covered with a good growth of timber – **well-timbered**
      Standing timber regarded as a commodity; the value of standing timber; the right to cut standing timber - **stumpage**
   The limit of altitude in mountainous regions beyond which trees do not grow – **timberline**; **timber line**
   A claim to the trees on property belonging to another – **timber right**
   The limit of northern or southern latitude beyond which trees cannot grow except as stunted forms – **tree line**
   An area restricted to the growing of forest trees – **wood lot**
   The cover formed by the upper branches of trees in a forest – **crown canopy**; **crown cover**
   Trees that cover an area after the removal of the original stand – **second growth**
   To clear away the trees or forest from – **deforest** (v.t.)
   A standing dead tree or tree stump, esp. one killed by fire – **rampike**
   Shaped like a tree – **arboreous**; **arborescent**; **dendriform**; **dendroid**
   The scientific cultivation of trees and shrubs – **arboriculture**
   The botanical study of trees – **dendrology**, adj. **dendrologic** or **dendrological**, n. **dendrologist**
      The branch of dendrology dealing with the gross and the minute structure of wood – **xylology**
   The study of growth rings in trees to date past events - **dendrochronology**

Trenches, one who digs – **trencher**

Trial – see Jury

Triangle:
Of, relating to or shaped like a triangle; having a triangle for a base – **triangular**
To divide into triangles; to make triangular; made up of or marked with triangles – **triangulate** (v.t./adj.)
Having an equilateral triangular cross section – **three-square**

Tribe, a member of a – **tribesman**, adj. **tribal**

Tropics, the inhabitants of the - **amphiscians**

Trout, a group of – **hover**

Truck:
The transport of goods by truck – **truckage**; **trucking**
The charge for the transport of goods by truck – **truckage**

Trust, willful betrayal of – **treachery**

Truth:
Expressing the truth – **veracious**; **veridic**; **veridical**
To determine or test the truth or accuracy of; to prove the truth of by the presentation of evidence or testimony – **verify** (v.t.), n. **verification**
To deny the truth or accuracy of – **refute** (v.t.) (q.v.)
Something that has the appearance of being true or real; the quality of appearing true or real – **verisimilitude**
A statement, principle or belief considered to be established and permanent truth; the condition or quality of being real, accurate and correct – **verity**
Adherence to the truth – **truthfulness**; **veracity**
To stray from or evade the truth – **prevaricate** (v.i.), n. **prevaricator**, n. **prevarication**
An obvious truth – **truism**
Incontestable because of having been demonstrated or proved to be true – **apodictic**
Intuitive apprehension of spiritual truths – **gnosis**, adj. **gnostic**

Tsar – see Czar

Tube:
A system of tubes; tubing as a whole; a length of tube – **tubing**
A slender, tubular process – **style**
Of, relating to or having the form of a tube; constituting or consisting of tubes – **tubular**; **tubulous**
Formed into or suggestive of a tube – **tubular**; **tubulate**; **tubulated**; **tubulous**
Having a tube – **tubate**; **tubulate**; **tubulated**
A very small tube – **tubule**
Having or consisting of tubules – **tubuliferous**
Shaped like a tube; reedlike – **fistulous**
A tube inserted into a bodily cavity to drain fluid or insert medication – **cannula**
Articles for the table, such as bowls, pitchers, etc., that are tubular or bowl-shaped – **hollowware**

Tuberculosis:
The care, treatment and study of tuberculosis – **phthisiology**
Of, relating to or afflicted with tuberculosis; having tubercles – **tubercular**; **tuberculous**
Resembling tuberculosis; resembling a tubercle – **tuberculoid**
Having a tubercle; characterized by tubercules – **tuberculate**; **tuberculated**; **tuberculed**; **tuberculose**
A tuberculous skin lesion – **tuberculid**; **tuberculoderm**

Characterized by the presence of tubercular lesions – **phthisic**; **phthisical**; **tubercular**; **tuberculoid**; **tuberculous**

A tubercular person – **phthisic**; **tubercular**

Tuberculosis of the lungs – **phthisic**; **phthisis**; **pulmonary tuberculosis**

The development of pulmonary tuberculosis – **phthisiogenesis** (adj. **phthisiogenic**), n. **phthisiologist**

The treatment of pulmonary tuberculosis – **phthisiotherapy**

Tumor:

The process of tumor formation and development – **oncogenesis** (adj. **oncogenic**); **tumorigenesis**

Causing tumors – **tumorigenic**

The medical study of tumors – **oncology**

A black-pigmented malignant tumor – **melanoma**

A benign tumor of chiefly fatty cells – **lipoma**

A malignant tumor derived from epithelial tissue – **carcinoma**

A tumor made up of nerve tissue – **neuroma**

A tumor composed of muscle tissue – **myoma**

A small hard tumor of the eyelid – **chalazion**

A tumor composed of immature and undifferentiated cells – **blastoma**

Tunnel:

To tunnel beneath – **undermine** (v.t.)

Turkey:

A male turkey – **gobbler**; **tom**

A female turkey – **hen**

A young turkey – **poult**

A group of turkeys – **flock**; **rafter**

Turn/Turning:

To turn or move increasingly away from a specified course or prescribed mode of behavior; to cause to turn aside or differ – **deviate** (v.i./v.t.), n. **deviation**

A deviation from the regular arrangement, general rule or usual method – **anomaly**, adj. **anomalous**

Turned or bent abruptly backward – **reflexed**; **retroflex**; **retroflexed**

A turning backward; the state of being turned back; the act or process of turning back – **retroversion**

The turning of one part within another – **introversion**, adj. **introversive**

The act of turning or the state of being turned – **torsion**

To turn (the palm or inner surface of the hand or forelimb) downward or backward – **pronate** (v.t.)

To turn away or ward off – **avert** (v.t.)

To turn outward or inside out – **evert** (v.t.)

Turned or directed downward – **retrorse**

To turn or become turned over; an upsetting or overturning – **overset** (v.t./v.i./n.)

Having turns or windings – **flexuose**; **flexuous**, n. **flexuosity**

Full of intricate turnings – **anfractuous**

Turnip, shaped like a – **napiform**

Turpentine:

Relating to, consisting of or resembling turpentine - **terebinthine**

Turret:

Equipped with a turret or turrets; shaped like a turret – **turreted**

Turtle – see Tortoise/Turtle

Tusks, an animal that has – **tusker**

Tweezers, to handle or extract with – **tweeze** (v.t.)

Twelve:
   Of, relating to or based on the number twelve; of or relating to twelfths; a twelfth part - **duodecimal**

Twenty:
   Relating to or based on the number twenty – **vicenary**; **vigesimal**
   Consisting of twenty; designating a notation system based on twenty – **vicenary**
   Proceeding or occurring in intervals of twenty – **vigesimal**

Twin:
   Bearing of twins; a pairing or union of two similar or identical things – **twinning**
   A pair of twins joined at the heads – **craniopagus**, pl. **craniopagi**

Twist:
   The act of twisting or the state of being twisted; stress produced when one end of an object is twisted in one direction
      and the other end is held motionless or twisted in the opposite direction – **torsion**
   Twisted or bent upon itself – **contorted**

Twilight (crepuscule; crepuscle):
   Becoming active at twilight or before sunrise (Zool.); of or like twilight – **crepuscular**

Two:
   Division into two usually contradictory parts or opinions – **dichotomy**
   To divide into two parts or classifications; to be or become divided into two parts or branches – **dichotomize** (v.t./v.i.)
   Divided into two equal parts by a median cleft – **bifid**
   Consisting of two parts or divisions – **binate**; **bipartite**; **dimeric**
   Having two distinct main parts – **bicorporeal**

Type:
   Relating to or serving as a type – **typal**; **typical**
   The study of types, as in a systematic classification – **typology**

Typhus:
   Of, relating to or afflicted with typhus or typhoid fever – **typhoid**
   Causing typhus - **typhogenic**

U

Ugly (see also Grotesque):
   To make ugly – **disfigure**; **uglify** (both v.t.)

Ulcer:
   To become affected with or as if with an ulcer – **ulcerate** (v.i.)
   The development of an ulcer; an ulcerous condition – **ulceration**
   Tending to cause the formation of ulcers – **ulcerogenic**
   Relating to or exhibiting ulcers – **ulcerous**

Umpire:
   The position, function or authority of an umpire – **umpirage**

Uncle:
   Of, relating to or similar to an uncle – **avuncular**

Under:
   To put (one thing) under another – **underlay** (v.t.)

Understand (see also Mind/Mental Processes):
   Easily understood – **lucid**
   Capable of being understood – **comprehensible**; **understandable**
   Capable of being clearly and readily understood - **perspicuous**
   Understood by only a few – **arcane**; **esoteric**; **occult**
   Beyond the realm of human understanding – **occult**
   Not easily understood – **abstruse**; **impalpable**; **mysterious**; **recondite**; **tenebrious**; **tenebrose**; **tenebrous**
   Having a limited degree of understanding, as of a technical subject – **semiliterate**
   Understanding of what is true, right or lasting – **wisdom** (q.v.)

Uneven, to make – **asperate** (v.t.)

Unidentified flying objects, the study of – **ufology**

Union – see Labor Union

Unite (see also Joints/Joining):
   The capacity of something to unite, react or interact with something else – **valence**; **valency**
   The uniting of related parts – **concrescence**
   Tending to promote unity or serving to unite – **unitive**

Universe (see also Astronomy):
   The total physical universe, including all galaxies – **metagalaxy**
   The scientific study of the chemical make-up of the universe – **cosmochemistry**
   The study of the evolution of the physical universe – **cosmogony**
   The study of the structure and dynamics of the universe – **cosmology**

Upward:
   Going, growing or moving upward – **ascending**, n. **ascension**, n. **ascent**

Urine:

Of or relating to urine – **uretic**; **uric**; **urinary**; **urinose**; **urinous**

Resembling or containing urine – **urinose**; **urinous**

Obtained from urine – **uric**

Promoting the excretion of uric acid in the urine – **uricosuric**

Chemical analysis of urine – **urinalysis**

Conveying urine – **uriniferous**

The formation or presence of urinary calculi (masses of inorganic material) – **urolithiasis**

The study of the urogenital tract – **urology**

The examination of urine with a microscope – **uroscopy**

Excessive discharge of urine – **diuresis**; **polyuria**

Tending to increase discharge of urine; an agent that does this – **diuretic**

Difficult or painful urination – **dysuria**

Involuntary urination – **bed-wetting**; **enuresis**

Excretion of abnormal quantities of sugar in the urine – **glycosuria**

A condition marked by excessive quantities of acid in the urine – **aciduria**

The presence of bacteria in the urine – **bacteriuria**

The presence of bacilli in the urine – **bacilluria**

The presence of albumin in the urine – **albuminuria**

The presence of blood or red blood cells in the urine – **hematuria**

Urn, shaped like a – **urceolate**

Use:

To use up – **consume**; **expend** (both v.t.)

A useful thing that a person constantly carries with him – **vade mecum**

Capable of being used advantageously – **serviceable**; **useful**

Lending itself to varied uses – **adaptable**; **pliant**

The quality or state of being useful; a useful article or device; designed primarily for practical use – **utility**

Relating to or based on utility – **utilitarian**

A discontinuance of use, practice, exercise or functioning - **desuetude**

Uterus (pl. uteri):

Of or concerning the uterus – **uterine**

Within the uterus – **intrauterine**

Inflammation of the uterus – **metritis**

An abnormal hemorrhage (excessive bleeding) of the uterus – **metrorrhagia**

Partial or complete surgical removal of the uterus – **hysterectomy**

Surgical incision of the uterus – **hysterotomy**

Uvula:

Relating to or associated with the uvula – **uvular**

Inflammation of the uvula – **uvulitis**

V

Vaccine:
To inoculate with a vaccine – **vaccinate** (v.t.)
Inoculation with a vaccine; a scar left on the skin by vaccinating - **vaccination**
Of or relating to vaccine or vaccination – **vaccinal**
A supplementary dose of a vaccine injected to maintain immunity – **booster**

Vacuum:
One who maintains that there are vacuums in nature – **vacuist**
One who maintains that there are no vacuums in nature – **plenist**

Vagina:
Of or relating to the vagina – **vaginal**
Inflammation of the vagina – **vaginitis**
Inflammation of the vaginal mucous membrane – **colpitis**
Surgical removal of all or part of the vagina – **vaginectomy**
A painful contractional spasm of the vagina – **vaginismus**

Value:
To estimate or decide the value of; to set a price or value for - **appraise** (v.t.) (n. **appraiser**); **valuate** (v.t.), n. **valuator**
Capable of being appraised – **appraisable**
An appraising or being appraised – **appraisal**
To rise in value – **appreciate** (v.i.)
According to the value – **ad valorem**
The value imprinted on a stock certificate or bond that provides the basis for bond interest, preferred stock dividend or share of equity capital – **face value**; **par value**
Without face value or par value – **no-par**; **no-par-value**
The philosophical study of the nature of values and value judgments – **axiology**, adj. **axiological**, n. **axiologist**

Valve:
Having valvelike parts – **valvate**
Relating to, having or operating by means of valves or valvelike parts – **valvular**
A small valve or valvelike structure – **valvule**
A small valve or tap for letting air enter or escape from a pipe, chamber, etc. – **air cock**
Having two valves – **bivalve**
Having three valves – **trivalve**
Having many valves; a shell or shellfish having many valves – **multivalve**; **plurivalve**
Inflammation of a valve (in the human body) – **valvulitis**

Vampire:
Of or like a vampire – **vampiric**
Belief in vampires; the practice or actions of vampires – **vampirism**

Vapor:
Of or relating to vapor – **vaporous**; **vapory**
The formation of vapor – **vaporescence**
Resembling or having the nature of vapor; producing or turning to vapor – **vaporific**; **vaporish**; **vaporous**; **vapory**
To convert or be converted into vapor – **vaporize** (v.t./v.i.), n. **vaporization**
To give off (vapor containing waste products) through the pores of the skin or the stomata of plant tissue – **transpire** (v.i.)

To dissipate like vapor – **evanesce** (v.i.)
Capable of being readily vaporized; evaporating readily at normal pressures and temperatures – **volatile**
    To remove volatile material from – **devolatize** (v.t.)

Variety:
    To give variety to; to make varied – **variegate** (v.t.)
    Of, indicating or characterizing a variety, esp. a biological variety – **varietal**

Vary:
    Something that varies or is prone to variation; a quantity capable of assuming any of a set of values; tending or apt to vary – **variable**
    Having two variables – **bivariate**
    To vary between alternate extremes – **oscillate** (v.i.) (Physics)

Vegetables (see also Diet):
    Raw vegetables served as an appetizer – **crudités**

Veil:
    Having or covered by a veil – **veiled**; **velate**

Vein:
    Of or relating to a vein or veins – **venose**; **venous**
    Having noticeable veins or veinlike markings – **venose**, n. **venosity**
    Having veins – **nervate** (used of leaves)
    The distribution or arrangement of veins – **nervation**; **veining**; **venation**
    A very small vein – **venule**
    Puncture of a vein, as for drawing blood, intravenous feeding or administration of medicine – **venipuncture**
    Within a vein or veins – **intravenous**
    Entry of foreign material into a vein – **intravenation**
    Inflammation of a vein – **phlebitis**
    Inflammation of a vein with the formation of a thrombus (stationary blood clot) – **thrombophlebitis**
    The medical study of the diseases and functioning of veins – **phlebology**
    The medical practice of opening a vein to draw blood – **phlebotomy** (v.t. **phlebotomize**); **venesection**
    Subcutaneous incision to cure varicose veins – **varicotomy**

Vermin:
    The condition of being infested with vermin; the breeding of vermin – **vermination**
    Of, relating to, of the nature of or infested with vermin – **verminous**

Verse – see Poetry

Vertebra (one of the segments of the spinal column; pl. vertebrae or vertebras; see also Spine):
    Located between vertebrae – **intervertebral**
    Inflammation of one or more of the vertebrae – **spondylitis**

Vessel:
    Of, characterized by or containing vessels for the transmission or circulation of plant or animal fluids – **vascular**

Vibration:
    Adapted to vibratory motion – **vibratile**
    Characterized by or capable of vibration – **vibratile**; **vibrative**; **vibratory**

Of, consisting of or causing vibration – **vibrating**; **vibrative**; **vibratory**
Without periodic vibrations - **aperiodic**

Victim:
    The study of the roles played by victims in the crimes committed against them – **victimology**

Victor/Victory:
    A victory that is offset by staggering losses – **Cadmean victory**; **Pyrrhic victory**
    A woman who is a victor – **victress**
    A victory or contest easily won – **walkaway**; **walkover**

Village, an inhabitant of a – **villager**

Villain, a woman who is a – **villainess**

Vine:
    An area or greenhouse for growing vines – **vinery**

Vinegar:
    Of, producing or like vinegar – **acetous**

Violence:
    Systematic use of violence, terror and intimidation to achieve an end – **terrorism**, n. **terrorist** or **terrorizer**, v.t.
        terrorize; n. **terrorization**, adj. **terroristic**
    Given to violence – **explosive**; **volatile**

Violet, of the color – **violaceous**

Violin, shaped like a – **pandurate** (Bot.)

Viper:
    Of, resembling or characteristic of a viper – **viperine**
    Suggestive of a viper or venomous snake – **viperous**
    A group of vipers – **nest**

Virtues:
    The "cardinal virtues": **justice**, **prudence**, **fortitude** and **temperance**

Virus:
    An agent that destroys or inhibits viruses – **viricide**; **virucide**
    The study of viruses and viral diseases – **virology**

Vision (see also Blindness and Eyes):
    The entire area visible to the immobile eyes at a given moment – **field of vision**; **visual field**
    Capable of being seen – **visible**
    Visible to the naked eye – **macroscopic**
    Having normal vision – **orthoscopic**
    Partial or total loss of vision from disease of the optic nerve, retina or brain without any perceptible external change in
        the eye – **amaurosis**, n. **amaurotic**
        An early stage of amaurosis - **amblyopia**
    Having poor vision; nearly or partly blind – **meropic**; **purblind**

Partial blindness - **meropia**

A defect of vision characterized by reduced visual capacity in bright lights – **day blindness**; **hemeralopia**

Spots before the eyes due to cells and cell fragments in the vitreous humor and lens – **muscae volitantes**

The state of the normal eye when parallel rays are focused precisely on the retina and vision is perfect - **emmetropia**

Improvement in near vision (through natural processes) – **senopia**

Having equality of refraction in both eyes – **isometropia**

Visual perception in three dimensions – **stereovision**

Nearsightedness – **myopia**, adj. **myopic**

    One who has myopia – **myope**

A condition in which parallel rays are focused behind the retina, so that vision is better for distant than near objects – **farsightedness**; **hyperopia** (adj. **hyperopic**); **hypermetropia**, adj. **hypermetropic** or **hypermetropical**

    One who has hyperopia – **hyperope**

A refractive defect in a lens that prevents focusing of sharply defined images – **astigmatism**

    Free from or corrected for astigmatism – **anastigmatic**

A visual defect in which one eye cannot focus with the other on an objective because of imbalance of the eye muscles – **strabismus**

    Strabismus in which one or both eyes turn outward – **divergent strabismus**; **exotropia**; **walleye**, adj. **walleyed**

    Strabismus in which one eye deviates inward - **esotropia**

The cutting of an ocular muscle or tendon to correct strabismus – **strabotomy**

The inability of the eye to focus sharply on nearby objects, as a result of hardening of the lens with advancing age – **presbyopia**

Weakness or rapid fatigue of the eyes – **asthenopia**

A blind or dark spot within the visual field – **scotoma**

A condition characterized by unequal refractive power of the eyes – **anisometropia**

A disorder that causes objects to appear double – **diplopia**; **double vision**

Imperfect refraction of the eye – **ametropia**

Conjunctivitis and deteriorated vision caused by sunlight reflected from snow or ice – **snow blindness**

Vision that is normal in daylight but abnormally weak when the light is poor – **night blindness**; **nyctalopia**

Dimness of vision without apparent defect or disease of the eye – **amblyopia**; **lazy eye**

Inability to see as clearly in bright light as in dim light – **hemeralopia**

The ability to see in dim light – **night-adaptive vision**; **scotopia**

A transient dimming or haziness of vision resulting from temporary impairment of cerebral circulation - **grayout**

Capable of distinguishing only two colors – **dichromatic**

Colorblindness – **achromatopia**; **achromatopsia**; **achromatopsy**

Red-green colorblindness – **daltonism**

Colorblindness marked by confusion of green, bluish-red and neutral – **deuteranopia**

A form of colorblindness in which red and bluish-green stimuli are confused with neutral stimuli and with each other – **protanopia**

The inability to distinguish the color blue – **tritanopia**

Loss of visual adjustment due to paralysis of the ciliary muscles of the eye – **cyclopegia**

The treatment of defective visual habits, defects of binocular vision, and muscle imbalance by reeducation of visual habits, exercise and visual training – **orthoptics**, adj. **orthoptic**

    A person who is trained in or practices orthoptics - **orthoptist**

Visit:

    The right of a parent to visit a child as specified in a divorce or separation order – **visitation**

    Of or relating to an official visitor or visit; having the right or power of visitation - **visitatorial**

Vitamin:

    A substance converted to a vitamin within the body – **provitamin**

Voice (see also Singing):
Of or relating to the voice; uttered or produced by the voice; having a voice; full of voices – **vocal**
The use of the voice in speaking or singing – **vocalism**
Loss of voice – **aphonia**, adj. **aphonic**

Void:
To make or declare void or invalid – **annul**; **nullify** (both v.t.)
Capable of being annulled – **defeasible**

Volcano (see also Rock):
Of, relating to or from a volcano or volcanic eruption – **vulcanian**
Volcanic force or activity – **volcanism**; **vulcanism**
To subject to or change by the effects of volcanic heat – **volcanize** (v.t.)
Of volcanic origin – **volcanogenic**
The science dealing with volcanic phenomena – **volcanology**; **vulcanology**
Of, relating to or being high-temperature deposits derived from magmatic emanations forced under pressure into place in pre-existing rock openings – **hypothermal**
A large crater formed by volcanic explosion or by collapse of a volcanic cone – **caldera**
To cause (molten lava) to pour forth from a volcanic vent – **extravasate** (v.t.)
Formed by rock fragmentation resulting from volcanic ejection – **pyroclastic**
A secondary volcanic cone of a volcano – **monticule**
A hole in a volcanic area from which smoke and gases arise – **fumarole**
A volcanic fissure (narrow crack or cleft) that emits sulfurous vapors, steam, etc. – **solfatara**
An opening in the earth from which gases escape, usually marking the last stage of volcanic activity; the gases that escape in this way – **mofette**; **moffette**
Molten rock that issues from a volcano or fissure in the earth's surface; the rock formed by the cooling and solidifying of such molten rock – **lava** (q.v.)
Rough fragments of burnt, crustlike lava – **scoria**
A volcano composed of lava and ash deposited in alternating conical layers – **stratovolcano**
A small air pocket or cavity formed in volcanic rock during solidification – **vesicle**
A mass of fragments of volcanic rocks fused by heat – **agglomerate**

Volume:
Of or relating to volume – **volumetric**
To reduce the volume of – **compress**; **condense** (both v.t.)

Volunteering one's services when they are neither requested nor needed – **meddlesome**; **officious**

Vomiting (emesis):
Of, relating to or causing vomiting – **emetic**; **vomitive**
An agent that causes vomiting – **emetic**
Vomited matter – **vomitus**
To make an effort to vomit; to strain to vomit – **retch** (v.i.)
Forceful but ineffective attempts at vomiting – **retching**; **vomiturition**
A stomach disturbance marked by feeling the need to vomit – **nausea**
To feel or cause to feel nausea – **nauseate** (v.i./v.t.)
Causing or affected with nausea – **nauseous**
Easily nauseated or sickened - **squeamish**

Voting – see Political Terms

Vowel – see Speech

Vulgar:
A vulgar person, esp. one who makes a conspicuous display of his or her money – **vulgarian**
A vulgar word or phrase – **vulgarism**
The condition or quality of being vulgar; an instance of vulgarism – **vulgarity**
To make vulgar – **vulgarize** (v.t.)

Vulture:
Of, relating to, characteristic of or suggestive of a vulture – **vulturine**; **vulturous**

Vulva:
Inflammation of the vulva – **vulvitis**
Simultaneous inflammation of the vulva and vagina - **vulvovaginitis**

W

Wagons, one who builds and repairs – **wainwright**

Walk/Walking:
    Walking or moving about – **ambulant**
    To walk or move about – **ambulate** (v.i.)
    Of, relating to or meant for walking; capable of walking; a sheltered place for walking – **ambulatory**
    Walking on the toes with the posterior part of the foot more or less raised; an animal that walks thus – **digitigrade**
    Walking with the entire lower surface of the foot on the ground; an animal that walks thus – **plantigrade**
    Moving on all fours – **pronograde**
    Adapted for walking; having legs adapted for walking – **gressorial**
    A halt in a person's walk – **claudication**; **limp**
    Dysfunction of muscular coordination in walking – **abasia**
    A stumbling or staggering gait characteristic of some nervous disorders – **titubation**
    To walk with short, unsteady steps; a slow, unsteady gait – **toddle** (v.i.)
    To walk with short steps that tilt the body from side to side – **waddle** (v.i.)
    To walk with an up and down movement, esp. in an affected manner intended to attract attention - **tittup**; **titup** (both v.i.)
    A walk (place for walking) that is shaded, esp. by alamo trees – **alameda**
    To convert (a street or area) into a pedestrian walkway or mall – **pedestrianize** (v.t.)
    Divination in which one walking in or around a circle falls from dizziness and prog-nosticates from the place of the fall – **gyromancy**

Wall:
    Relating to or forming the wall of a hollow structure – **parietal** (Biol.)
    To build into a wall, esp. to entomb in a wall – **immure** (v.t.)
    The lower part of an interior wall when finished in a material different from that of the upper part; to line or panel (a wall or room) thus – **wainscot** (n./v.t.)
        A wainscoted wall or walls – **wainscoting**; **wainscotting**
    A decorative band or strip on the upper part of a wall - **frieze**

Wander (expatiate):
    An exaggerated desire to wander – **dromomania**
    To wander about or stray from one place or subject to another – **divagate** (v.i.)
    Wandering from place to place and lacking a job or income; someone who wanders thus – **vagrant** (adj./n.)

War:
    One engaged or experienced in war – **warrior**
    Of, relating to, suggesting or resembling war; typical of or suitable for a warrior – **martial**, n. **martialism**, n. **martialist**
    Warlike in manner or temperament – **bellicose**; **combative**; **militant**
        Extremely militant – **ultramilitant**
    A nation associated but not allied with another or other nations waging war – **co-belligerent**
    One who advocates or attempts to stir up war – **warmonger**
    An act or event provoking, justifying, or used as an excuse for a declaration of war – **casus belli**
    Warfare marked by a lack of aggression or progress – **sitzkrieg**
    Opposed to war – **antiwar**
    An opposition to war or violence as a means of settling disputes – **pacifism**
    A war whose objective is of smaller scope than the total defeat of the enemy – **limited war**
    Happening after a war – **post-bellum**
    Belonging to the period before the American Civil War – **ante-bellum**

Out of combat; in a disabled condition – **hors de combat**
Extreme or disabling fear of war – **traumatophobia**

Warn/Warning:
    Cautionary advice or warning – **admonition**, adj. **admonitory**, v.t. **admonish**
    Serving as a warning or signal of danger – **sematic**

Warranty:
    A person to whom a warranty is made – **warrantee**
    A person who gives a warranty to another – **warrantor**

Wart:
    A wartlike projection – **verruca** (Biol.)
    Covered with warts or wartlike projections – **verrucose**; **verrucous**

Wasp:
    A group or colony of wasps or hornets – **nest**; **vespiary**
    Of, relating to or resembling a wasp – **vespine**

Wash:
    To wash or percolate the soluble matter from – **lixiviate** (v.t.), n. **lixiviation**
    A washing, esp. of a hollow organ, with repeated injections of water – **lavage**
    A washing of the body, esp. in a religious ceremony; the liquid used for such washing – **ablution**
    A woman employed to wash and iron clothes or linens – **laundress**

Waste/Wasting:
    Wasting away (of tissues, organs, etc.) – **abrosia**; **atrophy**
    Wasting away of the body, associated with inadequate or inadequately assimilated food – **marasmus**
    Progressive bodily wasting – **abrosia**; **tabes**
    A painfully urgent yet ineffectual attempt to defecate or urinate – **tenesmus**
    Functioning to carry waste matter out of the body – **emunctory**
    Allowance for waste – **tret**
    A person who wastes, esp. one who wastes money – **waster**; **wastrel**

Watch:
    One whose occupation is making or repairing watches – **watchmaker**
    A watch (lookout) kept during normal sleeping hours – **vigil**

Water (see also Wave):
    In the form of water – **aquiform**
    Of or like water – **aqueous**; **watery**
    Living on, done in or done on water - **aquatic**
    Growing or thriving in water – **aquatic**; **hydrophilous**, n. **hydrophily**
    Floating or swimming in water – **natant**
    Names of bodies of water – **hydronymy**
    A natural fountain or flow of water – **spring**
        A spring that is the source of a stream – **fountainhead**
    A sheet of water flowing over a dam or similar structure – **nappe**
    Of, relating to or living in moving water – **lotic**
    Capable of immersion in water without suffering damage – **immersible**
    Floating on or supported by water; transported by or transmitted in water – **waterborne**

Adapted for living or growing in or near water – **semiaquatic**

Capable of living at the bottom of a body of water in a wide range of depths – **eurybathic**

Movement of an organism in response to water – **hydrotropism**

Made up of both water and land – **terraqueous**

Water present in the soil and available for plant absorption – **chresard**

Water present in the soil and unavailable for plant absorption – **echard**

Water beneath the earth's surface between saturated soil and rock that supplies wells and springs – **ground water**; **groundwater**

  Of or related to ground water – **phreatic**

Of or relating to hot water – **hydrothermal**

Containing some salt – **brackish**; **briny** (both used of water)

Milky frozen water – **catice**

Of, relating to or being water that is located in the zone of aeration in the earth's crust above the ground water level – **vadose**

The depth or level below which the ground is saturated with water – **water table**

Contributing water to the zone of saturation and thereby sustaining or raising the water table – **influent**

A large area of open water surrounded by sea ice – **polynya**

A shallow body of water, esp. one separated from the sea by sandbars and coral reefs – **lagoon**

A long, narrow inlet from the sea between steep cliffs and slopes – **fiord**; **fjord**

An artificial channel for water fitted with a valve or gate for stopping or regulating the flow; a body of water pent up behind a floodgate or water gate; a device for letting water in or out or holding it back; a stream flowing through a floodgate; a conduit that serves to drain or carry off surplus water; to cause to flow or pour forth by or as if by floodgates; to flood or drench (an area of land, e.g.) by such a channel, floodgate, conduit or pent-up body of water; to pour from or as if from such a channel, floodgate, conduit or pent-up body of water – **sluice** (n./v.t/v.i.)

A channel for the overflow of water – **spillway**

An inclined channel for conveying water – **flume**

A powerful water current that usually moves in a circular direction with extreme rapidity, sucking in objects within a given radius – **maelstrom**; **whirlpool**

A narrow passage of water joining two larger bodies of water – **strait**; **straits**

In the direction opposite to that of the flow of water (over the land) – **upriver**

Slow addition to land by deposition of waterborne sediment – **accretion**

Silt deposited by a current of water – **sullage**

A stream or current of fresh water that flows into the sea – **freshet**

The washing of water against a shore or bank – **alluvion**

Clay, silt, sand, gravel or similar detrital material deposited by running water, esp. during recent geologic time – **alluvium**

  To cover with alluvium; to deposit alluvium – **alluviate** (v.t.), n. **alluviation**

Of, found in or made up of sand, clay, etc., deposited by flowing water, esp. along a river bed – **alluvial**

The gradual recession of water, leaving permanently dry land – **reliction**

The study of the properties, distribution and effects of water in the atmosphere, on the earth's surface and in soil and rocks – **hydrology**

The study of how groundwater moves through soil and rock – **hydrogeology**

The scientific description and analysis of the physical conditions, boundaries, flow and related characteristics of surface waters, as oceans, lakes and rivers, including the mapping of bodies of water – **hydrography**

The meteorology of the occurrence, motion and changes of state of atmospheric water – **hydrometeorology**, adj. **hydrometeorological**

To measure the depth of (water), esp. by means of a weighted line – **fathom**; **sound** (both v.t.)

A watercourse that channels water into a water wheel, mill or turbine – **headrace**

A water wheel with buckets attached to its rim that are used to raise water from a stream – **noria**

A mill with water-driven machinery – **water mill**

Moved or put into motion by the weight of water passing over and flowing from the top – **overshot**

Driven by water passing from below, as a water wheel – **undershot**

Skill in water-related activities such as managing boats or swimming – **watercraft**

The therapeutic use of water – **hydropathy**; **water cure**

Treatment of disease by copious and frequent use of water both internally and externally – **hydropathy**, adj. **hydropathic**

The treatment of disease or disability by the external application of water – **hydrotherapeutics**; **hydrotherapy**; **water cure**

To use a divining rod to find underground water; to search for water by or as if by this technique – **dowse** (v.i.)

A person who professes the ability to find underground water, esp. by means of a divining rod – **dowser**; **waterfinder**; **water witch**

To combine with water; a compound containing water combined in a definite ratio – **hydrate** (v.t./n.)

Chemically combined with water – **hydrated**

> Without water; not hydrated – **anhydrous**

Containing water, esp. that of crystallization or hydration – **hydrous**

To remove water from, for preservation; to lose water or moisture – **dehydrate** (v.t./v.i.)

Having an affinity for, absorbing, wetting smoothly with, tending to combine with, or capable of dissolving in water – **hydrophilic**

Readily absorbing water, as from the atmosphere – **hygroscopic**, n. **hygroscopicity**

Decomposition of a chemical compound by reaction with water – **hydrolysis**

> To subject to or undergo hydrolysis – **hydrolyze** (v.t./v.i.)

Unaffected by or impenetrable to water; made of or treated with a substance that resists water penetration; a material or fabric that is unaffected by or impenetrable to water or has been treated thus – **waterproof**; **watertight**

Resistant to water but not entirely waterproof – **water-repellent**; **water-resistant**

The right to draw water from a particular source; the right to navigate on particular waters – **water right**

The district of a town or city that borders the water, esp. a wharf district where ships dock – **waterfront**

Of, on or relating to the bank of a natural course of water – **riparian**

The right, as to fishing or the use of a riverbed, of one who owns riparian land – **riparian right** (Law)

The water system, including reservoirs, tanks, pumps and pipes, of a municipality; a single unit within such a system; an exhibition of moving water – **waterworks**

Found or occurring under water – **subaqueous**

Formed or adapted for underwater use – **subaqueous**; **submarine**

Growing or remaining under water – **submerged**; **submersed** (both Bot.)

Able to be plunged into water or remain under water – **submergible**; **submersible**

Setting and hardening under water – **hydraulic** (e.g., hydraulic cement)

A banging noise heard in a water pipe following an abrupt change of the flow – **water hammer**

To supply (dry land) with water by means of ditches, pipes or streams; to wash out (a canal or wound) with water – **irrigate** (v.t.), adj. **irrigable**

> To irrigate from beneath, as by underground pipes – **subirrigate** (v.t.)

Having or marked by a large amount of water or a vapor – **humid**

> To make humid – **humidify** (v.t.), n. **humidification**

Dampness, esp. of the air – **humidity**

A watertight structure in which underwater construction is effected – **caisson**

A temporary watertight enclosure built in the water and pumped dry to expose the bottom so that construction, as of piers, may be undertaken; a watertight chamber attached to a ship's side to facilitate underwater repairs – **cofferdam**

The sound made by rippling water – **purl**

A place were animals find water – **watering hole**; **watering place**

To soak or saturate with water – **waterlog** (v.t.) (adj. **waterlogged**); **water-soak** (v.t.)

To steep in hot water – **decoct** (v.t.)

Not requiring water, as a cooling system – **waterless**

A principal pipe in a system of pipes for conveying water, esp. one installed under-ground – **water main**

Divination by water, as by visions seen therein or the ebb and flow of tides – **hydromancy**

Divination involving the observation of water in a basin – **lecanomancy**

Extreme or irrational fear of water – **hydrophobia**, adj. **hydrophobic**

Wave:

The act or action of waving – **wafture**

To cause to move in a smooth, wavelike motion; to give a wavelike appearance or form to; to move in a wave or with a wavelike motion; to have a wavelike appearance or form – **undulate** (v.t./v.i.)

Having a wavy outline or appearance – **undulate**; **undulated**

Movement in waves; a wavelike form, outline or appearance; one of a series of waves – **undulation**

Resembling waves in occurrence, appearance or motion – **undulant**

A small wave or succession of small waves – **riffle**; **ripple**

Washed by waves; floating on waves – **awash**

To heave upward on a wave or swell; the rising movement of a ship on a wave or swell – **scend**; **send** (both v.i.)

A barrier that protects a harbor or shore from the full impact of waves – **breakwater**

The seaward return of water after the landward motion of a wave – **backrush**

A wave that oscillates in an enclosed body of water as a result of seismic or atmos-pheric disturbance - **seiche**

An ocean wave caused by an underwater earthquake or a volcanic eruption – **tidal wave**; **tsunami**

A high tidal wave in a narrow estuary – **bore**; **eager**; **eagre**

Any of numerous patterns of wave motion, as of acoustic waves – **mode**

Having different wavelengths or frequencies – **heterochromatic**

Wax:

Waxlike – **ceraceous**; **waxen**

Made of or covered with wax – **waxen**

Coated with wax – **cerated**; **waxed**

The art of making characters or designs in or with wax – **cerography**

A writing or engraving on wax – **cerograph**

Divination involving the dropping of melted wax into water – **ceromancy**

Weak/Weakness:

To weaken by wearing away a base or foundation – **undermine** (v.t.)

Abnormal bodily weakness – **debility**; **enervation**; **hyposthenia**

To make weak or feeble – **debilitate**; **enervate**; **weaken** (all v.t.)

Wealth:

Wealth or riches, esp. when dishonestly acquired – **pelf**

An excessive desire for wealth – **avarice** (adj. **avaricious**); **plutomania**

Excessive devotion to wealth – **plutolatry**

The scientific study or theory of wealth – **plutology**

Insanity characterized by delusions of wealth – **plutomania**

One who has recently become rich, esp. one who flaunts one's wealth – **nouveau riche**; **parvenu**

Of, relating to or occupied in the gaining of wealth – **chrematistic**

The study of wealth or a particular theory of wealth as measured in money – **chrematistic**; **chrematistics**

Weapons collectively – **weaponry** (see also Nuclear)

Wearing (friction):

The act of wearing away by rubbing or friction – **attrition**; **detrition**

Having attrition; worn or ground down by attrition – **attrite**; **attrited**

Weather:
    Delayed, halted or kept indoors by bad weather – **weather-bound**
    A broadcast of weather conditions – **weathercast**
    Weather forecasting – **aeromancy**
    A front along which an advancing mass of warm air rises over a mass of cold air – **warm front**
    The leading edge of a cold air mass that moves against and eventually replaces a warm air mass – **cold front**
    Development or intensification of a weather front – **frontogenesis**
    Disintegration of a weather front – **frontolysis**
    The study of the effects of climate on periodic biological phenomena such as breeding, flowering, migration, etc. –
        phenology

Weaving:
    A flexible shoot, as of a willow, used in weaving baskets or furniture; constructed, composed of or covered with this
        material – **wicker**
    Woven wicker – **wicker**; **wickerwork**
    Woven in; with a decorative pattern woven in – **inwrought**
    To weave into a fabric or design – **inweave** (v.t.)
    To unite by or as if by interweaving – **plait**; **pleach** (both v.t.)
    To renew by interweaving – **pleach** (v.t.) (used esp. of a hedge)
    To draw out and twist (a sliver of silk or other textile fiber) in preparation for spinning – **slub** (v.t.)

Wedge:
    Having the shape or form of a wedge – **cuneal**; **cuneate**; **cuneiform**; **sphenic**; **sphenoid**

Week (hebdomad):
    Occurring weekly – **hebdomadal**
    Two weeks – **fortnight**
    Occurring or issued twice a week – **biweekly**; **semiweekly**
    Occurring every two weeks – **biweekly**
    Occurring, done or appearing three times a week; three times a week; occurring every three weeks; every three weeks
        – **triweekly**

Weeping (see also Tears):
    Weeping or given to weeping; causing or tending to cause weeping – **lachrymal**, **lachrymose**, **lacrimal**
    Crying for mercy, esp. in the stress of battle – **recreant**

Weight:
    Of or relating to measurement by weight – **gravimetric**
    A weight that balances another – **counterbalance**; **counterpoise**
    To weigh down needlessly – **cumber** (v.t.)
    The weight of a container or wrapper deducted from the gross weight to obtain net weight – **tare**
    Physical exercise designed to facilitate weight loss – **slimnastics**
    The perception of weight by the cutaneous and muscle senses - **barognosis**
        Loss of barognosis – **baragnosis**

Welfare:
    The set of policies, practices and social attitudes associated with a welfare state – **welfarism**

West:
    Of or relating to the west – **Hesperian**
    At or toward the west; a direction or point toward the west; a region situated in or toward the west – **westward**

To move westward (used of a celestial body); to shift to the west (used of wind) – **wester** (v.i.)

Situated toward the west; from the west (used of wind) – **westerly**

Coming from the west – **western** (used of wind)

A native or inhabitant of the west – **westerner**

Farthest west – **westernmost**

A westward direction or movement – **westing**

To convert to the customs of Western civilization – **westernize** (v.t.)

Whale:

Of or like a whale, dolphin, etc. (member of the order Cetacea): **cetacean**; **cetaceous**

A group of whales – **gam**; **herd**; **pod**; **school**

A male whale – **bull**

A female whale – **cow**

A young whale – **calf**

One who hunts or processes whales; a whaling ship; a whale boat – **whaler**

Whale skin used for food – **muktuk**

The business or practice of hunting, killing or processing whales – **whaling**

A whale having a symmetrical skull, paired blowholes, and plates of whalebone instead of teeth – **mysticete**

The study of whales and related aquatic mammals - **cetology**

Wharf:

The use of a wharf or wharves; the charge for such use; wharves collectively – **wharfage**

The owner or manager of a wharf – **wharfinger**

Wheat:

Of, relating to or derived from wheat – **wheaten**

Dried cracked wheat prepared for food – **bulgur**

Wheel:

A wheel that regulates rate of movement in machine parts, as in a watch – **balance wheel**

One whose trade is the building or repairing of wheels – **wheelwright**

Shaped like a wheel – **rotate**; **rotiform**; **trochal**

Whim:

Determined by whim or impulse, not by reason or law – **arbitrary**

Whip:

To whip with or as if with nettles – **urticate** (v.t.)

A whip made from an animal's penis – **pizzle**

Shaped like or resembling a whip – **flagellate**; **flagelliform**

Whisper:

A whisper intended to be overheard – **stage whisper**

White:

Turning white – **albescent**; **canescent**

To cause to turn white or become pale or colorless – **blanch**; **bleach** (both v.t./v.i.)

Covered with whitish bloom, as a plum – **glaucous**

Whole:

Concerned with wholes rather than with analysis or dissection into parts – **holistic**

Wife (see also Woman):

Of, relating to or characteristic of a wife - **uxorial**

Excessively or irrationally submissive or devoted to one's wife – **uxorious**

A secondary wife in certain societies that permit more than one wife at a time – **concubine**

The practice or condition of having only one wife at a time – **monogyny**

The practice or condition of having more than one wife at a time – **polygyny**

Relating to the home territory of the wife's family or tribe – **matrilocal**

Will (choice or desire):

An act of willing, choosing or deciding – **volition**

The lowest level of volition; a mere wish unaccompanied by action or effort to obtain or realize it – **velleity**

Of, relating to or originating in the will – **volitive**

Belief in the primacy of the will – **voluntarism**

Arising from one's own free will – **voluntary**

A person who performs or gives his services of his own free will – **volunteer**

An advocate of the doctrine of free will – **libertarian**

Quick willingness; eager readiness – **alacrity**, adj. **alacritous**

Will (legal document):

One who makes a will – **legator**; **testator**

To perform, execute or sign (a will) – **make** (v.t.)

To leave or give by will – **bequeath** (v.t.)

Of, relating to or of the nature of a testament or will; given, bequeathed, done or appointed in a will; set forth or contained in a will – **testamentary**

Money or property bequeathed by a will – **bequest**; **legacy**

The inheritor of a legacy – **legatee**

The disposal by a testator of specific property bequeathed in his or her will so as to invalidate the bequest - **ademption**

To revoke (a legacy) by ademption **– adeem** (v.t.)

The recipient of benefits, as money or property, from a will – **beneficiary**

Having made a legally valid will before death – **testate**

The state of being testate – **testacy**

One who has made a legally valid will before death – **testator**

A woman who has made a legally valid will before death – **testatrix**

The neglect of a testator to mention a legal heir in his will – **preterition**

Having made no legal will; not disposed of by a legal will; one who dies without having made a legal will – **intestate**

One appointed to execute a will – **executor**

A woman appointed to execute a will – **executrix**

The remainder of a testator's estate after all claims, debts and bequests are satisfied – **residue**; **residuum**

Entitled to the residue of an estate – **residuary**

The act of transmitting or giving real property by will; the property or land transmitted by will – **devise**

A supplement or appendix to a will – **codicil**

A will primarily evidenced by the testator's oral declaration to a witness, as distinguished from a written will – **nuncupative will**

A will hand-written by the testator – **holographic will**

A will in which the signer, in the event of a terminal illness, requests to be allowed to die rather than be kept alive by medical life support systems – **living will**

Wind (see also Storm):

Carried or transmitted by the wind - **Aeolian**; **aeolian**; **Aeolic**; **Eolic**; **eolian**; **wind-borne**

Relating to or caused by the wind - **Aeolian**; **aeolian**; **Aeolic**; **Eolic**; **eolian**

In or toward the direction from which the wind blows – **upwind**; **windward**

Situated on or moving toward the side toward which the wind is blowing – **leeward**

The direction from which the wind blows; of or moving toward the direction from which the wind blows; of or on the side exposed to the wind or to prevailing winds – **windward**

The effect of wind on the course of a projectile; the disturbance of air caused by the passage of a fast-moving object – **windage**

Of or relating to the west wind – **favonian** (see also West)

A soft warm breeze from the west – **zephyr**

Coming from the west – **western** (used of wind)

A strong wind coming from the south – **souther**

A hot or warm southerly wind – **scirroco**; **sirocco**

A strong wind coming from the southwest – **southwester**

A light breeze – **waft**; **zephyr**

A wind with speeds of approximately:

    4 to 7 mph – **light breeze**

    8 to 12 mph – **gentle breeze**

    13 to 18 mph – **moderate breeze**

    19 to 24 mph – **fresh breeze**

    25 to 31 mph – **strong breeze**

    32 to 63 mph – **gale**

    32 to 38 mph – **moderate gale**

    39 to 46 mph – **fresh gale**

    47 to 54 mph – **strong gale**

    55 to 63 mph – **whole gale**

    64 to 72 mph – **storm**; **violent storm**

A sudden cold gale from the north – **norther**

Sand, dust or snow driven before the wind like sea spray – **spindrift**

An atmospheric disturbance marked by masses of air rapidly circulating around a low-pressure center, usually accompanied by stormy weather; a violent rotating windstorm – **cyclone**

    A severe tropical cyclone with winds exceeding approximately 74 mph – **hurricane**

A violent windstorm, esp. when accompanied by rain, snow or hail – **tempest**

    Relating to or characteristic of a tempest – **tempestuous**

A wind system that affects large climatic regions and reverses direction seasonally – **monsoon**

A whistling, violently cold wind – **sarsar**

A violent gust of cold wind blowing seaward from a mountainous coast; any sudden violent wind – **williwaw**

A wind blowing directly opposite to the course of an aircraft or ship – **head wind**

A consistent system of winds occupying most of the tropics, blowing northeasterly in the Northern Hemisphere and southeasterly in the Southern Hemisphere; any wind that is part of this system – **trade wind**

Winds that blow steadily above and opposite to the trade winds – **antitrades**

The study of winds – **anemology**

Window:

    The design and position of windows in a building – **fenestration**

    Having windows or windowlike openings – **fenestrated**

    An act of throwing something or someone out of a window – **defenestration**, v.t. **defenestrate**

    The vertical strip dividing the panes of a window – **mullion**

    One who cuts and fits window glass – **glazier**

Windpipe (trachea):

    Within the trachea – **endotracheal**

    Inflammation of the trachea – **tracheitis**

Wine:
   Contained in or derived from wine – **vinic**
   Made with wine; affected or caused by the consumption of wine; having the color of wine – **vinous**
   Of or relating to wine – **vinic**; **vinous**
   The yield of grapes from a particular vineyard (ground planted with cultivated grape vines) or district during one season; of or relating to such a yield of wine; wine identified as to year and vineyard or district of origin; the initial stages of winemaking; the year or place in which a particular wine is bottled – **vintage**
   One who owns or cultivates a vineyard and makes wine from the grapes - **winegrower**
   A producer or harvester of wine grapes – **vintager**
   A wine merchant; one who makes wines – **vintner**
   A wine-making establishment – **winery**
   The refuse of grapes left after the extraction of the juice in wine-making – **rape**
   Cheap red table wine – **vin ordinaire**
   Given to much drinking of wine; the habitual drinking of wine – **winebibbing**
   A cabinet for storing bottles of wine – **cellaret**; **cellarette**
   A wine steward in a restaurant – **sommelier**
   One who serves wine - **cupbearer**
   A lover or connoisseur of wine – **oenophile**; **oenophilist**
   The study of wines – **enology**; **oenology**

Wing (see also Falconry):
   Of wings – **alar**; **alary**
   Having wings – **alar**; **alary**; **alate**; **alated**; **pennate**; **pennated**; **winged**
   Having winglike attachments – **alate**; **alated**
   Having two winglike parts – **dipterous**
   Having four wings – **tetrapterous**
   Having no wings or winglike parts – **apteral**; **apterous**
   Having lost the wings – **dealate**; **dealated** (both used of certain insects that shed their wings after a mating flight)
   Having short wings, as certain insects – **brachypterous**
   Overlapping or crossing, as the wings of some insects when at rest – **cruciate**
   Shaped like a wing – **alar**; **alary**; **aliform**
   Wing-footed; having a winglike membrane connected with the feet, as in the bat - **aliped**

Winter:
   Of, relating to or characteristic of winter – **brumal**; **hibernal**; **hiemal**; **wintry**
   Occurring during the period of winter; to remain alive through the winter, as small game – **overwinter** (adj./v.i.)
   To pass the winter in a dormant or torpid state – **hibernate** (v.i.)

Wire:
   Capable of being drawn into wire – **ductile**
   A fine wire heated electrically to incandescence in an electric lamp – **filament** (q.v.)
   Fitted with or involving the use of two wires – **bifilar**
   To draw (metal) into wire – **wire- draw** (v.t.)
   Made of woven wire – **wire-wove**

Wisdom:
   To provide with spiritual wisdom – **enlighten** (v.t.)
   An act or means of enlightening; the state of being enlightened – **enlightenment**
   Belief in or proclamation of a special personal enlightenment – **illuminism**
   Hatred of enlightenment, reason, etc. - **misology**

Wit:
   One who has little wit – **witling**
   Sharp, lively wit – **salt**

Witch/Witchcraft (black magic; sorcery):
   Born of a witch or hag **– hagborn**
   A male witch or sorcerer – **warlock**
   An assembly of 13 witches – **coven**
   An orgy of witches, demons and sorcerers – **sabbat**; **witches' Sabbath**
   Witchcraft involving benevolent, nature-oriented practices derived from pre-Christian religions – **Wicca**; **wicca**, n.
      wiccan

Without which not – **sine qua non**

Wizard:
   The art, skill, practice or accomplishments of a wizard – **wizardry**
   A male wizard – **warlock**
   A chief wizard – **archimage**

Wolf:
   Resembling a wolf – **lupine**
   The supposed ability to assume the form and characteristics of a wolf – **lycanthropy**
   A male wolf – **dog wolf**
   A female wolf – **bitch**
   A young wolf – **cub**; **whelp**
   A group of wolves – **pack**; **rout**; **route**

Woman (see also Wife):
   The state of being a woman – **muliebrity**; **womanhood**
   The qualities characteristic of women – **muliebrity**
   Women collectively – **femineity**; **femininity**; **womanhood**; **womankind**
   Woman's nature – **womanhood**
   A woman sharing the same racial, cultural or national background as another; a female relative – **kinswoman**
   A woman whose husband has died and who has not remarried; to make such a woman of (someone) – **widow** (n./v.t.)
      Of or relating to widowhood (viduity) – **vidual**
   A woman divorced or separated from her husband – **grass widow**
   A married woman acting or contracting with respect to her separate estate – **feme sole**, pl. **femes sole** (Law)
   A married woman – **feme covert** (pl. **femes covert**); **femme couverte**, pl. **femmes couvertes** (Law)
   Fondness for women – **philogyny**
   Masculine mentality and psychology in a woman – **viraginity**
   A large, strong and courageous woman – **virago**
   Acting like an old woman – **anile**, n. **anility**
   A woman adviser or companion – **egeria**
   A woman who suckles another woman's child – **wet nurse**
      To serve as a wet nurse for (someone) – **wet-nurse** (v.t.)
   A woman who travels with troops to sell them food, supplies and liquor – **vivandière**
   An attractive woman who may lead a man into a compromising or dangerous situation; a charming, mysterious woman
      – **femme fatale**, pl. **femmes fatales**
   A doctrine advocating for women the same rights granted men; the movement supporting this doctrine - **feminism**
   The social practice of regarding women as common property – **hetaerism**; **hetairism**, n. **hetaerist**
   Hatred of women – **misogynism**; **misogyny**, adj. **misogynic**, n. **misogynist**

The branch of medicine that deals with diseases, reproductive physiology and endocrinology in women – **gynecology**, adj. **gynecologic** or **gynecological**, n. **gynecologist**
Any of various diseases peculiar to women – **gynecopathy**
Treatment of diseases peculiar to women – **gyniatrics**
Extreme or irrational fear of women – **gynephobia**

Wood:
Made of wood – **treen**; **wooden**
Any small object made entirely of wood – **treen**
Of or resembling wood – **ligneous**; **xyloid**
Composed of or having the appearance or texture of wood – **ligneous**; **woody**
To form or turn into wood through the formation and deposit of lignin in cell walls – **lignify** (v.t.)
Dry, easily ignited wood – **lightwood**
The act, process or art of working with wood – **woodcraft**
The art or process of shaping wood into forms on a lathe – **woodturning**
To cut or shape wood with a knife; to cut small bits or pare shavings from (a piece of wood) – **whittle** (v.t./v.i.)
Wood as a building material – **lumber**; **timber**
   Uncut marketable timber; the value of or price paid for timber as it stands uncut in the woods - **stumpage**
A notch in timber to receive part of another timber; to cut such a notch – **dap** (n./v.t.)
A crack made in young timber by the wind – **anemosis**; **wind shake**
One employed at sawing wood – **sawyer**
A flat piece of wood used to punish school children; punishment with such a piece of wood – **ferula**; **ferule**
A contorted knot in wood - **knurl**
Wood that has been steamed until pliable, then bent and shaped – **bentwood**
Wood that has been preserved in a peat bog – **bog wood**
Feeding on wood – **xylophagous**
Feeding on the wood of trees – **dendrophagous**
The process or technique of cutting a design on wood – **woodcut**; **wood engraving**; **xylography**
An engraving on wood – **woodcut**; **wood engraving**; **xylograph**
A print made from engraving on wood – **woodcut**; **wood engraving**
The art of printing texts or illustrations from wood blocks – **xylography**
Preparation of cross sections of wood for microscopic study – **xylotomy**
Divination by means of pieces of wood – **xylomancy**

Woodpeckers, a group of – **descent**

Wool:
Having wool – **laniferous**
The annual yield of wool – **wool-clip**
A sheepskin with the wool still on it – **woolskin**
A dealer in wool; a person who sorts wool by the quality of the staple (length and fineness) or fiber – **wool-stapler**
Reclaimed wool of low quality – **mungo**
Low-grade, irregular wool – **cast**
Composed of or containing wooly masses; having a fluffy or wooly appearance – **flocculent**

Word (see also Language, Repeat/Repetition, and Syllable):
Of, relating to or associated with words; concerned with words rather than the facts or ideas they represent; using or consisting of words alone without action – **verbal**
One skilled in the use of words; one who favors words over ideas or facts – **verbalist**
To express in words; to express oneself in words – **verbalize** (v.t./v.i.)
The way in which one expresses oneself in words - **diction**; **verbiage**

Word for word – **literal**; **textual**; **verbal**; **verbatim**

A prefix, suffix or infix (collective term) – **affix**

    The adding of affixes - **affixation**

The formation of words by a combination of compounding and adding an affix - **parasynthesis**

A new word created by removing from an existing word what is mistakenly thought to be an affix, as *laze* from *lazy* – **back-formation**

The very word – **ipsissima verba**

A word or term having only one meaning - **univocal**

Words in excess of those needed for clarity or precision – **verbiage**; **wordiness**

Using or containing an excessive number of words - **verbose**; **wordy**

Words addressed to a person or thing, whether absent or present, generally in an exclamatory tone and as a digression in a speech or literary writing – **apostrophe**, adj. **apostrophic**

Of or relating to the words or vocabulary of a language – **lexical**

The study of the lexical components of a language – **lexicology**

Using or marked by the use of few words – **concise** (n. **conciseness**); **laconic** (n. **laconism**); **terse**, n. **terseness**

A word having a meaning similar to that of another word in the same language – **synonym**, adj. **synonymous**, n. **synonymy**

    One who studies or discriminates synonyms – **synonymist**

    To provide or analyze the synonyms of (a word) – **synonymize** (v.t.)

A newly coined word, phrase or expression; a meaningless word or phrase used by a psychotic – **neologism**; **neology**

Use of a newly coined word, phrase or expression or of a new meaning for an already established word – **neology**

A word frequently used without regard to its precise meaning, or that has a broad and vague range of meaning – **counter word**; **counterword**

A word occurring, invented or used just for a particular occasion – **nonce word**

A word formed by merging the sounds and meanings of two different words, e.g., *smog* (smoke + fog) – **portmanteau word**

A word that has come into a language through the perpetuation of a misreading of a manuscript, a typographical error or a misunderstanding – **ghost word**

A word placed at the head of a column or page, as in a dictionary, to indicate the first or last entry on the page - **catchword**

An ambiguous word used to lessen the force of a statement or evade a direct commitment – **weasel word**

The use of more words than are necessary to express an idea; an instance of this – **pleonasm**; **redundancy**; **tautology**

The most exact and suitable word or expression – **mot juste**

A word whose elements are derived from different languages – **hybrid**

A word or form occurring only once in the recorded corpus of a given language – **hapax legomenon**

A nonstandard word usage or grammatical construction – **solecism**, n. **solecist**

A sign, abbreviation, letter or character standing for words in ancient manuscripts or on coins or medals – **siglum**, pl. **sigla**, adj. **siglarian**

A word formed by the initial letters of a name – **acronym**, adj. **acronymic** or **acronymous**

A group of words arranged in a square that reads the same vertically and horizontally – **acrostic**; **word square**

One of two or more words having the same spelling but differing in origin and meaning – **homograph**

A word having more than one meaning – **polysemant**

Multiplicity of meaning - **polysemy**

One of two or more words having the same sound, and often the same spelling, but differing in meaning – **homonym**, adj. **homonymic**

One of two or more words having the same sound but differing in spelling, origin and meaning – **homophone**

Having the same sound as another word – **homophonic**

One of two words having identical spelling but different meanings and pronunciation – **heteronym**, adj. **heteronymous**

The addition of a phoneme at the beginning of a word to ease pronunciation or to form a new word – **prothesis**, pl. **protheses**

The addition of a sound or syllable to the end of a word – **paragoge**

The addition of a sound or syllable to a word, esp. by prefixing – **prosthesis**, pl. **prostheses**

The carrying forward of a final sound or letter to a following sound – **provection**

The changing of a word by adding, subtracting or transposing letters or syllables – **metaplasm**

The occurrence in a phrase or line of speech or writing of two or more words having the same initial sound – **alliteration**, v.i./v.t. **alliterate**, adj. **alliterative**

A change in the form of a word indicating grammatical features such as number, person, tense, etc.; a word element involved in such a change; such a word form – **inflection**, v.i./v.t. **inflect**

The union or fusion into one of two or more originally different inflectional forms - **syncretism**

The use of a word, as an adjective or verb, in grammatical agreement with only one of two nouns by which it is governed – **syllepsis**, pl. **syllepses**

A word having similar derivation or the same stem as another word – **paronym**, adj. **paronymous**

Transposition within a word of letters, sounds or syllables – **metathesis**

A word adopted from another language and at least partly adopted into general use – **loan**; **loan-word**; **loanword**

An unintentional transposition of sounds of two or more words – **spoonerism**

The study of words and expressions having similar or associated concepts and a basis for being grouped - **onomasiology**

A preoccupation or obsession with words or names, or their meanings or sounds; a mania for repeating certain words or sounds – **onomatomania**

A word, phrase, verse or sentence that reads the same backward or forward – **palindrome**

A word regarded only as a sequence of sounds or letters instead of as a unit of meaning voiced or spoken – **vocable**

To describe (a word, e.g.) grammatically by stating the part of speech and explaining the inflection and syntactical relationships – **parse** (v.t.)

A word or phrase formed by rearranging the letters of another word or phrase – **anagram**, adj. **anagramatic** or **anagrammatic**

To make an anagram of – **anagrammatize** (v.t.)

A word puzzle, as an anagram- **logogriph**

Substitution of an inoffensive or agreeable word or phrase for one considered offensive; a word or expression so substituted – **euphemism**, v.i./v.t. **euphemize**

A word believed by its user to be socially preferable to a common synonym – **genteelism**

Substitution of a disagreeable, offensive or disparaging word or phrase for an agreeable or inoffensive one; a word or phrase so substituted - **dysphemism**

Omission of the conjunctions that ordinarily join coordinated words or clauses – **asyndeton**, pl. **asyndeta** or **asyndetons**

Related by derivation from the same root – **paronymous** (used of words)

A paronymous word – **paronym**

A word functioning as a phrase or sentence – **holophrase**, adj. **holophrastic**

The use of words or phrases in a sense opposite to the proper one – **antiphrasis**

An antiquated or ancient word, phrase, expression, etc. – **archaism**

A short, pointed and instructive saying – **apophthegm**; **apothegm**

The loss of one or more sounds or letters at the beginning of a word – **aphaeresis**; **apheresis**

Apheresis consisting of the loss of a short unaccented vowel at the beginning of a word - **aphesis**, adj. **aphetic**

The loss of a short unaccented vowel at the beginning of a word – **aphesis**, v.t. **aphetize**

The historical process by which the semantic and connotative status of a word tends to rise – **melioration**

The process by which the semantic status of a word changes for the worse over a period of time – **pejoration**

The formation of words from other words that retain their original forms and meanings – **agglutination**, adj. **agglutinative**, v.i./v.t. **agglutinate**

A change undergone by a word as it passes from language to language; the linguistic change of a morpheme from one construction to another – **modification**

The expression of the ideas of a phrase or sentence in one word – **holophrasis**

The expression of an idea by two nouns connected by *and* – **hendiadys**

An adjective used as a noun (e.g., the lame, the blind) – **adnoun**

The introduction of an esp. nonstandard sound or letter into a word – **epenthesis**

    Epenthesis of a vowel – **anaptyxis**, adj. **anaptyctic** or **anaptyctical**

A linguistic element that always occurs as part of another word – **bound form**

The omission of one of two similar adjacent syllables or sounds in a word – **haplology**

The accidental omission of a letter group that should be repeated in writing – **haplography**

A meaningless battle of words; a dispute about words – **logomachy**

The use of a wrong word in a context; the misuse of words - **catachresis**

Ludicrous misuse of a word – **malapropism**, adj. **malapropian**

The cutting off or dropping of the last sound, letter or syllable of a word – **apocope**

    To shorten by apocope – **apocopate** (v.t.)

    Shortened by apocope – **apocopate**; **apocopated**

The shortening of a word by dropping a sound, letter or syllable from the middle of a word, e.g., *bos'n* for *boatswain* – **syncope**; **syncopation**

To drop (a letter or sound) from the spelling or pronunciation of a word; to shorten (a word) thus – **syncopate** (v.t.)

Separation of the parts of a compound word by one or more intervening words, e.g., *where I go ever* instead of *wherever I go* – **tmesis**

Word play, esp. a pun – **paronomasia**, adj. **paronomastic** or **paronomasial**

A word or words serving to define another word or expression, as in a dictionary entry – **definiens**

    A word or expression defined by a definiens – **definiendum**

The study of the origins and forms of words, or of proper names – **onomastics** (sing./pl.)

The formation or use of words that imitate what they denote – **echoism**; **onomatopoeia**, adj. **onomatopoeic** or **onomatopoetic**

A word or expression capable of two interpretations; ambiguity of meaning arising from such language – **double entendre**

A study and description of word-formation in a language; the system of word-forming elements and processes in a language – **morphology**

The science of defining technical terms – **orismology** (adj. **orismologic** or **orismological**); **terminology**

A mania for words; excessive use of or obsession with words – **verbomania**, n. **verbomaniac**

One whose mental imagery consists of words – **verbile**

Use of words to convey the opposite of their literal meaning; an expression or utterance marked by deliberate contrast between apparent and intended meaning – **irony**, adj. **ironic** or **ironical**

    A user of irony, esp. a writer – **ironist**

The worship of words or letters; a devotion to the letter, as in law or Scripture – **grammaolatry**

The use of ambiguous words – **parisology**, adj. **parisological**

A list of words with their definitions – **glossary**

    A word explained in a glossary – **lemma**

    The writing and compilation of glossaries – **glossography**

A patterned change in root vowels of verb forms indicating changes in tense, aspect or function - **ablaut**

Limited by person, number, tense and mood and capable of serving as a predicate – **finite** (used of verbs)

A term used as a descriptive substitute for a person's name or title; a derogatory or abusive word or phrase – **epithet**

To double (the initial syllable or all of a root word) to make an inflectional or derivational form; to form (a new word) by doubling all or part of a word – **reduplicate** (v.t.)

    Reduplication of letters or syllables in writing, printing, etc., as through error – **dittography**

      An instance of dittography; a passage containing reduplicated syllables, letters, etc. – **dittograph**

Having only one form to indicate either male or female sex – **epicene** (used of a noun)

A mark or marks showing omission of letters, words or other material; the omission of a word or phrase required for a complete syntactical construction but not necessary for understanding; an example of this – **ellipsis**, pl. **ellipses**

Spaced periods (usu. three) used to mark an omission of a word or group of words from a written context –
suspension periods; **suspension points**

Dots over the second of two adjacent vowels to indicate that it is pronounced separately, as in *naïve* – **dieresis**

Work (see also Labor):

An association of wage earners formed to help its members secure satisfactory wages, benefits and working conditions – **labor union** (q.v.); **trade union**

A business, industrial establishment, etc., in which workers are employed without regard to labor union membership – **open shop**

An increase in labor required of industrial workers without a commensurate pay increase – **stretch-out**

Laborious work, study, thought, etc., esp. at night; the result of such activity – **lucubration**, v.i. **lucubrate**

Working together – **cooperating**; **cooperative**; **synergetic**; **synergic**

To work untiringly and continuously; exhausting work – **toil** (v.i./n.)

Marked by or requiring toil – **toilsome**

A worker expected to serve in several capacities – **utility man**

One who has served an apprenticeship in a trade or craft and is a qualified worker in another's employ – **journeyman**

The work of a journeyman – **journeywork**

The chief work of a person's lifetime – **lifework**

An unskilled laborer or farm worker of Latin America or the southwestern United States; such a worker bound in servitude to a landlord creditor – **peon**

The condition of being a peon – **peonage**; **peonism**

The breakdown of skilled jobs or operations into separate processes requiring little or no skill to perform – **dilution**

An unskilled worker performing a task previously a part or process of a skilled operation – **dilutee**

One who loves work – **ergophile**

Excessive devotion to work, esp. as a symptom of mental disorder – **ergomania**

An onerous or unpleasant and unavoidable task - **corvée**

Hatred of or aversion to work – **ergophobia**, n. **ergophobe**

A contrivance to hide or counteract defective work – **dutchman**, pl. **dutchmen**

A position or office requiring little or no work but providing a salary – **sinecure**

The practice of granting sinecures – **sinecurism**

World:

Of, relating to or typical of this world – **mundane**

Before the creation of the world – **antemundane**

A comprehensive world view, esp. from a specified standpoint; a conception of the universe and of life –
Weltanschauung, pl. **Weltanschauungs** or **Weltanschauungen**

A little world; a small, representative system more or less analogous to a larger system in constitution, configuration or development – **microcosm**

The great world; the universe in its entirety – **macrocosm**

Worldly rather than spiritual – **laic**; **secular**, n. **secularity**, v.t. **secularize**

Worm:

Of or relating to worms – **helminthic**; **vermicular**

Caused by worms – **vermicular**

Of or relating to parasitic intestinal worms – **helminthic**

Acting to expel or destroy intestinal worms – **anthelminthic**; **anthelmintic**

An agent used to kill worms – **vermicide**

An agent that expels or destroys intestinal worms - **anthelminthic**; **anthelmintic**; **vermifuge**

The condition of being infested with worms – **vermiculation**; **vermination**

Infested with worms – **vermiculate**

Infestation with parasitic worms – **verminosis**

Infestation with pinworms – **oxyuriasis**
Having the shape of a worm – **vermiform**; **vermicular**
Resembling a worm or solex (head of a tapeworm) – **scolecoid**
Having a wormlike motion or wormlike markings – **vermicular**; **vermiculate**
Resembling an earthworm – **lumbricoid**
Motion resembling that of a worm; wormlike marks or carvings - **vermiculation**
The breeding of worms – **vermination**
Feeding on worms – **vermivorous**
Producing wormlike young – **vermiparous**
The study of worms, esp. parasitic worms – **helminthology**

Worry:
Causing anxiety or worry; tending to worry – **worrisome**

Wren:
A group of wrens – **herd**
A female wren – **jenny**

Writing:
Writing done by the hand; the writing typical of a particular person – **calligraphy**; **handwriting**
The art, skill or manner of handwriting – **chirography**; **penmanship**
A rapid handwriting system utilizing symbols to represent words, letters and phrases – **brachygraphy**; **shorthand**;
    stenography; **tachygraphy**
    Ancient Greek and Roman stenography - **tachygraphy**
A system of shorthand based on phonetic transcription – **phonography**
Incorrect or bad handwriting – **cacography**
One who has poor penmanship – **cacographer**
Impairment of the ability to write – **dysgraphia**
A disorder marked by the inability to write – **agraphia**
A condition in mental disorder or brain injury in which words or letters other than those intended are written –
    paragraphia
To write in a scholarly way – **lucubrate** (v.i.), n. **lucubration**
To write, print or engrave (letters or words) on a surface – **inscribe** (v.t.), n. **inscription**
The study of ancient modes of writing, including inscriptions – **paleography**, n. **paleographer**
The study of handwriting, esp. that of individuals as a means of analyzing character – **graphology**, n. **graphologist**
A descending letter or character (e.g., *g* or *j*); the descending part of a descending letter – **descender**
To write or type a copy of; to write out fully, as from notes – **transcribe** (v.t.), n. **transcription**
    Transcribed matter – **transcript**
To write in correct form – **redact** (v.t.)
To write or insert between lines already written or printed; to make such insertions – **interline** (v.t.)
Written beneath; a distinguishing character or symbol written directly beneath or next to and slightly below a letter or
    number – **subscript** (adj./n.)
A writer paid according to the amount of space his material occupies in print – **space writer**
Tending to write at great length – **prolix**, n. **prolixity**
The procedures, processes, methods, etc., used to translate or interpret secret writings and codes for which the key is
    unknown – **cryptanalysis** (n. **cryptanalyst**); **cryptography** (n. **cryptographer**); **cryptologist**
The writing of alternate lines in opposite directions – **boustrophedon**; **boustropheidon**
A system of secret writing – **cipher**; **cryptograph**; **cryptography**
Spirit writing – **psychography**
The use of written characters that represent syllables – **syllabism**
The art of fine writing – **calligraphy**

Of or relating to a form of writing believed to be intermediate between picture writing and phonetic writing in which pictures or signs stand not for objects themselves but for their names considered as phonetic elements only – **iconomatic**; **ikonomatic**

Iconomatic writing – **iconomaticism**; **iconomatography**; **ikonomatography**

The omission in writing or copying of one of two or more adjacent and similar letters, syllables, words or lines – **haplography**

A cramp chiefly affecting the muscles of the thumb and two adjacent fingers after prolonged writing – **graphospasm**; **writer's cramp**

Abnormally large handwriting – **macrography**

The profession or occupation of writing – **authorship**

An act of rewriting; something that is rewritten – **rescript**

Writing executed in gold letters; to write in letters of gold – **chrysograph** (n./v.t.)

X

X-ray (see also Radiation):

To subject to the action of x-rays – **roentgenize** (v.t.)

The use of a radiosensitive surface to produce an image by radiation other than visible light, esp. by x-rays passed through an object – **radiography**, v.t./n. **radiograph**

Radiography of a part or organ in motion – **cinematoradiography**

A photograph made with x-rays – **roentgenogram**; **roentgenograph**

Photography with the use of x-rays – **roentgenography**

The therapeutic use of x-rays in treating disease – **radiotherapy**; **roentgenotherapy**

The technique of making x-ray photographs of the kidneys, renal pelvis and ureters, using injection of opaque solutions or radiopaque dyes – **pyelography**

X-ray of arteries following an injection of a radiopaque dye – **arteriography**

X-ray examination of the bile ducts – **cholangiography**

Anatomical examination with the use of a fluoroscope (a fluorescent screen on which the internal structure of an optically opaque object may be continuously viewed by transmission of x-rays through the object) – **fluoroscopy**

The production of x-ray pictures of a predetermined plane section of a solid object by blurring out the images of other planes – **tomography**, n. **tomogram** or **tomograph**

Y

A y-shaped object – **wye**

Yacht:
   A person who sails in or owns a yacht – **yachtsman**
   The sport of sailing in yachts – **yachting**

Yawning, the act of – **oscitancy**

Year (see also Anniversary):
   Recurring, done or performed every year – **annual**; **yearly**
   Every year – **annually**; **yearly**
   Lasting through one year – **yearlong**
   Occurring or issued twice a year – **biyearly**; **semiannual**; **semiyearly**
   Living or growing for only one year or season; a publication appearing yearly; a plant whose life cycle is one year or season – **annual**
   Lasting or active through the year or through many years; having a life span of more than two years - **perennial**
   A two-year period – **biennium**
   Occurring every two years – **biennial**; **biyearly**
   Lasting or living for two years – **biennial**
   Occurring every third year; lasting three years; an event occurring every three years – **triennial**
   A three-year period – **triennium**
   A four-year period – **quadrennium**
   Occurring once in four years; lasting four years; an event occurring every four years – **quadrennial**
   A five-year period – **lustrum**; **quinquennial**; **quinquennium**
   Occurring once every five years; lasting for five years – **quinquennial**
   Occurring every six years; relating to or lasting six years – **sexennial**
   Occurring every seven years; relating to or lasting seven years; an event that occurs every seven years – **septennial**
   Occurring every eight years; relating to or lasting eight years – **octennial**
   A period of ten years – **decade**; **decennium**
   Of or relating to ten years or a ten-year period – **decennary**; **decennial**
   Occurring once every ten years; lasting for ten years – **decennial**
   Occurring once every 15 years; lasting 15 years – **quindecennial**
   Occurring once every twenty years; existing or lasting for twenty years – **vicennial**
   Year of wonders – **annus mirabilis**
   The time required for one complete revolution of the earth around the sun (365 days, 6 hours, 9 minutes and 9.54 seconds in units of mean solar time) – **sidereal year**
   Of or relating to a leap year; of or relating to the extra day falling in a leap year – **bissextile**
   A period of 100 years – **centenary**; **century**
   Lasting from century to century – **secular**
   Of or relating to a 100-year period; occurring once every 100 years – **centenary**; **centennial**
   Occurring once every 200 years; lasting for 200 years – **bicentennial**
   Of or relating to a 300-year period – **tercentenary**; **tercentennial**; **tricentennial**
   Of or relating to a 600-year period – **sexcentenary**
   A period of a thousand years – **chiliad**; **millennium**
   Of or relating to a thousand years – **millenarian**; **millenary**; **millennial**

Yellow:
   Turning yellow – **flavescent**
   Yellowish staining of the eyes, skin and body fluids by bile pigment – **jaundice** (q.v.), adj. **jaundiced**

Yoga, one who practices – **yogi**

Young:
   The state of being or growing young or youthful – **juvenescent**, n. **juvenescence**

Z

Zebra:
  A group of zebras – **herd**
  A young zebra – **colt**; **foal**

Zinc:
  Zinc in the form of ingots, slabs or plates – **spelter**
  To coat (iron or steel) with rust-resistant zinc – **galvanize** (v.t.)
  The process of engraving zinc in printing plates – **zincography**
    A prepared zinc plate used in zincography; a print or picture obtained from such a plate – **zincograph**

Zone:
  Divided into zones; of or associated with a zone – **zonary**; **zonal**
  Having zones; belted, striped or ringed – **zonate**; **zonated**
  Arrangement or formation in zones – **zonation**
  Not restricted to a particular zone or region; not local – **azonic**

About the Author

Dr. Donges is a retired land use planner and academic researcher. His previous publications include *Policymaking for the Mentally Handicapped* (Gower, 1982), co-winner of the University of Aberdeen's George Adam Smith Prize (1983), and *Salo Flohr's Best Games of Chess* (Thinkers' Press, 1985).